# FREE Study Skills Videos/DVD Offer

Dear Customer,

Thank you for your purchase from Mometrix! We consider it an honor and a privilege that you have purchased our product and we want to ensure your satisfaction.

As part of our ongoing effort to meet the needs of test takers, we have developed a set of Study Skills Videos that we would like to give you for FREE. These videos cover our *best practices* for getting ready for your exam, from how to use our study materials to how to best prepare for the day of the test.

All that we ask is that you email us with feedback that would describe your experience so far with our product. Good, bad, or indifferent, we want to know what you think!

To get your FREE Study Skills Videos, you can use the **QR code** below, or send us an **email** at studyvideos@mometrix.com with *FREE VIDEOS* in the subject line and the following information in the body of the email:

- The name of the product you purchased.
- Your product rating on a scale of 1-5, with 5 being the highest rating.
- Your feedback. It can be long, short, or anything in between. We just want to know your impressions and experience so far with our product. (Good feedback might include how our study material met your needs and ways we might be able to make it even better. You could highlight features that you found helpful or features that you think we should add.)

If you have any questions or concerns, please don't hesitate to contact me directly.

Thanks again!

Sincerely,

Jay Willis
Vice President
jay.willis@mometrix.com
1-800-673-8175

# NCE

**Exam Preparation 2022 and 2023 Secrets**

# 650+ Practice Test Questions

National Counselor Study Guide with Step-by-Step Video Tutorials

**3rd Edition**

Written and edited by Mometrix Test Prep

Printed in the United States of America

This paper meets the requirements of ANSI/NISO Z39.48-1992 (Permanence of Paper).

Mometrix offers volume discount pricing to institutions. For more information or a price quote, please contact our sales department at sales@mometrix.com or 888-248-1219.

Paperback
ISBN 13: 978-1-5167-2123-8
ISBN 10: 1-5167-2123-3

# DEAR FUTURE EXAM SUCCESS STORY

First of all, **THANK YOU** for purchasing Mometrix study materials!

Second, congratulations! You are one of the few determined test-takers who are committed to doing whatever it takes to excel on your exam. **You have come to the right place.** We developed these study materials with one goal in mind: to deliver you the information you need in a format that's concise and easy to use.

In addition to optimizing your guide for the content of the test, we've outlined our recommended steps for breaking down the preparation process into small, attainable goals so you can make sure you stay on track.

We've also analyzed the entire test-taking process, identifying the most common pitfalls and showing how you can overcome them and be ready for any curveball the test throws you.

Standardized testing is one of the biggest obstacles on your road to success, which only increases the importance of doing well in the high-pressure, high-stakes environment of test day. Your results on this test could have a significant impact on your future, and this guide provides the information and practical advice to help you achieve your full potential on test day.

### Your success is our success

**We would love to hear from you!** If you would like to share the story of your exam success or if you have any questions or comments in regard to our products, please contact us at **800-673-8175** or **support@mometrix.com**.

Thanks again for your business and we wish you continued success!

Sincerely,
The Mometrix Test Preparation Team

---

**Need more help? Check out our flashcards at:**
**http://mometrixflashcards.com/NCE**

# TABLE OF CONTENTS

# Introduction

**Thank you for purchasing this resource!** You have made the choice to prepare yourself for a test that could have a huge impact on your future, and this guide is designed to help you be fully ready for test day. Obviously, it's important to have a solid understanding of the test material, but you also need to be prepared for the unique environment and stressors of the test, so that you can perform to the best of your abilities.

For this purpose, the first section that appears in this guide is the **Secret Keys**. We've devoted countless hours to meticulously researching what works and what doesn't, and we've boiled down our findings to the five most impactful steps you can take to improve your performance on the test. We start at the beginning with study planning and move through the preparation process, all the way to the testing strategies that will help you get the most out of what you know when you're finally sitting in front of the test.

We recommend that you start preparing for your test as far in advance as possible. However, if you've bought this guide as a last-minute study resource and only have a few days before your test, we recommend that you skip over the first two Secret Keys since they address a long-term study plan.

If you struggle with **test anxiety**, we strongly encourage you to check out our recommendations for how you can overcome it. Test anxiety is a formidable foe, but it can be beaten, and we want to make sure you have the tools you need to defeat it.

# Secret Key #1 – Plan Big, Study Small

There's a lot riding on your performance. If you want to ace this test, you're going to need to keep your skills sharp and the material fresh in your mind. You need a plan that lets you review everything you need to know while still fitting in your schedule. We'll break this strategy down into three categories.

## Information Organization

Start with the information you already have: the official test outline. From this, you can make a complete list of all the concepts you need to cover before the test. Organize these concepts into groups that can be studied together, and create a list of any related vocabulary you need to learn so you can brush up on any difficult terms. You'll want to keep this vocabulary list handy once you actually start studying since you may need to add to it along the way.

## Time Management

Once you have your set of study concepts, decide how to spread them out over the time you have left before the test. Break your study plan into small, clear goals so you have a manageable task for each day and know exactly what you're doing. Then just focus on one small step at a time. When you manage your time this way, you don't need to spend hours at a time studying. Studying a small block of content for a short period each day helps you retain information better and avoid stressing over how much you have left to do. You can relax knowing that you have a plan to cover everything in time. In order for this strategy to be effective though, you have to start studying early and stick to your schedule. Avoid the exhaustion and futility that comes from last-minute cramming!

## Study Environment

The environment you study in has a big impact on your learning. Studying in a coffee shop, while probably more enjoyable, is not likely to be as fruitful as studying in a quiet room. It's important to keep distractions to a minimum. You're only planning to study for a short block of time, so make the most of it. Don't pause to check your phone or get up to find a snack. It's also important to **avoid multitasking**. Research has consistently shown that multitasking will make your studying dramatically less effective. Your study area should also be comfortable and well-lit so you don't have the distraction of straining your eyes or sitting on an uncomfortable chair.

 The time of day you study is also important. You want to be rested and alert. Don't wait until just before bedtime. Study when you'll be most likely to comprehend and remember. Even better, if you know what time of day your test will be, set that time aside for study. That way your brain will be used to working on that subject at that specific time and you'll have a better chance of recalling information.

Finally, it can be helpful to team up with others who are studying for the same test. Your actual studying should be done in as isolated an environment as possible, but the work of organizing the information and setting up the study plan can be divided up. In between study sessions, you can discuss with your teammates the concepts that you're all studying and quiz each other on the details. Just be sure that your teammates are as serious about the test as you are. If you find that your study time is being replaced with social time, you might need to find a new team.

# Secret Key #2 – Make Your Studying Count

You're devoting a lot of time and effort to preparing for this test, so you want to be absolutely certain it will pay off. This means doing more than just reading the content and hoping you can remember it on test day. It's important to make every minute of study count. There are two main areas you can focus on to make your studying count.

## Retention

It doesn't matter how much time you study if you can't remember the material. You need to make sure you are retaining the concepts. To check your retention of the information you're learning, try recalling it at later times with minimal prompting. Try carrying around flashcards and glance at one or two from time to time or ask a friend who's also studying for the test to quiz you.

To enhance your retention, look for ways to put the information into practice so that you can apply it rather than simply recalling it. If you're using the information in practical ways, it will be much easier to remember. Similarly, it helps to solidify a concept in your mind if you're not only reading it to yourself but also explaining it to someone else. Ask a friend to let you teach them about a concept you're a little shaky on (or speak aloud to an imaginary audience if necessary). As you try to summarize, define, give examples, and answer your friend's questions, you'll understand the concepts better and they will stay with you longer. Finally, step back for a big picture view and ask yourself how each piece of information fits with the whole subject. When you link the different concepts together and see them working together as a whole, it's easier to remember the individual components.

Finally, practice showing your work on any multi-step problems, even if you're just studying. Writing out each step you take to solve a problem will help solidify the process in your mind, and you'll be more likely to remember it during the test.

## Modality

*Modality* simply refers to the means or method by which you study. Choosing a study modality that fits your own individual learning style is crucial. No two people learn best in exactly the same way, so it's important to know your strengths and use them to your advantage.

For example, if you learn best by visualization, focus on visualizing a concept in your mind and draw an image or a diagram. Try color-coding your notes, illustrating them, or creating symbols that will trigger your mind to recall a learned concept. If you learn best by hearing or discussing information, find a study partner who learns the same way or read aloud to yourself. Think about how to put the information in your own words. Imagine that you are giving a lecture on the topic and record yourself so you can listen to it later.

For any learning style, flashcards can be helpful. Organize the information so you can take advantage of spare moments to review. Underline key words or phrases. Use different colors for different categories. Mnemonic devices (such as creating a short list in which every item starts with the same letter) can also help with retention. Find what works best for you and use it to store the information in your mind most effectively and easily.

# Secret Key #3 – Practice the Right Way

Your success on test day depends not only on how many hours you put into preparing, but also on whether you prepared the right way. It's good to check along the way to see if your studying is paying off. One of the most effective ways to do this is by taking practice tests to evaluate your progress. Practice tests are useful because they show exactly where you need to improve. Every time you take a practice test, pay special attention to these three groups of questions:

- The questions you got wrong
- The questions you had to guess on, even if you guessed right
- The questions you found difficult or slow to work through

This will show you exactly what your weak areas are, and where you need to devote more study time. Ask yourself why each of these questions gave you trouble. Was it because you didn't understand the material? Was it because you didn't remember the vocabulary? Do you need more repetitions on this type of question to build speed and confidence? Dig into those questions and figure out how you can strengthen your weak areas as you go back to review the material.

 Additionally, many practice tests have a section explaining the answer choices. It can be tempting to read the explanation and think that you now have a good understanding of the concept. However, an explanation likely only covers part of the question's broader context. Even if the explanation makes perfect sense, **go back and investigate** every concept related to the question until you're positive you have a thorough understanding.

As you go along, keep in mind that the practice test is just that: practice. Memorizing these questions and answers will not be very helpful on the actual test because it is unlikely to have any of the same exact questions. If you only know the right answers to the sample questions, you won't be prepared for the real thing. **Study the concepts** until you understand them fully, and then you'll be able to answer any question that shows up on the test.

It's important to wait on the practice tests until you're ready. If you take a test on your first day of study, you may be overwhelmed by the amount of material covered and how much you need to learn. Work up to it gradually.

On test day, you'll need to be prepared for answering questions, managing your time, and using the test-taking strategies you've learned. It's a lot to balance, like a mental marathon that will have a big impact on your future. Like training for a marathon, you'll need to start slowly and work your way up. When test day arrives, you'll be ready.

Start with the strategies you've read in the first two Secret Keys—plan your course and study in the way that works best for you. If you have time, consider using multiple study resources to get different approaches to the same concepts. It can be helpful to see difficult concepts from more than one angle. Then find a good source for practice tests. Many times, the test website will suggest potential study resources or provide sample tests.

# Practice Test Strategy

If you're able to find at least three practice tests, we recommend this strategy:

## UNTIMED AND OPEN-BOOK PRACTICE

Take the first test with no time constraints and with your notes and study guide handy. Take your time and focus on applying the strategies you've learned.

## TIMED AND OPEN-BOOK PRACTICE

Take the second practice test open-book as well, but set a timer and practice pacing yourself to finish in time.

## TIMED AND CLOSED-BOOK PRACTICE

Take any other practice tests as if it were test day. Set a timer and put away your study materials. Sit at a table or desk in a quiet room, imagine yourself at the testing center, and answer questions as quickly and accurately as possible.

Keep repeating timed and closed-book tests on a regular basis until you run out of practice tests or it's time for the actual test. Your mind will be ready for the schedule and stress of test day, and you'll be able to focus on recalling the material you've learned.

# Secret Key #4 – Pace Yourself

Once you're fully prepared for the material on the test, your biggest challenge on test day will be managing your time. Just knowing that the clock is ticking can make you panic even if you have plenty of time left. Work on pacing yourself so you can build confidence against the time constraints of the exam. Pacing is a difficult skill to master, especially in a high-pressure environment, so **practice is vital**.

Set time expectations for your pace based on how much time is available. For example, if a section has 60 questions and the time limit is 30 minutes, you know you have to average 30 seconds or less per question in order to answer them all. Although 30 seconds is the hard limit, set 25 seconds per question as your goal, so you reserve extra time to spend on harder questions. When you budget extra time for the harder questions, you no longer have any reason to stress when those questions take longer to answer.

Don't let this time expectation distract you from working through the test at a calm, steady pace, but keep it in mind so you don't spend too much time on any one question. Recognize that taking extra time on one question you don't understand may keep you from answering two that you do understand later in the test. If your time limit for a question is up and you're still not sure of the answer, mark it and move on, and come back to it later if the time and the test format allow. If the testing format doesn't allow you to return to earlier questions, just make an educated guess; then put it out of your mind and move on.

On the easier questions, be careful not to rush. It may seem wise to hurry through them so you have more time for the challenging ones, but it's not worth missing one if you know the concept and just didn't take the time to read the question fully. Work efficiently but make sure you understand the question and have looked at all of the answer choices, since more than one may seem right at first.

Even if you're paying attention to the time, you may find yourself a little behind at some point. You should speed up to get back on track, but do so wisely. Don't panic; just take a few seconds less on each question until you're caught up. Don't guess without thinking, but do look through the answer choices and eliminate any you know are wrong. If you can get down to two choices, it is often worthwhile to guess from those. Once you've chosen an answer, move on and don't dwell on any that you skipped or had to hurry through. If a question was taking too long, chances are it was one of the harder ones, so you weren't as likely to get it right anyway.

On the other hand, if you find yourself getting ahead of schedule, it may be beneficial to slow down a little. The more quickly you work, the more likely you are to make a careless mistake that will affect your score. You've budgeted time for each question, so don't be afraid to spend that time. Practice an efficient but careful pace to get the most out of the time you have.

# Secret Key #5 – Have a Plan for Guessing

When you're taking the test, you may find yourself stuck on a question. Some of the answer choices seem better than others, but you don't see the one answer choice that is obviously correct. What do you do?

The scenario described above is very common, yet most test takers have not effectively prepared for it. Developing and practicing a plan for guessing may be one of the single most effective uses of your time as you get ready for the exam.

In developing your plan for guessing, there are three questions to address:

- When should you start the guessing process?
- How should you narrow down the choices?
- Which answer should you choose?

## When to Start the Guessing Process

Unless your plan for guessing is to select C every time (which, despite its merits, is not what we recommend), you need to leave yourself enough time to apply your answer elimination strategies. Since you have a limited amount of time for each question, that means that if you're going to give yourself the best shot at guessing correctly, you have to decide quickly whether or not you will guess.

Of course, the best-case scenario is that you don't have to guess at all, so first, see if you can answer the question based on your knowledge of the subject and basic reasoning skills. Focus on the key words in the question and try to jog your memory of related topics. Give yourself a chance to bring the knowledge to mind, but once you realize that you don't have (or you can't access) the knowledge you need to answer the question, it's time to start the guessing process.

It's almost always better to start the guessing process too early than too late. It only takes a few seconds to remember something and answer the question from knowledge. Carefully eliminating wrong answer choices takes longer. Plus, going through the process of eliminating answer choices can actually help jog your memory.

**Summary**: Start the guessing process as soon as you decide that you can't answer the question based on your knowledge.

7

# How to Narrow Down the Choices

The next chapter in this book (**Test-Taking Strategies**) includes a wide range of strategies for how to approach questions and how to look for answer choices to eliminate. You will definitely want to read those carefully, practice them, and figure out which ones work best for you. Here though, we're going to address a mindset rather than a particular strategy.

Your odds of guessing an answer correctly depend on how many options you are choosing from.

| Number of options left | 5 | 4 | 3 | 2 | 1 |
|---|---|---|---|---|---|
| Odds of guessing correctly | 20% | 25% | 33% | 50% | 100% |

You can see from this chart just how valuable it is to be able to eliminate incorrect answers and make an educated guess, but there are two things that many test takers do that cause them to miss out on the benefits of guessing:

- Accidentally eliminating the correct answer
- Selecting an answer based on an impression

We'll look at the first one here, and the second one in the next section.

To avoid accidentally eliminating the correct answer, we recommend a thought exercise called **the $5 challenge**. In this challenge, you only eliminate an answer choice from contention if you are willing to bet $5 on it being wrong. Why $5? Five dollars is a small but not insignificant amount of money. It's an amount you could afford to lose but wouldn't want to throw away. And while losing

$5 once might not hurt too much, doing it twenty times will set you back $100. In the same way, each small decision you make—eliminating a choice here, guessing on a question there—won't by itself impact your score very much, but when you put them all together, they can make a big difference. By holding each answer choice elimination decision to a higher standard, you can reduce the risk of accidentally eliminating the correct answer.

The $5 challenge can also be applied in a positive sense: If you are willing to bet $5 that an answer choice *is* correct, go ahead and mark it as correct.

**Summary**: Only eliminate an answer choice if you are willing to bet $5 that it is wrong.

# Which Answer to Choose

You're taking the test. You've run into a hard question and decided you'll have to guess. You've eliminated all the answer choices you're willing to bet $5 on. Now you have to pick an answer. Why do we even need to talk about this? Why can't you just pick whichever one you feel like when the time comes?

The answer to these questions is that if you don't come into the test with a plan, you'll rely on your impression to select an answer choice, and if you do that, you risk falling into a trap. The test writers know that everyone who takes their test will be guessing on some of the questions, so they intentionally write wrong answer choices to seem plausible. You still have to pick an answer though, and if the wrong answer choices are designed to look right, how can you ever be sure that you're not falling for their trap? The best solution we've found to this dilemma is to take the decision out of your hands entirely. Here is the process we recommend:

**Once you've eliminated any choices that you are confident (willing to bet $5) are wrong, select the first remaining choice as your answer.**

Whether you choose to select the first remaining choice, the second, or the last, the important thing is that you use some preselected standard. Using this approach guarantees that you will not be enticed into selecting an answer choice that looks right, because you are not basing your decision on how the answer choices look.

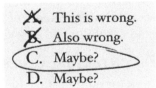

This is not meant to make you question your knowledge. Instead, it is to help you recognize the difference between your knowledge and your impressions. There's a huge difference between thinking an answer is right because of what you know, and thinking an answer is right because it looks or sounds like it should be right.

**Summary**: To ensure that your selection is appropriately random, make a predetermined selection from among all answer choices you have not eliminated.

# Test-Taking Strategies

This section contains a list of test-taking strategies that you may find helpful as you work through the test. By taking what you know and applying logical thought, you can maximize your chances of answering any question correctly!

It is very important to realize that every question is different and every person is different: no single strategy will work on every question, and no single strategy will work for every person. That's why we've included all of them here, so you can try them out and determine which ones work best for different types of questions and which ones work best for you.

## Question Strategies

### ☑ READ CAREFULLY

Read the question and the answer choices carefully. Don't miss the question because you misread the terms. You have plenty of time to read each question thoroughly and make sure you understand what is being asked. Yet a happy medium must be attained, so don't waste too much time. You must read carefully and efficiently.

### ☑ CONTEXTUAL CLUES

Look for contextual clues. If the question includes a word you are not familiar with, look at the immediate context for some indication of what the word might mean. Contextual clues can often give you all the information you need to decipher the meaning of an unfamiliar word. Even if you can't determine the meaning, you may be able to narrow down the possibilities enough to make a solid guess at the answer to the question.

### ☑ PREFIXES

If you're having trouble with a word in the question or answer choices, try dissecting it. Take advantage of every clue that the word might include. Prefixes can be a huge help. Usually, they allow you to determine a basic meaning. *Pre-* means before, *post-* means after, *pro-* is positive, *de-* is negative. From prefixes, you can get an idea of the general meaning of the word and try to put it into context.

### ☑ HEDGE WORDS

Watch out for critical hedge words, such as *likely, may, can, sometimes, often, almost, mostly, usually, generally, rarely,* and *sometimes.* Question writers insert these hedge phrases to cover every possibility. Often an answer choice will be wrong simply because it leaves no room for exception. Be on guard for answer choices that have definitive words such as *exactly* and *always.*

### ☑ SWITCHBACK WORDS

Stay alert for *switchbacks.* These are the words and phrases frequently used to alert you to shifts in thought. The most common switchback words are *but, although,* and *however.* Others include *nevertheless, on the other hand, even though, while, in spite of, despite,* and *regardless of.* Switchback words are important to catch because they can change the direction of the question or an answer choice.

**10**

## ⊘ Face Value

When in doubt, use common sense. Accept the situation in the problem at face value. Don't read too much into it. These problems will not require you to make wild assumptions. If you have to go beyond creativity and warp time or space in order to have an answer choice fit the question, then you should move on and consider the other answer choices. These are normal problems rooted in reality. The applicable relationship or explanation may not be readily apparent, but it is there for you to figure out. Use your common sense to interpret anything that isn't clear.

# Answer Choice Strategies

## ⊘ Answer Selection

The most thorough way to pick an answer choice is to identify and eliminate wrong answers until only one is left, then confirm it is the correct answer. Sometimes an answer choice may immediately seem right, but be careful. The test writers will usually put more than one reasonable answer choice on each question, so take a second to read all of them and make sure that the other choices are not equally obvious. As long as you have time left, it is better to read every answer choice than to pick the first one that looks right without checking the others.

## ⊘ Answer Choice Families

An answer choice family consists of two (in rare cases, three) answer choices that are very similar in construction and cannot all be true at the same time. If you see two answer choices that are direct opposites or parallels, one of them is usually the correct answer. For instance, if one answer choice says that quantity $x$ increases and another either says that quantity $x$ decreases (opposite) or says that quantity $y$ increases (parallel), then those answer choices would fall into the same family. An answer choice that doesn't match the construction of the answer choice family is more likely to be incorrect. Most questions will not have answer choice families, but when they do appear, you should be prepared to recognize them.

## ⊘ Eliminate Answers

Eliminate answer choices as soon as you realize they are wrong, but make sure you consider all possibilities. If you are eliminating answer choices and realize that the last one you are left with is also wrong, don't panic. Start over and consider each choice again. There may be something you missed the first time that you will realize on the second pass.

## ⊘ Avoid Fact Traps

Don't be distracted by an answer choice that is factually true but doesn't answer the question. You are looking for the choice that answers the question. Stay focused on what the question is asking for so you don't accidentally pick an answer that is true but incorrect. Always go back to the question and make sure the answer choice you've selected actually answers the question and is not merely a true statement.

## ⊘ Extreme Statements

In general, you should avoid answers that put forth extreme actions as standard practice or proclaim controversial ideas as established fact. An answer choice that states the "process should be used in certain situations, if..." is much more likely to be correct than one that states the "process should be discontinued completely." The first is a calm rational statement and doesn't even make a definitive, uncompromising stance, using a hedge word *if* to provide wiggle room, whereas the second choice is far more extreme.

### ☑ BENCHMARK

As you read through the answer choices and you come across one that seems to answer the question well, mentally select that answer choice. This is not your final answer, but it's the one that will help you evaluate the other answer choices. The one that you selected is your benchmark or standard for judging each of the other answer choices. Every other answer choice must be compared to your benchmark. That choice is correct until proven otherwise by another answer choice beating it. If you find a better answer, then that one becomes your new benchmark. Once you've decided that no other choice answers the question as well as your benchmark, you have your final answer.

### ☑ PREDICT THE ANSWER

Before you even start looking at the answer choices, it is often best to try to predict the answer. When you come up with the answer on your own, it is easier to avoid distractions and traps because you will know exactly what to look for. The right answer choice is unlikely to be word-for-word what you came up with, but it should be a close match. Even if you are confident that you have the right answer, you should still take the time to read each option before moving on.

## General Strategies

### ☑ TOUGH QUESTIONS

If you are stumped on a problem or it appears too hard or too difficult, don't waste time. Move on! Remember though, if you can quickly check for obviously incorrect answer choices, your chances of guessing correctly are greatly improved. Before you completely give up, at least try to knock out a couple of possible answers. Eliminate what you can and then guess at the remaining answer choices before moving on.

### ☑ CHECK YOUR WORK

Since you will probably not know every term listed and the answer to every question, it is important that you get credit for the ones that you do know. Don't miss any questions through careless mistakes. If at all possible, try to take a second to look back over your answer selection and make sure you've selected the correct answer choice and haven't made a costly careless mistake (such as marking an answer choice that you didn't mean to mark). This quick double check should more than pay for itself in caught mistakes for the time it costs.

### ☑ PACE YOURSELF

It's easy to be overwhelmed when you're looking at a page full of questions; your mind is confused and full of random thoughts, and the clock is ticking down faster than you would like. Calm down and maintain the pace that you have set for yourself. Especially as you get down to the last few minutes of the test, don't let the small numbers on the clock make you panic. As long as you are on track by monitoring your pace, you are guaranteed to have time for each question.

### ☑ DON'T RUSH

It is very easy to make errors when you are in a hurry. Maintaining a fast pace in answering questions is pointless if it makes you miss questions that you would have gotten right otherwise. Test writers like to include distracting information and wrong answers that seem right. Taking a little extra time to avoid careless mistakes can make all the difference in your test score. Find a pace that allows you to be confident in the answers that you select.

## ⊘ Keep Moving

Panicking will not help you pass the test, so do your best to stay calm and keep moving. Taking deep breaths and going through the answer elimination steps you practiced can help to break through a stress barrier and keep your pace.

# Final Notes

The combination of a solid foundation of content knowledge and the confidence that comes from practicing your plan for applying that knowledge is the key to maximizing your performance on test day. As your foundation of content knowledge is built up and strengthened, you'll find that the strategies included in this chapter become more and more effective in helping you quickly sift through the distractions and traps of the test to isolate the correct answer.

Now that you're preparing to move forward into the test content chapters of this book, be sure to keep your goal in mind. As you read, think about how you will be able to apply this information on the test. If you've already seen sample questions for the test and you have an idea of the question format and style, try to come up with questions of your own that you can answer based on what you're reading. This will give you valuable practice applying your knowledge in the same ways you can expect to on test day.

**Good luck and good studying!**

# Professional Practice and Ethics

## Ethics

### HISTORY AND DEVELOPMENT OF ETHICAL STANDARDS

In 1961, the American Personnel and Guidance Association (APGA) adopted **ethical standards** of the mental health counseling profession. In 1964, the Association for Counselor Education and Supervision (ACES) provided training standards for secondary school counselors. In 1973, the Standards for Preparation of Counselors and other Personnel Services Specialists were embraced by the ACES association. In 1977, standards were agreed on that met master's and doctoral degree requirements.

The American Mental Health Counselors Association (AMHCA) also wrote standards for mental health counseling programs. In 1995, these ethical standards went through a thorough process of revision. These new standards have been adopted by other groups that provide certification. AMHCA Standards are applied and enforced by the AMHCA Ethics Committee. The most stringent of these enforcements are found in the regulations that allocate expulsion from the association.

> **Review Video: Ethics**
> Visit mometrix.com/academy and enter code: 629669

### INCORPORATION OF ETHICS INTO CURRICULA

It was not until after 1990 that **ethics courses** were incorporated into the counselors' graduate degree programs. The American Psychological Association played an important part in the 1970's to change the curricula offered in doctoral programs by requiring colleges to teach ethics. This requirement was necessary before the college could be granted accreditation privileges. Those in the field prior to 1990 had to depend upon their supervisors' ability to both model and train in ethical procedures and conduct. This was an inefficient method for a number of reasons. The supervisor may not have been aware of the ethical code that applied to a given situation, or the supervisor may not have had a good understanding of sound ethical principles. Instruction in ethical principles should not be the sole responsibility of the clinical supervisor.

### HISTORY AND DEVELOPMENT OF THE CODE OF ETHICS

The original **Code of Ethics** for counselors was introduced in 1990 and gave specific solutions to specific problems; however, it had ambiguous interpretations in areas not specifically spelled out. The ambiguity is seen in the way that the code does not specify the meaning of exact terms. The National Board for Certified Counselors sought in 1997 to provide a less ambiguous wording for the Code of Ethics, so it is no longer seen as abstract rules that do not apply to real situations and real people. Problem-solving models and appreciation for the philosophical basis of each code has been applied to the more comprehensive ethical courses available in colleges today. The American Counseling Association's most recent Code of Ethics was released in 2014 to include the elements of distance counseling, technology, and social media. This code is very similar to the National Board for Certified Counselors Code of Ethics (2016), which contains 95 directives for ethical standards to be upheld by all certified counselors.

## ACA's 2014 Code of Ethics

Elements addressed within the American Counseling Association (ACA) Code of Ethics (2014) include the following:

- **Counseling relationship**: Informed consent, prohibited sexual and/or romantic relationships, professional boundaries, roles with individuals and groups, payment issues, business practices, and termination and referrals.
- **Confidentiality and privacy**: Right to privacy and exceptions, such as the serious and foreseeable harm requirements, information sharing, record keeping, and client access.
- **Professional responsibility**: Issues of competency, advertising, soliciting clients, professional qualifications, and responsibilities to public.
- **Relationships with other professionals**: Respect and equity in professional relationships with colleagues, employers, and employees, and provisions of consultation.
- **Evaluation, assessment, and interpretation**: Assessment, diagnosis, instrument selection, and conditions and issues related to assessment.
- **Supervision, training, and teaching**: Responsibilities of the supervisor and educator roles.
- **Research and publication**: Guidelines for carrying out research, informing clients, and protecting clients.
- **Distance counseling, technology, and social media**: Laws/regulations for both the counselor's place of work and client's place of residence may apply. Clients should be aware that privacy and security of electronic transmission may be breached. The counselor must verify the client's identity at every session.
- **Resolving ethical issues**: Reporting violations and cooperating with ethics committees.

### INFORMED CONSENT

Provisions of the ACA Code of Ethics (2014) regarding **informed consent** in the counseling relationship include the following:

- Clients should be informed of the nature of all services both in writing and verbally and should be apprised of fees. Clients should be included in discussions even if they are themselves unable to give informed consent.
- Language used to obtain informed consent must be clear, understandable, and culturally appropriate.
- Informed consent must be obtained for all assessments, and recipients of assessment results must be identified.
- If supervising another counselor, the supervisee must be made aware of clients' rights, and the client must give consent for supervision.
- Clients must have informed consent for any research they are involved in and have the right to refuse participation.
- Clients must be informed about risks of breach of security when utilizing distance counseling and should be apprised of the location of the counselor's practice, risks and benefits of participation, anticipated response times (such as for text messaging), times when counselor is available, and issues related to payment or nonpayment of third-party payors.

## ETHICAL DILEMMAS
### ETHICAL ISSUES THAT COUNSELORS MAY FACE

The counselor is obligated to uphold ethical standards. The nature of the work presents the counselor with ongoing **challenges that test the counselor's ethical positions** about a problem.

Counselors not only have to consider the ethical position they should take when a problem presents, but must also consider how the solution will be of benefit to the client. The client cannot be damaged from the solution. Therefore, the consequences of the solution should be weighed carefully. There does exist a tendency for counselors to do nothing when an ethical issue is involved. This tendency may be due to the fact that the counselor feels unsure of how to proceed in the situation, or it may be that the counselor is reluctant to proceed in general. Self-awareness when this hesitation occurs is vital in ensuring proper handling of ethical dilemmas.

## PROBLEM-SOLVING FOR ETHICAL DILEMMAS

There are nine steps used in the problem-solving model for ethical dilemmas designed by Koocher and Keith-Spiegel in 1998:

- **Step 1**: Determine the ethical problem.
- **Step 2**: Review the ethical guidelines available that pertain to the problem at hand, including possible solutions that have previously worked with other clients.
- **Step 3**: Peruse the impact that other sources may have on the decisions that should be made to resolve the problem.
- **Step 4**: Consult with trusted professionals about the problem and possible solutions.
- **Step 5**: Assess the human rights and civil liberties of the client, which may be impacted by the solution to the problem, and consider possible consequences of the solution for the problem at hand.
- **Step 6**: Create a number of avenues that may be explored in the solution to the problem.
- **Step 7**: Evaluate the possible consequences that can be the result of each solution applied to the problem at hand.
- **Step 8**: Make a decision about one solution to be implemented.
- **Step 9**: Follow through with the decision that was made.

Koocher and Keith-Spiegel's approach can be applied to many ethical dilemmas that a counselor faces in his or her daily professional life. This model is currently in use in the instruction of ethical principles in degree programs throughout the country.

## MULTIPLE RELATIONSHIPS

In 1974, Arnold Lazarus was a renowned psychotherapist who supported **multiple relationships** in his ethical decision-making model (multi-modal therapy). Lazarus thought that the client could benefit from the development of both a therapeutic and social relationship with the counselor. In 1993, M.C. Gottlieb responded with his own five-step model:

- **Step 1**: Consider the element of power, where the client feels inferior to the counselor and may find a long-standing relationship harmful.
- **Step 2**: Consider the duration of the relationship by predicting how the relationship and the balance of power may change over time.
- **Step 3**: Consider the clarity of termination, which involves compatibility between the client and the counselor, and consequences that can occur when the client and counselor roles are conflicting and harmful.
- **Step 4**: Gain the perspective and advice of a professional associate.
- **Step 5**: Present the relationship change to the client, and give him or her time to make a decision about this change in the relationship.

## SMALL-TOWN PHENOMENON

Some multiple relationships are unavoidable. For instance, the **small-town phenomenon** describes a situation in which the therapist may have to come into contact with clients within the social structures of a community. A small-town therapist may belong to the same religious organization as a client. The small-town therapist may find that their clients live in the same neighborhood or have children in the same school as their own. The small-town therapist may belong to the same charitable organizations or attend the same functions.

## DEONTOLOGY VS. UTILITARIANISM

Two of the most common schools of thought when approaching ethical decision-making and ethical dilemmas are the deontological view and the utilitarian view.

- Immanuel Kant is most commonly associated with the **deontological view** of ethics. One foundational philosophy developed by Kant was his categorical imperative. Deontological perspectives deal in universal truths, where everyone receives equal treatment. Therefore, when a counselor believes that privacy should be part of their service, then that privacy is applied to all clients in every situation. There is no room for exceptions to the rule. Likewise, there is no need to consider consequences in this philosophy, as all people are treated equally. The Golden Rule is at the heart of deontology ("Do unto others as you would have them do unto you").
- **Utilitarianism** was presented by John Stuart Mill. He believed that the consequences had to be looked at in relation to the resulting outcomes. The overall goal is to create as many constructive and positive consequences as possible for the majority of people.

## CONFIDENTIALITY IN THE COUNSELOR-CLIENT RELATIONSHIP

### APPLICATION OF HIPAA CONCEPTS IN THE COUNSELING PROFESSION

Counselors who electronically submit any type of protected health information for third-party payments for services must be **HIPAA** compliant with the privacy rule, which then applies to all protected health information (PHI), even that not transmitted. Once compliance with the privacy rule is triggered, compliance with the security rule is also required:

- **Privacy rule**: Protected information includes any information included in the medical record (electronic or paper), conversations between the doctor and other healthcare providers, billing information, and any other form of health information. Procedures must be in place to limit access and disclosures.
- **Security rule**: Any electronic health information must be secure and protected against threats, hazards, or non-permitted disclosures, in compliance with established standards.

Individual states may have even more restrictive regulations and may have consent requirements, so the counselor must be aware of all pertinent laws and regulations. Therapy notes that are separate from the rest of the medical record have increased protection from disclosure. PHI may be disclosed without consent to report abuse, to prevent serious harm to person or public, and in response to legal subpoenas or court orders.

> **Review Video: What is HIPAA?**
> Visit mometrix.com/academy and enter code: 412009

### BREAKING CONFIDENTIALITY

John Stuart Mill proposed that the utilitarian should **break confidentiality** when it benefited the majority of the people. In 1976, a lawsuit was brought to the California Supreme Court to contest the deontological perspective against the utilitarian perspective. In the case of *Tarasoff versus the Board of Regents of the University of California*, the courts supported the utilitarian perspective on breaking confidentiality for the good of the majority. The court allowed that keeping confidentiality in this case could have caused injury to others. However, some counselors do tend to believe that confidentiality should be an absolute right of the client.

> **Review Video: Ethics and Confidentiality in Counseling**
> Visit mometrix.com/academy and enter code: 250384

## VIRTUE ETHICS

The **virtue ethics** philosophy holds that people with high ethical standards have the ability to make good ethical judgments. This philosophy is also known as value ethics or principle ethics. Lazarus' decision-making model is based on the virtue ethics philosophy. The counselor can find that having a strong philosophy of virtue ethics can assist them in their work. Virtue ethics helps the counselor to be motivated to make the best decision for their client and helps the counselor to understand their responsibility to act in a positive manner and to implement an ethical solution to a problem. Virtue ethics help the counselor in their appraisal of possible consequences that can arise in a given solution. The counselor with a strong philosophy in virtue ethics has a strong moral character. Virtue ethics is based on **beneficence** and **nonmaleficence**, which are the basis of the **Hippocratic Oath** that states, "First, do no harm." This means that the counselor works to help the client and does not want any damage to come to the client. The decisions that are made in counseling must not disregard the principles maintained in virtue ethics.

### ROLE OF CARE AND COMPASSION IN VIRTUE ETHICS AND COUNSELING

Care and compassion take the principles behind beneficence one step further. In 1982, Gilligan described caring as a bonding process that created a sense that the counselor had the ability to understand and to identify with how the client was feeling. Gilligan also proposed that the counselor was able to react quickly and favorably in meeting the needs of the client. Gilligan went on to state that the counselor exhibited a compassionate and concerned commitment to their client. The counselor performs these acts of caring in a professional manner. The counselor should not try to practice counseling methods that fall outside their scope of expertise and training. The counselor may violate an ethical principle by not realizing their own incompetence in an area. Some violations occur out of arrogance, over-involvement, or control issues with the client.

### INHERENT DANGERS ASSOCIATED WITH VIRTUE ETHICS AND WAYS TO ENHANCE AN ETHICAL PERSPECTIVE

Virtue ethics are essential in the role that the counselor performs. However, a note of caution: No one source can be trusted to **maintain a virtue ethics perspective**. Therefore, supervisors, ethical codes, decision-making models, utilitarian perspectives, and deontological perspectives should all be understood and reviewed when making ethical decisions.

- The counselor should seek to internalize sound virtue ethics principles.
- The counselor should recognize virtue ethics and seek to live by those ethics in all areas of life.
- The counselor should seek to gain additional education and training to ensure that they gain competency in a variety of areas.
- The counselor should seek out an ethical support group.
- The counselor should seek to establish sound ethical philosophies that reflect virtue ethics principles.

## COMPETENCE

Competence is the ability to do something to a compulsory set of standards. However, this denotes the most basic level of competency. In the counselor's role, **competence** must be reached at its uppermost levels. This regard for excellence in performance levels follows the perspective held in virtue ethics. Therefore, the counselor takes on a life-long commitment to achieving competency levels in their profession. In 1996, Pope and Brown proposed that there were two types of competence to be achieved.

- The first type involves **intellectual competence**, which consists of education and training.
- The second type involves **emotional competence**. The counselor is self-aware of prejudices held, emotional stability, and competence levels. The counselor seeks professional supervision and referrals when it is necessary.

### SELF-KNOWLEDGE

Self-knowledge is an area in which a counselor should make a daily assessment. Some psychoanalytically-trained therapists must undergo counseling therapy as part of their training. This is not always the case, however. **Self-knowledge** is essential in developing competency in an area. Competency is a considerable part of value ethics. Self-knowledge is also supported by supervisory personnel in the field. Peers or colleagues can be sought out to gain advice on ethical dilemmas. Some counselors violate virtue ethics by becoming too absorbed in the client's problem. Caring and compassion is taken to unhealthy emotional levels. One condition that can arise from this violation is post-traumatic stress disorder. The counselor has the tendency to develop hypervigilance in response to stressful situations that arise daily. The counselor may experience burnout or withdraw from their family. The counselor may also experience physical or emotional symptoms.

## RESPECT

The counselor must treat all clients with **respect**. Respect involves accuracy in reporting details, loyal devotion, honesty, confidence, reliability, keeping promises, and valuing the client's personal independence. The counselor relays to the client an accurate representation of the counselor's role, the client's rights, confidentiality rights, and any negative consequences that can result in a prescribed treatment plan. A handout and simple explanation do not ensure client understanding. The client and legal guardians must give informed consent before treatment can be applied. Clients with a legal guardian must have the guardian's consent to the therapy. Informed consent involves confidentiality in the counselor-client relationship. Confidentiality is maintained in individual counseling sessions unless the client is a danger to himself or others. This harm must be identified by method and time. Confidentiality is not assured in a group setting or in cases of child abuse.

## JUSTICE AND ACCOUNTABILITY

The counselor is aware of their role in providing clients with a fair and just program of treatment. Fairness involves the same equal treatment of all clients, as each receives a fair amount of the counselor's time and attention. The virtue of **justice** may be violated when the counselor is in denial or when the counselor tries to rationalize their actions.

**Accountability** is part of the virtue ethics philosophy. This means that the counselor takes responsibility for their actions and that of others in their field. Unethical behavior in others can be handled professionally and emphatically. Confrontations need to be approached with respect and a sense of fair play. The goal of the confrontation is to achieve a positive result. The counselor should role-play or rehearse confrontations to ensure that possible responses and consequences can be responded to on a professional level.

## ETHICS-BASED APPROACHES WHEN SERVICES A CLIENT REQUIRES ARE LIMITED

Many HMO's and other third-party influences may cause the counselor to question whether virtue ethics principles are being followed in the client's care. The counselor may believe that the client is in need of more sessions that are not covered under the client's insurance policy. The counselor can follow a series of actions to maintain the virtue ethics principles of beneficence and nonmaleficence. The counselor may appeal to the insurance company for additional sessions. The counselor may also continue to see the client at a reduced price, giving additional sessions at an affordable rate, or issue a referral to the client to seek free services from a government agency or reputable charity. These actions reflect a sense of caring for the client that follows ethical guidelines.

# Regulatory Standards

## HISTORY OF PROFESSIONAL COUNSELING CERTIFICATION

The **Commission on Rehabilitation Counselor Certification (CRCC)** was established in 1973. In 1976, the CRCC initiated its first national assessment. Currently, the CRCC boasts over 30,000 certifications and over 15,000 valid certification holders.

The **National Academy of Certified Clinical Mental Health Counselors** was founded by AMHCA in 1979. The first 50 candidates had to provide a clinical work sample and pass the national assessment exam. Throughout the years, the exacting standards for this voluntary credential have kept the numbers of credentialed counselors low.

In 1982, the **National Board of Certified Counselors (NBCC)** was established under the APGA. This organization offered a generic counseling certificate to mental health counselors. In 1983, the NBCC gave the assessment to certify over 2,200 mental health counselors.

In 1985, the **National Counsel for the Credentialing of Career Counselors (NCCC)** offered a professional certification. However, this certification is no longer available. The NCCC does maintain the NCCC credential previously achieved by its candidates who passed the assessment given.

In the latter part of the 1990s, the National Academy of Certified Clinical Mental Health Counselors joined the National Board for Certified Counselors. The joint entity offers the National Certified School Counselor (NCSC) and the Master Addictions Counselor (MAC) certificates. There is now one generic certification available to mental health counselors, which remains suitable for a broad range of positions. There are now five specialty certifications available on a national or international level, in addition to minor types of certification in place.

## CREDENTIALING PROCESS

The credentialing process depends on the counselor's work setting and specialty. Generally, credentialing begins with the student obtaining a master's degree of 48-60 semester hours in psychology or education. Some states still accept a bachelor's degree with additional post-graduate courses in counseling, or for substance abuse and behavior counselors in certain settings, a high school diploma and certification. There are generally eight **core areas of study**:

- Professional counseling orientation and ethical practice
- Social and cultural diversity
- Human growth and development
- Career development
- Counseling and helping relationships
- Group counseling and group work
- Assessment and testing
- Research and program evaluation

Student counselors complete a supervised clinical experience, usually 3,000 hours or 2 years, and obtain two letters of professional endorsement. Licensure differs state by state. The candidate must pass a state exam. Most licenses require annual continuing education credits for maintenance. The counselor agrees to follow certain standards and ethical codes. Some jobs require additional credentials, for example, a school counselor must have both a teaching certificate and a counseling certificate, in addition to teaching experience.

## ACCREDITATION

Accreditation is quality control for the programs that train mental health counselors. Most universities observe **accreditation standards** in each academic department. Not all private schools, colleges, and universities that offer counseling courses are accredited. A student will probably not be able to obtain an internship to complete their practicum or obtain a license if they did not attend an accredited school. Internship positions are usually found in organizations such as hospitals, community mental health centers, clinics, and schools, many of which require accreditation. The stakeholders involved in accreditation include the following:

- Pre-service programs
- Professional preparation programs
- Local agencies
- State agencies
- Federal agencies

Accreditation is founded on a set of standards that can be tied to either the professional standards or to a general set of standards. The program and the standards must be defined in such a way that the accreditation is acceptable to future employers.

## CACREP ACCREDITATION

The ACES (Assessment, Counseling, and Educational Services) developed a manual for training counselors in the field of mental health in 1978. This manual was used in five regional workshops in 1979 for a pilot program. Then, the American Personnel and Guidance Association (APGA) and ACES began developing an accreditation program for mental health counselors. In 1981, the **Council for the Accreditation of Counseling and Related Educational Programs (CACREP)** was founded as an independent organization that could provide accreditation to the mental health counselor. As of 2018, over 400 universities boast of CACREP accredited educational programs in their schools. These universities have increased the number of master's and doctoral level programs that they now offer. Many other universities are in pursuit of the CACREP accreditation for their programs. Many states mandate the necessity of the CACREP accreditation as a requirement for obtaining a license.

## CHANGES IN THE COUNSELING EDUCATION AND PROGRAM ACCREDITATION

The increase in both long- and short-term psychotherapies wrought a number of **changes in the education system**. Those responsible for the educational needs of counselors changed curricula and techniques to improve the quality of education. Education counselors added the courses to the counselor's curricula to address the changing demographics and needs of the country, with courses focused on multicultural counseling, brief therapy, and ethical issues. Counselors began learning about conflict resolution, community consultations, case management, and client advocacy, in addition to sound business practices. Counselor education programs have been encouraged to seek accreditation privileges from the Council for Accreditation of Counseling and Related Educational Programs (CACREP). The accredited program's objectives and curriculum must follow approved standards with clinical instruction. Faculty and staff must meet prescribed CACREP standards regarding organizations and administrative structures. In addition, the college must be willing to undergo program evaluations set by CACREP standards.

## CACREP STANDARDS FOR PROFESSIONAL COUNSELING EDUCATION PROGRAMS

In 2016, the **Standards of the Council for the Accreditation of Counseling and Related Educational Programs (CACREP)** were organized into six sections. These six sections include:

- The learning environment
- Professional counseling identity
- Professional practice
- Evaluation in the program
- Entry-level specialty areas (including addictions, career, clinical mental health, clinical rehabilitation, college counseling and student affairs, marriage/couple/family, and school counseling)
- Doctoral standards for counselor education and supervision

According to the CACREP, these standards were written "with the intention to simplify and clarify the accreditation requirements and to promote a unified counseling profession." The CACREP standards provide sequencing and clinical experience that can make a solid foundation for the professional counselor's education. The standards help the counselor to develop a professional identity. The student learns about social and cultural diversity, human development and growth, career development, helping relationships, group work, assessment, research, and program evaluation. The student receives clinical instruction and experience at a supervised practicum and internship opportunities, in addition to the theory. The number of clinical hours, the type of supervision, and supervisory credentials are included in the **CACREP standards**. Curriculum development can also be improved with contributions made by counseling practitioners.

## STANDARDS OF PROFESSIONAL PRACTICE

The professional practice standards for counselors require significant command of mental health care theory and its application. Graduate students must be prepared to accept entry level positions to become proficient and competent in all skills. A standard set of criteria is used to assess whether or not the graduate student has reached the level of professional proficiency. The criteria include the following:

- Meeting accreditation requirements
- Following ethical practice standards* for the public good
- Achieving competencies required in entry level positions
- Satisfactory completion of all academic classes
- Satisfactory completion of a supervised clinical experience (usually 3,000 hours)
- Meeting all certification provisions (e.g., two professional endorsement letters)

*Ethical standards apply to testing of humans and animals and refraining from sexual or other harmful relationships with clients. Ethical standards stipulate scrutiny and disciplinary actions for violators.

## LICENSING

### STATE LICENSING BOARDS

State licensing boards supervise mental health professionals in their work. **State licensing boards** set internship hours, supervisor qualifications, and the amount of direct client contact required, as well as monitor ethics. When a board finds that a counselor acted unethically, then the state can suspend or revoke the counselor's license and apply penalties. Counselors who wish to renew their licenses may be required to complete continuing education credits and pay additional fees to the state board. If a counselor is discovered practicing without a legal license, then he or she can be charged and prosecuted. Each state posts its minimum education and work experience standards for statutory certification, and every counselor in the state must meet them. The counselor can use the civil law system to fight the state board's charges and to sue for monetary restitution.

## LICENSURE AND PROFESSIONAL CERTIFICATION REQUIREMENTS

Counselors receive state authorization to work as mental health practitioners either through **licensure** or **professional certification**. Licensure is the law in most of the country. Some states do not issue licenses; instead, they recognize professional certification as the practice credential, meaning the candidate obtained the National Certified Counselor designation through the National Board for Certified Counselors, Inc. National certification is voluntary. It is distinct from a state license and requires a separate exam and 100 hours of continuing education every 5 years. The Commission on Rehabilitation Counselor Certification is required for rehab counselors, and includes an exam every 5 years or 100 hours of education, an internship, and work experience in rehabilitation if the counselor graduated with another specialization.

## LICENSURE LAWS

In 1976, the Virginia Counselors Association passed **licensure laws**. This was the result of a lawsuit by an unlicensed counselor. In 1979, Arkansas and Alabama passed licensure laws also. By the end of 1985, more than 13 states had passed similar licensure laws. Currently, all states, the District of Colombia, and Puerto Rico now have counseling licensure laws. Licensure laws give the public a sense of protection that their therapists are qualified professionals who have met the requirements of the state to hold those positions. All states mandate a written assessment and some also have oral assessments in place. The professional who gains a license is a Licensed Professional Counselor, Licensed Clinical Mental Health Counselor, or Certified Professional Counselor. Ethical violators are penalized by the legal system. Exemptions are given to those in private and public practice who counsel in related professional groups.

## FUTURE OF COUNSELOR CREDENTIALING

The efforts of the AMHCA have had a profound affect upon the licensure laws for counselors in the mental health field. Counselor education programs have applied more exacting standards to their courses. Managed care options in the insurance industry have also changed the counselor's standing within the profession. This change has benefited the equality that mental health counselors desire to be accepted by other professionals. Legislation has also been passed to grant professional counselors equal standing. The credentials and licensure laws will continue to change as government bodies are influenced by the efforts of AMHCA. The future promises to be one in which more opportunities are presented to the counselors who have achieved the appropriate credentials required in their state of operation. New counseling professions will emerge as the need for more specialized counselors arises.

# Legal and Political Issues

## LEGISLATIVE PROCESS

### PROPOSING AND PROMOTING A BILL

The **legislative process** begins with a proposed bill. This proposed bill must be assessed to determine what strategies are applicable to get the bill to pass and become law. The bill must be presented to the legislature. This calls for some consideration about the most receptive body. Some bills do well in the House of Representatives, and other bills are more suited to the Senate. Still others perform well in both the House and the Senate. The political representative who is chosen must be the best advocate for the particular cause. Special interest groups may help promote the bill through legislative contacts, after it has been presented to the legislative body. Lobbyists work to establish relationships with key committee members. The bill must go through the committee before it can be voted on.

### PASSING A BILL TO BECOME LAW

Most bills that are introduced to a legislative body never make it out of committee. The bill that does make it out of committee must still be given support by the majority of the legislative body to be **approved**. The approved bill can then be sent to the **executive branch** of the government. The executive branch on the state level is the governor. The executive branch on the national level is the president. The executive branch representative has the responsibility of signing the bill into law and may veto or reject a bill. The executive branch is subject to lobbying efforts. The **legislative process** is expensive and time-consuming. The American Mental Health Counselors Association (AMHCA) sees it as their responsibility to take on this complex process to ensure that counselors are recognized and credentialed by each state.

## INFLUENCES OF THE POLITICAL SYSTEM ON COUNSELING

The United States has a **political system** that allows its citizens to voice their issues and concerns publicly. A wide spectrum of communication systems is available to help in this endeavor. The individual may present their issues/concerns to others through speeches, telephone calls, emails, or the internet (blogs, social media, etc.). The AMHCA recognizes the need to bring issues important to mental health counselors to light and works jointly with the American Counseling Association (ACA) to send lobbyists to Washington D.C. to represent mental health counselors. As early as 1982, the AMHCA has managed to enlist the services of a renowned lobbyist to represent its interests in the political arena. Today, the AMHCA continues on this endeavor, and provides resources to mental health counselors on how to stay informed on proposed legislation, contact their local legislator, and appropriately lobby either as an individual or part of a group.

## AVENUES THE AMHCA ESTABLISHED IN THEIR POLITICAL NETWORK

Mental health counselors were taught how to represent themselves as **political advocates and lobbyists** in the grassroots campaigns set up by the AMHCA. The AMHCA and the ACA have worked diligently to establish a network that is competent in issuing timely emails, written correspondence, phone calls, and face-to-face communications to promote its political agenda. The successes of the lobbying efforts have been critical in the licensure legislation set up in the majority of states, and it is expected that the AMHCA and the ACA will turn their efforts to equality issues for the mental health counselor. The problem of recognition exists on the corporate level. Private corporate third-party payers and some insurance companies have yet to recognize the high standards and expertise that exist in the mental health counselors' professional credentials.

## ESTABLISHING RELATIONSHIPS OF INFLUENCE WITH POLITICAL OFFICIALS

Mental health professionals may consider a relationship that is built on campaign contributions as ethically suspect. However, the time-honored tradition of donating money to a candidate's election campaign is effective in gaining the attention of **elected government officials**. The government official takes a donation to mean that an individual or group is a member of their campaign and that they support their position as a representative for the state. This puts the contributor in a privileged and influential position. A campaign donation may be enough for one to gain faster access into the government official's office. Any relationship that is built should be given the necessary attention to maintain it. Be persistent with communication efforts, even when no lobbying agenda is in place.

## RELATIONSHIPS THAT UNPAID LOBBYISTS MUST DEVELOP

The **unpaid lobbyist** works to influence political entities and representatives who have the power to pass a bill. The counselor assigned as a lobbyist creates a rapport with elected government officials face-to-face and develops it through telephone calls, letters, and email correspondence. The intended result of this diligent communication effort is to remind the official about issues that are important to the counselor. The face-to-face visit can be accomplished during visits to the official's office in the home state. This setting gives the official a chance to connect with their constituents and to engage in conversation on key issues.

## IMPORTANCE OF VOTES AND FINANCIAL BACKING IN LOBBYING EFFORTS

Politicians are elected based on how many votes they receive from their constituents. This means that the politician finds great worth in the **power of the voter**. Constituents who are part of an organized group can mean a great many votes on election day. The politician will pay attention to the lobbyist who represents large numbers of constituents. The Political Action Committees (PAC) had a strong influence on the political system in the past. However, today this influence has diminished. PACs and many lobbying committees are careful to keep a low profile because of the negative attitudes that voters have about paid lobbyists and large corporations. Counselor lobbyists do not have much in the way of financial resources but do have the grassroots support of other counselor voters that are responsible for electing government officials into office.

## PRESENTING ISSUES TO POLICY MAKERS

### COMMUNICATION STYLE

The importance of **communicating to policy makers in succinct terms** cannot be overstated. The unpaid lobbyist must make his or her point quickly and succinctly to be heard. Otherwise, the unpaid lobbyist risks "the brush off," or is not understood by the official. The best way to present an issue is through brief telephone calls, emails, or formally written letters. Hand-written notes should be written on paper that bears personal letterhead. Emails are not as effective but benefit from an appropriate subject and respectful tone. Communication should clearly state how the bill will make a positive impact on the voting constituents. Data points, signature lists of supporters, and other attachments are helpful to include in these communication efforts. Keep the client's needs at the forefront of one's mind. Represent these needs accurately to the elected government official. The official needs to understand how the bill will improve counseling services for the client.

## TIMING

Timing is another issue that should be addressed in the life of an unpaid lobbyist. Activate the communication network system among fellow counselor supporters whenever there is a vote in front of a legislative committee. The support of other counselors within the organized network should impact this vote in a positive way. The bill cannot go to the floor for a vote by the larger body of legislators until it is passed by the committee. The chain needs to be activated again when the bill comes up for a vote on the floor. This is a critical time, as the vote must pass to go on to the next step in the legislative process. The final stop is at the executive branch. This is also a critical time for the communication network to make their opinions known to their elected governmental leader.

# Research

## RESEARCH PROCESS

The key steps in the research process are as follows:

1. **Problem or issue identification**: Includes a literature review to further define the problem and to ensure that the problem has not already been studied
2. **Hypothesis formulation**: Creating a clear statement of the problem or concern, worded in a way that it can be operationalized and measured
3. **Operationalization**: Creating measurable variables that fully address the hypothesis
4. **Study design selection**: Choosing a study design that will allow for the proper analysis of the data to be collected

## DATA

### OBJECTIVE VS. SUBJECTIVE DATA

Both **subjective (qualitative)** and **objective (quantitative)** data are used for research and analysis, but the focus is quite different:

| Subjective Data | Objective Data |
| --- | --- |
| Subjective data depend on the opinions of the observer or the subject. Data are described verbally or graphically, depending upon observers to provide information. Interviews may be used as a tool to gather information, and the researcher's interpretation of data is important. Gathering this type of data can be time-intensive, and it usually cannot be generalized to a larger population. This type of information gathering is often useful at the beginning of the design process for data collection. | Objective data are observable and can be tested and verified. Data are described in terms of numbers within a statistical format. This type of information gathering is done after the design of data collection is outlined, usually in later stages. Tools may include surveys, questionnaires, or other methods of obtaining numerical data. |

### DATA COLLECTION

Key points in data collection include the following:

- Data should ideally be collected close to the time of intervention (delays may result in variation from forgetfulness, rather than from the intervention process).
- Frequent data collection is ideal, but subject boredom or fatigue must be avoided as well. Thus, make the data collection process as easy as possible (electronic devices can sometimes help).
- Keep the data collection process short to increase subject responsiveness.
- Standardize recording procedures (collect data at the same time, place, and method to enhance ultimate data validity and reliability).
- Choose a collection method that fits the study well (observation, questionnaires, logs, diaries, surveys, rating scales, etc.) to optimize the data collection process and enhance the value of the data obtained.

## STUDY DESIGNS
### SELECTING A STUDY DESIGN
Key considerations that guide the selection of a study design include the following:

- **Standardization**: Whether or not data can be collected in an identical way from each participant (eliminating collection variation)
- **Level of certainty**: The study size needed to achieve statistical significance (determined via power calculations)
- **Resources**: The availability of funding and other resources needed
- The **time frame** required
- The capacity of subjects to provide **informed consent** and receiving **ethics approval** via Human Subjects Review Committees and Institutional Review Boards

### COMMON STUDY DESIGNS
The three common study designs used in the research process include the following:

- An **exploratory research design** is common when little is known about a particular problem or issue. Its key feature is flexibility. The results comprise detailed descriptions of all observations made, arranged in some kind of order. Conclusions drawn include educated guesses or hypotheses.
- When the variables chosen have already been studied (e.g., in an exploratory study), further research requires a **descriptive survey design**. In this design, the variables are controlled partly by the situation and partly by the investigator, who chooses the sample. Proof of causality cannot be established, but the evidence may support causality.
- **Experimental studies** are highly controlled. Intervening and extraneous variables are eliminated, and independent variables are manipulated to measure effects in dependent variables (e.g., variables of interest)—either in the field or in a laboratory setting.

### ETHICAL CONCERNS WITH STUDY DESIGN SELECTION
Ethical concerns involved with selecting a study design include the following:

- Research must not lead to harming clients.
- Denying an intervention may amount to harm.
- Informed consent is essential.
- Confidentiality is required.

### SINGLE SYSTEM STUDY DESIGNS
Evaluation of the efficacy and functionality of a practice is an important aspect of quality control and practice improvement. The most common approach to such an evaluation is the **single system study approach**. Selecting one client per system ($n = 1$), observations are made prior to, during, and following an intervention.

The **research steps** are:

1. Selection of a problem for change (the target)
2. Operationalizing the target into measurable terms
3. Following the target during the baseline phase, prior to the application of any intervention
4. Observing the target and collecting data during the intervention phase, during which the intervention is carried out (There may be more than one phase of data collection.)

Data that are repeatedly collected constitute a single system study "time series design." Single system designs provide a flexible and efficient way to evaluate virtually any type of practice.

## BASIC SINGLE SYSTEM DESIGN AND ADDITIONAL TYPES OF CASE STUDY OR PREDESIGNS

The most basic single system design is the **A-B design**. The baseline phase (A) has no intervention, followed by the intervention phase (B) with data collection. Typically, data are collected continuously through the intervention phase. Advantages of this design include the following:

- Versatility
- Adaptability to many settings, program styles, and problems
- Clear comparative information between phases

A significant limitation, however, is that causation cannot be demonstrated.

Three additional types of **case study or predesigns** are:

- **Design A,** an observational design with no intervention
- **Design B,** an intervention-only design without any baseline
- **Design B-C,** a "changes case study" design (where no baseline is recorded, a first intervention [B] is performed and then changed [C] and data are recorded)

## COMMON SINGLE SYSTEM EXPERIMENTAL DESIGNS

Common single system experimental designs are described below:

- The **A-B-A design** begins with data collection in the pre-intervention phase (A) and then continuously during the intervention phases (B). The intervention is then removed (returning to "A") and data are again collected. In this way an experimental process is produced (testing without, with, and then again without intervention). Inferences regarding causality can be made, and two points of comparison are achieved. However, the ethics of removing a successful intervention leaves this study poorly recommended.
- The **A-B-A-B study** overcomes this failure by reintroducing the intervention ("B") at the close of the study. Greater causality inferences are obtained. However, even temporary removal of a successful intervention is problematic (especially if the client drops out at that time), and this design is fairly time-consuming.
- The **B-A-B design** (the "intervention repeat design") drops the baseline phase and starts and ends with the intervention (important in crisis situations and where treatment delays are problematic), saving time and reducing ethical concerns.

## SAMPLING
### TERMS USED IN SAMPLING

In sampling, the following concepts are considered:

- A **population** is the total set of subjects sought for measurement by a researcher.
- A **sample** is a subset of subjects drawn from a population (as total population testing is usually not possible).
- A **subject** is a single unit of a population.
- **Generalizability** refers to the degree to which specific findings obtained can be applied to the total population.

## SAMPLING TECHNIQUES

The following are types of sampling techniques:

| Simple random sampling | Any method of sampling wherein each subject selected from a population has an equal chance of being selected (e.g., drawing names from a hat). |
|---|---|
| Stratified random sampling | Dividing a population into desired groups (age, income, etc.) and then using a simple random sample from each stratified group. |
| Cluster sampling | A technique used when natural groups are readily evident in a population (e.g., residents within each county in a state). The natural groups are then subjected to random sampling to obtain random members from each county. The best results occur when elements within clusters are internally heterogeneous and externally (between clusters) homogeneous, as the formation of natural clusters may introduce error and bias. |
| Systematic sampling | A systematic method of random sampling (e.g., randomly choosing a number $n$ between 1 and 10—perhaps drawing the number from a hat) and then selecting every $n$th name of a randomly generated or already existing list (such as the phone book) to obtain a study sample. |

## MEASUREMENTS

### CATEGORIES OF MEASUREMENT

The four different categories of measurement are as follows:

| Nominal | Used when two or more named variables exist (male/female, pass/fail, etc.) |
|---|---|
| Ordinal | Used when a hierarchy is present but when the distance between each value is not necessarily equal (e.g., first, second, third place) |
| Interval | Hierarchal values that are at equal distance from each other |
| Ratio | One value divided by another, providing a relative association of one quantity in terms of the other (e.g., 50 is one half of 100) |

### STATISTICS AND MEASURES OF CENTRAL TENDENCY

A statistic is a numerical representation of an identified characteristic of a subject.

- **Descriptive statistics** are mathematically derived values that represent characteristics identified in a group or population.
- **Inferential statistics** are mathematical calculations that produce generalizations about a group or population from the numerical values of known characteristics.

Measures of central tendency identify the relative degree to which certain characteristics in a population are grouped together. Such measures include:

- The **mean**, or the arithmetic average
- The **median**, or the numerical value above which 50% of the population is found and below which the other 50% is located
- The **mode**, or the most frequently appearing value (score) in a series of numerical values

| Review Video: **Mean, Median, and Mode** |
|---|
| Visit mometrix.com/academy and enter code: 286207 |

32

## MEASURES OF VARIABILITY AND CORRELATION

Measures of variability (or variation) include the following:

- The **range**, or the arithmetic difference between the largest and the smallest value (idiosyncratic "outliers" often excluded)
- The **interquartile range**, or the difference between the upper and lower quartiles (e.g., between the 75th and 25th percentiles)
- The **standard deviation,** or the average distance that numerical values are dispersed around the arithmetic mean

Correlation refers to the strength of relatedness when a relationship exists between two or more numerical values, which, when assigned a numerical value, is the **correlation coefficient** ($r$). A perfect (1:1) correlation has an $r$ value of 1.0, with decimal values indicating a lesser correlation as the correlation coefficient moves away from 1.0. The correlation may be either positive (with the values increasing or decreasing together) or negative (if the values are inverse and move opposite to each other).

> **Review Video: Standard Deviation**
> Visit mometrix.com/academy and enter code: 419469

## STATISTICAL SIGNIFICANCE

Statistical tests presume the null hypothesis to be true and use the values derived from a test to calculate the likelihood of getting the same or better results under the conditions of the null hypothesis (referred to as the "observed probability" or "empirical probability," as opposed to the "theoretical probability"). This likelihood is referred to as **statistical significance**. Where this likelihood is very small, the null hypothesis is rejected. Traditionally, experimenters have defined a "small chance" at the 0.05 level (sometimes called the 5% level) or the 0.01 level (1% level). The Greek letter alpha ($\alpha$) is used to indicate the significance level chosen. Where the observed or empirical probability is less than or equal to the selected alpha, the findings are said to be "statistically significant," and the research hypothesis would be accepted.

## TESTS

Three examples of tests of statistical significance are:

- The **chi square test** (a nonparametric test of significance), which assesses whether or not two samples are sufficiently different to conclude that the difference can be generalized to the larger population from which the samples were drawn. It provides the degree of confidence by which the research hypothesis can be accepted or rejected, measured on a scale from 0 (impossibility) to 1 (certainty).
- A *t*-test is used to compare the arithmetic means of a given characteristic in two samples and to determine whether they are sufficiently different from each other to be statistically significant.
- **Analysis of variance**, or **ANOVA** (also called the "*F* test"), which is similar to the *t*-test. However, rather than simply comparing the means of two populations, it is used to determine whether or not statistically significant differences exist in multiple groups or samples.

## STATISTICAL ERROR

Types of statistical error include the following:

- **Type I error**: Rejecting the null hypothesis when it is true
- **Type II error**: Accepting the null hypothesis when it is false and the research hypothesis is true (concluding that a difference doesn't exist when it does)

## DATA ANALYSIS

Data analysis involves the examination of testing results within their context, assessing for correlations, causality, reliability, and validity. In testing a hypothesis (the assertion that two variables are related), researchers look for correlations between variables (a change in one variable associated with a change in another, expressed in numerical values). The closer the correlation is to +1.0 or –1.0 (a perfect positive or negative correlation), the more meaningful the correlation. This, however, is not causality (change in one variable responsible for change in the other). Since all possible relationships between two variables cannot be tested (the variety approaches infinity), the "null hypothesis" is used (asserting that no relationship exists) with probability statistics that indicate the likelihood that the hypothesis is "null" (and must be rejected) or can be accepted. Indices of "reliability" and "validity" are also needed.

## RELIABILITY AND VALIDITY

Reliability refers to consistency of results. This is measured via test–retest evaluations, split-half testing (random assignment into two subgroups given the same intervention and then comparison of findings), or in interrater situations, where separate subjects' rating scores are compared to see if the correlations persist.

Validity indicates the degree to which a study's results capture the actual characteristics of the features being measured. Reliable results may be consistent but invalid. However, valid results will always be reliable. **Methods for testing validity** include the following:

| Concurrent validity | Comparing the results of studies that used different measurement instruments but targeted the same features |
| Construct validity | The degree of agreement between a theoretical concept and the measurements obtained (as seen via the subcategories of (a) convergent validity, the degree of actual agreement on measures that should be theoretically related, and (b) discriminant validity, the lack of a relationship among measures which are theoretically not related) |
| Content validity | Comprising logical validity (i.e., whether reasoning indicates it is valid) and face validity (i.e., whether those involved concur that it appears valid) |
| Predictive validity | Concerning whether the measurement can be used to accurately extrapolate (predict) future outcomes |

---

**Review Video: Testing Validity**
Visit mometrix.com/academy and enter code: 315457

---

# Research in Counseling

## RELEVANCE OF RESEARCH TO COUNSELING THERAPY

All counselors today receive training in how to apply theories and methods that have been discovered through **research**. The foundations to applying research to counseling are as follows:

- The counselor learns how to **evaluate** the clinical interventions that have been applied in therapy.
- The counselor **remains objective** in their examination of the data.
- The counselor maintains **ethical procedures** and is **accountable** for their actions. This means that the counselor is careful to document their work.
- The counselor is **competent** in their use of terminology and can make a sound interpretation of the research obtained.
- The counselor and the researcher work for the **client's benefit**. The client must not be harmed. The counselor and the researcher recognize that the client has a choice to determine his or her own actions. The counselor and the researcher are fair and loyal to the client. Both desire to help the client develop steps that will assist in the solution of the problem.

## STEPS RESEARCHERS TAKE TO HELP CLIENTS

The researcher takes different steps than the counselor in helping the client:

1. The first research step is to **identify the problem** with a series of questions. These questions are used to formulate a research design.
2. The **research design** will utilize the goals that are essential to the researcher's investigation process.
3. The **treatment or interventions** that will be applied are considered in the choice of measuring instruments to be used. The interventions are implemented so that the researcher can collect data on the various interventions and results of each.
4. The **data is then evaluated** to determine the desired outcome. The data is interpreted in accordance with prescribed criteria.
5. The **conclusions** that are reached are used to help increase the knowledge that the research was used to develop. Counselors may use knowledge gleaned from previous research to help a client with his or her problem.

## POSITIVISTIC RESEARCH

Positivism is a scientific method that can be applied in social science research. The researcher uses the method to make predictions about what may happen in the future. The researcher takes care in designing experiments that can be disproved or supported by observations of the conditions that occur. The research is accomplished by comparing groups. The numerical data obtained is taken from random samples of a population. The numerical data is compared to the group findings. **Positivistic research** investigates causality by comparing the group members in one group with another group. The variables that are different in each group are known as variable X or variable Y. Typically, variable X refers to an independent variable. Variable Y is known as the dependent variable that can change with the application or the withdrawal of variable X.

## POST-POSITIVISM PARADIGM APPLIED TO SOCIAL SCIENCE RESEARCH

The belief of those researchers who support **post-positivism** is that truth cannot ever be fully revealed. The post-positivist will collect data and perform methodical examinations of the data. These examinations help the researcher to develop a probability about the results. Probability is defined as a prediction, which is founded on hypothesized truths that are generally believed. The post-positivism researcher does not deal in absolutes. Instead, the researcher will apply statistical tests that will support their hypothesized and inconclusive information. They refrain from making an assertion about the absolute truth of an answer to the problem. The researcher will state a number of close approximations to the truth based on quantitative research. The term "quantitative" refers to the quantity or the amount, which is described in numerical terms of measurement. Qualitative research is different, in that it uses narrative forms of data.

## Lab Research Versus Field Research

**Lab research** has a high internal validity value because it is more easily controlled in terms of the cause-and-effect relationships of the variables applied under specific conditions. It also eliminates other explanations that can be attributed to a change in the results. However, lab research has a low external validity, in that generalization to other people, places, or time frames may not be so easy to accomplish. Generalization means that the action can be repeated in other situations.

**Field research** is more easily accomplished because it is done in a natural setting or environment; the researcher travels to the field of study. Field research demonstrates low internal validity because of the lack of control over external variables. Field research has high external validity because it can be generalized to other situations and settings.

## Barriers to Research Efforts

Cost has become an issue in the mental health care system, directly affecting the **research efforts** in this field. This issue has increased the need for counselors to be accountable in their work. Accountability is found in the documentation and data collection methods used by counselors. The National Institute of Mental Health (NIMH) issues funding grants to various research institutions. The research is performed on clients in the daily practice of mental health counselors. The research is concerned with gaining insight into the practicality of the counseling interventions applied in the daily life of the client. Therefore, it is necessary for research courses to be offered in college programs. Research courses may be used to instruct the student in standardized tests and evaluation, experimental research design, descriptive and inferential statistics, and the critique of research designs.

# Careers in Counseling

## EVOLUTION OF PERCEPTIONS OF COUNSELING

Counselors have had an influx of clients in recent years. Part of the reason for this influx in clients can be found in the **changes in attitudes and perceptions** of other professionals towards counseling:

- **Human resources departments** recognize that counselors can assist employees by providing short-term counseling to address work performance issues.
- **Psychiatrists** recognize that counselors provide a necessary component in treatment, along with input regarding medications and capacity for compliance to medication regimens.
- **Managed care plans** pushed for counseling treatments.
- Organizations, such as **Mothers Against Drunk Driving (MADD)**, have worked toward increasing alcohol and drug programs provided by counselors.
- The **internet** has provided counselors with different counseling formats, particularly through telehealth.
- **State licensure boards** give clients reassurance about the treatment they will receive under the care of a licensed professional counselor.

## PROFESSIONAL COUNSELORS

Professional counselors provide similar services to those of the psychologist or social worker. However, the professional counselor does provide a distinctive professional service in its own right. The nature of a professional counselor is defined by the following **criteria**:

- A clear list of **objectives** for the professional counselor position and instruction on how to meet those defined objectives
- **Training techniques** to be applied to meet an individual's needs (These techniques are part of a subset of intellectual procedures. These intellectual procedures or techniques are founded within the principles of science, theology, and law, and these procedures cannot easily be applied by untrained personnel.)
- **Membership** in a professional organization
- **Ethical operation** that is service-oriented for the betterment of others

> **Review Video: Becoming a Professional Counselor**
> Visit mometrix.com/academy and enter code: 334798

## MENTAL HEALTH COUNSELORS

The mental health counselor only received limited recognition in the early 1980's. This limited recognition originated from the efforts of the Office of Civilian Health and Medical Program for the Uniformed Services (now known as TRICARE), who refused to recognize the **mental health counselor** as the fifth core service provider. Opponents found the lack of a universal licensure or certification system for mental health counselors to be problematic. However, managed care programs have helped this process. The managed care systems' demand for licensed mental health counselors caused the states to appropriately respond by passing licensure legislation.

The professional counselor and mental health counselor titles gained popularity from 1980-1990. The mental health counselor's role was defined in the AMHCA's 1981 manual. In 1984, the mental health counselor's job description was listed in the Dictionary of Occupational Titles and the Occupational Outlook Handbook. This allowed the role of counselor to then be added to the core provider list for mental health services. Previously, the list included only psychiatrists, psychologists, psychiatric nurses, and clinical social workers. Today, the list has been expanded to include licensed professional counselors, family counselors, pastoral counselors, and marriage counselors. Recognition can now be given to the counselor in forms of reimbursement payments for services rendered.

> **Review Video: Careers in Counseling**
> Visit mometrix.com/academy and enter code: 363115

## COUNSELOR EDUCATORS

**Counselor educators** can become bridge builders who create an understanding between mental health practitioners and those that do research. Educators seek to help their students see the rationale behind research. Likewise, the educator strives to help the researching student to see the relevance of understanding sound counseling practices. One way that this is accomplished is to provide the student with an assignment that delves into the procedures used in cognitive therapy. The student counselor learns to appreciate research and its applications. The research student will find that an assignment in qualitative research provides ample opportunity to use counseling techniques. The current accountability movement makes it imperative for the counselor and the research student to share outcome data obtained in these areas. The practicing counselor will find that research is relevant to client counseling and the techniques used.

## PSYCHIATRISTS

Psychiatrists are medical doctors with four years of residency in psychiatry. **Psychiatrists** assess and prescribe treatment for more complex mental disorders, and provide expert consultation for other mental health service providers. Psychiatrists are qualified to conduct psychotherapy and psychoanalysis, to order laboratory tests, to hospitalize clients, and prescribe all legal drugs. Psychotherapy provides the client and family with a series of discussions involving treatment methods proven to be effective in resolving behavioral problems. Psychoanalysis includes psychotherapy and medications for an extended period of time. Prescription drugs help correct chemical imbalances at the root of emotional problems. In cases where medication is ineffective, the psychiatrist provides an alternative treatment, such as electroconvulsive therapy.

## PSYCHIATRIC NURSES

Psychiatric nurses are the only mental health professionals besides psychiatrists who have experience in the medical field, along with mental health instruction and training. The **psychiatric nurse** works closely with individuals suffering from severe emotional problems. The psychiatrist holds the psychiatric nurse responsible for providing quality medical care and for the administration of prescribed medications. The psychiatrist may delegate some therapeutic counseling and intervention program responsibilities to the psychiatric nurse. A psychiatric nurse can provide a client with outpatient care that is easily accessible. Insurance accepts claims for these services because of the licensure and training requirements associated with this position. Usually, psychiatric nurses do not open independent private practices within a community.

## CLINICAL PSYCHOLOGISTS

Clinical psychologists work in the following settings to assist a wide range of individuals/groups: physical rehabilitation departments, family or marriage counseling centers, independent practices, group practices, and hospitals. **Clinical psychologists** may be needed after a surgical procedure or other life-altering event, such as divorce, separation, death of a loved one, stroke, brain injury, paralysis, spinal cord injury, or debilitating illnesses. Psychologists conduct psychotherapy, but cannot order lab tests, and most cannot prescribe drugs. Only the states of New Mexico, Illinois,

Idaho, Iowa, and Louisiana have laws that give clinical psychologists permission to prescribe medications.

## SOCIAL WORKERS

Demand for social workers increased when their roles expanded to providing care in the community. They are classified as Clinical or Licensed Clinical Social Workers. Educational requirements are stringent. Most **social workers** obtain a master's degree in social work, with a specialization in psychiatry, as the minimum requirement for employment. Most social workers provide assistance to children and families in schools, homes, or within the community. Some social workers assist with support groups geared to teenage mothers, the elderly, at-risk students, and unemployed or untrained workers. Social workers can hold the titles of child welfare social worker, family service social worker, child protective social worker, occupational social worker, or gerontology social worker.

# Counseling Settings

## ELEMENTARY AND SECONDARY SCHOOL SETTING

In the past, certified school counselors filled guidance positions in both the **elementary and secondary school systems**. Over the past two decades, special programs have been initiated to counter non-educational problems that students experience, such as drug and alcohol addictions and teenage pregnancy, which both lead to student drop out. Individual counseling is usually conducted on a weekly basis to help students cope with problems they are having at home, school, or in their communities. Some students benefit from group therapy counseling sessions that present skills in socialization, behavior management, and problem solving in the context of their family situations.

Mental health counselors may consult with educators, principals, administrators, guidance counselors, and other school staff to help a child deal with life roles. Some students require specialized interventions to alleviate a crisis situation. Crisis services may help a student who has a behavior problem at school, who is on the verge of committing suicide, or who is inflicting self-injury. Crisis situations cause the student's educational performance to deteriorate. Therefore, the school counselor has a responsibility to evaluate students' academic successes and failures. The mental health counselor seeks to identify the career interests and aptitudes of at-risk students. The counselor assists in college selection and in the general social development of the student. In some states, Licensed Professional Counselors (LPC's) are engaged for teen pregnancy preventions, employment, GED testing, individual and group counseling, support groups, and classroom education.

## COLLEGE SETTING

Counselors may seek employment with **college students** in individual or group counseling, on a consultation basis, or as a liaison between the faculty and students. Students self-refer to the counselor. However, if a student is in significant need of ongoing care, the counselor may refer the student to an outside agency for mental health care services. Cost-cutting has reduced college staffing, yet the need still exists to provide qualified counselors to cope with emergency situations and make the needed referrals. Career center counselors may prepare resumes, interest and aptitude assessments, job placement services, and career counseling services. Some counselors specialize in proactive drug and alcohol prevention programs.

## HOSPICE SETTING

Hospice centers opened in the 1970's. The professional counselor seeking a **hospice care position** can expect to deal with families experiencing a crisis situation of catastrophic illness and the impending death of a loved one. The professional counselor helps the family through the end-of-life experience and grieving. Ideally, the family comes to terms with the situation prior to the death, and the client gains insights and coping skills regarding death and dying. The counselor helps the client deal with living wills, financial concerns, family of origin issues, and other associated problems that may need to be handled. The goal of the counselor is to help the client and his or her family to experience caring in the dying process and to maintain their dignity.

## MEDICAL REHABILITATION SETTING

Counselors may seek employment in a **rehabilitation program**. Rehabilitation counselors work to help a person gain skills to compensate for a disability. The effects of the disability may impair the person's personal, occupational, or social life and psychological well-being. The counselor must examine the strengths and weaknesses of the client to determine the course of treatment to be followed. The counselor works to collect personal information and data regarding training programs that will fit the individual's needs. Long range planning goals are established. The title of these counselors is **Certified Rehabilitation Counselor (CRC)**. Most CRC's have a graduate degree in rehabilitation counseling. Rehabilitation work is a growth area for counselors because of the increasing age of the population.

## COMMUNITY MENTAL HEALTH SETTING

Community mental health counselors can expect to have a variety of age groups in their treatment programs. One specialized area where the young and the old alike need treatment is domestic abuse. **Community mental health counselors** also work to provide assessment and treatment for clients with drug and alcohol addictions. Some community mental health counselors help families during child adoption interviews and the assessment process. Some counselors work in geriatric treatment centers with the elderly, while others may work in AIDS treatment and support service centers. Some families require conflict resolution and psychoeducational services. Still other counselors find work as employment counselors, helping others to find work by assessing clients' interests and aptitudes. Community mental health counselors must understand the community within which they function.

## ELDER CARE SETTINGS

The skills that a professional counselor needs in positions which serve the **elderly** are numerous. The counselor must receive training in the following:

- Cognitive and emotional assessments specifically geared to the elderly population
- Grief and bereavement counseling procedures
- How to establish a good rapport with an elderly individual
- Looking at the client holistically and noting any medical problems or medications that impact a client's daily functioning
- Laws that apply to treatment

The counselor listens to the concerns of family members involved in the client's care. The counselor is aware of the services and facilities that would benefit the client, and acts as a referral resource regarding lawyers, medical doctors, financial advisors, insurance specialists, and community support services.

## BUSINESS AND INDUSTRY SETTINGS

Employers hire professional counselors to help improve job performance through **employee assistance programs**. Ongoing counseling in the business/industry setting helps to do the following:

- Alleviate job discontent
- Enhance coping skills for dealing with family problems
- Provide drug and alcohol addiction treatment
- Resolve work problems
- Ameliorate retirement issues

Some counselors provide contract training and educational workshops and seminars addressing job satisfaction, work productivity, and family and personal problems. The counselor may work as a consultant to directly support supervisors, managers, and employees, and refers them to outside resources when necessary. Some counselors work on-call to provide crises interventions on job sites, including catastrophic workplace accidents, deaths on the job, violence at work, sexual harassment, and layoffs or terminations of employees. Brief counseling is a cost-effective way to help employees cope with the transition process.

## CRIMINAL JUSTICE SYSTEM SETTING

The number of professional counselors in the state-run criminal justice system has recently increased to alleviate some of the overpopulation found in prisons. The **criminal justice counselor** serves the following individuals:

- Prison inmates
- Detainees
- The accused on trial
- Recovering drug addicts and alcoholics

The job titles for this counselor include probation officer, juvenile offender officer, and prison counselor. The entry requirement is a bachelor's degree including criminology, counseling, psychology, social work, family relations, or theology, and a one-year internship. The counseling segregation trend replaces models that previously incarcerated all prisoners together, regardless of the nature of their crimes. Addiction centers are specifically designed to treat criminals with drug addictions who commit crimes to support their habits. Career criminals and sexual predators are now separated from young offenders. Criminal justice counselors have high-stress but rewarding jobs.

## PERSONAL COACHING

Professional counselors may find employment as a **personal coach**. Coaching certification, insurance, and job restrictions vary from state to state. Generally, a coach provides a client with the following services:

- Provides advice and coping strategies for specific issues
- Helps the client to focus on life goals
- Helps the client to realize potential
- Helps the client recognize their own value and self-worth

The coach can perform his or her duties in face-to-face interviews, online, or on the telephone, so the coach has more freedom than a licensed professional counselor. The coach may expect to find an increase in employment opportunities in the future.

# Private Practices

## PRIVATE PRACTITIONER
### CONSULTATION SERVICES

The private practitioner engages in two kinds of **consultation services**: unpaid and paid.

- **Unpaid consultation** involves communication between two professionals about the private practitioner's client. The counselor does not pay for or accept money for this exchange of information. The counselor that requested consultation must obtain a signed release of information consent form to protect the client's right to privacy. The consultation relationship with other professionals can lead to additional referrals for services.
- The private practitioner offers **paid consultations** to schools, agencies, industries, hospitals, vocational programs, nursing homes, or community organizations. These services can benefit those who cannot afford full-time counseling services. Payment may be received based on renewable contractual agreements made for a specific period of time.

### COUNSELING SERVICES

Counseling is the main source of income for the private practitioner. The counselor must evaluate potential needs to be addressed in the community being served. Good contacts to make within the community include pastors, social workers, school counselors, medical personnel, helping agencies, and employers. Other private practitioners in nearby geographic areas, (that are not competitors), may provide additional insights into the business. Some counselors are generalists. Others specialize in individual or group counseling sessions, marriage or family counseling, children/teenagers, elders, rehabilitation counseling, and drug and alcohol abuse counseling. It is also an option to choose a variety of different deliveries to ensure a more lucrative practice.

### COMMUNITY INVOLVEMENT

Visibility within the community is good for the business. If a private practitioner provides some free services to **community groups**, it creates bonds and respectful relationships with the community members that could lead to paying referrals. Some organizations that may be in need of free services include Parent Teacher Associations, diabetes and other illness support groups, and local church groups. Groups may require the services of a counselor to conduct seminars on bereavement, violence, or other social problems experienced in the community. All counselors should provide some community service as a demonstration of their ethics, but it can be especially difficult to fit volunteerism into a private practitioner's role.

### SUPERVISORY ROLES

The private practitioner performs **supervisory roles** to obtain additional credentials, or education credits required for licensing. When providing clinical advice and supervision to other professionals in the field, the private practitioner must keep their own skills up to date. The complexity of some client's cases requires the counselor to seek advice from peer supervision groups. These groups meet periodically to converse about cases and to review procedures. Insurance carriers and HMOs often require private practitioners to have some supervision by a licensed psychologist or psychiatrist. The licensed professional counselor, clinical social worker, or marriage and family therapist receives payments based on the decisions of the overseeing psychologist or psychiatrist and the insurer. Not every private practitioner finds supervision acceptable, and many turn down work that necessitates this relationship with a supervisor.

## WORK SETTINGS

The three work settings of the private practitioner include the following:

- **Incorporated office groups** share the same workspace, and the members are not personally liable for legal judgments against the corporation.
- **Expense-sharing groups** share resources and costs but not office space. Counselors can benefit from local, state, and national counseling group relationships. Group practice gives the counselor an outlet from the isolation and burnout associated with private practice.
- **Sole proprietorship** indicates a single person is in charge of the business and is liable to pay business damages out of personal funds, if sued successfully. This business owner is not entirely alone, as he or she must continue to network with other mental health professionals.

The private practitioner should select a work setting based on which type of work fits their life and occupational goals. Choices will be influenced by the opportunities available in the geographic region and limited by the practitioner's type of training and licensing.

## RECOMMENDATIONS FOR DAY-TO-DAY BUSINESS

Recommendations for the private practitioner in running day-to-day business include the following:

- Have a **set schedule** that includes face-to-face therapy time with clients, research and preparation time, answering client phone calls and emails, coping with ethical issues, and handling everyday paperwork and operations.
- **Plan** ahead and **budget** for cancellations and payment problems that cause financial losses.
- Do not **overextend** resources, either in time or in financial considerations.
- Make **referrals** based on confidence in one's level of training and understanding of the client's needs.
- Evaluate what **types of mental health services** are delivered in the community. There are four types of services, which include counseling, consultation, supervision, and community involvement.
- Provide a **flexible model** to make services more attractive to the community.

## BILLABLE HOURS

The **private practitioner** must be dedicated to the business at hand, whether it is run as a part-time or full-time operation, because the start-up time and effort is significant in both cases. Use the following standard calculation to determine the number of hours needed to bill for: Multiply the hours spent directly with the client by two to account for the additional office hours not in the company of the client spent doing paperwork and preparing for treatment. For example, if a practitioner has 15 clients, each of whom is booked weekly for an hour-long session, then they will spend 30 hours a week working. Make a realistic commitment for work-life balance.

## CONSIDERATIONS IMPORTANT IN THE DECISION TO OPEN A PRIVATE PRACTICE

When deciding whether to open a private practice, the counselor must consider the following:

- Consider **problems associated with charging fees** for services in the mental health industry in perspective. A counselor in private practice must first find out which services are offered free in their community and not duplicate them.
- They must survey the surrounding geographic areas to find out which **mental health service models** colleagues use. Assess how to deliver mental health services to the consumer based on this comparative survey. Private practice has a multitude of service options for the counselor to explore. They should make practical decisions about the delivery model that will be used, because the model selected has financial implications for the business.
- Thoroughly understand the **advantages and disadvantages** of setting up and running a private practice and understand how insurance companies work in regard to reimbursement for services delivered.
- Balance **financial concerns** with sound ethical background.

## PRACTICAL CONSIDERATIONS FOR BEGINNING A PRIVATE PRACTICE

The first practical consideration for beginning a private practice is the type of office space required. The next consideration should be the length of time the practitioner plans to remain in private practice. They may rent space on a part-time basis from other mental health providers in the area, which would provide them with an already established location and recognized business address that may be more prestigious than what could be afforded alone. Sharing office equipment will minimize start-up costs. However, if financial resources permit, a practitioner may choose to purchase office space or a separate building. They may also choose to open a home office if space and money for office furniture, a computer, phone and internet service, answering machine, fax, office supplies, liability insurance, and restroom facilities for clients and their families are all available.

**Practical issues** associated with opening a private practice decrease the time spent on personal activities and with paying clients:

- A home business opens the family to intrusions by insistent clients, undesirables, or criminals.
- Time may be spent making structural changes to satisfy the insurance company and accountant. Set up a record keeping system to last at least seven years from the last time the client was seen.
- Avoid feeling shut off from the mental health network by establishing connections and maintaining contacts.
- Keep equipment functional and learn new software that meets the growing needs of the office. It is legally required that you record a referral number for clients who cannot contact you by phone in an emergency (usually the nearest hospital that offers 24-hour mental health services or the locum tenens).
- Instruct answering services in all procedures to be followed during emergency situations, and how to contact locum tenens when sick, on vacation, or attending training.

## INCORPORATED OFFICE GROUP

Incorporated office groups are mental health specialists who have signed on as legal partners with shares in a business. The specialists can include psychologists, psychiatrists, social workers, and professional counselors. Their salaries can be weekly, bi-weekly, or monthly payments, based on

45

time spent on the job, the status of the specialist in the business, and the initial investment of the professional as a partner. The legal arrangements include an exit plan for leaving the practice, relocation of the practice, and expected changes in the practice. Consult an attorney to help thoroughly scrutinize and understand all aspects of the legal contract before making the commitment to become a partner. This understanding may prevent the business from making costly and illegal decisions.

## BENEFITS AND RISKS ASSOCIATED WITH PRACTICING IN A GROUP SETTING

**Benefits** associated conducting private practice in a group setting include having:

- Vacation and sick coverage by a trusted colleague (locum tenens)
- Quick access to consultation and referrals by other members
- Specialized services offered by other members
- Protection if a client becomes violent or makes threats
- Centralized bookings, accounting, and filing, if a clerk is affordable
- Higher group practice rates negotiated with insurance companies under a single tax number
- Better equipment than afforded alone

There are also **risks** involved in working with a group:

- If a group member is sued or has legal issues, the consequences impact the whole group.
- Staff supervision, consultations, and office meetings detract from therapy time with the clients.

Ask an attorney and accountant to address these possible risks in the initial business legal documents. Write a clear policies and procedures manual for staff.

## EXPENSE SHARING GROUPS

Expense sharing groups consist of mental health specialists who have not signed on as legal partners in a corporation. Their contractual agreements should define their financial and business relationships and costs incurred by each person in the group. A clear understanding prevents future misunderstandings and legal entanglements. The specialists can include psychologists, psychiatrists, social workers, and professional counselors. Their salaries are paid in the same way that a sole proprietor is paid. The group fees pay for office expenses and any consulting fees charged by other professionals. However, the private practitioner does not share his or her counseling payments received from clients or other agencies for services rendered. The legal options for the private practitioner include remaining in the group, incorporating the group, or leaving to start his or her own private practice.

## GOAL SETTING

Goal setting involves a yearly evaluation. The private practitioner should set goals in the following areas:

- Gear **professional growth goals** to those that can be accomplished within one year's time. Determine how many cases or clients will be served annually and break that figure into monthly and weekly averages. Evaluate the types of clients the business will be willing to handle. The types include individuals, couples, families, and groups. Evaluate which skills must be improved or gained in order to obtain these clients. Monitor supervision to determine if enough time has been devoted to this task.
- The private practitioner should set goals for **financial growth** by the number of clients that they have the ability to serve. The number is limited by opportunities, time constraints, and voluntary performance.
- **Skill development** requires the practitioner to make a financial and time investment in university courses or seminar training. Professional organizations within the mental health community may make demands for professional counselors to obtain increased training in specialized areas.
- Plan time for **family and personal life activities**, because clients model their behavior of "wellness" after that of their counselor. The professional counselor must stay balanced in both professional and personal life.

## ESTABLISHING A REFERRAL BASE

The practical needs of setting up an office cannot overshadow the need to establish a **referral base**. A private practice will grow out of referrals from the community. Referrals can come from educational facilities, private and public organizations, churches, corporations, manufacturing firms, other mental health providers, hospitals, medical physicians, and rehabilitation programs. Professional counselors increase public awareness of their services by writing for publications. Enhance public image by volunteering individual or group counseling, consultation services, support groups, workshops, or seminars. School personnel, medical professionals, and other community professionals seeking free services for an individual are good contacts to widen a referral base. A strong referral system is an investment in future revenue opportunities.

## MENTAL HEALTH INSURANCE OPTIONS AND PAYMENT SYSTEMS

Mental health insurance coverage and payment options are complex. There are three kinds of insurance plans in which the client may be involved:

- **Indemnity plans** reimburse the client directly after the client has paid for a service. The client usually pays a deductible as a qualification before any additional reimbursements are paid by the insurance company.
- A **preferred provider organization (PPO)** offers the client the ability to visit any caregiver within their network provider list at a low fee, but if the client goes to a caregiver not on the list, the client must pay more. The PPO establishes set fees that the counselor can charge the client.
- A **health maintenance organization (HMO)** contracts with the provider for bulk discount care. A referral must be obtained from the client's general practitioner or other gatekeeper before commencing service. Outpatient mental health care is extremely limited at an HMO.

### PPOS AND HMOS

The **PPO** establishes what fees the counselor can charge the client. The client usually pays co-payments and deductibles to the provider, and the PPO pays the remainder owed to the provider.

The **HMO** is like a PPO, except that the primary care physician pre-certifies the need for mental health services in an HMO. Some health maintenance organizations demand that the counselor submit a prescribed treatment plan as part of the pre-certification process. The provider sends the plan to the insurance company for pre-certification. The care and insurance coverage restricts the client to only going to an in-network provider for services. The HMO has a set fee for services. There usually is not a deductible with an HMO, but there is co-pay required. Normally, the premiums for an HMO are lower than other insurance plans.

## LIABILITY INSURANCE, MALPRACTICE INSURANCE, AND ATTORNEY SERVICES

**Liability insurance** is a policy that provides protection against negligent acts and omissions, such as failure to remove ice from a walkway that results in a client's accidental injury. **Malpractice insurance** provides protection against injurious conduct by the counselor when acting in his or her professional capacity, like misdiagnosis or incorrect treatment. Office equipment and the office space itself need separate policies. Most groups require a new partner to obtain these types of insurance before work begins.

**Attorney services** are enlisted to protect the practitioner's business and financial investments. Hire an attorney who is knowledgeable about mental health legalities. Ask the attorney to explain HIPAA duties (a law that protects the privacy of the client). The attorney may hire counselors to consult in custody or abuse cases, which can bring in revenue for the business as well.

## ROLE OF AN ACCOUNTANT IN PRIVATE PRACTICE

An accountant helps the professional counselor to set up and maintain accounting and billing systems for the business, to fill out Internal Revenue Service (IRS) paperwork and file income taxes. An accountant offers good advice regarding sound financial investments, selecting a retirement plan, business goals and growth plans for the business. An accountant can help the counselor determine projected income for the following year. Projected income is vital to know how much time should be allocated to counseling services, consultation services, and other professional time use. The IRS will not consider the practice to be a viable business if it does not make income within three years of operation.

# Managed Care

## INTEGRATED CARE MODEL OF MANAGED CARE

Integrated care is defined by AHRQ as "the care a patient experiences as a result of a team of primary care and behavioral health clinicians, working together with patients and families, using a systematic and cost-effective approach." The **integrated care model** for treatment is increasing in mental health service delivery and is directed towards providing services to those in underserved populations. Within the integrated care module of a managed care program, the counselor is responsible for:

- Giving an appropriate assessment and diagnosis of the client's mental state
- Supplying psychoeducational services
- Offering brief-structured counseling sessions

Integrated care models require the counselor to be able to do the following:

- **Accurately diagnose** the mental health of the client
- Be apprised of brief-structured **counseling methods** that utilize **pharmacological interventions** and individual and group approaches
- Follow specific guidelines in **reporting procedures**
- **Write a grant application** to compete for contractual agreements
- **Network and collaborate** with other service professionals

## IMPACT OF MANAGED CARE ON SERVICE DELIVERY SYSTEM

Mental health services are impacted by the need for cost-effective service deliveries. Managed care programs implement treatment plans that are supervised under case managers and review boards. Under the managed care programs, it is not uncommon for treatment plans to be restricted to a limited number of visits. Many counselors have switched to fee-for-service contractual agreements. These agreements are made with medical facilities, agencies, and private businesses to reduce the cost of having a salaried counselor on staff. Counselors had to change their business plans to compete for government contracts and insurance reimbursements. This change provides the counselors with a more secure source of income for services rendered.

## ETHICAL ISSUES THAT MAY BE INFLUENCED UNDER MANAGED CARE PROGRAMS

Managed care programs have strict guidelines for treatment plans. These guidelines are used to restrict and limit the number of visits that a counselor can prescribe for treatment. Due to these restrictions, the counselor may face ethical dilemmas in being able to fully provide for the needs of the client. Dilemmas may include the following:

- These guidelines do not take into account any difficulties that may need to be addressed in establishing relationships between different cultures or races.
- These guidelines may not allow for differentiation specific to the competing needs of the client.
- The managed care program's reporting structure may compromise the confidentiality of the client.

The counselor may need to review their own personal identity principles to alleviate the stress that results from these types of compromises. To alleviate some of these stresses, the counselor should receive instruction in therapeutic relationships, contextual care in the community or private practice, writing case notes, informed consent issues, treatment plan development, selection of counseling interventions, and applying ethical decisions.

## COMPONENTS OF MANAGED CARE WITHIN COUNSELING EDUCATION PROGRAMS

Mental health counseling education programs should include these topics in relation to **managed care treatment**:

- Diagnosis and treatment of clients
- Treatment plans
- Methods of brief and goal directed counseling sessions
- Standards of practice for groups and families
- Pharmacological interventions that can be offered to the client
- Networking and consultation skills
- Record keeping procedures
- Understanding evidence-based research
- Practicum placement in a managed care setting during their internship experience

## INCORPORATION OF MANAGED CARE INTO CURRICULUM

Counselor educators have not been strong supporters of incorporating the managed care component into the **curriculum**. There have been some attempts to include the managed care component, but overall, the changes to the curriculum have not been enough. A stronger component that addresses the following concerns in managed care restrictions is imperative:

- Minimum competencies
- Ethical standards
- Informed consent
- Confidentiality issues
- Reporting procedures
- Citing appropriate diagnosis
- How to terminate management when problems cannot be resolved

If managed care is incorporated into the curriculum, then the counselor will be better prepared to work in that setting.

# Technology in Counseling

## ADVANCEMENTS IN TECHNOLOGY

Technical advancements over the last century have resulted in changes to almost every professional field of study. Mental health professionals can expect to see these technological advancements applied in a number of ways. Clients have new ways to access services. Counselors and clients will continue to find new formats for interaction. Management procedures may also change to support the technological structures. Training may be altered or delivered via different formats or systems. The latest research may increase in consumption due to the methods of accessing research data. The counselor will need to be competent in technological literacy and the applications of technology in the field.

## TECHNOLOGICAL ADVANCES IN COUNSELING

Technological advances allow clients to have more control over their therapy and allow the counselor/client to better track progress. **Technological advances** include the following:

- **Greenspace**: This website matches clients and counselors and allows clients to plot their own progress by answering questions, such as about their level of depression, through email or messaging. The result graphs can be accessed by both client and counselor.
- **Apple Watch and other devices**: Can be used to track behavioral changes and to send information to the counselor. For example, Muse is a headband that is used to facilitate meditation through sensing brain activity.
- **Mobile device apps**: Multiple apps, such as MoodTracker, Mood Path, Calm, Calming Circles, and Mind Body Awareness Project, can be used to help clients relax, sleep, or carry out exercises. Alarm apps can remind the clients to take medications or keep appointments. Many apps, such as LoseIt, are available to assist with weight loss.

## TECHNOLOGICAL LITERACY

Technological literacy can be described as the ability to comprehend the use of technology and to select the appropriate applications used in a variety of systems.

- The counselor who is technologically literate will be able to make an **informed decision** about the use of technology in a given area.
- The technologically literate counselor will have the **basic skill level** that is needed in a variety of technological environments.
- The technologically literate counselor will be able to **access technology** at work, at home, and in the community environment.
- The technologically literate counselor will understand that there are certain **security risks** associated with the use of technology and will be able to make sound judgments about ethical dilemmas that can arise through the use of technology.
- The technologically literate counselor will be able to **critically examine new advancements** for their potential counseling uses.

## INTEGRATION OF TECHNOLOGY INTO CONSULTATION, COLLABORATION, AND SHARED DECISION-MAKING

The counselor must be able to collaborate and work with a wide group of people through **technologically-based systems**. The counselor can access others through electronic devices such as the internet or intranet. Email is used on a day-to-day basis by many individuals. Electronic communications can be accomplished on anywhere from internal to global scales.

- In the **discussion group format**, units are formed to talk about topics regarding specific activities, goals, or projects.
- In the **data collection and organizational activities format**, databases are used to organize, share, and retrieve information. Information can be given in the form of references, curriculum projects, research papers, and an exchange of contact information.
- In the **document or file sharing format**, the capability exists to allow each person in the group to work on a project at the same time, in synchronous collaboration.

## INTEGRATING SOCIAL MEDIA INTO THE BUSINESS OF COUNSELING

It's essential that personal and professional **social media** accounts be kept strictly separate and that clients never be "friended" or accepted as friends on personal sites. The counselor should use privacy settings to shield personal information. The counselor should always avoid making any comments about work or clients on personal sites. For professional sites, such as LinkedIn, counselor should make a clear plan for use, ensuring that confidentiality is maintained. For example, the counselor may use social media to post information about office hours, to provide information (such as articles about treatment and mental health), and to schedule appointments. If clients can interact with the counselor on social media sites, such as by making Facebook posts, this can establish a legal responsibility to respond. Additionally, if non-clients post questions asking for advice to which the counselor responds, this can establish a counselor-client relationship that the counselor did not intend.

## SYNCHRONOUS AND ASYNCHRONOUS COMMUNICATION

In **synchronous communication**, real time is incorporated to allow users to accomplish text chats with each other or video conferences between the counselor and the client. When documents are involved, annotations systems (such as in Microsoft Word) can be employed to allow the users to comment and edit the project. Online communication brings people together in an electronic format. A network of colleagues is formed to alleviate some of the isolation many counselors experience. Inclusion is promoted.

**Asynchronous communication** is a sharing of ideas at different times. This can be a benefit to the counselor who needs an opportunity to reflect on new ideas. Social media platforms, such as Twitter, Facebook, Snapchat, or LinkedIn, allow for the asynchronous communication of ideas, along with online blogs. An additional benefit is found in the sharing of solutions within the collaborative community. Online collaboration can save time and money. It is easily accessible and increases productivity, as the counselor doesn't have to leave their own office.

## COLLABORATION TOOLS FOR ONLINE COMMUNICATION

With the technology boom, many free **video chat options** are available for clients to meet with their counselors through a digital avenue. The most important consideration in these various options is that **HIPAA privacy laws** are maintained. While there are different specifics to each video chat product, most will incorporate audio, video, and text communication. The user can exchange information in various ways. Graphics are exchanged on an electronic whiteboard. Files can be transferred. The benefits to video conferences include flexibility, comfort, price (perhaps

simply saving on transportation costs), and an increased likelihood of consistently making scheduled meetings.

## ONLINE SURVEYS

Online surveys can be used for a number of different purposes:

- **To assess needs in a community**: The survey may be targeted to a specific population or to the community as a whole to help, for example, to determine the need for certain types of programs.
- **To gain specific feedback**: A counselor may ask brief post-counseling questions to ascertain the client's perceived reaction to the session and to plan further sessions.
- **To assess satisfaction**: A survey may be sent to all clients to ask about satisfaction with services provided as part of a quality improvement initiative.

Careful consideration must be given to development of the survey, the target population, and issues of privacy and confidentiality. The goal of the survey and how the results will be utilized should be clearly established and the survey written clearly, avoiding medical jargon, leading questions ("How helpful is our messaging service?"), double questions, and open-ended questions, which are difficult to quantify. When possible, the counselor should establish **benchmarks** in order to better interpret results.

## WEB COUNSELING

Web counseling is a popular format for counselors working in the current technological age and working specifically with clients of the generations raised on technical literacy. The American Counseling Association recommends that counselors who are providing assistance through **web counseling** always assess the client prior to offering this service to ensure it is the appropriate method of care. Counselors must also warn clients of the limitations, risks, and benefits of web counseling prior to initiating the service. There is a mixture of perceptions about how web counseling is performed, but there is no formal definition for this structure. Some think that this is not a viable way to accomplish counseling, because there is limited body language visible on a web cam. Some fear that online personalities differ from personalities encountered in real life. Others fear that generalization of coping strategies may not allow them to materialize in the life of the client. Some see web counseling as being beneficial as a supplemental tool to face-to-face counseling sessions, and are embracing this new structure.

### ADVANTAGES TO WEB COUNSELING

There are many advantages to web counseling, including the following:

- Web counseling has increased both the **efficiency and accessibility** for persons seeking counseling services. For instance, individuals with physical disabilities or those located in remote locations may find that this medium is more accessible. Limitations of the worldwide COVID-19 pandemic required many counseling services to move to a web-based format. This was a necessary transition as mental health was greatly impacted by the isolation and loss experienced during the pandemic, in addition to the focus placed on struggling marriages/relationships that were forced to face issues head on during shutdowns.
- Some individuals may find that this medium is **less intrusive** upon their privacy, especially if it is by text alone. These clients may be more comfortable in disclosing private thoughts and feelings in the virtual environment.

- Counselors can provide **electronic file transfers** or links that connect clients to available research, or other information, in a direct manner.
- Counselors can seek help from colleagues in **collaborative efforts**.
- Assessment, instruction, and informational **resources** are available via the internet.
- Virtual environments give counselors and clients a **forum** to answer questions, gain social support, and conduct virtual counseling sessions.
- Marriage and family counseling can be conducted with clients from **different parts of the globe**.
- **Supervision** can be conducted through anecdotal evidence shown in emails. Increased communication between student counselor and supervisor counselor can be accomplished.

## DISADVANTAGES OF WEB COUNSELING

Disadvantages of web counseling also exist, and must be considered when deciding on the best medium for counseling services:

- **Certification and licensure issues** pose a complication to the concept of web counseling, as the counselor may be licensed in one state, while treating a client in another.
- Virtual environments **may not be conducive to building trust, concern, and authentic working relationships** between client and counselor.
- The **client's identity cannot be established** with verification procedures in the virtual environment. Clients could potentially disguise their gender, race, or other pertinent details about their life.
- The client's identity is at risk for **breaches of privacy**. Encryption and security measures can fail, increasing the risk that confidentiality is breached. Counselors must provide all possible and reasonable security measures in an effort to protect their clients.
- **Ethical standards** as they apply to web counseling have yet to be fully established.
- The counselor and the client **may not be proficient in their computer skills**. Keyboarding, electronic file transfers, and other computer skills are required.
- The **fluidity of the internet** and the changes that can occur in technology may have future implications on mental health service delivery that have yet to be realized. Therefore, training and educational programs may not be effective in preparing the mental health counselor to conduct web counseling.
- **Geographical, community, or cultural factors** may be ignored. Natural disasters in one part of the country may not be so readily understood in other parts of the country. The counselor should research the client's locale to anticipate geographical factors that may be of significance to the client.
- Web counseling inherently caters to individuals with the means to have access to a computer, internet, or other form of technology, therefore **disadvantaging those in lower socioeconomic categories**.
- The internet has also introduced new **negative habits** that the counselor must be aware of and prepared to assist with, such as compulsive shopping, gambling, pornography, online marital affairs, online bullying, online stalking, and hatred-based websites.

## VIRTUAL MEETINGS

Virtual meetings allow counselors and clients to conduct audiovisual meetings using the internet and video conferencing. Options include:

- **WebEx**: Allows voice and video conferencing and the ability to not only see each other but to share a screen so that both can, for example, discuss a graph showing a client's progress. Multiple individuals in different areas can participate in group discussions.
- **BetterHelp**: This online counseling service with over 15,000 counselors allows clients to pay a flat fee to unlimited sessions with a counselor at the times of their choosing. BetterHelp allows 24-hour a day texting that is not in real time but also offers real-time texting, and video sessions. Unlimited access costs $60-90 per week but is usually not covered by insurance.
- **Talkspace**: This site is similar to BetterHelp, and costs are similar. It offers matching with a personal counselor, unlimited text messaging, and video conferencing on request.

## ETHICAL CONSIDERATIONS WHEN INTEGRATING TECHNOLOGY INTO COUNSELING

The ethical considerations critical to the integration of technology into counseling remain similar to those for other aspects of counseling:

- **Beneficence/Nonmaleficence**: The use of technology should not result in harm to the client. The counselor should assess the client to determine appropriateness of technology and should assess the remote location for videoconferencing to determine if privacy can be assured.
- **Fidelity/Responsibility**: Technology should promote trust and responsibility rather than impairment. The counselor should do a risk assessment regarding technology to ensure it is secure and the client's information is protected.
- **Integrity/Justice**: The counselor should keep commitments, be honest with clients, and be fair. The counselor must ensure that information exchanged through technology cannot be misused.
- **Privacy/Confidentiality**: Technology must have secure settings if information is exchanged. Counselors should obtain written permission to use technology, such as video conferencing, and should use only secure networks and password protected access. If information exchange (text messages, video/audio messages) is to be retained as part of client records, the clients should be made aware of this.

# Professional Practice and Ethics Chapter Quiz

**1. The reflection of the subject matter in the content of the test is known as:**
   a. Content validity
   b. Face validity
   c. Predictive validity
   d. Construct validity

**2. The immediate comparison of test results with the results from other sources that measure the same factors in the same short time span is known as:**
   a. Construct validity
   b. Face validity
   c. Concurrent validity
   d. Content validity

**3. How many steps are included in Koocher and Keith-Spiegel's problem-solving model for ethical dilemmas (1998)?**
   a. 9
   b. 7
   c. 5
   d. 3

**4. Which of the following is at the heart of the deontological view of ethics?**
   a. Jung's "Shadow" archetype
   b. Gottlieb's multi-modal therapy
   c. Mill's *A System of Logic*
   d. "The Golden Rule"

**5. Which court case supported the utilitarian perspective on breaking confidentiality for the good of the majority?**
   a. *United States v. Hearst*
   b. *Tarasoff v. Regents of University of California*
   c. *Jaffee v. Redmond*
   d. *Roper v. Simmons*

**6. Which of the following is the most basic single system experimental designs?**
   a. A-B-A-B design
   b. A-B design
   c. B-C design
   d. B-A-B design

**7. Which of the following is NOT a key step in the research process?**
   a. Problem or issue identification
   b. Hypothesis formulation
   c. Generalization
   d. Study design selection

**8. Which of the following is NOT one of the three common study designs used in the research process?**

    a. Exploratory research
    b. Confirmation analysis
    c. Descriptive survey
    d. Experimental study

**9. The total set of subjects sought for measurement by a researcher refers to which of the following?**

    a. Sample
    b. Habitat
    c. Population
    d. System

**10. Which of the following $r$ values refer to a perfect correlation?**

    a. 1.0
    b. 10.0
    c. 100.0
    d. 1,000.0

# Intake, Assessment, and Diagnosis

## Human Growth and Development

### MASLOW'S HIERARCHY OF NEEDS

American psychologist Abraham Maslow defined human motivation in terms of needs and wants. His hierarchy of needs is classically portrayed as a pyramid sitting on its base divided into horizontal layers. He theorized that, as humans fulfill the needs of one layer, their motivation turns to the layer above.

| Level | Need | Description |
|---|---|---|
| Physiological | Basic needs to sustain life—oxygen, food, fluids, sleep | These basic needs take precedence over all other needs and must be dealt with first before the individuals can focus on other needs. |
| Safety and security | Freedom from physiological and psychological threats | Once basic needs are met, individuals become concerned about safety, including freedom from fear, unemployment, war, and disasters. Children respond more intensely to threats than adults. |
| Love/Belonging | Support, caring, intimacy | Individuals tend to avoid isolation and loneliness and have a need for family, intimacy, or membership in a group where they feel they belong. |
| Self-esteem | Sense of worth, respect, independence | To have confidence, individuals need to develop self-esteem and receive the respect of others. |
| Self-actualization | Meeting one's own sense of potential and finding fulfillment | Individuals choose a path in life that leads to fulfillment and contentment. |

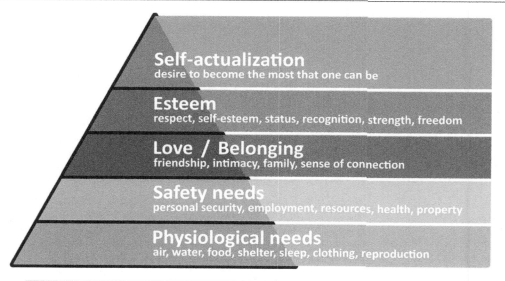

**Review Video: Maslow's Hierarchy of Needs**
Visit mometrix.com/academy and enter code: 461825

58

# FREUD'S PSYCHOANALYTIC THEORY

## MOTIVATIONAL FORCES OF THE UNCONSCIOUS MIND THAT SHAPE BEHAVIOR

Freud's psychoanalytic theory postulates that behavior is influenced not only by environmental stimuli (i.e., physical influences) and external social constrains and constructs (i.e., taboos, rules, social expectations), but also by four specific unconscious elements as well. These elements exist only in the unconscious mind, and individuals remain substantively unaware of all the forces, motivations, and drives that shape their thoughts and behavioral decisions. The **four elements** are:

- Covert desires
- Defenses needed to protect, facilitate, and moderate behaviors
- Dreams
- Unconscious wishes

## LEVELS OF THE MIND

The three levels of the mind that Freud proposed include the following:

- The **conscious mind** is comprised of various ideas and thoughts of which we are fully aware.
- The **preconscious mind** is comprised of ideas and thoughts that are outside of immediate awareness, but can be readily accessed and brought into awareness.
- The **unconscious mind** is comprised of thoughts and ideas that are outside of our awareness and that cannot be accessed or brought into full awareness by personal effort alone.

## PRIMARY FOCUS OF PSYCHOANALYSIS

The primary focus of psychoanalysis is on the unconscious mind and the desires, defenses, dreams and wishes contained within it. Freud proposed that the key features of the unconscious mind arise from experiences in the past and from problems in the development of the personality. Consequently, a focus on the unconscious mind requires the psychoanalytic process to also focus on the **past**—specifically on those repressed infant and childhood memories and experiences that served to create the desires, defenses, dreams, and wishes that invariably manifest through the thoughts and behaviors of every individual.

## FREUD'S STRUCTURAL THEORY OF PERSONALITY DEVELOPMENT

Freud proposed a three-level structure of personality, composed of the id, the ego, and the super-ego:

| | |
|---|---|
| **Id** | The level of personality that comprises basic instinctual drives and is the only part of personality present at birth. The id seeks immediate gratification of primitive needs (hunger, thirst, libido) and adheres to the "pleasure principle" (i.e., seek pleasure, avoid pain). |
| **Ego** | Develops secondarily and allows for rational thought, executive functions, and the ability to delay gratification. The ego is governed by the "reality principle" and mediates the desires of the id with the requirements of the external world. |
| **Super-ego** | Develops last and incorporates the higher concepts of morality, ethics, and justice into the personality, allowing concepts of right, wrong, and greater good to override base instincts and purely rational goals. |

### SUPER-EGO, CONSCIENCE, AND EGO IDEAL

The **super-ego** is comprised of the conscience and the ego ideal, which are constructed from the restraints and encouragements provided by caregivers (parents, teachers, other role models). The **conscience** focuses on cognitive and behavioral restrictions (i.e., the "should nots") while the **ego ideal** focuses on perfection, including spiritual attainment and higher-order goals (the "shoulds" of thought and behavior).

The super-ego works in opposition to the id, produces feelings of guilt for inappropriate drives, fantasies, and actions, and encourages refinement, aspirations, and higher-order goals. Freud theorized that the super-ego emerges around age five, and is not the dominant feature of the personality in a healthy person (which would result in overly-rigid, rule-bound behavior).

The strongest part of the personality is the ego, which seeks to satisfy the needs of the id without disrupting the super-ego.

## PSYCHOSEXUAL STAGES OF DEVELOPMENT

Freud proposed that children develop through five stages that he referred to as the psychosexual stages of development. They are as follows:

| Stage | Description |
|---|---|
| Oral (Birth to 1.5 years) | Gratification through mouth/upper digestive tract. |
| Anal (1.5 to 3 years) | The child gains control over anal sphincter and bowel movements. |
| Phallic (3 to 6 years) | Gratification through genitalia. Major task is resolution of Oedipal complex and leads to development of superego, which begins about age 4. During this time child's phallic striving is directed toward the opposite-sex parent and in competition with same-sex parent. Out of fear and love, child renounces desire for the opposite sex parent and represses sexual desires. Child then identifies with same-sex parent and internalizes their values, etc. This leads to development of superego and ability to experience guilt. |
| Latency (6 to 10 years) | Sublimation of the oedipal stage, expression of sexual-aggressive drives in socially acceptable forms |
| Genital (10 years to adulthood) | Acceptance of one's genitalia and concern for others' wellbeing. |

## ADULT PERSONALITY TYPES

Freud's adult personality types are based on his psychosexual stages and include the following:

| Personality Type | Characteristics |
|---|---|
| Oral | Infantile, demanding, dependent behavior; preoccupation with oral gratification. |
| Anal | Stinginess, excessive focus on accumulating and collecting. Rigidity in routines and forms, suspiciousness, legalistic thinking. |
| Phallic | Selfish sexual exploitation of others, without regard to their needs or concerns. |

## PROCESSES AND STAGES RELEVANT TO DEVELOPMENT OF THE PERSONALITY

Freud identified two primary elements that contribute to the development of the personality:

1. Natural growth and maturational processes (biological, hormonal, and time-dependent processes)
2. Learning and experiential processes (coping with and avoiding pain, managing frustration, reducing anxiety, and resolving conflicts).

According to Freud, psychopathology will result if all 5 stages of psychosexual development are not fully mastered, or if fixation at a particular stage develops (resulting if needs at a particular stage are either over- or under-gratified). If significant developmental frustration is experienced in a later stage, the developmental process may fall back to an earlier stage by means of the defense mechanism known as regression.

## CATHEXIS AND ANTI-CATHEXIS

According to Freud's theory, the individual's mental state emerges from the process of reciprocal exchange between two forces: cathexis and anti-cathexis:

- Freud used the term **cathexis** to refer to the psychic energy attached to an object of importance (i.e., person, body part, psychic element). He also used this term to refer to what he called urges, or psychic impulses (e.g., desires, wishes, pain), that drive human behavior.
- In contrast to the driving urges of cathexis, there is a checking force he referred to as **anti-cathexis**. It serves to restrict the urges of the id and also to keep repressed information in the unconscious mind.

## ERIK ERIKSON'S PSYCHOSOCIAL STAGES OF DEVELOPMENT

Erik Erikson was one of the first theorists to address human development over the entire life span. The eight developmental stages in his theory of psychosocial development are:

| Stage | Description |
|---|---|
| **Trust vs. Mistrust (Birth to 1.5 years)** | <ul><li>Same ages as Freud's oral stage.</li><li>Infants develop a sense of trust in self and in others.</li><li>Psychological dangers include a strong sense of mistrust that later develops and is revealed as withdrawal when the individual is at odds with self and others.</li></ul> |
| **Autonomy vs. Shame (1.5 to 3 years)** | <ul><li>Same ages as Freud's anal stage.</li><li>In this phase, rapid growth in muscular maturation, verbalization, and the ability to coordinate highly conflicting action patterns is characterized by tendencies of holding on and letting go.</li><li>The child begins experiencing an autonomous will, which contributes to the process of identity building and development of the courage to be an independent individual.</li><li>Psychological dangers include immature obsessiveness and procrastination, ritualistic repetitions to gain power, self-insistent stubbornness, compulsive meek compliance or self-restraint, and the fear of a loss of self-control.</li></ul> |

| Stage | Description |
|---|---|
| **Initiative vs. Guilt (3 to 6 years)** | • Same ages as Freud's phallic stage.<br>• Incursion into space by mobility, into the unknown by curiosity, and into others by physical attack and aggressive voice.<br>• This stage frees the child's initiative and sense of purpose for adult tasks.<br>• Psychological dangers include hysterical denial or self-restriction, which impede an individual from actualizing inner capacities. |
| **Industry vs. Inferiority (6 to 11 years)** | • Same as Freud's latency stage.<br>• The need of the child is to make things well, to be a worker, and a potential provider.<br>• Developmental task is mastery over physical objects, self, social transaction, ideas, and concepts.<br>• School and peer groups are necessary for gaining and testing mastery.<br>• Psychological dangers include a sense of inferiority, incompetence, self-restraint, and conformity. |
| **Identity vs. Role Confusion (Adolescence)** | • Same age range as Freud's genital stage.<br>• Crucial task is to create an identity, reintegration of various components of self into a whole person—a process of ego synthesis.<br>• Peer group is greatly important in providing support, values, a primary reference group, and an arena in which to experiment with various roles.<br>• Psychological dangers include extreme identity confusion, feelings of estrangement, excessive conformity or rebelliousness, and idealism (a denial of reality, neurotic conflict, or delinquency). |
| **Intimacy vs. Isolation (Early adulthood)** | • Task is to enter relationships with others in an involved, reciprocal manner.<br>• Failure to achieve intimacy can lead to highly stereotyped interpersonal relationships and distancing. Can also lead to a willingness to renounce, isolate, and destroy others whose presence seems dangerous. |
| **Generativity vs. Stagnation (Adulthood)** | • Key task is to develop concern for establishing and guiding the next generation, and the capacity for caring, nurturing, and concern for others.<br>• Psychological danger is stagnation. Stagnation includes caring primarily for oneself, an artificial intimacy with others, and self-indulgence. |
| **Ego integrity vs. Despair (Late adulthood)** | • Task is the acceptance of one's life, achievements, and significant relationships as satisfactory and acceptable.<br>• Psychological danger is despair. Despair is expressed in having the sense that time is too short to start another life or to test alternative roads to integrity.<br>• Despair is accompanied by self-criticism, regret, and fear of impending death. |

The stages are hierarchical and build upon each other. The resolution of the fundamental "crisis" of each prior stage must occur before one can move on to the next stage of growth. Although individual attributes are primary in resolving the crisis associated with each stage, the social environment can play an important role as well.

## ERIKSON'S EGO STRENGTH

The ego essentially mediates irrational impulses related to the id (drives, instincts, needs). The concept of ego strengths derives from Erikson's (1964, 1985) 8 psychosocial stages and includes hope, will, purpose, competence, fidelity, love, care, and wisdom. Ego strength results from the overcoming of crises in each stage of development and allows the individual to maintain good mental health despite challenges and cope with conflict. Ego strength is assessed through questioning and observation. Characteristics of **ego strength** include the ability to:

- Express a range of feelings and emotions without being overwhelmed by them
- Deal effectively with loss
- Gain strength from loss
- Continue to engage in positive and life-affirming activities
- Exhibit empathy and consideration of others
- Resist temptation and exercise self-control
- Admit responsibility for own actions and avoid blaming others
- Show acceptance of the self
- Set limits in order to avoid negative influences and outcomes

## JEAN PIAGET'S THEORY OF COGNITIVE AND MORAL DEVELOPMENT
### KEY CONCEPTS

Jean Piaget believed that development was progressive and followed a set pattern. He believed the child's environment, their interactions with others in that environment, and how the environment responds help to shape the child's cognitive development. **Key concepts of Piaget's theory of cognitive and moral development** are defined below:

- **Action** is overt behavior.
- **Operation** is a particular type of action that may be internalized thought.
- **Activity in Development** refers to the fact that the child is not a passive subject, but an active contributor to the construction of her or his personality and universe. The child acts on her or his environment, modifies it, and is an active participant in the construction of reality.
- **Adaptation** includes accommodation and assimilation. Accommodation entails adapting to the characteristics of the object. Assimilation is the incorporation of external reality into the existing mental organization.

## STAGES OF COGNITIVE AND MORAL DEVELOPMENT

The stages of Piaget's theory of cognitive and moral development are as follows:

| Stage | Description |
|---|---|
| **Sensorimotor (Birth to 2 years)** | • Infant cannot evoke representations of persons or objects when they are absent—symbolic function.<br>• Infant interacts with her or his surroundings and can focus on objects other than self. Infant learns to predict events (door opening signals that someone will appear). Infants also learn that objects continue to exist when out of sight and learn a beginning sense of causality. |
| **Pre-operational (2 to 7 years)** | • Developing of symbolic thought draws from sensory-motor thinking.<br>• Conceptual ability not yet developed. |
| **Concrete operational (7 to 11 years)** | • Child gains capacity to order and relate experience to an organized whole.<br>• Children can now explore several possible solutions to a problem without adopting one, as they are able to return to their original outlook. |
| **Formal operational (11 years to adolescence)** | • Child/youth can visualize events and concepts beyond the present and is able to form theories. |

## LAWRENCE KOHLBERG'S THEORY OF MORAL DEVELOPMENT

Lawrence Kohlberg's theory of moral development is characterized as the following:

- Kohlberg formulated his theory to extend and modify the work of Piaget, as he believed that moral development was a longer and more complex process. He postulated that infants possess no morals or ethics at birth and that moral development occurs largely independently of age. Kohlberg asserted that children's experiences shape their understanding of moral concepts (i.e., justice, rights, equality, human welfare).
- Kohlberg suggested a process involving three levels, each with two stages. Each stage reveals a dramatic change in the moral perspective of the individual.
- In this theory, moral development is linear, no stage can be skipped, and development takes place throughout the life span.
- Progress between stages is contingent upon the availability of a role model who offers a model of the principles of the next higher level.

## LEVELS AND STAGES OF MORAL DEVELOPMENT

The levels and stages of Kohlberg's theory of moral development are as follows:

| Stage | Level | Description |
|---|---|---|
| 1 | Pre-conventional | The individual perspective frames moral judgments, which are concrete. The framework of Stage 1 stresses rule following, because breaking rules may lead to punishment. Reasoning in this stage is egocentric and not concerned with others. |
| 2 | Pre-conventional | Emphasizes moral reciprocity and has its focus on the pragmatic, instrumental value of an action. Individuals at this stage observe moral standards because it is in their interest, but they are able to justify retaliation as a form of justice. Behavior in this stage is focused on following rules only when it is in the person's immediate interest. Stage 2 has a mutual contractual nature, which makes rule-following instrumental and based on externalities. There is, however, an understanding of conventional morality. |
| 3 | Conventional | Individuals define morality in reference to what is expected by those with whom they have close relationships. Emphasis of this stage is on stereotypic roles (good mother, father, sister). Virtue is achieved through maintaining trusting and loyal relationships. |
| 4 | Conventional | In this stage, the individual shifts from basically narrow local norms and role expectations to a larger social system perspective. Social responsibilities and observance of laws are key aspects of social responsibility. Individuals in this stage reflect higher levels of abstraction in understanding laws' significance. Individuals at Stage 4 have a sophisticated understanding of the law and only violate laws when they conflict with social duties. Observance of the law is seen as necessary to maintain the protections that the legal system provides to all. |
| 5 | Post-conventional | The individual becomes aware that while rules and laws exist for the good of the greatest number, there are times when they will work against the interest of particular individuals. Issues may not always be clear-cut and the individual may have to decide to disregard some rules or laws in order to uphold a higher good (such as the protection of life). |
| 6 | Post-conventional | Individuals have developed their own set of moral guidelines, which may or may not fit with the law. Principles such as human rights, justice, and equality apply to everyone and the individual must be prepared to act to defend these principles, even if it means going against the rest of society and paying the consequences (i.e., disapproval or imprisonment). Kohlberg believed very few, if any, people reached this stage. |

## PARENTING STYLES

Although children are born with their own temperament, the parenting style they grow up with can influence how this temperament manifests over time.

**Authoritarian (autocratic)** parents desire obedience without question. They tend toward harsh punishments, using their power to make their children obey. They are emotionally withdrawn from their children and enforce strict rules without discussing why the rules exist. These children tend to have low self-esteem, be more dependent, and are introverted with poor social skills.

**Authoritative (democratic)** parents provide boundaries and expect obedience, but use love when they discipline. They involve their children in deciding rules and consequences, discussing reasons for their decisions, but they will still enforce the rules consistently. They encourage independence and take each child's unique position seriously. These children tend to have higher self-esteem, good social skills, and confidence in themselves.

**Indulgent (permissive)** parents stay involved with their children, but have few rules in place to give the children boundaries. These children have a difficult time setting their own limits and are not responsible. They disrespect others and have trouble with authority figures.

**Indifferent (uninvolved)** parents spend as little time as possible with their children. They are self-involved, with no time or patience for taking care of their children's needs. Guidance and discipline are lacking and inconsistent. These children tend toward delinquency, with a lack of respect for others.

## ATTACHMENT AND BONDING

Attachment is the emotional bond that develops between an infant and parent/caregiver when the infant responds to the nonverbal communication of the parent/caregiver and develops a sense of trust and security as the infant's needs are met. Nonverbal communication includes eye contact, calm and attentive facial expressions, tender tone of voice, touch, and body language.

Bonding is especially important during the child's first 3 years, and the failure to develop an attachment bond may impact the child's development and the family dynamics. Infants that have bonded generally exhibit stranger anxiety at about 6 months and separation anxiety by one year. While the parent/caregiver can nurture the emotional connection with the child at later ages, those infants who failed to attach in the first year may have increased difficulty doing so later. Children who have bonded with parents/caregivers tend to develop according to expectations, meeting expected milestones, while those who are deprived may exhibit growth and development delays and well as poor feeding.

> **Review Video: Factors in Development**
> Visit mometrix.com/academy and enter code: 112169

## LEARNING THEORY AND BEHAVIOR MODIFICATION
### PAVLOV'S WORK

Pavlov learned to link experimentally manipulated stimuli (or conditioned stimuli) to existing natural, unconditioned stimuli that elicited a fixed, **unconditioned response**. Pavlov accomplished this by introducing the **conditioned response** just prior to the natural, unconditioned stimulus. Just before giving a dog food (an autonomic stimulus for salivation), Pavlov sounded a bell. The bell then became the stimulus for salivation, even in the absence of food being given. Many conditioned responses can be created through continuing reinforcement.

### SKINNER'S WORK

B. F. Skinner developed the **empty organism concept**, which proposes that an infant has the capacity for action built into his or her physical makeup. The infant also has reflexes and motivations that will set this capacity in random motion. Skinner asserted that the **law of effect** governs development. Behavior of children is shaped largely by adults. Behaviors that result in satisfying consequences are likely to be repeated under similar circumstances. Halting or discontinuing behavior is accomplished by denying satisfying rewards or through punishment. Skinner also theorized about **schedules of reinforcement**. He posited that rather than reinforcing every instance of a correct response, one can reinforce a fixed percentage of correct responses, or space reinforcements according to some interval of time. Intermittent reinforcement will reinforce the desired behavior.

## FEMINIST THEORY

Feminist theory views inequity in terms of gender with females as victims of an almost universal patriarchal model in which the sociopolitical, family, and religious institutions are dominated by males. Proponents of feminist theory focus on areas of interest to females, including social and economic inequality, power structures, gender discrimination, racial discrimination, and gender oppression. Feminists often point to the exclusion of women in the development of theories about human behavior, research, and other academic matters. Some feminists believe that oppression of women is inherent to capitalism, where females are often paid less than males, but others believe that it is inherent in all forms of government because they are all based on patriarchal models. Feminists recognize that gender, social class, and race are all sources of oppression with ethnic minorities and those in the lower social classes often suffering the most oppression. Feminists note that the idea that families headed by women are dysfunctional is based on patriarchal ideals.

### CAROL GILLIGAN'S MORALITY OF CARE

Carol Gilligan's morality of care is the feminist response to Kohlberg's moral development theory. Kohlberg's theory was based on research only on men. Gilligan purports that a morality of care reflects women's experience more accurately than one emphasizing justice and rights. Key concepts include the following:

- **Morality of care** reflects caring, responsibility, and non-violence, while **morality of justice and rights** emphasizes equality.
- The two types of moralities give two distinct charges, to not treat others unfairly (justice/rights) and to not turn away from someone in need (care). Care stresses interconnectedness and nurturing. Emphasizing justice stems from a focus on individualism.
- **Aspects of attachment**: Justice/rights requires individuation and separation from the parent, which leads to awareness of power differences. Care emphasizes a continuing attachment to parent and less awareness of inequalities, not a primary focus on fairness.

## OLDER ADULTHOOD
### HOW THE ELDERLY DEAL WITH LIFE TRANSITIONS

Typically, the elderly population seeks to cope with whatever problem comes their way without the benefit of mental health care. In 1991, Butler and Lewis developed a definition for **loss** in relation to the elderly. Elderly can experience a range of emotions whenever loss or death occurs. Examples of loss could be loss of friends, loss of significant others or spouse, a loss of social roles within the community, a loss of work or career, a loss of a prestigious role, a loss of income, a loss of physical vigor, or a loss of health. Some may experience personality changes or changes in sexual appetites. Elderly people may have a situational crisis that puts a strain on their resources. The resiliency of this population is evident by the large number of seniors who live independently with only a little support. Only 4-6% live in nursing homes or assisted living facilities, and 10-15% receive homecare.

## FACTORS PREVENTING THE ELDERLY FROM RECEIVING MENTAL HEALTH SERVICES

While mental illness is often overestimated in the elderly population, it is still prevalent, with one in five elderly individuals experiencing some sort of mental illness. The most significant **mental illnesses** experienced by the elderly are anxiety, severe cognitive impairment, and mood disorders. Anxiety is the most prevalent of these problems. These numbers may be skewed by the fact that the elderly may not be seeking help when needed. Sadly, suicide rates are higher in this population than in any other population. The older a person gets, the higher the rate of suicide. Anxiety and depression cause much suffering in the elderly.

There are a number of factors that **prevent the elderly from receiving mental health services**. Part of the problem lies in the strong values which guide the elderly to solve their own problems. Other seniors feel they should keep quiet about private issues. Still others feel a negative connotation from past stigmas attached to those who needed mental health care. Baby boomers approaching old age have been bombarded with literature on psychology and healthy lifestyles. Therefore, the baby boomer generation may take on a healthier attitude about receiving the appropriate mental health care for their needs. A limited number of counselors, social workers and therapists are trained in geriatric care. Providers for the elderly have difficulties working with payment policies and insurance companies. In addition, seeing the client's aging problems may cause unpleasant personal issues about aging to surface for the provider.

# Human Behavior in the Social Environment

## PERSON-IN-ENVIRONMENT THEORY

The **person-in-environment** theory considers the influence the client has on their environment and the influence that multiple environments (social, economic, family, political, cultural, religious, work, ethnic, life events) have on the client. This is an interactive model that is central to many professional helping relationships and recognizes the impact of oppression and discrimination on the client. The person-in-environment theory supports the goals of providing personal care for the client and furthering the cause of social justice. The person-in-environment theory is the basis for the strengths-based perspective in which the initial focus is placed on the personal strengths of the client and the strengths within the client's environment. It involves utilizing psychosocial interventions and assessing behavior on the basis of interactions between the client and the environment because the client's life situation results from the relationship between the client and the environment.

## HILDEGARD PEPLAU'S THEORY OF INTERPERSONAL RELATIONS

Hildegard Peplau developed the theory of interpersonal relations in 1952, applying Sullivan's theory of anxiety to nursing practice, developing a framework for psychiatric nursing. The model, however, can be applied to other helping disciplines. The relationship comprises the helping professional (counselor, social worker, or nurse) who has expertise and the individual (client or patient) who wants relief from suffering/problems.

According to Peplau, the professional-individual relationship evolves through 4 phases:

| Phase | Details |
|---|---|
| Preorientation | The helping professional prepares, anticipating possible reactions and interventions. |
| Orientation | Roles and responsibilities are clarified in the initial interview. |
| Working | The professional and individual explore together and promote the individual's problem-solving skills. |
| Termination | The final phase consists of summarizing and reviewing. |

The helping professional uses process recording, which includes observing, interpreting, and intervening to help the client, but also self-observation to increase self-awareness. Peplau believed that individuals deserved human care by educated helpers and should be treated with dignity and respect. She also believed that the environment (social, psychosocial, and physical) could affect the individual in a positive or negative manner. The helping professional can focus on the way in which clients react to their problems and can help them to use those problems as an opportunity for learning and maturing.

## SYSTEMS THEORY

**Systems theory** derives its theoretical orientation from general systems theory and includes elements of organizational theory, family theory, group behavior theory, and a variety of sociological constructs. Key **principles** include the following:

- Systems theory endeavors to provide a methodological view of the world by synthesizing key principles from its theoretical roots.
- A fundamental premise is that key sociological aspects of clients, families, and groups cannot be separated from the whole (i.e., aspects that are systemic in nature).
- All systems are interrelated, and change in one will produce change in the others.

- Systems are either open or closed: Open systems accept outside input and accommodate, while closed systems resist outside input due to rigid and impenetrable barriers and boundaries.
- Boundaries are lines of demarcation identifying the outer margins of the system being examined.
- Entropy refers to the process of system dissolution or disorganization.
- Homeostatic balance refers to the propensity of systems to reestablish and maintain stability.

## ECOSYSTEMS THEORY

Ecosystems (or life model) theory derives its theoretical orientation from ecology, systems theory, psychodynamic theory, behavioral theory, and cognitive theory. Key principles include the following:

- There is an interactive relationship between all living organisms and their environment (both social and physical).
- The process of adaptation is universal and is a reciprocal process by individuals and environments mutually accommodating each other to obtain a "goodness of fit."
- Changes in individuals, their environments, or both can be disruptive and produce dysfunction.
- This theory works to optimize goodness of fit by modifying perceptions, thoughts, responsiveness, and exchanges between clients and their environments.
- On a larger (community) level, treatment interventions by the ecosystems approach are drawn from direct practice and include educating, identifying and expanding resources, developing needed policies and programs, and engaging governmental systems to support requisite change.

## IMPACT OF FAMILY ON HUMAN BEHAVIOR
### FAMILY TYPES

A **family** consists of a group of people that are connected by marriage, blood relationship, or emotions. There are many different variations when referring to the concept of family.

- The **nuclear family** is one in which two or more people are related by blood, marriage, or adoption. This type of family is typically parents and their children.
- The **extended family** is one in which several nuclear families related by blood or marriage function as one group.
- In a **single-parent structure**, there is only one parent caring for the children in the household.
- In a **blended family** a parent marries or remarries after he or she has already had children. Blended families are often referred to as stepfamilies because they consist of a parent, a stepparent, and one or more children.

A **household** consists of an individual or group of people residing together under one roof. The practitioner will often interact with families on many different levels. This may involve meeting the family once during treatment or establishing a long-term relationship with the family over the course of long-term treatment.

### FUNCTIONAL FAMILY

A functional family will be able to change roles, responsibilities, and interactions during a stressful event. This type of family can experience **nonfunctional behaviors** if placed in an acute stressful

event; however, they should be able to reestablish their family balance over a period of time. The functional family will have the ability to deal with **conflict and change** in order to deal with negative situations without causing long-term dysfunction or dissolution of the family. They will have completed vital life cycle tasks, keep emotional contact between family members and across generations, over-closeness is avoided, and distance is used to resolve issues. When two members of the family have a conflict, they are expected to **resolve** this conflict between themselves and there is **open communication** between all family members. Children of a functional family are expected to achieve age-appropriate functioning and are given age-appropriate privileges.

## FAMILY LIFE CYCLE

The family life cycle comprises the states typical individuals go through from childhood to old age. Stages include:

| Stage | Details |
|---|---|
| Independence | Individuals begin to separate from the family unit and develop a sense of their place in the world. Individuals may begin to explore careers and become increasingly independent in providing for self needs. Individuals often develop close peer relationships outside of the family. |
| Coupling | Individuals develop intimate relationships with others and may live together or marry, moving toward interdependence, joint goal setting and problem-solving. Individuals learn new communication skills and may have to adjust expectations. |
| Parenting | Individuals make the decision to have or adopt children and adjust their lives and roles accordingly. Relationships may change and be tested, and parents may shift focus from themselves to their children. |
| Empty nest | Individuals may feel profound loss and stress at this change, especially since this is also the time when health problems of age and the need to care for parents arise. Relationships with children evolve. |
| Retirement | Individuals may undergo many changes and challenges and must deal with deaths of family and friends and their own mortality. |

## CHANGE IN FAMILY ROLES OF MEN AND WOMEN IN UNITED STATES

The family roles of men and women in the United States have changed drastically over the past several decades. Women were traditionally the primary caretakers of children, so they were expected to maintain the household while the men worked to provide for the family. However, this is no longer the case, as there has been a drastic increase in the number of women entering the work force in the recent years. This change is partially due to the fact that it has become more difficult for families to live off of one income. It can be extremely difficult for a family to find the time and money to care for a child, especially if that child has a disability, because both parents are typically required to work.

## HOW A FAMILY AIDS THE DEVELOPMENT, EDUCATION, AND FUNCTION OF ITS MEMBERS

A family can aid the development, education, and function of its members in two major ways. First, parents and grandparents typically pass their heritage down to their children and teach them what is considered acceptable through their actions, customs, and traditions. In other words, a person typically acquires culture through his or her family, and that culture helps the person function in society and interact socially with other people. Second, a person's family can act as an effective support network in many situations. A family may be able to provide some of the emotional, financial, or other types of support a person needs.

## EFFECTS OF MENTAL ILLNESS ON FAMILY

Families with a member that has a **chronic mental illness** will provide several functions that those without mentally ill members may not need. These functions can include providing support and information for care and treatment options. They will also monitor the services provided the family member and address concerns with these services. Many times, the family is the biggest **advocate** for additional availability of services for mental health clients. There can often be disagreements between the care providers and the family members concerning the dependence of the client within the family. Parents can often be viewed as overprotective when attempting to encourage a client's independence and self-reliant functioning. They will need support and reassurance if the client leaves home. On the other hand, many parents will provide for their child for as long as they live. Once the primary care provider dies, the client may be left with no one to care for them and they may experience traumatic disruptions.

## INCONGRUOUS HIERARCHY

An incongruous hierarchy is a family relationship in which a minor figure controls the family dynamic. The control engine may be the exhibition of inappropriate behavior at crucial times. It is a "tail wags the dog" type of scenario. A child throws an entire family into turmoil by ranting and throwing a fit each evening at bedtime. The child's father reacts by attempting to soothe her, offering her candy and letting her stay up late. The child's mother is angry with the father for doing so, and begins shouting at him and withholding affection. An older brother loses sleep because of the daily hysterics, and subsequently performs poorly in school. This type of family dysfunction is called incongruous hierarchy.

## FAMILY VIOLENCE

Family violence can include physical, emotional, sexual, or verbal behaviors that occur between members of the same family or others living within the home. This behavior can include both abuse and neglect and involve the elderly, spouses, and children. Family violence is often kept a secret and may be the main issue with many family problems. Many times, actions that would be considered unacceptable to strangers or friends are often the norm between family members. Violence and abuse occur due to the unique interactions between the family members based upon personality differences, situational variations, and sociocultural influences.

### CHARACTERISTICS OF VIOLENT FAMILIES

Violent families will often share many of the same characteristics. Many times, the abusive family member will have suffered abuse from their family while growing up. This type of abuse is a **multigenerational transmission** and is a cycle of violence. These abusers have learned to believe that violent behavior is a way to solve problems. Violent families are also usually socially isolated so that others such as friends, teachers, neighbors, or law enforcement officials do not become aware that the abuse is occurring. The abuser will also use and abuse power to **control** the victim. They may be considered a person of authority, such as a parent would be to a child. Power is a very important factor with abuse of an intimate partner. The abuser is often very controlling of their partner and will attempt to dominate every aspect of their life. Another commonality among abusers is **substance abuse**; however, one is not dependent upon the other. Many times, the use of alcohol or drugs may escalate violent behaviors by decreasing inhibitions.

## FAMILY LIFE EDUCATION

Family life education, which can include parenting and financial management classes, aims to give people the information and tools they need in order to strengthen family life. Approaches to family life education include:

- **Strength-based**: Assisting clients to identify their strengths and those of their environment in order to increase their sense of personal power and engagement.
- **Cultural**: Focusing on cultural norms and the diverse needs of different populations as well as utilizing communication and activities that correspond to different cultures.
- **Selective**: Aiming at specific groups, such as LGBTQ parents or grandparents, in order to ascertain their unique needs and to provide appropriate education. Some programs may be designed for at-risk groups, such as those in court-ordered education programs because of abuse or neglect.
- **Universal**: Universal education focuses on all members of a particular population, such as all parents, despite differences among the parents. These programs often focus on general information, such as growth and development, and cover a range of topics.

## DEVELOPMENTAL MODEL OF COUPLES THERAPY

The developmental model of couples therapy (Bader & Pearson) accepts the inevitable change in relationships and focuses on both individual and couple growth and development. The goal is to assist the couple to recognize their stage of development and to gain the skills and insight needed to progress to the next stage. Problems may especially arise if members of the couple are at different stages. Stages include:

| Stage | Details |
|---|---|
| Bonding | Couples meet, develop a romantic relationship, and fall in love, focusing on similarities rather than differences. Sexual intimacy is an important component. |
| Differentiating | Conflicts and differences begin to arise, and couples must learn to work together to resolve their problems. |
| Practicing | Couples become more independent from each other, establish outside friendships, and develop outside interests. |
| Rapprochement | Couples move apart and then together again, often increasing intimacy and feeling more satisfied with the relationship. |
| Synergy | Couples become more intimate and recognize the strength of their union. |

## ANNA FREUD'S DEFENSE MECHANISMS

According to Anna Freud, defense mechanisms are an unconscious process in which the ego attempts to expel anxiety-provoking sexual and aggressive impulses from consciousness. Defense mechanisms are attempts to protect the self from painful anxiety and are used universally. In themselves they are not an indication of pathology, but rather an indication of disturbance when their cost outweighs their protective value. Anna Freud proposed that defense mechanisms serve to protect the ego and to reduce angst, fear, and distress through irrational distortion, denial, and/or obscuring reality. Defense mechanisms are deployed when the ego senses the threat of harm from thoughts or acts incongruent with rational behavior or conduct demanded by the super-ego.

The following are terms that pertain to **Anna Freud's defense mechanisms**:

| | |
|---|---|
| **Compensation** | Protection against feelings of inferiority and inadequacy stemming from real or imagined personal defects or weaknesses. |
| **Conversion** | Somatic changes conveyed in symbolic body language; psychic pain is felt in a part of the body. |
| **Denial** | Avoidance of awareness of some painful aspect of reality. |
| **Displacement** | Investing repressed feelings in a substitute object. |
| **Association** | Altruism; acquiring gratification through connection with and helping another person who is satisfying the same instincts. |
| **Identification** | Manner by which one becomes like another person in one or more respects; a more elaborate process than introjection. |
| **Identification with the Aggressor** | A child's introjection of some characteristic of an anxiety evoking object and assimilation of an anxiety experience just lived through. In this, the child can transform from the threatened person into the one making the threat. |
| **Introjection** | Absorbing an idea or image so that it becomes part of oneself. |
| **Inversion** | Turning against the self; object of aggressive drive is changed from another to the self, especially in depression and masochism. |
| **Isolation of Affect** | Separation of ideas from the feelings originally associated with them. Remaining idea is deprived of motivational force; action is impeded and guilt avoided. |
| **Intellectualization** | Psychological binding of instinctual drives in intellectual activities, for example the adolescent's preoccupation with philosophy and religion. |
| **Projection** | Ascribing a painful idea or impulse to the external world. |
| **Rationalization** | Effort to give a logical explanation for painful unconscious material to avoid guilt and shame. |
| **Reaction Formation** | Replacing in conscious awareness a painful idea or feeling with its opposite. |
| **Regression** | Withdrawal to an earlier phase of psychosexual development. |
| **Repression** | The act of obliterating material from conscious awareness. This is capable of mastering powerful impulses. |
| **Reversal** | Type of reaction formation aimed at protection from painful thoughts/feelings. |
| **Splitting** | Seeing external objects as either all good or all bad. Feelings may rapidly shift from one category to the other. |
| **Sublimation** | Redirecting energies of instinctual drives to generally positive goals that are more acceptable to the ego and superego. |
| **Substitution** | Trading of one affect for another (e.g., rage that masks fear) |
| **Undoing** | Ritualistically performing the opposite of an act one has recently carried out in order to cancel out or balance the evil that may have been present in the act. |

# Biological Theories

## COLOR VISION AND COLOR BLINDNESS THEORIES

There are two basic **theories of color vision**.

- Young-Helmholtz proposed a **trichromatic theory**, stating that there are color receptors for the three primary colors (red, green, blue). According to this theory, all other colors are based on variations and combinations of these three.
- The **opponent-process theory** of Ewald Hering proposed that there are three receptors, but they are red-green, yellow-blue, and white-black. Cells in these receptors are stimulated one way or the other, and the overall pattern in their stimulation creates differences in color perception.

Neither trichromatic nor opponent-process theory adequately explains color perception, so the current consensus is that at the retinal level trichromatic theory holds, while the thalamus operates on an opponent-process model.

**Color blindness** occurs when an individual has a recessive trait on the X chromosome. Males are more likely than females to be colorblind.

## WEBER'S LAW, FECHNER'S LAW, AND STEVENS' POWER LAW

**Weber's law** states that the more intense a stimulus, the greater will be the increase in stimulus intensity necessary for the stimulus to be perceived over time.

Fechner built on Weber's law and was able to determine the exact relationship between the magnitude of a stimulus and the magnitude of the reaction. **Fechner's law** states that stimulus changes are logarithmically related to psychological sensations.

Stevens determined that the work of Weber and Fechner was only good for studying stimuli of moderate intensity. In order to examine extreme stimuli, Stevens had to develop his **Power law**, which describes sensation as an exponential function of stimulus intensity. Stevens' work depended on a system of magnitude estimation, in which subjects assigned numerical values to the intensities of various stimuli.

## SYNESTHESIA AND PSYCHOPHYSICS

Synesthesia is when the stimulation of one sensory modality triggers the stimulation of another sensory modality. Synesthetic individuals report being able to see the color of words or taste shapes. There is no clear understanding of the etiology of **synesthesia**, although many researchers believe that it is caused by "cross-wiring" in the brain.

The study of the relationship between physical stimulus magnitudes and their corresponding psychological sensations is called **psychophysics**. An important part of psychophysics is the determination of absolute thresholds (minimum stimulation needed to produce a sensation) and difference thresholds (smallest unit of stimulus intensity needed to recognize a difference in stimulus intensity).

# Assessment Process

## IMPORTANCE OF INDIVIDUAL ASSESSMENT IN COUNSELING

Counselors hold the belief that the individual has a specific blueprint of behaviors, genetic characteristics, and life circumstances that make them a unique person. The **individual assessment** is the first step in both the counselor and the client gaining insight into the individual. Counseling is designed to help the client gain a perspective on how he or she behaves through the following:

- The counselor works to establish a **rapport** with the client and to develop the client's positive self-esteem.
- The client is made to understand how **genetics** can influence a person's characteristics and behaviors and is encouraged to gain perspective about negative circumstances in early life.
- **Self-knowledge** is used to help the client learn how to make better decisions and to take responsibility for his or her own actions.
- The client learns **coping strategies** to deal with unpleasant circumstances or memories.

## THE ROLE OF OBSERVATION IN ASSESSMENT

### LEVELS OF OBSERVATION

One form of assessment involves nonstandard procedures that are used to provide individualized assessments. Nonstandard assessment procedures include observations of client behaviors and performance. There are three **levels of observation** techniques that can be applied:

- The first level is **casual informational observation**, where the counselor gleans information by watching the client during unstructured activities throughout the day.
- The second level is **guided observation**, an intentional style of direct observation accomplished with a checklist or rating scale to evaluate the performance or behavior seen.
- The third level is the **clinical level**, where observation is done in a controlled setting for a lengthy period of time. This is most often accomplished on the doctoral level with applied instrumentation. Clinical predictions are then based on the intuition and experience of the observing clinician.

## INSTRUMENTS USED DURING THE OBSERVATION PROCESS

The following **instruments** can be used in an observation:

- The **checklist** is used to check off behaviors or performance levels with a plus or minus sign to indicate that the behavior was observed or absent. The observer can converse with the client as they mark the checklist.
- The **rating scale** is a more complex checklist that notes the strength, frequency, or degree of an exhibited behavior. Likert scales are applied using the following ratings: 1. Never; 2. Rarely; 3. Sometimes; 4. Usually; and 5. Always. The evaluator of the behavior makes a judgment about whatever question has been asked on the rating scale.
- The **anecdotal report** is used to record subjective notes describing the client's behavior during a specified time or in a specified setting, and is often applied to evaluate a suspected pattern.

Structured interviews, questionnaires, and personal essays or journals may also be useful in the observation process, depending on the client's ability to participate in these exercises.

**Review Video: Basic Skills of a Counselor**
Visit mometrix.com/academy and enter code: 965456

## ASSESSING CHILDREN

In order to obtain a useful interview from a child, the clinician must establish a good **rapport** and maintain the cooperation of the child. Establish rapport by:

- Using **descriptive** statements to encourage the child (e.g., "You're doing well.")
- Using **reflective** statements that encourage the child to think about what he or she has said (e.g., "You sound very angry about that.")
- **Praising** the child specifically for those things that contribute to a good interview
- Avoiding criticism
- When relevant, using **play**, such as anatomically correct dolls to help children discuss issues of sexual function and abuse or medical issues and interventions

## THEMATIC ASSESSMENT

Thematic assessment appraises major themes that have happened over the lifetime of a client. As the client discusses or describes the life events, the therapist makes notes of the themes or predominant topics that create a pattern. The predominant themes are then related to the assessment, which attempts to bring into focus a better understanding of what these themes mean. The assessment can be in the form of a pencil-and-paper test, a behavioral assessment, or a clinical interview.

- One type of paper-and-pencil test is the **Minnesota Multiphasic Personality Inventory (MMPI)**, with the most recent version updated in 2020, the MMPI-3.
- **Behavioral chart assessments** can be used to document a person's habitual, explosive, angry episodes.
- **Clinical interviews** are used for cognitive imagery assessments.

**Review Video: Life Stages in Client Assessment**
Visit mometrix.com/academy and enter code: 535888

## SPHERES OF INFLUENCE IN TERMS OF CLIENT ASSESSMENT

The spheres of influence of a client progress outward from the self and should be carefully assessed by the counselor:

- **Self**: Personal beliefs, values, thoughts, and behaviors influence the client's response to therapy and willingness to interact with the counselor.
- **Family**: Family values, expectations, and behavioral norms that may affect the client's thought processes and behavior. Parents, children, and partners having the strongest effect (positive or negative), although extended family may also affect the client.
- **Friends/Neighbors**: The influence may vary widely, depending on the closeness of the relationship, the client's response to peer pressure, and the need or desire to conform to norms.
- **School/Work**: Clients may feel pressured to attain certain goals and conflicted about doing so. These conflicts and pressures may influence the goals that clients set for themselves.

- **Community/Government**: Community organizations, government assistance, laws and regulations may all affect a client's understanding of themselves, their rights, and their belief systems.
- **Country/World**: Broad cultural norms bring expectations that may affect the client.

## ASSESSING A CLIENT'S READINESS TO CHANGE

The counselor must assess the client's readiness to change in order to determine the best therapeutic approach. If, for example, a client is in court-ordered therapy or in therapy because of family intervention, the client may lack motivation to change and is not likely to actively engage in therapy. Clients may state directly that they have no problem or may simply fail to follow through. Some may feel that they need to change but don't yet have the will to do so. These clients often state an intent to work on the problem at a future time, "I'm going to cut down on my drinking after I change jobs." Some clients may recognize a problem and have a clear plan, while others actively begin to make changes. The counselor should begin by asking clients if they believe they have a problem and, if so, when they intend to take action to change. The goal of therapy for most clients should be to help the client to move toward an acceptance of the need for change and to making plans, as most clients entering therapy are not yet ready to take action.

## ASSESSING MEMBERS OF CULTURALLY DIVERSE POPULATIONS

Guidelines that psychologists should remember when assessing members of culturally diverse populations include the following:

- Clarify the purpose of the evaluation for the examinee.
- Be sensitive to any test material that unfairly discriminates against individuals of a particular culture.
- Use an alternate method of assessment that is more appropriate to the individual, if necessary. Consider an interpreter or a professionally translated paper-and-pencil test if the client's primary language is not English.
- Before beginning an assessment, become familiar with the norms and values of the examinee's culture.
- Recognize that the job is to establish a good rapport with the examinee and call a replacement psychologist if good rapport is not possible.

## ASSESSING INTELLIGENCE

### THEORETICAL APPROACHES TO INTELLIGENCE

There are various theoretical approaches to intelligence:

- **Spearman** proposed the existence of a general intelligence factor (G) and any number of specific intelligence factors (S) unique to a task.
- **Horn and Cattell** adjusted this model by dividing (G) into two categories:
  - *Crystallized intelligence (Gc):* The knowledge and skills acquired through education and experience
  - *Fluid intelligence (Gf):* The ability to solve new problems
- **Sternberg** asserted that successful intelligence is composed of analytical, practical, and creative elements, and argued that standardized tests focus almost exclusively on analytical elements.
- **Gardner** proposed eight different kinds of intelligence: Linguistic, musical, logical-mathematical, spatial, bodily-kinesthetic, interpersonal, intrapersonal, and naturalistic.

## INTELLIGENCE THROUGHOUT THE LIFESPAN

Research efforts have been interested in the growth and decline of intelligence over the lifespan, and how that correlates with the same measures of one's IQ. **The Seattle Longitudinal Study** was conducted by Schaie et al. at seven-year intervals from 1956 to 2005. The study concluded that "there is no uniform pattern of age-related changes across all intellectual abilities, and that studies of an overall index of intellectual ability (IQ) therefore do not suffice to monitor age changes and age differences in intellectual functioning for either individuals or groups." Subsequent research in this line indicates perceptual speed is the only area in which the elderly experience significant decline.

Research conducted by Horn indicated that while **crystallized intelligence** will continue to increase throughout life, **fluid intelligence** will peak in adolescence and decline thereafter. Decline in fluid intelligence has been linked to diminished processing speed, stemming from reductions in working memory.

## EFFECTS OF HEREDITY AND ENVIRONMENT ON INTELLIGENCE

Research has shown that individuals with a genetic similarity have similar levels of intelligence. Heritability estimates for intelligence range from about 0.6 to 0.8, meaning that 32-64% of the variability in intelligence comes from **genetic factors**.

Other research has sought to describe the link between environment and intelligence. One environmental factor that has been consistently linked to performance on intelligence tests is **socioeconomic status**.

The **Flynn effect** describes the gradual increase in IQ test scores that has occurred worldwide over time, as nations become more industrialized. The Flynn effect does not seem to involve genetic factors and therefore is solely based on the environment and evolving resources.

## EVALUATION AND DECISION MAKING IN THE ASSESSMENT PROCESS

Evaluation is the process of analyzing accumulated data in order to improve a counselor's ability to make a decision based on reliable standards. The accumulated data is given careful consideration and appraisal by the evaluator (the counselor) to ensure that it is complete and accurate. The evaluator must make some kind of interpretation or inference about the data that has been collected. This inference is known as a **value judgment** and is a common task for the counselor. The counselor uses a methodical and well-organized system to help make these value judgments.

**Decision making** is a process in which the collected data has been weighed against possible consequences and test results. Decisions must be made regarding prioritization of interventions, risk or danger the client may be in that must be addressed, identification of approaches that are failing and succeeding, and the creation of a counseling plan specific to the client's personality, life experiences, and problem(s) at hand.

# Client Interviews

## OBTAINING A CLIENT HISTORY AND DATA FROM MULTIPLE SOURCES

During the admissions assessment, information about the **client's history** should be gathered. The interview should occur in a space that allows for privacy, but it should not be isolated in case the client becomes violent or threatening. Asking open-ended questions in a nonjudgmental manner (e.g., What problem brings you here today?) is more effective than asking yes or no questions. Questions should focus on one problem or symptom at a time (e.g., Tell me about your sleeping habits.). Depending on the client's condition, information may be obtained by:

- Directly interviewing the client
- Observing the client's behavior and interactions with others
- Reviewing previous hospitalization and discharge records
- Interviewing family or caregivers, ideally without the client present so caregivers can speak freely (Care should be taken not to violate the client's right to privacy and the client should be asked for their permission to speak with others.)
- Interviewing police (if involved) and requesting a copy of police reports
- Interviewing EMS personnel and reviewing their written reports

## SUBJECTIVE AND OBJECTIVE INFORMATION

There are two types of information that medical providers will receive from clients: subjective and objective. Information obtained through these means is what the health care provider will utilize in documentation.

- **Subjective information** includes what the client tells the provider. This information is based on their description or opinion and is usually received verbally or through writing.
- **Objective information** is what the health care provider actually observes. This includes client behaviors as well as any findings during physical assessment.

## INTERVIEWING PRE-SCHOOL AGED CLIENTS

In most cases, it is better to interview the parent and child **separately**, though this may occur in the company of one another before the child is of school-age. Children can usually give better information about what they are feeling, and parents give better information on their external behavior. When talking with young children, speak in simple terms and short sentences. Convey a neutral attitude. Most children between the ages of 1-4 understand more than they can communicate. Children may not be able to communicate **absolute ideas**. Assessing the child during **play** may give insight into real world experiences that the child cannot verbalize through questions alone. Play will often allow for evaluation of physical and cognitive development, adaptability, social and moral development, and coping abilities. It may give great insight into the child's perceptions of social relationships and family. Play may include drawing, dolls, puppets, dress up clothes, or modeling clay.

## INTERVIEWING SCHOOL-AGED CLIENTS

The interview of the school-aged client usually takes place with the client sitting on a couch or in a chair. Talking with the client is the best way to build rapport. At this age, children are gaining more **independence** and it is important to respect that. Starting the interview with a casual conversation about school and their interests, such as their friends or video games, can help to lighten the mood. Asking about their favorite subjects in school and what they like the most and least about school can open the door to gaining some insight on their school performance. Most school-aged clients can provide their own medical history, depending upon the severity of their illness. At this age, the parent or guardian of the client should be present to confirm or clarify any medical history to ensure it is accurate. The client's history of academic performance, including any disciplinary issues at school, should be confirmed with the parent or guardian.

## INTERVIEWING ADOLESCENT CLIENTS

Establishing a healthy rapport with the adolescent client is essential in order to obtain an open, honest history. Regardless of where the client sits, the interviewer should sit to place themselves at the **same level** as the client. Initially, **client confidentiality** should be explained to the adolescent client and specifically what can and cannot be kept confidential. Any statements about wanting to hurt themselves or someone else cannot be kept confidential. The majority of the visit with an adolescent client should be done without the parent or guardian present unless it is necessary. The interview should contain open-ended questions that cover their home life, education or employment, activities alone and with friends, any drug use or dieting habits, sexuality, suicide and depression, and safety issues. When discussing any drug use with the adolescent client, make sure to ask about their friends' habits, also.

## INTERVIEWING ADULT CLIENTS

Within the first few minutes of the interview of the adult client, it is important that introductions are completed and are clear. Try to sit during the interview to not seem to be towering over the client and place yourself at the **same level** as them. Provide **active listening** to the client's concerns, empathy for these concerns, and concern for the client as an individual. When a client knows that that their concerns are taken seriously, they are more likely to be more active in their healthcare. Ask about job satisfaction, involvement in community activities, and social support to evaluate for possible signs of depression. Providing reassuring touch or a shared silence with the client may put them more at ease and let them know that their problems matter. It is important to not be quick to move onto the next question, and rather, let the client fully answer a question without interrupting them. Finally, while some of the problems expressed by the client may not seem medically significant, they should still be addressed to some degree to validate them.

## INTERVIEWING ELDERLY CLIENTS

The interview of the elderly client differs from that of the adult client because the interviewer is trying to identify what the client can do versus what they should be able to do or would like to be able to do. In order to gather this information, it is important to spend the time necessary with the client and provide patience in listening to their **complete history**. Hearing loss, vision changes, and dementia can affect communication with the client, so more **time** may need to be spent with these clients and/or their family members. Important elements to consider in the interview process are the general health status of the client, their mental health status, the activities of daily living, their social support system, the future outlook, and any family concerns they may have. Identifying their reliance on community services that are available can help to identify the client's ability to care for themselves. There is a high incidence of depression and dementia amongst the elderly, and identification of these symptoms can help to determine in which area of living they need assistance.

## MEDICATION RECONCILIATION

When obtaining an in-home medication list, known as a medication reconciliation, the first step is to ask if the client has a list of medications or has brought current medications. If so, the health care provider should review each medication, including the **dose and frequency**. If the medicine is available, the **date** should be checked on the medicine bottle as clients often keep medications for long periods of time and should assess the amount of remaining medication in relation to the dispensing date. If necessary, the client, family, or caregivers should be asked to provide information about their medication(s), asking detailed questions about the drugs. Other questions can include the duration of treatment, reasons for taking the drugs, names of prescribing physicians, and the dispensing pharmacies. Specific questions should be asked about any complementary treatments (e.g., vitamins, probiotics) and over-the-counter medications, and specific categories of drugs (e.g., pain medicines, antacids, laxatives, stool softeners, antihistamines) used both frequently and infrequently.

# Assessment Tests and Tools

## PSYCHOLOGICAL ASSESSMENT TERMINOLOGY

A **standardized test** is one in which the questions and potential responses from all tests can be compared with one another. Every aspect of the test must remain consistent.

A **behavioral assessment** assumes that an individual can only be evaluated in relation to his or her environment. Behavioral assessments must include a stimulus, organism, response, and consequences (SORC).

A **dynamic assessment** involves systematic deviation from the standardized test to determine whether the individual benefits from aid. This includes the process called "testing the limits," in which an examinee is provided with a sequence of extra clues.

**Domain-referenced testing** breaks evaluation into specific domains of ability—for instance, reading or math ability.

## MEASUREMENT AND TESTS IN THE ASSESSMENT PROCESS

The mental health care provider develops a representation of the client through the collection of facts. Psychometric instruments are used to collect pertinent data on the client. **Measurement** is a numerical value that has been allocated to a mannerism, attribute, or characteristic on the instrument. The measurement used must be one that is commonly understood by the general population.

A **test** is a task or series of tasks used to examine a psychomotor behavior or action that is indicative of a state of being. The state of being can be cognitively based or affective in nature. Answering written questions is a typical test scenario. The student goes through the task of answering academically based questions to indicate that cognitive learning has been accomplished in an academic class. The teacher grades the test and makes the inference that the student has learned on a cognitive or affective level.

## TEST SELECTION AND ADMINISTRATION

The primary concern in test selection should be the client's needs and wants. Out of this consideration, the mental health care provider makes an informed decision about which **tests and psychometric techniques** to apply. A provider should suggest testing if there is a need to gain further information, but testing is not necessarily required. The client may perceive the testing to be some kind of threat or manipulative tool. In that case, the client should be reassured and educated about the real purpose of the test. **Competency level** should also be considered when selecting, administering, measuring, and evaluating the test results, including legal issues involving a particular assessment, and any **ethical issues** that may be associated with an assessment. The mental health care provider may require additional training in test procedures before giving and assessing a particular test.

### USING THE INTERNET FOR TEST SELECTION

The internet provides an excellent search tool for the mental health provider. The internet can be used to locate specific tests that are applicable to the client's needs and wants. The **decision-making model** presented by Drummond in 1996 can be used to help select the most appropriate test. Any tests being considered should be evaluated for dimension, traits, and attributes. The decision should be based on what kind of information is anticipated to be the most useful. This involves a thorough perusal of the information already available at hand. The internet can also be used to search through objective evaluations given by others. Prospective tests should also be appraised for validity and reliability. The test and its results must provide the mental health care provider and the client with a practical use.

## ISSUES IMPACTING TEST SELECTION

The test-related issues that may impact the selection of a test include validity, reliability, and norm standards.

- The issue of **validity** in a test involves an effective examination that gives the desired results. Tests used within the mental health profession should have well founded, criterion-based content that measures what it is supposed to measure.
- Before using a test, make sure it has received an independent appraisal from established sources, and is considered **reliable**, meaning that the test results should be able to stand up over a period of time. The test should give a precise and accurate score. The entire test should be evaluated for its *reliability coefficient* and *standard of error measurement*. The test may present a split-half reliability that measures internal consistency among other assessment instruments.
- The test should follow the **norm-referenced criteria** for the client's age, sex, ethnic origin, culture, and socioeconomic status.

## PAPER-AND-PENCIL TESTS VS. PERFORMANCE TESTS

Another choice in test selection is that between administering a paper-and-pencil test vs. a performance test.

- **Paper-and-pencil tests** are used by a variety of test takers. One drawback is found when the client cannot read at the same level at which the test is written.
- **Performance tests** are given with a verbal request. The verbal request elicits a response that measures whether the client can follow the instruction given.

Paper-and-pencil and performance tests can either be applied in group settings or in individual treatments. Group-administered tests may be given by untrained proctors in a variety of settings. Typically, the group completes a paper-and-pencil test. Individuals may take the test under the supervision of an administrator. The administrator understands the complexities involved in giving the test, scoring the test, and interpreting the test results. Paper-and-pencil tests or performance tests are used to collect data about an exhibited behavior. The data is then evaluated. Paper-and-pencil tests are used to provide a fast, inexpensive, and objective grade. Test publishers develop most of the commercial grade paper-and-pencil assessment tests available. The administrator or proctor of the paper-and-pencil test will distribute materials, read the directions to the group, time the test, and collect the test.

## USING COMPUTERS IN PSYCHOLOGICAL ASSESSMENTS

The computer has gained popularity over paper-and-pencil tests and has changed the field of assessment through a wide range of mechanically based scoring mechanisms. The analog computer has been incorporated in tallying the score of the Strong Vocational Interest Blank, now called the Strong Interest Inventory, developed by Edward Kellog Strong in 1946. Computer software capabilities have given way to school-based vocational preference instruments. National testing organizations like the Educational Testing Service (ETS) uses computers to administer multiple college-admissions tests like the GRE and to score them. The computer is also used to administer and interpret some psychological instruments like the Rorschach and the MMPI tests.

### NORM-REFERENCED VS. CRITERION-REFERENCED TESTS

Tests can be **norm-referenced** or **criterion-referenced**. Both require that the test is graded with a raw score. The raw score indicates the number of right answers or a pattern found. The client's raw score is then compared to a group score. The raw score in a criterion-related test is compared to a criterion that can determine mastery or minimum competency levels within a subject.

### STRUCTURED VS. UNSTRUCTURED TESTS

The difference found between a **structured** and an **unstructured test** is the range or degree of structure applied. For instance, the Strong Interest Inventory is a structured vocational preference test that only allows the client to give one of six possible answers. The Rorschach inkblot test allows the client to answer with any response that comes to mind.

### STANDARDIZED ASSESSMENT TOOLS USED IN EVALUATION PROCESS

The five standardized assessment tools or tests are the achievement test, the aptitude test, the intelligence test, the vocational preference instrument, and the personality test:

- The **achievement test** is used to measure what has been learned in academics, vocation, or other life experience.
- The **aptitude test** is used to make a prediction on the subject's future performance in a given field of study.
- The **intelligence test** predicts a person's academic performance in the future by determining the person's mental potential.
- The **vocational preference instrument** is used to discover a pattern of characteristics that describe the individual's preferences or inclination to do something in leisure, work, and educational settings.
- The **personality test** describes the person's behavior, attitudes, beliefs, and values, and is used to diagnose psychopathology or in relationship counseling.

### ASSESSING TRAITS, STRENGTHS, AND WEAKNESSES

An assortment of tests is available to **delineate capabilities, tendencies, and personalities**:

- The selection category can include tests like the Graduate Record Exam (GRE) or the Law School Admissions Tests (LSAT). **Selection tests** may also include vocational preference tests or personality tests used in educational and occupational counseling.
- **Placement tests** are used to determine where a client belongs in a program. Colleges may use these tests to determine in which class a student should start a program of study.
- **Diagnostic tests** use a combination of psychometric techniques and tests to evaluate human performance levels, and incorporate the DSM diagnostic labels to determine a remediation program for a client. Many insurance carriers also require this DSM label before payment is released for services rendered. Individual progress is also typically measured using psychometric instruments to help evaluate progress toward a goal.

## INTELLIGENCE TESTS
### STANFORD-BINET INTELLIGENCE SCALES

The Stanford-Binet intelligence scales (SB5) measure cognitive ability, assist in psychoeducational evaluation, diagnose developmental disabilities, and perform various assessments for individuals 2 to 85+. The SB5 test measures five **categories of intelligence**:

- Fluid reasoning
- Knowledge
- Quantitative reasoning
- Visual-spatial processing
- Working memory

SB5 measures each of these domains through both verbal and nonverbal activities. Subtests indicate which components of the SB5 are appropriate for the examinee. These subtest scores are combined to give four kinds of **composite score**:

- Factor index
- Domain
- Abbreviated battery
- Full-scale IQ

The standardization sample of the SB5 was based on 4,800 participants of various ages, socioeconomic statuses, geographic regions, and races.

## WAIS-IV
### MAIN INDEX SCORES OF WAIS-IV

The fourth edition of the **Wechsler Adult Intelligence Scale (WAIS-IV, 2008)** is used to measure the intellectual ability of late-adolescents and adults. The newest edition, WAIS-V, is currently under the clinical validation phase and has not yet been released. Wechsler considered intelligence to be a global ability made up of a number of interrelated functions. This interrelationship between the various types of intelligence is described in the current test in terms of four index scores:

- Verbal Comprehension Index (VCI)
- Perceptual Reasoning Index (PRI)
- Working Memory Index (WMI)
- Processing Speed Index (PSI)

### CORE SUBTESTS OF WAIS-IV

There are **ten core subtests** on the WAIS-IV:

- VCI: Similarities (abstract reasoning)
- VCI: Vocabulary (semantic knowledge)
- VCI: Information (general knowledge)
- PRI: Block Design (spatial processing)
- PRI: Matrix Reasoning (inductive reasoning)
- PRI: Visual Puzzles (spatial reasoning)
- WMI: Digit Span (working memory)
- WMI: Arithmetic (quantitative reasoning)
- PSI: Symbol Search (processing speed)
- PSI: Coding (associative memory)

## ADMINISTRATION AND SCORING OF WAIS-IV

There are 2 **broad scores** in the WAIS-IV.

- **Full Scale IQ (FSIQ)**: Based on the combined scores for the ten VCI, PRI, WMI and PSI subtests
- **General Ability Index (GAI)**: Based only on the six subtests that test VCI and PRI

The **administration** of the test begins with picture completion and then a series of alternating verbal and nonverbal subtests. The only exception to this is that the digit span and information subtests are administered together. Some tests will be timed, while others will be allowed to go on until the examinee has finished. The raw **scores** for each subtest are converted into scaled scores with a standard conversion table. In the subtests, the mean score is 10 and the standard deviation is 3. For the full-scale performance and verbal IQs and factor indices, the mean is 100 and the standard deviation is 15.

## SUPPLEMENTAL SUBTESTS OF THE INTELLIGENCE SCALES OF THE REVISED WAIS-IV

Additional supplemental subtests are included with each intelligence scale in the WAIS-IV:

- Verbal Comprehension (VCI) Supplemental Subtest: Comprehension
- Perceptual Reasoning (PRI) Supplemental Subtests: Picture Completion and Figure Weights
- Working Memory (WMI) Supplemental Subtest: Letter-Number Sequencing
- Processing Speed (PSI) Supplemental Subtest: Cancellation

## GROUP INTELLIGENCE TESTS

Many different organizations, from schools to the armed forces, administer **group intelligence tests**:

- The **Kuhlman-Anderson Test (KA)** is for children in grades K-12; it measures verbal and quantitative intelligence. This test is unique in that it relies less on language than do other individual and group tests.
- The **Woodcock Johnson IV** consists of a test of cognitive abilities and a test of achievement; the latter of which measures oral language and academic achievement.
- The **Wonderlic Personnel Test (WPT-R)** takes about 12 minutes to fill out with paper and pencil; it purports to measure the mental ability of adults. The Wonderlic is a good predictor of performance, but some critics maintain that it unfairly discriminates against some cultural groups in certain jobs.

## TESTS FOR COGNITIVE AND INTELLECTUAL DEVELOPMENT IN CHILDREN
## WISC-V AND WPPSI-IV

The **WISC-V** is a variation of the WAIS made especially for children between the ages of 6 and 17. WISC-V is closely based on neurocognitive models of information processing, and gives scores through five indexes:

- Verbal comprehension
- Visual-spatial
- Fluid reasoning
- Working memory
- Processing speed

Highly asymmetrical scores on the subtests are used to diagnose autism, ADHD, and other learning disorders.

The **WPPSI-IV** (released in 2012) is made for children between the ages of 2.5 and 7.25. For children that are either 2 or 3 years old, the test can measure verbal comprehension, and perceptual organization; for older children, processing speed can also be measured.

## INFANT AND PRESCHOOL TESTS

Tests administered to children aged 2 or younger are good at screening for developmental delays and disabilities, but have poor predictive validity. **The Denver II** screens for developmental delays by observing a child's performance in four developmental domains:

- Personal-social
- Fine motor adaptive
- Language
- Gross motor

If a child fails an item that 90% of younger children pass, he or she is scored as having a **developmental delay**.

The **Bayley Scales of Infant Development (BSID-III)** assess the development of children 1 to 42 months old on mental, motor, and behavior rating scales.

The **Fagan Test of Intelligence** tries to gauge the information processing speed of an infant, in order to predict childhood IQ. It does this by introducing novel stimuli and observing the reaction time of the child.

## KAUFMAN TEST OF EDUCATIONAL ACHIEVEMENT, COGNITIVE ASSESSMENT SYSTEM, AND SLOSSON TESTS

The **Kaufman Test of Educational Achievement (KTEA-3)** measures academic ability in children grades 1-12. It provides scores in three core areas:

- Reading
- Math
- Written Language

Verbal instructions and responses should be minimized on these tests to make them fair for all cultures.

The **Cognitive Assessment System (CAS2)** is based on the *PASS* (planning, attention, simultaneous processing, and sequential processing) model of intelligence, and is appropriate for children between the ages of 5 and 18 of all cultures and ethnicities.

The **Slosson tests** were designed to be fast ways of estimating intelligence in order to identify children at risk of educational failure.

## ASSESSMENT OF INTELLECTUAL DISABILITY

Intellectual disability is defined as limitations in mental functioning mirrored by significant limitations in everyday functioning that are present early in life and before the age of 18.

- The **Individuals with Disabilities Act** states that all disabled individuals under the age of 25 need to be evaluated, and an *individualized educational plan (IEP)* needs to be developed for each child in order to provide education in the least restrictive environment.
- The case **Larry P. vs. Riles** established that IQ tests can be *racially discriminatory* and should not be used to place African-Americans in special education classrooms.
- The **Vineland Behavior Scales** measure communication, daily living skills, and socialization, for the purpose of developing *special education programs.*
- The **AAIDD Adaptive Behavior Scales** assess personal self-sufficiency, community self-sufficiency, personal-social responsibility, social adjustment, and personal adjustment for individuals ages 4-21.

## VANDERBILT ADHD

Vanderbilt ADHD is used to assess whether a child has attention deficit hyperactivity disorder. The tool has 3 parts:

- Assessment by a parent
- Assessment by a teacher
- Follow-up assessment by a parent

The parental assessment evaluates 47 symptoms that may be associated with ADHD and 8 performance measures. The teacher assessment evaluates 35 symptoms, 3 academic performances (reading, math, written expression), and 5 classroom performance behaviors. The follow-up parental assessment evaluates 18 symptoms, 8 performance measures, and 12 possible side effects.

## ACADEMIC ABILITY TESTING

Ability tests measure current status and predict future academic achievement. Types of **ability testing** include:

- **Curriculum-based measurement** is any form of assessment that focuses on the student's ability to perform the work of the school curriculum. Usually, a teacher will set a minimum standard for performance and provide remedial attention for any student who performs below this level.
- **Performance-based assessment** evaluates students on their execution of a task or creation of a product. It is meant to be egalitarian and culture-fair.
- The **Scholastic Achievement Test (SAT)** measures verbal and mathematical reasoning skills; it is used to predict the college success of high school students. Studies show that the SAT is more effective as a predictor when it is combined with grade-point average.
- The **Graduate Record Exam (GRE)** measures general scholastic abilities and may be taken in lieu of a normal secondary course of study.

## PERSONALITY TESTS

### STRUCTURED PERSONALITY TESTS

A structured personality test (as opposed to a projective test) measures emotional, social, and personal traits and behaviors through a series of multiple-choice questions or other unambiguous stimuli. There are four common strategies for structured personality tests:

- **Logical content method** bases its questions on deductive logic and a systematic theory of personality.
- **Theoretical method** measures the prevalence of the personality structures identified by a particular theory of personality.
- **Empirical criterion keying** has questions that are administered to different criterion groups; there are items that distinguish between the groups in the test.
- **Factor analysis tests** administer a large number of items to a large group of examinees, and then analyze their answers for any correlations.

## MMPI-3

### VALIDITY SCALES

The **Minnesota Multiphasic Personality Inventory-3 (MMPI-3)** was originally developed to diagnose psychiatric patients. The attitude of the examinee towards the test is indicated by his or her scores on various validity measures. In general, the validity scales can be grouped into three measurements: those that detect inconsistent response or non-response, those that detect the exaggerated self-reporting of the prevalence/severity of psychological symptoms, and those meant to detect those under-reporting psychological symptoms. Validity scales include:

- **Inconsistent/Non-Response:** CNS ("cannot say"), VRIN (Variable response inconsistency, TRIN (True response inconsistency).
- **Exaggerated Response**: F (Infrequency, or "faking bad" in the first half of the test); Fb (F Back; "faking bad" in the second half of the test); Fp (F-Psychopathology (frequency of presentation).
- **Downplayed Response:** L (Lie; "faking good"); K (Defensiveness, denial); S (Superlative Self-Presentation).

### SCORING, INTERPRETATION, AND PROFILE ANALYSIS

The MMPI-3 takes raw scores and converts them into T-scores with a mean of 50 and a standard deviation of 10. If a person scores above a 65, it is considered to be clinically significant. The most common use of the MMPI-3 is as an assessment of personality and behavior through profile analysis. Most of the time, the code is simply the two highest scores on the various subtests. The validity scales are then used to ensure that the profile is the result of an honest attempt at the test. The standardization sample approximated the 2020 US census in age, gender, race, and social class.

### RORSCHACH INKBLOT AND TAT PROJECTIVE PERSONALITY TESTS

**Projective personality tests** assume that unstructured and ambiguous stimuli can elicit meaningful responses from individuals, particularly about personality and underlying conflicts. Projective tests are typically open-ended and therefore less susceptible to faking. The most famous projective test is the **Rorschach Inkblot Test**, in which a person is presented with ten cards containing bilaterally symmetrical inkblots and asked to free associate on the design. Scoring the Rorschach is very complex, but relies on the following dimensions of the individual's response:

- Location (as in where the subject sees whatever he or she describes)
- Determinants (why the subjects saw what they saw)
- Form quality (resemblance of the response to the inkblot)
- Content
- Frequency of occurrence

The Rorschach may provide interesting results, but its use in clinical work is dubious.

Another projective test is the **Thematic Apperception Test (TAT),** in which the examinee is asked to make up a story based on a random presentation of picture cards.

## EPPS, 16 PF-5, NEO-3

The **Edwards Personal Preference Schedule**, based on the personality theory of Murray, contains 225 items that present an either-or choice to the examinee. This test strives to prevent examinees from responding in ways that they know are socially desirable. The test provides ipsative scores, meaning that the strengths of the candidate are given comparative, rather than absolute, value.

The **Sixteen Personality Factor Questionnaire (16PF 5th Ed)** is a factor analysis-based exam that identifies 16 primary personality traits and 5 secondary traits.

The **NEO-Personality Inventory (NEO-PI-3)** attempts to gauge an individual's level of the Big Five personality traits (extraversion, agreeableness, conscientiousness, neuroticism, and openness to experience). These traits are then broken down into facets, for example, neuroticism contains anxiety and depression.

## TESTS FOR DEMENTIA, ATTENTION, AND DELIRIUM
### MMSE

The mini-mental state exam (MMSE), also known as the **Folstein test**, is a commonly used assessment tool for evaluating cognition. It is typically used to evaluate for the presence and severity of **dementia**. The MMSE consists of a 30-point questionnaire that evaluates immediate and short-term memory recall, orientation, arithmetic, the ability to follow simple commands, language, and other functional abilities such as copying a drawing. In clinical settings, it is very useful to detect initial impairment or follow responses over the course of an illness and/or treatment. This tool establishes a score based on education level and age. This score can be placed on a scale to determine **functionality** of the individual. A total possible score of 30 can be achieved. A score of 24 or greater is considered a normal functioning level. The lower the score, the greater the degree of dementia or mental dysfunction. It is possible that simple physical limitations such as the inability to read or hear or decreased motor function may negatively affect the total score.

### TRAIL MAKING TEST

The Trail Making Test (Parts A and B) assesses brain function and indicates increasing dementia. It is useful for detecting early Alzheimer's disease, and those who do poorly on part B often need assistance with activities of daily living (ADLs). The individual is given a demonstration of each part before beginning:

- **Part A** has 25 sequentially-numbered scattered circles across the page, and the individual is advised to use a pencil/pen to draw a continuous line to connect in ascending order the circles (starting with 1 and ending with 25).
- **Part B** is slightly more complex and has circles with numbers (1-12) and circles with letters (A-L) scattered about the page. The individual is advised to draw a continuous line alternating between numbers and letters in ascending order (1-A-2-B....).

The test is scored according to the number of seconds required for completion:

- **A**: 29 seconds is average, and >78 indicates deficiency.
- **B**: 75 seconds is average, and >273 seconds indicates deficiency.

## TIME AND CHANGE TEST

The Time and Change Test assesses **dementia** in adults and is effective in diverse populations. First, the individual is shown a clock face set at 11:10 and has one minute to make two attempts at stating the correct time. Next, the individual is given change (7 dimes, 7 nickels, and 3 quarters) and asked to give the clinician $1.00 from the coins. The individual has two minutes and two attempts to make the correct change. Failing either or both tests is indicative of dementia.

## DIGIT REPETITION TEST

The Digit Repetition Test is used to assess **attention**. The individual is told to listen to numbers and then repeat them. The clinician starts with two random single-digit numbers. If the individual gets this sequence correct, the clinician then states three numbers and continues to add one number each time until the individual is unable to repeat the numbers correctly. People with normal intelligence (without intellectual disability or expressive aphasia) can usually repeat 5-7 numbers, so scores <5 indicate impaired attention.

## CONFUSION ASSESSMENT METHOD

The Confusion Assessment Method is used to assess the **development of delirium** and is intended for those without psychiatric training. The tool covers 9 factors. Some factors have a range of possibilities and others are rated only as to whether the characteristic is present, not present, uncertain, or not applicable. The tool provides room to describe abnormal behavior. Factors indicative of delirium include:

- **Onset**: Acute change in mental status
- **Attention**: Inattentive, stable, or fluctuating
- **Thinking**: Disorganized, rambling conversation, switching topics, or illogical
- **Level of consciousness**: Altered, ranging from alert to coma
- **Orientation**: Disoriented (person, place, time)
- **Memory**: Impaired
- **Perceptual disturbances**: Hallucinations, illusions
- **Psychomotor abnormalities**: Agitation (tapping, picking, moving) or retardation (staring, not moving)
- **Sleep-wake cycle**: Awake at night and sleepy in the daytime

The tool indicates delirium if there is an acute onset with fluctuating inattention and disorganized thinking or altered level of consciousness.

## TESTS FOR ANXIETY AND DEPRESSION

### HAMILTON ANXIETY SCALE

The Hamilton Anxiety Scale (HAS or HAMA) is utilized to evaluate the anxiety related symptomatology that may present in adults as well as children. It provides an evaluation of overall **anxiety** and its degree of severity. This includes **somatic anxiety** (physical complaints) and **psychic anxiety** (mental agitation and distress). This scale consists of 14 items based on anxiety produced symptoms. Each item is ranked 0-4 with 0 indicating no symptoms present and 4 indicating severe symptoms present. This scale is frequently utilized in psychotropic drug evaluations. If performed before a particular medication has been started and then again at later visits, the HAS can be helpful in adjusting medication dosages based in part on the individual's score. It is often utilized as an outcome measure in clinical trials.

## GAD-7

General Anxiety Disorder-7 (GAD-7) is used to assess the severity of an individual's anxiety and focuses on the previous 2 weeks. The questions are as follows:

1. Feeling nervous, anxious, on edge?
2. Unable to stop/control worrying?
3. Worrying excessively about different things?
4. Having trouble relaxing?
5. Being excessively restless?
6. Easily annoyed/irritated?
7. Fearful something terrible will occur?

Responses are scored as 0 (not at all), 1 (several days), 2 (more than half of days), or 3 (nearly every day). Scores and assessment:

- **5-9 mild anxiety**, requires monitoring.
- **10-14 moderate anxiety**, requires further diagnostic tests, including MMSE and referral to a professional.
- **15+ severe anxiety**, requires active treatment.

### BECK DEPRESSION INVENTORY

The Beck Depression Inventory (BDI) is a widely utilized, self-reported, multiple-choice questionnaire consisting of 21 items, which measures the **degree of depression**. This tool is designed for use in adults between the ages of 17 and 80 years of age. It evaluates physical symptoms such as weight loss, loss of sleep, loss of interest in sex, and fatigue, along with attitudinal symptoms such as irritability, guilt, and hopelessness. The items rank in four possible answer choices based on an increasing severity of symptoms. The test is scored with the answers ranging in value from 0 to 3. The total score is utilized to determine the degree of depression. The usual ranges include: 0-9 no signs of depression, 10-18 mild depression, 19-29 moderate depression, and 30-63 severe depression.

## GERIATRIC DEPRESSION SCALE

The Geriatric Depression Scale (GDS) is a self-assessment tool to identify older adults with depression. The test can be used with those with normal cognition and those with mild to moderate impairment. The test poses 15 questions to which individuals answer "yes" or "no" and a point is assigned for each answer that indicates depression. A score of >5 points is indicative of depression:

1. Are you basically satisfied with your life?
2. Have you dropped many of your activities and interests?
3. Do you feel your life is empty?
4. Do you often get bored?
5. Are you in good spirits most of the time?
6. Are you afraid that something bad is going to happen to you?
7. Do you feel happy most of the time?
8. Do you often feel helpless?
9. Do you prefer to stay at home rather than going out and doing new things?
10. Do you feel you have more problems with memory than most?
11. Do you think it is wonderful to be alive now?
12. Do you feel pretty worthless the way you are now?
13. Do you feel full of energy?
14. Do you feel that your situation is hopeless?
15. Do you think that most people are better off than you are?

## CHILDREN'S DEPRESSION RATING SCALE-REVISED

The Children's Depression Rating Scale-Revised (CDRS-R) evaluates a child for depressive disorders and monitors treatment response. CDRS-R includes 17 items, 14 of which are assessed during an interview, and 3 of which are assessed by the clinician's interpretation of the individual's nonverbal cues. The CDRS-R is designed specifically for individuals aged 6-12 but may also be used during an interview with the individual's parents, caregivers, and teachers. The items included in the interview include the following: schoolwork, capacity to have fun, social withdrawal, sleep, appetite or eating patterns, excessive fatigue, physical complaints, irritability, guilt, self-esteem, depressed feelings, morbid ideation, suicidal ideation, weeping, depressed affect, tempo of speech, and hypoactivity.

## PHQ-9

Patient Health Questionaire-9 (PHQ-9) is used to determine the severity of depression and focuses on answers to questions related to the previous 2 weeks. The questions are as follows:

1. Little interest/pleasure in activities?
2. Feelings of depression or hopelessness?
3. Sleeping difficulties?
4. Tiredness of lack of energy?
5. Poor appetite or excessive eating?
6. Feelings of being a failure or letting down self/others?
7. Difficulty concentrating?
8. Speaking/moving slowly or fidgeting?
9. Suicidal ideation?

Responses are scored as 0 (not at all), 1 (several days), 2 (more than half of days), or 3 (nearly every day). Scores and assessment:

- **0-4: minimal or no depression**—monitor but likely does not need treatment
- **5-9: mild depression**—may need treatment
- **10-15: moderate depression**—may need treatment
- **15-19: moderately severe depression**—treatment required
- **20-27: severe depression**—treatment required

Suicide risk assessment should be carried out for any individuals indicating suicidal ideation.

## MULTIPLE APTITUDE TEST BATTERIES AND SPECIAL BATTERIES

Multiple aptitude test batteries measure ability in a number of different areas; one of their weaknesses is that they often lack adequate differential validity, meaning that the various parts of the test do not have different validities for different categories.

- **Differential aptitude tests (DAT)** identify job-related abilities and are used for career counseling and employee selection.
- The **general aptitude test battery (GATB)** was developed by the US Employment Service for vocational counseling and job placement. There are other tests used to measure special aptitudes.
- **Psychomotor tests** are used to assess speed, coordination, and general movement responses. These typically have low validity coefficients because they are highly specific and susceptible to practice effects.
- **Mechanical aptitude tests** are used to assess dexterity, perceptual and spatial skills, and mechanical reasoning. The different skills that fall within this category are relatively independent.

## ASSESSMENT OF INDIVIDUALS WITH PHYSICAL DISABILITIES

The **Americans with Disabilities Act of 1990** declares that any test administered to a disabled job applicant or employee should reflect only the person's ability on the test, and not his or her disability. Employers are also required to make reasonable accommodations for disabled employees.

- The **Columbia Mental Maturity Scale (CMMS)** is a test of general reasoning ability that does not require fine motor skills or verbal responses. It is useful for assessing students with cerebral palsy, brain damage, intellectual disability, and speech impediments.
- The **Peabody Picture Vocabulary Test (PPVT-5)** measures receptive vocabulary without requiring verbal responses.
- The **Haptic Intelligence Scale (HIS)** uses tactile stimuli, so it is good for assessing blind and partially-sighted individuals.
- The **Hiskey-Nebraska Test of Learning Aptitude (H-NTLA)** contains twelve nonverbal subtests which can be administered verbally or in pantomime; it is good for assessing children with hearing impairments.

## *WORLD HEALTH ORGANIZATION DISABILITY ASSESSMENT SCHEDULE 2.0*

The World Health Organization Disability Assessment Schedule 2.0 (WHODAS 2.0), is the DSM-5 recommended tool for assessing **global impairment and functioning**. It is based on ICD and ICF classifications. In previous versions of the DSM, global disability was assessed by the Global Assessment of Functioning (GAF) scale. WHODAS comes as a self-report tool with either 12 or 36 questions, taking around 7-15 minutes to administer. These questions help to assess the individual's performance in 6 domains over the last 30 days. The **six domains** are: cognition, participation, mobility, self-care, life activities, and interacting with other people. Using the questionnaire, the tool produces a score that represents the individual's global disability. Pros of the tool include that it is reliable and valid, even across cultures. Cons include that due to the self-report nature of the tool, there is no way to check the validity of the individual's responses to the questions.

## NEUROPSYCHOLOGICAL ASSESSMENTS

The **Benton Visual Retention Test (BVRT)** assesses visual memory, spatial perception, and visual-motor skills in order to diagnose brain damage. The subject is asked to reproduce from memory the geometric patterns on a series of ten cards.

The **Beery Developmental Test of Visual-Motor Integration (Beery-VMI-6)** assesses visual-motor skills in children; like the BRVT, it involves the reproduction of geometric shapes.

The **Wisconsin Card Sorting Test (WSCT)** is a screening test that assesses the ability to form abstract concepts and shift cognitive strategies; the subject is required to sort a group cards in an order that is not disclosed to him or her.

The **Stroop Color-Word Association Test (SCWT)** is a measure of cognitive flexibility; it tests an individual's ability to suppress a habitual reaction to stimulus.

The **Halstead-Reitan Neuropsychological Battery (HRNB)** is a group of tests that are effective at differentiating between normal people and those with brain damage. The clinician has control over which exams to administer, though he or she is likely to assess sensorimotor, perceptual, and language functioning. A score higher than 0.60 indicates brain pathology.

The **Luria-Nebraska Neuropsychological Battery (LNNB)** contains 11 subtests that assess areas like rhythm, visual function, and writing. The examinee is given a score between 0 and 2, with 0 indicating normal function and 2 indicating brain damage.

The **Bender Visual-Motor Gestalt Test (Bender-Gestalt II)** is a brief examination that involves responding to 16 stimulus cards containing geometric figures, which the examinee must either copy or recall.

## AIMS

The abnormal involuntary movement scale (AIMS) is an assessment tool that can be utilized to assess **abnormal physical movements**. These movements can often be the resulting side-effects of certain antipsychotic medications and can be associated with tardive dyskinesia or chronic akathisia. These motor abnormalities can also be associated with particular illnesses. Based on a five-point scale, the movements of three specific physical areas are evaluated to determine a total score. These areas are the face and mouth, trunk area, and the extremities. The AIMS has been established as a reliable assessment tool and also has a very simple design that provides a short assessment time. This allows it to be easily utilized in an inpatient or outpatient setting to provide an objective record of any abnormal physical movements that can change over the course of time.

## BRIEF PSYCHIATRIC RATING SCALE FOR CHILDREN

The Brief Psychiatric Rating Scale for Children (BPRS-C) is designed to identify presenting symptoms and annotate the severity of each symptom, on a scale ranging from "not present" to

"extremely severe." BPRS-C is used to diagnose psychiatric disorders for both children and adolescents through an interview with the child and parent(s).

Symptoms evaluated on the scale include:

- **Behavioral symptoms**, such as uncooperativeness and hostility
- **Mood symptoms**, such as depressive mood and anxiety
- **Sensory symptoms**, such as hallucinations, delusions, and speech characteristics
- **Symptoms of awareness and alertness**, such as disorientation, hyperactivity, distractibility, and others
- **Symptoms of affect**, such as emotional withdrawal and blunted affect

The BPRS-C assessment tool is a cursory look at many symptoms typically displayed with mental disorders.

## YALE-BROWN OBSESSIVE-COMPULSIVE SCALE

The Yale-Brown Obsessive-Compulsive Scale (Y-BOCS) is a useful tool for identifying and diagnosing obsessive-compulsive disorders. Y-BOCS aims to identify obsessions, including: aggressive, contamination, sexual, hoarding/saving, religious, need for symmetry, somatic, and miscellaneous obsessions such as cleaning/washing, checking, repeating, and counting. Y-BOCS asks the individual to rate the time he or she spends on obsessions and compulsions during the week prior to the clinician's interview. It asks the individual how much control he or she has over the compulsion/obsession, and how much distress it causes him or her. Y-BOCS has questions about resistance and interference. The clinician can ask for clarification and if the individual volunteers information, it is included in the assessment. The final rating is based on the clinician's judgment.

## COMMUNICATING TEST RESULTS

Test results must be communicated to the client in an ethical manner that will be of benefit to the client. This information should not add to the client's sense of bewilderment, embarrassment, unworthiness, or be perceived as critical in nature. The mental health care provider should provide significant results to the client out of a sincere desire to help. The client should understand the reason for giving the test and what information will be gleaned from its results. Then, the results and the scores should be discussed in relation to the questions asked on the test. The client should be encouraged to make his or her own interpretation of the results discussed. This can alleviate an attitude of passive acceptance or a more defensive rejection concerning the outcome of the test. The client should be affirmed by the communication efforts of the provider.

# Diagnostic Tests

## PET Scan

**Positron-emission tomography (PET)** involves injecting the individual with a radioactive glucose tracer that is taken up by active brain cells. By analyzing images of brains that have been injected with radioactive glucose, doctors can gauge regional cerebral blood flow, glucose metabolism, and oxygen consumption, all of which correlate with the brain's level of activity. PET scans are often used by clinicians to assess the cerebral damage that has been done by cerebrovascular disease, major neurocognitive disorder (formerly dementia), schizophrenia, Alzheimer's disease, and other disorders. Researchers often use PET scans to determine which areas of the brain are active during certain functions.

## CT Scan

The procedure known as **neuroimaging** has vastly improved scientists' ability to assess the structure and function of living brains. The two most common techniques of neuroimaging are computed axial tomography (CT or CAT) and magnetic resonance imaging (MRI). In **CT scans**, an x-ray is taken of various horizontal cross-sections of the brain. CT scans are good for diagnosing pathological conditions like tumors, blood clots, and multiple sclerosis.

### HEAD CT FOR AN INDIVIDUAL WITH ALTERED MENTAL STATUS

The **CT scan** is a common imaging technique used to diagnose individuals who present with altered mental status. The CT scan can identify **traumatic brain injury** and **mass lesions**, such as brain tumors or hematomas, as well as cerebral edema, so it may be invaluable for neurological disorders, but it is primarily used to **rule out differential diagnoses** rather than to diagnose mental health disorders. CT scans may also be used in addition to other tests to help confirm a possible diagnosis. For example, individuals with schizophrenia tend to have enlarged ventricles with increased CSF and a concomitant reduction in brain volume with sulci that are more widened than in a non-schizophrenic brain. Despite these findings, the CT alone cannot be used for diagnosis, and no specific pattern of abnormality has been noted with depression or bipolar disorder, although there is evidence that the frontal cortex shrinks in size with uncontrolled bipolar disease and depression and increases with treatment, so long-term monitoring may show differences.

## MRI

An MRI uses magnetic fields and radio waves to produce cross-sectional images. MRIs are able to produce more detailed images than CT scans, and MRIs can produce images from any angle, not just horizontally. MRIs are able to construct three-dimensional representations of brains.

## EEG TESTING IN AN INDIVIDUAL WITH ALTERED LEVEL OF CONSCIOUSNESS

The **electroencephalogram (EEG)** is sometimes used to test individuals with altered level of consciousness in order to evaluate the individuals' **electrical impulses** (brain waves). EEG is indicated for suspected seizure activity, encephalopathies, infarcts, and altered consciousness. The purpose is to identify abnormal electrical activity, which may be noted as slowing, which occurs where there has been injury or an infarct. Waves include delta (1-4 Hz), alpha (8-13 Hz), theta (4-7

Hz), beta (12-40 Hz), sleep spindles (12-14 Hz), and spikes and waves (variable frequency). Spikes and waves indicate that tissue is irritated. Findings indicate:

- **Metabolic encephalopathy**: Intermittent slowing with triphasic waves
- **Cerebral anoxic damage**: Generalized slowing in delta and theta range
- **Coma state**: Prognosis poor if EEG shows unchanging alpha waves with stimulation
- **CNS depressant overdose**: Transient periods of absence of electrical activity
- **Epilepsy**: Unusual electrical activity within the brain, partial seizures evident from only some of the electrodes while generalized seizures evident from all electrodes
- **ADHD**: A 20-minute EEG procedure FDA-approved to diagnose children with ADHD

## TESTING FOR DELIRIUM

**Appropriate testing** for an individual presenting with delirium, transient confusion and alterations in consciousness depends on the age and circumstances. **Delirium** is most common in older adults in response to illness or surgery but can occur at any age. **Hyperactive delirium** may be associated with alcohol withdrawal or drug toxicity. **Hypoactive delirium** may result from disease processes, such as hepatic encephalopathy. Some have mixed symptoms, becoming more agitated during the evening and night. Testing includes:

- **Confusion Assessment Method (CAM) or CAM-ICU** helps to differentiate confusion from other causes of altered consciousness.
- The **CAM-S** form of the CAM test is used to determine the severity of delirium.
- A **Delirium Symptom Interview** also helps to identify delirium.
- **Laboratory tests**: If the cause of the individual's confusion is not evident, numerous tests may be done to rule out other causes, including CBC, blood glucose, renal and liver function tests, drug and alcohol screening, sed-rate, thyroid function tests, HIV, and thiamine and vitamin $B_{12}$ levels.

## LABORATORY TESTS FOR PSYCHIATRIC ILLNESSES

At the current time, diagnosis of psychiatric illnesses is based almost completely on symptoms and history, and no laboratory tests have been FDA approved for diagnosis; however, **biochemical markers** have been identified for some psychiatric disorders, including schizophrenia, bipolar disorder, and depression. Some companies have collected data and applied for FDA approval for these tests and are now marketing tests. This testing is not in common use because its use is not yet reimbursed by Medicare/Medicaid or insurance companies. Some researchers believe that genetic testing and imaging (PET, MRI) may also have larger roles in diagnosis in the future. Currently, **laboratory tests** are used for primarily two reasons:

- Rule out differential diagnoses and identify concomitant disorders. Many different tests may be used, but in many cases the results of tests don't alter the original diagnosis, so testing is done selectively, based on individual's age, history, and physical exam.
- Monitor serum levels of drugs during therapy, such as lithium levels.

## LABORATORY TESTS FOR INDIVIDUALS PRESENTING WITH NEW ONSET PSYCHIATRIC ISSUE

When individuals present with a new onset psychiatric issue, a series of **laboratory tests** may be conducted to determine potential causes, rule out differential diagnoses, and identify concomitant disorders:

- **Blood alcohol level and urine drug screening** to determine if the individual is experiencing overdosing, withdrawal symptoms, or toxic reaction
- **Blood glucose level** to determine if the individual has hypoglycemia or hyperglycemia that may be affecting mental status
- **Urinalysis and urine culture** to determine if an infection is present (may result in confusion in older adults)
- **Pregnancy testing** to determine if females are pregnant before initiating treatment.
- **Liver and kidney function tests** to evaluate for hepatic and renal encephalopathy
- **CBC** to assess for anemia, infection, or other abnormalities
- **HIV antibodies** to rule out HIV/AIDS
- **Lyme antibodies** to rule out neuropsychological symptoms related to Lyme disease
- **Lumbar puncture** to examine cerebrospinal fluid for suspected infection

# Indicators for Risk to Self or Others

## COMPONENTS OF A RISK ASSESSMENT

A risk assessment evaluates the client's condition and their particular situation for the presence of certain risk factors. These risks can be influenced by age, ethnicity, spirituality, or social beliefs. They can include risk for suicide, harming others, exacerbation of symptoms, development of new mental health issues, falls, seizures, allergic reactions, or elopement. This assessment should occur within the first interview and then continue to be an ongoing process. The client's specific risks should be prioritized and documented, and then interventions should be put into place to protect this client from these risks.

## SUICIDAL IDEATION

Danger to the self or suicidal ideation occurs frequently in clients with mood disorders or depression. While females are more likely to attempt suicide, males actually successfully commit suicide 3 times more than females, primarily because females tend to take overdoses from which they can be revived, while males choose more violent means, such as jumping from a high place, shooting, or hanging. Risk factors include psychiatric disorders (schizophrenia, bipolar disorder, PTSD, substance abuse, and borderline personality disorder), physical disorders (HIV/AIDS, diabetes, stroke, traumatic brain injury, and spinal cord injury), and a previous violent suicide attempt. Passive suicidal ideation involves wishing to be dead or thinking about dying without making plans while active suicidal ideation involves making plans. Those with active suicidal ideation are most at risk. People with suicidal ideation often give signals, direct or indirect, to indicate they are considering suicide because many people have some ambivalence and want help. Others may act impulsively or effectively hide their distress.

## *SUICIDE RISK ASSESSMENT*

A suicide risk assessment should be completed and documented upon initial interview, with each subsequent visit, and any time suicidal ideations are suggested by the client. This risk assessment should evaluate and score the following criteria:

- Would the client sign a contract for safety?
- Is there a suicide plan, and if so, how lethal is the plan?
- What is the elopement risk?
- How often are the suicidal thoughts?
- Have they attempted suicide before?

Any associated symptoms of hopelessness, guilt, anger, helplessness, impulsive behaviors, nightmares, obsessions with death, or altered judgment should also be assessed and documented. A higher score indicates a higher the risk for suicide.

## WARNING SIGNS OF SUICIDE

The warning signs of suicide include the following:

- Depression
- Prior suicide attempts
- Family suicide history
- Abrupt increase in substance abuse
- Reckless and impulsive behavior
- Isolation
- Poor coping
- Support system loss
- Recent or anticipated loss of someone special
- Verbal expression of feeling out of control
- Preoccupation with death
- Behavioral changes not otherwise explained (a sudden changed mood from depressed to happy, the giving away of one's personal belongings, etc.)

Where **risk of suicide is suspected**, the client should be questioned directly about any thoughts of self-harm. This should be followed by a full assessment and history (particularly family history of suicide). Where the threat of suicide is not imminent, one commonly used intervention is the no-suicide contract, in which the client signs a written agreement promising to contact the suicide hotline or a counselor, social worker, or other specified professional rather than carry out an act of suicide. While commonly used, these contracts have not been proven to reduce suicide attempts and therefore should not be used in isolation as an intervention for suicide risk, nor should they be used when threat of suicide is high. When a client already has a plan for suicide, or has multiple risk factors, hospitalization must be arranged. If any immediate attempt has already been made, a medical evaluation must occur immediately.

## SIGNS AND RISK FACTORS OF CLIENT'S DANGER TO OTHERS

Violence and aggression are not uncommon among clients and pose a danger to others. Risk factors include mental health disorders, access to weapons, history of personal or family violence, abuse, animal cruelty, fire setting, and substance abuse. Violence and aggression should be handled as follows:

- **Violence** is a physical act perpetrated against an inanimate object, animal, or other person with the intent to cause harm. Violence often results from anger, frustration, or fear and occurs because the perpetrators believe that they are threatened or that their opinion is right and the victim is wrong. It may occur suddenly without warning or following aggressive behavior. Violence can result in death or severe injury if the individual attacks, so anyone in the presence of an actively violent client should back away and seek safety.
- **Aggression** is the communication of a threat or intended act of violence and will often occur before an act of violence. This communication can occur verbally or nonverbally. Gestures, shouting, speaking increasingly loudly, invasion of personal space, or prolonged eye contact are examples of aggression requiring the client be redirected or removed from the situation.

## FIVE-PHASE AGGRESSION CYCLE

The five-phase aggression cycle is as follows:

| Triggering | Client responds to a triggering event with anger or hostility. Client may exhibit anxiety, restlessness, and muscle tension. Other signs include rapid breathing, perspiration, loud angry voice, and pacing. |
|---|---|
| Escalation | Client's responses show movement toward lack of control. Client's face flushes and he or she becomes increasingly agitated, demanding, and threatening, often swearing, clenching fists, and making threatening gestures. Client is unable to think clearly or resolve problems. |
| Crisis | Client loses emotional and physical control. Client throws objects, hits, kicks, punches, spits, bites, scratches, screams, shrieks, and cannot communicate clearly. |
| Recovery | Client regains control. Client's voice lowers, muscle tension relaxes, and client is able to communicate more rationally. |
| Post-crisis | Client may attempt reconciliation. Client may feel remorse, apologize, cry, or become quiet or withdrawn. Client is now able to respond appropriately. |

## MANAGING ACTIVE THREATS OF HOMICIDALITY BY CLIENTS

A client may be deemed a threat to others if:

- Client makes a serious threat of physical violence.
- The threat is made against one or more specifically named individuals.

When a threat meeting these criteria is made, even in the context of a privileged-communication relationship, a duty to protect is generated. In such a situation, the professional is required not only to notify appropriate authorities and agencies charged to protect the citizenry, but also to make a good-faith effort to warn the intended victim or, failing that, someone who is reasonably believed to be able to warn the intended victim.

The duty to warn stems from the 1976 legal case *Tarasoff v. Regents of the University of California*, where a therapist heard a credible threat and called only law enforcement authorities, failing to notify the intended victim. The murder occurred, and the case was appealed to the California Supreme Court, from which the rubric of duty to protect an intended victim has been established.

# Intake, Assessment, and Diagnosis Chapter Quiz

**1. Which of the following is NOT an unconscious element that influences behavior according to Freud?**

    a. Covert desires
    b. Taboos
    c. Dreams
    d. Defenses

**2. Which of the following developmental stages occurs between ages 6-11 according to Erikson?**

    a. Trust vs. Mistrust
    b. Autonomy vs. Shame
    c. Initiative vs. Guilt
    d. Industry vs. Inferiority

**3. Who of the following developed the empty organism concept?**

    a. Skinner
    b. Kohlberg
    c. Peplau
    d. Pavlov

**4. The _____ contains 11 subtests that assess areas like rhythm, visual function, and writing.**

    a. HRNB
    b. SCWT
    c. LNNB
    d. BVRT

**5. The fourth edition of the Wechsler Adult Intelligence Scale has which four indexes?**

    a. VCI, PLI, WMI, PSI
    b. TSM, PRI, VHS, PSI
    c. VCI, PRI, WMI, PSI
    d. WMI, VCI, PSI, NMI

**6. Bader and Pearson are known for which of the following?**

    a. Theory of moral development
    b. Developmental model of couples therapy
    c. Person-in-environment theory
    d. Theory of interpersonal relations

**7. Seeing external objects as either all good or all bad refers to which of the following defense mechanisms?**

    a. Identification
    b. Sublimation
    c. Splitting
    d. Displacement

**8. Which of the following describes the defense mechanism of introjection?**

    a.  Replacing in conscious awareness a painful idea or feeling with its opposite.

    b.  Somatic changes conveyed in symbolic body language; psychic pain is felt in a part of the body.

    c.  Turning against the self; object of aggressive drive is changed from another to the self, especially in depression and masochism.

    d.  Absorbing an idea or image so that it becomes part of oneself.

**9. The third level of observation where observation is done in a controlled setting for a lengthy period of time is known as**

    a.  Casual informational observation

    b.  Clinical level observation

    c.  Truman level observation

    d.  Guided observation

**10. Which of the following is NOT a group intelligence test?**

    a.  Denver II

    b.  Kuhlman-Anderson Test

    c.  Woodcock Johnson IV

    d.  Wonderlic Personnel Test

# Areas of Clinical Focus

## Psychiatric Disorders and Diagnosis

### DSM-5 CLASSIFICATIONS

The major DSM-5 classifications are as follows:

- Neurodevelopmental disorders
- Schizophrenia spectrum and other psychotic disorders
- Bipolar and related disorders
- Depressive disorders
- Anxiety disorders
- Obsessive-compulsive and related disorders
- Trauma- and stressor-related disorders
- Dissociative disorders
- Somatic symptom and related disorders
- Feeding and eating disorders
- Elimination disorders
- Sleep-wake disorders
- Sexual dysfunctions
- Gender dysphoria
- Disruptive, impulse-control, and conduct disorders
- Substance-related and addictive disorders
- Neurocognitive disorders
- Personality disorders
- Paraphilic disorders
- Other mental disorders
- Medication-induced movement disorders
- Other conditions that may be a focus of clinical attention

### INTELLECTUAL DISABILITIES

Very few (approximately 5%) cases of intellectual disability are **hereditary**. Hereditary forms of intellectual disability include Tay-Sachs, fragile X syndrome, and phenylketonuria. Most cases of intellectual disability (about 30%) are due to **mutations in the embryo** during the first trimester of pregnancy. Babies born with Down syndrome or those exposed to environmental toxins while in the uterus fall into this category. About 10% of cases of intellectual disability are due to **pregnancy or perinatal problems**, like fetal malnutrition, anoxia, and HIV. About 5% of those with intellectual disability have **general medical conditions** (like lead poisoning, encephalitis, or malnutrition) suffered during infancy or childhood. Approximately 20% are intellectually disabled because of either **environmental factors** or **other mental disorders** (e.g., sensory deprivation or autism). In the remaining 30%, etiology is **unknown**.

### PKU

Phenylketonuria (PKU) is one cause of intellectual disability. It occurs when an infant lacks the enzyme to metabolize the amino acid phenylalanine, found in high-protein foods and aspartame sweetener. PKU is a rare recessive genetic disorder diagnosed at birth by a simple blood test. It affects mostly blue-eyed, fair babies. Expectant mothers can reduce the hazard of PKU by

106

maintaining a diet low in phenylalanine. Untreated PKU typically leads to some form of intellectual disability. Some of the symptoms common to individuals with PKU are impaired motor and language development and volatile, erratic behavior. PKU can be treated if it is diagnosed in a timely fashion. Individuals must monitor their diet to keep phenylalanine blood levels at 2-10 mg/dL. Some phenylalanine is required for growth.

## DOWN SYNDROME

Down syndrome (Trisomy 21) occurs when a person has three #21 chromosomes instead of two. **Down syndrome** causes 20-30% of all cases of moderate and severe intellectual disability (1:800 births). Around 80% of Trisomy 21 pregnancies end in miscarriage. Classic physical characteristics associated with Down syndrome are slanted, almond-shaped eyes with epicanthic folds; a large, protruding tongue; a short, bent fifth finger; and a simian fold across the palm. Individuals with Down syndrome age rapidly. Medical conditions that often accompany Down syndrome and cause individuals to have a shorter life expectancy than normal, or poor quality of life, include heart lesions, leukemia, respiratory and digestive problems, cataracts, and Alzheimer's disease.

## COMMUNICATION DISORDERS

A number of disorders are lumped together under the heading of **communication disorders**:

- Language disorders
- Speech sound disorders
- Childhood-onset fluency disorders (stuttering)
- Social communications disorders

**Childhood-onset fluency disorder** (stuttering) typically begins between the ages of 2 and 7, and is more common in males than females. Research shows stuttering can be controlled through the removal of psychological stress in the home. Children who are constantly told not to stutter tend to stutter all the more. Many children find success through controlled and regular breathing exercises, accompanied by positive encouragement. In most cases, though, the child will spontaneously stop stuttering before the age of 16.

Many conditions that previously fell under the DSM-IV category of **pervasive developmental disorders** meet the criteria for **communication disorders** in DSM-5. Because autism spectrum disorder has social and communication deficits as part of its defining characteristics, it is important to note that communication disorders should not be diagnosed when there are repetitive behaviors or narrowed interests or activities.

## LEARNING DISORDERS AND ASSOCIATED CONDITIONS

A specific learning disorder is diagnosed as learning and academic difficulty, as evidenced by at least one of the following for at least six months (after interventions have been tried):

- Incorrect spelling
- Problems with math reasoning
- Problems with math calculation and number sense
- Difficulty reading
- Problems understanding what is read
- Difficulty using grammar and syntax

A child will be diagnosed with a learning disorder when he or she scores substantially lower than expected on a standardized achievement test and confirmed by a clinical assessment. The expectation for the child's score should be based on age, schooling, and intelligence, and the definition of "substantially lower" is a difference of two or more standard deviations. Learning disorders are frequently attended by delays in language development or motor coordination, attention and memory deficits, and low self-esteem. Learning disorders can be graded by severity as mild, moderate, or severe.

### PROGNOSIS AND ETIOLOGY OF LEARNING DISORDERS

Specific learning disorders include specific learning disorder with **impairment in reading**, specific learning disorder with **impairment in mathematics**, and specific learning disorder with **impairment in written expression**. Research has shown that boys are more likely to develop specific learning disorders with impairment in reading than girls. Although learning disorders are typically diagnosed during childhood or adolescence, they do not go away without treatment, and indeed may become more severe with time. Children who have a learning disorder with impairment in reading are far more likely than others to display antisocial behavior as an adult. At present, many researchers believe that reading disorders derive from problems with **phonological processing**.

Proposed **causes of learning disorders** include:

- Incomplete dominance and other hemispheric abnormalities
- Cerebellar-vestibular dysfunction
- Exposure to toxins, like lead

## AUTISM SPECTRUM DISORDER
### SYMPTOMS

There are two categories of symptoms necessary for a diagnosis of autism spectrum disorder. The first category is **deficits in social interaction and social communication**, which includes:

- Absence of developmentally appropriate peer relationships
- Lack of social or emotional reciprocity
- Marked impairment in nonverbal behavior
- Delay or lack of development in spoken language
- Marked impairment in the ability to initiate or sustain conversation
- Stereotyped or repetitive use of language or idiosyncratic language
- Lack of developmentally appropriate play

The other category of symptoms necessary for diagnosis of autism spectrum disorder is **restricted, repetitive patterns of behavior (RRBs), interests, and activities**. These include:

- Preoccupation with one or more stereotyped and restricted patterns of interest
- Inflexible adherence to nonfunctional routines or rituals
- Stereotyped and repetitive motor mannerisms
- Persistent preoccupation with the parts of objects

### DIAGNOSIS

Both categories of symptoms will be present in the ASD diagnosis. **Severity levels** are: **Level 1** (requiring support), **Level 2** (requiring substantial support), and **Level 3** (requiring very substantial support). Of note, ASD encompasses four disorders that were previously separate under DSM-IV: autistic disorder, Asperger's disorder, childhood integrative disorder, and pervasive developmental disorder. Individuals with ASD associated with other known conditions or

environmental factors should have the diagnosis written: autism spectrum disorder associated with (name of condition).

## PROGNOSIS

Autism spectrum disorder (ASD) is frequently first suspected when an infant does not respond to his or her caregiver in an age-appropriate manner. Babies with ASD are not interested in cuddling, do not smile, and do not respond to a familiar voice. They are often misdiagnosed as profoundly deaf. The current scientific consensus is that four different disorders previously believed to be separate are actually just different **degrees** on the autism spectrum. Many children with ASD severity level 1 may escape diagnosis until a much later age. At the higher end of the spectrum (which was once referred to as Asperger's syndrome), individuals have impairment in social interactions and a limited repertoire of behaviors, interests, and activities, but they do not display other significant delays in language, self-help skills, cognitive development, or curiosity about the environment. They are extremely sensitive to touch, sounds, sights, and tastes, and have strong clothing preferences. The prognosis of the individual with ASD will largely depend on where they are on the spectrum. Unfortunately, even a small degree of improvement in ASD takes a great deal of work. Only one-third of children with autism will achieve some **independence** as adults. Those with ASD who have developed the ability to communicate verbally by age 5-6 and have an IQ over 70 have the best chance for future independence.

## CHARACTERISTIC BEHAVIOR PATTERNS

Some very noticeable, specific behavior patterns characteristic of autism spectrum disorder include:

- Lack of eye contact and disinterest in the presence of others
- Infants who rarely reach out to a caregiver
- Hand-flapping
- Rocking
- Spinning
- Echolalia (the imitating and repeating the words of others)
- Obsessive interest in a very narrow subject, like astronomy or basketball scores
- Heavy emphasis on routine and consistency, and violent reactions to changes in their normal environment

One half of people with autism remain mute for their entire lives. The speech that does develop may be abnormal. The majority of people with autism have an IQ in the intellectual disability range.

## ETIOLOGY AND TREATMENT

There are a few structural abnormalities in the brain that have been linked to autism spectrum disorders. These include a **reduced cerebellum** and **enlarged ventricles**. Research has also suggested that there is a link between autism and abnormal levels of **norepinephrine**, **serotonin**, and **dopamine**. The support for a genetic etiology of ASD has been increased by studies indicating that siblings of children with autism are much more likely have autism themselves. As for treatment, the most successful interventions focus on teaching individuals with autism the practical skills they will need to survive independently. Therapy should also include development of social skills and the reduction of undesirable behavior. Individuals with autism who reach a moderate level of functioning can be given direct vocational training.

> **Review Video: Autism**
> Visit mometrix.com/academy and enter code: 395410

## ADHD

### DIAGNOSIS

Attention-deficit/hyperactivity disorder, commonly known as ADHD, can be diagnosed only if a child displays at least six symptoms of inattention or hyperactivity-impulsivity. Their onset must be before the age of 12, and they must have persisted for at least 6 months. The symptoms must not be motivated by anger or the wish to displease or spite others.

| Inattentiveness Symptoms (must have 6 for diagnosis for children) | Impulsivity/Hyperactivity Symptoms (must have 6 for diagnosis for children) |
| --- | --- |
| • Forgetful in everyday activity<br>• Easily distracted (often)<br>• Makes careless mistakes and doesn't give attention to detail<br>• Difficulty focusing attention<br>• Does not appear to listen, even when directly spoken to<br>• Starts tasks but does not follow through<br>• Frequently loses essential items<br>• Finds organizing difficult<br>• Avoids activities that require prolonged mental exertion | • Frequently gets out of chair<br>• Runs or climbs at inappropriate times<br>• Frequently talks more than peer<br>• Often moves hands and feet, or shifts position in seat<br>• Frequently interrupts others<br>• Frequently has difficulty waiting on turn<br>• Frequently unable to enjoy leisure activities silently<br>• Frequently "on the go" and seen by others as restless<br>• Often finishes other's sentences before they can |

### ASSOCIATED FEATURES

Even though they are found to have **average or above-average intelligence**, children with ADHD typically score lower than average on **IQ tests**. Almost every child with ADHD will have some trouble in school, with about a quarter having major problems in **reading**. Also, **social adjustment** can be difficult for children with ADHD. Various reports give the co-diagnosis of Conduct Disorder with ADHD occurring 30-90% of the time. Other common co-diagnoses include **Oppositional Defiant Disorder**, **Anxiety Disorder**, and **Major Depression**. About half of all children who are diagnosed with ADHD are also suffering from a learning disorder.

### SUBTYPES

There are three subtypes of ADHD:

- **Predominantly Inattentive Type** is diagnosed when a child has six or more symptoms of inattention and fewer than six symptoms of hyperactivity-impulsivity.
- **Predominantly Hyperactive-Impulsive Type** is diagnosed when there are six or more symptoms of hyperactivity-impulsivity and fewer than six of inattention.
- **Combined Type** is diagnosed when there are six or more symptoms of both hyperactivity-impulsivity and inattention.

ADHD is 4-9 times more likely to occur in boys than in girls, although the gender split is about half and half for Predominantly Inattentive Type. The rates of ADHD among adults appear to be about equal for both males and females.

### ETIOLOGY

The theory that ADHD is a **genetic disorder** is supported by data that shows slightly higher rates of the disorder occur among biological relatives than among the general population, and there are higher rates among identical twins, rather than fraternal twins. ADHD is associated with structural abnormalities in the brain, like subnormal activity in the frontal cortex and basal ganglia, and a relatively small caudate nucleus, globus pallidus, and prefrontal cortex. Symptoms of ADHD vary widely, depending on the child's environment. Repetitive or boring environments encourage symptoms, as do those in which the child is given no chance to interact. One theory of ADHD asserts that it is the result of an inability to distinguish between important and unimportant **stimuli** in the environment.

## PROGNOSIS

The behavior of children with ADHD is likely to remain consistent until **early adolescence**, when they may experience diminished overactivity, but continue to suffer from attention and concentration problems. ADHD adolescents are much more likely to participate in antisocial behaviors and to abuse drugs. More than half of all children who are diagnosed with ADHD will continue to suffer from it as **adults**. These adults are more susceptible to divorce, work-related trouble, accidents, depression, substance abuse, and antisocial behavior. Children with ADHD who are co-diagnosed with Conduct Disorder are especially likely to have these problems later in life.

## TREATMENT

Somewhat counterintuitively, central nervous system stimulants like **methylphenidate (Ritalin)** and **amphetamine (Dexedrine)** control the symptoms of ADHD. Side effects include headaches, gastrointestinal upset, anorexia, sleep difficulty, anxiety, depression, blood sugar and blood pressure increase, tics, and seizures. Research has consistently shown that **pharmacotherapy** works best when it is combined with **psychosocial intervention**. Many teachers have used the basic elements of **classroom management** to control the symptoms of ADHD. This involves laying out clear guidelines and contingencies for behavior, so that students do not have to speculate on what will happen in class or what they should be doing. Therapy that tries to increase the child's ability to **self-regulate behavior** has been shown to be less successful. It is always helpful when **parents** are involved in the treatment program.

## CONDUCT DISORDER

### DIAGNOSIS

**Conduct disorder criteria** are as follows:

| Criteria A | Persistent pattern of behavior in which significant age-appropriate rules or societal norms are ignored, and others' rights and property are violated (theft, deceitfulness); aggression to people and animals and destruction of property are common. To meet diagnosis criteria individuals will display three of the fifteen possible symptoms over the course of a year. All the symptoms can be categorized as belonging to one of the four categories below: <ul><li>Aggression to people or animals</li><li>Destruction of property</li><li>Deceitfulness or theft</li><li>Serious violations of rules</li></ul> |
|---|---|
| Criteria B | The patterns of behavior cause academic, social, or other impairments. |
| Criteria C | The behaviors couldn't better be classified as antisocial personality disorder. |

Individuals with conduct disorder persistently violate either the rights of others or age-appropriate rules. They have little remorse about their behavior, and in ambiguous situations, they are likely to interpret the behavior of other people as hostile or threatening.

## ETIOLOGY

According to Moffitt, there are two basic **types** of conduct disorder:

- **Life-course-persistent type** begins early in life and gets progressively worse over time. This kind of conduct disorder may be a result of neurological impairments, a difficult temperament, or adverse circumstances.
- **Adolescence-limited type** is usually the result of a temporary disparity between the adolescent's biological maturity and freedom. Adolescents with this form of conduct disorder may commit antisocial acts with friends. It is quite common for children with adolescence-limited conduct disorder to display antisocial behavior persistently in one area of life and not at all in others.

## TREATMENT FOR CONDUCT DISORDER AND OPPOSITIONAL DEFIANT DISORDER

Research suggests that conduct disorder **interventions** are most successful when they are administered to preadolescents and include the immediate family members. Some therapists have developed programs of **parent therapy** to help adults manage the antisocial behavior of their children, as this has been demonstrated to have good success. Most programs advise rewarding good behavior and consistently punishing bad behavior.

**Oppositional Defiant Disorder** is similar to conduct disorder and is characterized by:

- Patterns of negative or hostile behavior towards authority figures
- Frequent outbreaks of temper and rages
- Deliberately annoying people
- Blaming others
- Spite and vindictiveness

This pattern of negative, hostile, defiant behavior, and vindictiveness however, is less serious violations of the basic rights of others that characterize conduct disorders. Behavior is motivated by interpersonal reactivity or resentful power struggle with adults.

## MOTOR DISORDERS

Motor disorders are a type of neurodevelopmental disorder. **Motor disorders** can be classified as developmental coordination disorders, stereotypic movement disorders, and tic disorders. **Tic disorders** are further classified as Tourette's disorder, persistent motor or vocal tic disorder, and provisional tic disorder. **Tics** are defined in the DSM as "sudden, rapid, recurrent, nonrhythmic, stereotyped motor movements or vocalizations that feel irresistible yet can be suppressed for varying lengths of time."

## TOURETTE'S SYNDROME

Tourette's syndrome is a neurological disorder characterized by at least one vocal tic and multiple motor tics that appear simultaneously or at different times, and appears before the age of 18. Those with **Tourette's syndrome** typically have multiple motor tics and one or more vocal tics. Those with chronic motor or vocal tic disorder have either motor or vocal tics. Individuals with Tourette's syndrome are likely to have obsessions and compulsions, high levels of hyperactivity, impulsivity, and distractibility.

### TREATMENT

Most successful treatments for Tourette's syndrome include **pharmacotherapy**. The antipsychotics **haloperidol (Haldol)** and **pimozide (Orap)** are successful in relieving the symptoms of Tourette's

syndrome because they inhibit the flow of dopamine in the brain; their success has led many scientists to speculate that Tourette's Disorder is caused by an excess of dopamine. In some cases, psychostimulant drugs amplify the tics displayed by the individual. In these cases, a doctor may treat the hyperactivity and inattention of Tourette's with **clonidine** or **desipramine**. The former of these is a drug usually used to treat hypertension, while the latter is typically used as an antidepressant.

## ENURESIS AND ENCOPRESIS

Encopresis and enuresis make up the two major categories of elimination disorders. **Enuresis** is repeated urinating during the day or night into the bed or clothes at least twice a week for three or more months. Most of the time this urination is involuntary. Enuresis is diagnosed only when the child has reached an age at which continence can be reasonably expected (at least age five for DSM-5 criteria), and he or she does not have some other medical condition that could be to blame, like a urinary tract infection. Enuresis is treated with a night alarm, which makes a loud noise when the child urinates while sleeping. This is effective about 80% of the time, especially when it is combined with techniques like behavioral reversal and overcorrection. Desmopressin acetate (DDAVP) nasal spray, imipramine, and oxybutynin chloride (Ditropan) may help control symptoms. **Encopresis** is the involuntary fecal soiling in children who have already been toilet trained. Encopresis diagnosis cannot be made until the child is at least 4 years of age per DSM-5 criteria.

## PICA AND RUMINATION DISORDER

Pica is the persistent eating of non-food substances such as paint, hair, sand, cloth, pebbles, etc. Those with **pica** do not show an aversion to food. In order to be diagnosed, the symptoms must persist for at least a month without the child losing an interest in regular food. Also, the behavior must be independent and not a part of any culturally acceptable process. Pica is most often manifested between the ages of 12 and 24 months. Pica has been observed in developmentally disabled children, pregnant women, and people with anemia.

**Rumination disorder** is the regurgitation and re-chewing of food.

## AVOIDANT/RESTRICTIVE FOOD INTAKE DISORDER
### DIAGNOSIS
The **criteria for avoidant/restrictive food intake disorder** are as follows:

| Criteria A | A disruption in eating evidenced by not meeting nutritional needs and failure to gain expected weight or weight loss, nutritional deficiency requiring nutritional supplementation, or interpersonal interference. |
|---|---|
| Criteria B | This disruption is not due to lack of food or culture. |
| Criteria C | There does not appear to be a problem with the individual's body perception. |
| Criteria D | The disturbance can't be explained by another medical condition. |

## *ANOREXIA NERVOSA*

### DIAGNOSIS

The characteristics of **anorexia nervosa** are:

| Criteria A | Extreme restriction of food, lower than requirements, leading to low body weight |
|---|---|
| Criteria B | An irrational fear of gaining weight or behaviors that prevent weight gain, despite being at low weight |
| Criteria C | Distorted body image or a lack of acknowledgement of severity of current weight |

A general standard used to determine the minimum healthy body weight is that it should be at least 85% of the norm for the individual's height and weight. People with restricting type anorexia lose weight through fasting, dieting, and excessive exercise. People with binging/purging type anorexia lose weight by eating a great deal and then either vomiting it or inducing immediate defecation with laxatives. People with anorexia are preoccupied with food. The physical symptoms of **starvation** are constipation, cold intolerance, lethargy, and bradycardia. The physical problems associated with **purging** are anemia, impaired renal function, cardiac abnormalities, dental problems, and osteoporosis.

### GENDER, AGE, ETIOLOGY, AND TREATMENT

The vast majority of people with anorexia are **female**, and the onset of anorexia is usually in **mid-to-late adolescence**. Onset may be associated with a stressful life event. Some studies associated anorexia with middle- and upper-class families that have a tendency towards competition and success. Girls with anorexia are likely to be introverted, nonassertive, and conscientious. Their mothers are likely to also be very concerned about food intake and weight. The immediate goal of any treatment program is to help the individual gain weight. Sometimes this requires hospitalization. **Cognitive therapy** is also often employed to correct the individual's misconceptions about healthy weight and nutrition.

## *BULIMIA NERVOSA*

### DIAGNOSIS

The characteristics of **bulimia nervosa** are:

| Criteria A | Cyclical periods of binge eating characterized by discretely consuming an amount of food that is larger than most individuals would eat in the same time period and situation. The individual feels a lack of control over the eating. |
|---|---|
| Criteria B | Characterized by binge eating followed by purging via self-induced vomiting/laxatives/fasting/vigorous exercise in order to prevent weight gain |
| Criteria C | At least one binge eating episode per week for three months |
| Criteria D | It is marked by a persistent over-concern with body shape and weight. |
| Criteria E | The eating and compensatory behaviors do not only occur during periods of anorexia nervosa. |

**Binges** are often caused by interpersonal stress and may entail a staggering caloric intake. The **medical complications** associated with bulimia are fluid and electrolyte disturbances, metabolic alkalosis, metabolic acidosis, dental problems, and menstrual abnormalities.

<u>GENDER, AGE, ETIOLOGY, AND TREATMENT</u>

As with anorexia, the vast majority of people with bulimia are **female**. The onset is typically in **late adolescence** or **early adulthood**, and may follow a period of dieting. There are indications of a **genetic etiology** for bulimia. Also, there are links between bulimia and low levels of the endogenous opioid beta-endorphin, as well as low levels of serotonin and norepinephrine. The main point of any treatment for bulimia is encouraging the individual to get control of eating, and modifying unhealthy beliefs about body shape and nutrition. Treatment often involves **cognitive-behavioral techniques** like self-monitoring, stimulus control, cognitive restructuring, problem-solving, and self-distraction. Some antidepressants, like imipramine, have been effective at reducing instances of binging and purging.

## ANXIETY DISORDERS

Types of anxiety disorders include the following:

| Panic disorder | Recurrent brief but intense fear in the form of panic attacks with physiological or psychological symptoms |
|---|---|
| Specific phobia | Fear of specific situations or objects |
| Generalized anxiety disorder | Chronic psychological and cognitive symptoms of distress and excessive worry lasting at least 6 months |
| Separation anxiety disorder | Excessive anxiety related to being separated from someone the individual is attached to |
| Selective mutism | Inability to speak in social settings (when it would seem appropriate) though normally able to speak |
| Social anxiety disorder | Anxiety about social situations |
| Agoraphobia | Anxiety about being outside of the home or in open places |

> **Review Video: Anxiety Disorders**
> Visit mometrix.com/academy and enter code: 366760

### *PANIC DISORDER*

<u>DIAGNOSIS</u>

An individual may be diagnosed with **panic disorder** if he or she suffers recurrent unexpected panic attacks, and one of the attacks is followed by one month of either persistent concern regarding the possibility of another attack or a significant change in behavior related to the attack. **Panic attacks** are brief, defined periods of intense apprehension, fear, or terror. They develop quickly, and usually reach their greatest intensity after about ten minutes. Attacks must include at least 4 characteristic **symptoms**, which include:

Palpitations or accelerated heart rate (tachycardia)
Sweating
Chest pain
Nausea
Dizziness
Derealization
Paresthesia (pins and needles or numbness)

Shaking
Shortness of breath
Fear of losing control
Fear of dying
Chills or heat sensation
Feeling of choking

115

## PREVALENCE AND GENDER ISSUES

The consensus of research is that 1-2% of the population will suffer panic disorder at some point during their lives, and 30-50% of these individuals will also suffer **agoraphobia**. Panic disorder has a higher rate of diagnostic comorbidity when it is accompanied by agoraphobia. Panic disorder is far more likely to occur in **females** than males, and females with a panic disorder have a 75% chance of also having agoraphobia. There is a great deal of variation in the age of onset, but the most frequent ages of occurrence are in adolescence and the mid-30s. Children can experience the physical symptoms of a panic attack, but are unlikely to be diagnosed with panic disorder because they do not have the wherewithal to associate their symptoms with catastrophic feelings. The individual can be diagnosed with agoraphobia even if they are not diagnosed with panic disorder, but the two are commonly diagnosed together.

## TREATMENT AND DIFFERENTIAL DIAGNOSIS

The most effective treatment for panic attacks appears to be controlled in vivo exposure with response prevention, known as **flooding**. Flooding is typically accompanied by cognitive therapy, relaxation, breathing training, or pharmacotherapy. **Antidepressant medications** are often prescribed to relieve the symptoms of panic disorder. If stand-alone drug treatment is used, the risk of relapse is very high. Differential diagnoses for panic disorder include social phobia, and medical conditions like hyperthyroidism, hypoglycemia, cardiac arrhythmia, and mitral valve prolapse. Panic disorder can be distinguished from social phobia by the fact that attacks will sometimes occur while the individual is alone or sleeping.

## *PHOBIAS*
### DIAGNOSIS

A specific phobia is a marked and persistent fear of a particular object or situation, other than those associated with social phobia or agoraphobia. When an individual with a phobia is exposed to the feared object or event, he or she will have a panic attack or some other anxiety response. Adults with a specific phobia should be able to recognize that their fear is irrational and excessive. The onset of a specific phobia is typically in childhood or in the mid-20s. According to the DSM-5, there are five **subtypes** of specific phobia:

- Animal
- Natural environment
- Situational
- Blood-injection-injury
- Other

The blood-injection-injury subtype has different physical symptoms than the others. Individuals with blood-injection-injury phobia have a brief increase in heart rate and blood pressure, followed by a drop in both, often ending in a brief loss of consciousness (fainting). Other phobic reactions just entail the increase in heart rate and blood pressure, without loss of consciousness.

### DISTINGUISHING SYMPTOMS OF AGORAPHOBIA

Symptoms that distinguish panic disorder from **agoraphobia** include the fear of being in a situation or place from which it could be difficult or embarrassing to escape, or of being in a place where help might not be available in the event of a panic attack. Agoraphobia usually manifests when the individual is alone outside of the home, is in a crowd, or is traveling in a train or automobile. Those who suffer from agoraphobia will typically go to great lengths to avoid problematic situations, or they will only be able to enter certain situations with a companion and under heavy distress. One of the main problems with agoraphobia is that it causes the individual to severely limit the places they are willing to go. These individuals often become reclusive.

## ETIOLOGY AND TREATMENT

The **two-factor theory** proposed by Mower asserts that phobias are the result of avoidance conditioning, when an individual associates a neutral or controlled stimulus with an anxiety-causing, unconditioned stimulus. The phobia reinforces a strategy of avoidance because it prevents anxiety (even though the neutral stimulus was not to blame for the anxiety in the first place). Another theory for the etiology of phobias is offered by **social learning theorists**, who state that phobic behaviors are learned by watching avoidance strategies used by one's parents. As with panic disorder, **in vivo exposure** is considered the best treatment for a specific phobia. **Relaxation and breathing techniques** are also helpful in dispelling fear and controlling physical response.

## GENERALIZED ANXIETY DISORDER

Individuals may be diagnosed with generalized anxiety disorder (GAD) if they have excessive anxiety about multiple events or activities. This anxiety must have existed for at least six months and must be difficult for the individual to control. The anxiety must be disproportionate to the feared event. Anxiety must include at least three of the following:

- Restlessness
- Fatigue on exertion
- Difficulty concentrating
- Irritability
- Muscle tension
- Sleep disturbance

The treatment for GAD usually entails a **multicomponent cognitive-behavioral therapy**, occasionally accompanied by pharmacotherapy. **SSRI** antidepressants and the anxiolytic buspirone have both demonstrated success in diminishing the symptoms of GAD.

## SEPARATION ANXIETY DISORDER

### ONSET

Many children who suffer from separation anxiety disorder will refuse to go to school, and may claim physical ailments to avoid having to leave the home. In some cases, the child will actually develop a headache or stomachache as a result of anxiety about separation from the home or from an individual to whom they are attached. The refusal to go to school may begin as early as 5 or as late as 12. If the separation anxiety occurs after the age of 10, however, it is quite possibly the result of depression or some more severe disorder. There are various treatment plans for separation anxiety disorder, all of which recommend that the child immediately resume going to school on a normal schedule.

### SYMPTOMS

Separation anxiety disorder is characterized by age-inappropriate and excessive anxiety that occurs when an individual is separated or threatened with separation from his or her home or family unit. In order to be diagnosed with separation anxiety disorder, the child must exhibit **symptoms** for at least four weeks and onset must be before the age of 18. Individuals with separation anxiety disorder will manifest some of the following symptoms:

- Excessive distress when separated from home or attachment figures
- Persistent fear of being alone
- Frequent physical complaints during separation

Children with separation anxiety tend to be from loving, stable homes. For many, the disorder begins to manifest after the child has suffered some personal loss.

## SOCIAL ANXIETY DISORDER

The characteristics of social anxiety disorder or **social phobia** are a marked and persistent fear of social situations or situations in which the individual may be called upon to perform. Typically, the individual fears criticism and evaluation by others. The response to the feared situation is an immediate panic attack. Those with social phobia either avoid the feared situation or endure it with much distress. The fear and anxiety regarding these social situations have a negative impact on the individual's life, and is present for at least six months. Adults should be able to recognize that their fear is excessive and irrational. As with other phobias, social phobia is best treated with **exposure** in combination with **social skills and cognitive therapy**. Antidepressants and the beta-blocker propranolol are helpful for treating social phobia.

## OBSESSIVE-COMPULSIVE DISORDER

The following are the **criteria for obsessive-compulsive disorders:**

| Criteria A | The individual exhibits obsessions, compulsions, or both. **Obsession**: continuous, repetitive thoughts, compulsions, or things imagined that are unwanted and cause distress. The individual will try to suppress thoughts, ignore them, or do a compulsive behavior. **Compulsion**: recurrent behavior or thought the individual feels obliged to perform after an obsession to decrease anxiety; however, the compulsion is usually not connected in an understandable way to an observer. |
|---|---|
| Criteria B | The obsessions and compulsions take at least one hour per day and cause distress. |
| Criteria C | The behavior is not caused by a substance. |
| Criteria D | The behavior could not better be explained by a different mental disorder. |

Note if the criteria are met with good insight (individual realizes OCD beliefs are not true), poor insight (individual thinks the OCD beliefs are true), or absent insight (individual is delusional, truly believing OCD beliefs are true). Note if the individual has ever had tic disorder.

Other obsessive-compulsive and related disorders include:

- Body dysmorphic disorder
- Hoarding disorder
- Trichotillomania (hair-pulling disorder)
- Excoriation (skin-picking disorder)

## GENDER ISSUES, ETIOLOGY, AND TREATMENT

OCD is equally likely to occur in adult males and adult females. The average age of onset is lower for males, so the rates of OCD among male children and adolescents are slightly higher than among females. Evidence suggests that OCD is caused by low levels of **serotonin**. Structurally, OCD seems to be linked to overactivity in the **right caudate nucleus**. The most effective treatment for OCD is exposure with response prevention in tandem with medication, usually either the tricyclic clomipramine or an SSRI. Therapies that provide help with stopping thought patterns seem to be especially successful in battling OCD. When drugs are used alone, there remains a high risk of relapse.

> **Review Video: <ins>Obsessive-Compulsive Disorder (OCD)</ins>**
> Visit mometrix.com/academy and enter code: 499790

## PTSD

### DIAGNOSIS

An individual may be diagnosed with post-traumatic stress disorder (PTSD) if he or she develops symptoms after exposure to an extreme trauma. Examples of extreme trauma include: witnessing the death or injury of another person, experiencing injury to self, learning about the unexpected or violent death or injury of a family member or friend, or repeatedly being exposed to trauma (such as first responders or military soldiers). The traumatic event must elicit a reaction of intense fear, helplessness, or horror. The **characteristic symptoms** of PTSD are:

- Persistent re-experiencing of the event
- Persistent avoidance of stimuli associated with the trauma
- Persistent symptoms of increased arousal (difficulty concentrating, staying awake, or falling asleep)

These symptoms must have been present for at least a month; symptoms may not begin until three or more months after the event.

### TREATMENT

The preferred treatment for PTSD is a **comprehensive cognitive-behavioral approach** that includes:

- Exposure
- Cognitive restructuring
- Anxiety management
- SSRIs to relieve symptoms of PTSD and comorbid conditions

Some psychologists criticize single-session psychological debriefings, because they believe one session amplifies the effects of a traumatic event. Another controversial therapy used to treat PTSD is eye movement desensitization and reprocessing; the positive benefits of this therapy may be more to do with the exposure that goes along with it than with the eye movements themselves.

## ACUTE STRESS DISORDER

Acute stress disorder has symptoms similar to those of post-traumatic stress disorder. Acute stress disorder is distinguished by symptoms that occur for more than 3 days and but less than one month. An individual is diagnosed with acute stress disorder when he or she has 9 or more **symptoms** from any of the following 5 categories, which begin after the trauma:

- Intrusion
- Negative mood
- Avoidance symptoms
- Dissociative symptoms
- Arousal symptoms

An individual with acute stress disorder persistently relives the traumatic event, to the point where he or she takes steps to avoid contact with stimuli that bring the event to mind, and experiences severe anxiety when reminiscing about the event.

> **Review Video: What is Acute Stress Disorder?**
> Visit mometrix.com/academy and enter code: 538946

## ADDITIONAL TRAUMA- AND STRESSOR-RELATED DISORDERS

Additional trauma- and stress-related disorders include:

| | |
|---|---|
| **Reactive attachment disorder** | Child rarely seeks or responds to comfort when upset, usually due to neglect of emotional needs by caregiver (e.g., children who are institutionalized or in foster care). Reactive attachment disorder is characterized by a markedly disturbed or developmentally-inappropriate social relatedness in most settings. This condition typically begins before the age of five. In order to definitively diagnose this disorder, there must be evidence of pathogenic care, which may include neglect or a constant change of caregivers that made it difficult for the child to form normal attachments. |
| **Disinhibited social engagement disorder** | Child has decreased hesitations regarding interacting with unfamiliar adults. Does not question leaving normal caregiver to go off with a stranger. |
| **Adjustment disorder** | The individual has behavioral or emotional changes occurring within 3 months of a stressor. These changes cause distress for the individual and are disproportional to the actual stressor. |

## SOMATOFORM DISORDERS
### CONVERSION DISORDER

Conversion disorder is a somatoform disorder characterized by either loss of bodily functions or symptoms of a serious physical disease. The individual becomes blind, mute, or paralyzed in response to an acute stressor. Occasionally, individuals develop hyperesthesia, analgesia, tics, belching, vomiting, or coughing spells. These symptoms do not conform to physiological mechanisms, and testing reveals no underlying physical disease. The sensory loss, movement loss, or repetitive physical symptoms are not intentional. The individual is not malingering to avoid work, or factitiously trying for financial gain. The symptoms of a conversion disorder can often be removed with **hypnosis** or **Amytal interview**. Some researchers believe that simply suggesting that these symptoms will go away is the best way to relieve them. The individual can develop complications, like seizures, from disuse of body parts.

## PRIMARY GAIN, SECONDARY GAIN, AND DIFFERENTIAL DIAGNOSES

The **etiology of conversion disorder** is explained in terms of two psychological mechanisms:

- A conversion disorder may be used for **primary gain** when the symptoms keep an internal conflict or need out of the consciousness.
- A conversion disorder is used for **secondary gain** when the symptoms help the individual avoid an unpleasant activity or obtain support from the environment.

In order to diagnose a conversion disorder, there must be evidence of *involuntary* psychological factors. Conversion disorder is occasionally confused with factitious disorder and malingering, both of which are voluntary.

## SOMATIC SYMPTOM DISORDER

Somatic symptom disorder is a somatoform disorder, meaning that it suggests a medical condition but is not fully explainable by the medical condition, substance abuse, or other medical disorder. Individuals with somatic symptom disorder often describe their problems in dramatic, overstated, and ambiguous terms. They excessively worry or think about the symptoms and spend much time and energy worrying about health issues. Somatic symptom disorders cause clinically significant distress or impairment, and are not produced intentionally. A somatic symptom disorder involves recurrent multiple somatic complaints and though no one symptom has to be continuous, some symptoms are present for at least six months. Medical attention has been sought, but no physical explanation has been found.

## ILLNESS ANXIETY DISORDER

Individuals with illness anxiety disorder (formerly hypochondriasis) have an unrealistic preoccupation with having or getting a serious illness that is based on a misappraisal of bodily symptoms. This preoccupation is disproportional to symptoms or medical evidence. Individuals with illness anxiety disorder likely know a great deal about their condition, and frequently go to a number of different doctors searching for a professional opinion that confirms their own. They likely either experience frequent health related checks (either by doctors or by self-checks) or avoidance of doctors and healthcare facilities. The symptoms of this disorder have been present for at least six months, however the specific illness that the individual fears may change.

## DELIRIUM

Delirium is characterized by a clinically significant deficit in cognition or memory as compared to previous functioning. In order for delirium to be diagnosed, the individual must have disturbances in consciousness and either a change in personality or the development of perceptual abnormalities. These changes in cognition may appear as losses of memory, disorientation in space and time, and impaired language. The perceptual abnormalities associated with delirium include hallucinations and illusions. Delirium usually develops over a few hours or days, and may vary in intensity over the course of the days and weeks. If the cause of the delirium is alleviated, it may disappear for an extended period of time.

The **criteria** for delirium are as follows:

| Criteria A | A disturbance in consciousness or attention |
| --- | --- |
| Criteria B | Develops over a short period of time, and fluctuates throughout the day |
| Criteria C | Accompanied by changes in cognition |
| Criteria D | Not better explained by another condition |
| Criteria E | Caused by a medical condition or is substance related |

Five groups of people at **high risk** for delirium:

- Elderly people
- Those who have a diminished cerebral reserve due to major neurocognitive disorder (formerly dementia), stroke, or some other medical condition
- Those who have recently undergone cardiotomy
- Burn victims
- Individuals who are drug-dependent and in withdrawal

Delirium can also be **caused** by:

- Systemic infections
- Metabolic disorders
- Fluid and electrolyte imbalances
- Postoperative states
- Head trauma
- Long hospital stays, such as those in the intensive care unit

The **treatment** for delirium usually aims at curing the underlying cause of the disorder and reducing the agitated behavior. Antipsychotic drugs can be good for reducing agitation, delusions, and hallucinations, while providing a calm environment can decrease the appearance of agitation.

## NEUROCOGNITIVE DISORDERS

Major and minor neurocognitive disorders (NCD) may be due to any of the following: Alzheimer's disease, Frontotemporal lobar degeneration, Lewy body disease, vascular disease, traumatic brain injury, substance or medication use, HIV Infection, prion disease, Parkinson's disease, Huntington's disease, another medical condition, and multiple etiologies. **Criteria** are as follows:

| Criteria A | A change in cognitive ability from baseline. This information can be determined by the individual, a well-informed significant other, family member, or caretaker, or it can be determined by neuropsychology testing. |
| --- | --- |
| Criteria B | For a major neurocognitive disorder, the cognitive change interferes with ADLs and independence. For a minor neurocognitive disorder, the cognitive change doesn't interfere with normal ADLS and independence, if accommodations are used. |
| Criteria C | The cognitive change cannot be defined as delirium only. |
| Criteria D | The cognitive change is not better described as another mental disorder. |

## DIFFERENTIAL DIAGNOSIS

Some of the cognitive symptoms of major depressive disorder are very similar to those of **neurocognitive disorders**. Indeed, this kind of depression is frequently referred to as pseudodementia. One difference is that the **cognitive deficits** typical of neurocognitive disorders will get progressively worse, and the individual is unlikely to admit that he or she has impaired cognition.

**Pseudodementia**, on the other hand, typically has a very rapid onset and usually causes the individual to become concerned about his or her own health. There are also differences in the quality of memory impairment in these two conditions: Individuals with **neurocognitive disorders** have deficits in both recall and recognition memory, while individuals who are **depressed** only have deficits in recall memory.

## DIAGNOSIS

Individuals who suffer from neurocognitive disorders are likely to manifest a few **cognitive deficits**, most notably memory impairment, aphasia, apraxia, agnosia, or impaired executive functioning. Depending on the etiology of the neurocognitive disorders, these deficits may get progressively worse or may be stable.

These individuals could have both **anterograde** and **retrograde amnesia**, meaning that they find it difficult both to learn new information and to recall previously learned information. There may be a decrease in language skill, specifically manifested in an inability to recall the names of people or things. Individuals may also have a hard time performing routine motor programs, and may be unable to recognize familiar people and places. Abstract thinking, planning, and initiating complex behaviors are difficult.

## NEUROCOGNITIVE DISORDER DUE TO ALZHEIMER'S DISEASE

Particular kinds of **Alzheimer's disease** have been linked with specific genetic abnormalities. For instance, those with early-onset familial Alzheimer's often have abnormalities on **chromosome 21**, while individuals whose onset is later are likely to have irregularities on **chromosome 19**. Those with Alzheimer's disease have also been shown to have significant **aluminum deposits** in brain tissues, a malfunctioning **immune system**, and a low level of **acetylcholine**. Some of the drugs used to treat Alzheimer's increase the cholinergic activity in the brain. These drugs, which include the trade names **Cognex** and **Aricept**, can temporarily reverse cognitive impairment, though these improvements are not sustained when the drugs are removed.

## STAGES OF ALZHEIMER'S DISEASE

Over half of all cases of neurocognitive disorder are caused by Alzheimer's disease. Alzheimer's begins slowly and may take a long time to become noticeable. Researchers have outlined **three stages** of Alzheimer's disease:

- **Stage 1** usually comprises the first 1-3 years of the condition. The individual suffers from **mild anterograde amnesia**, especially for declarative memories. He or she is likely to have **diminished visuospatial skill**, which often manifests itself in wandering aimlessly. Also common to this stage are indifference, irritability, sadness, and anomia.
- **Stage 2** can stretch between the second and tenth years of the illness. The individual suffers increasing **retrograde amnesia**, restlessness, delusions, aphasia, acalculia, ideomotor apraxia (the inability to translate an idea into movement), and a generally flat mood.
- In **Stage 3** of Alzheimer's disease, the individual suffers **severely impaired intellectual functioning**, apathy, limb rigidity, and urinary and fecal incontinence. This last stage usually occurs between the eighth and twelfth years of the condition.

Alzheimer's disease is quite difficult to diagnose directly, so it is usually only diagnosed once all the other possible causes of major neurocognitive disorder (formerly dementia) have been eliminated. A brain biopsy that indicates extensive neuron loss, amyloid plaques, and neurofibrillary tangles can give solid evidence of Alzheimer's disease. Individuals who develop Alzheimer's disease usually only live about ten years after onset. The disease is more common in females than males, and is more likely to occur after the age of 65.

## TREATMENT

Though Alzheimer's disease is a degenerative condition with no known cure, there are a number of different **treatments** that can provide help to those who suffer from the disease:

- Group therapy that focuses on orienting the individual in reality and encourages him or her to reminisce about past experiences
- Antidepressants, antipsychotics, and other pharmacotherapy
- Behavioral techniques to fight the agitation associated with Alzheimer's
- Environmental manipulation to improve memory and cognitive function
- Involving the individual's family in interventions

## *NEUROCOGNITIVE DISORDER DUE TO HIV INFECTION*

Individuals with AIDS develop a particular form of neurocognitive disorder. In its early stages, the **Human Immunodeficiency Virus** causes major neurocognitive disorder (formerly dementia), which appears as forgetfulness, impaired attention, and generally decelerated mental processes. **Neurocognitive disorders** due to HIV progresses include poor concentration, apathy, social withdrawal, loss of initiative, tremor, clumsiness, trouble with problem-solving, and saccadic eye movements. One of the ways that neurocognitive disorders due to HIV is distinguished is by motor slowness, the lack of aphasia, and more severe forms of depression and anxiety. It shares these features with neurocognitive disorders due to Parkinson's and Huntington's diseases.

## *NEUROCOGNITIVE DISORDER DUE TO VASCULAR DISEASE*

In order to be diagnosed with neurocognitive disorder due to **vascular disease**, the individual must have **cognitive impairment** and either **focal neurological signs** or **laboratory evidence of cerebrovascular disease**. Neurocognitive disorder has varying symptoms, depending on where the brain damage lies. Focal neurological signs may include exaggerated reflexes, weaknesses in the extremities, and abnormalities in gait. Symptoms gradually increase in severity. Risk factors for vascular neurocognitive disorder are hypertension, diabetes, tobacco smoking, and atrial fibrillation. In some cases, an individual may be able to recover from neurocognitive disorder due to vascular disease. Stroke victims, for instance, will notice a great deal of improvement in the first six months after the cerebrovascular accident. Most of this improvement will be in their physical, rather than cognitive, symptoms.

## NEUROCOGNITIVE DISORDER DUE TO HUNTINGTON'S DISEASE

Individuals with **Huntington's disease** suffer degeneration of the GABA-producing cells in their substantia nigra, basal ganglia, and cortex. This inherited disease typically appears between the ages of 30 and 40. The **affective symptoms** of Huntington's disease include irritability, depression, and apathy. After a while, these individuals display **cognitive symptoms** as well, including forgetfulness and dementia. Later, **motor symptoms** emerge, including fidgeting, clumsiness, athetosis (slow, writhing movements), and chorea (involuntary quick jerks). Because the affective symptoms appear in advance of the cognitive and motor symptoms, many people with Huntington's are misdiagnosed with depression. Individuals in the early stages of Huntington's are at risk for suicide, as they are aware of their impending deterioration, and will have the loss of impulse control associated with the disease.

## NEUROCOGNITIVE DISORDER DUE TO PARKINSON'S DISEASE

The following symptoms are commonly associated with neurocognitive disorder due to **Parkinson's disease**:

- Bradykinesia (general slowness of movement)
- Resting tremor
- Stoic and unmoving facial expression
- Loss of coordination or balance
- Involuntary pill-rolling movement of the thumb and forefinger
- Akathisia (violent restlessness)

Most people with Parkinson's will suffer from **depression** at some point during their illness, and 20-60% will develop major neurocognitive disorder (formerly dementia). Research indicates that those with Parkinson's have a deficiency of **dopamine-producing cells** and the presence of **Lewy bodies** in their substantia nigra. Many doctors now believe that there is some **environmental cause** for Parkinson's, though the etiology is not yet clear. The medication L-dopa (Dopar, Larodopa) alleviates the symptoms of Parkinson's by increasing the amount of dopamine in the brain.

## SCHIZOPHRENIA
### DIAGNOSIS

Schizophrenia is a psychotic disorder. Psychotic disorders are those that feature one or more of the following: delusions, hallucinations, disorganized speech or thought, or disorganized or catatonic behavior. Schizophrenia **diagnostic criteria** are as follows:

| | |
|---|---|
| **Criteria A** | Diagnosis requires at least two of the following symptoms, one being a core positive symptom:<br>• Hallucinations (core positive symptom)<br>• Delusions (core positive symptom)<br>• Disorganized speech (core positive symptom)<br>• Severely disorganized or catatonic behavior<br>• Negative symptoms (i.e., avolition, diminished expression) |
| **Criteria B** | Individual's level of functioning is significantly below level prior to onset. |
| **Criteria C** | If the individual has not had successful treatment there are continual signs of schizophrenia for more than six months. |
| **Criteria D** | Depressive disorder, bipolar disorder, and schizoaffective disorder have been ruled out. |
| **Criteria E** | The symptoms cannot be attributed to another medical condition or a substance. |
| **Criteria F** | If the individual has had a communication disorder or Autism since childhood, a diagnosis of schizophrenia is only made if the individual has hallucinations or delusions. |

### ETIOLOGY

Both twin and adoption studies have suggested that there is a **genetic component** to the etiology of schizophrenia. The rates of instance (concordance) among first-degree biological relatives of people with schizophrenia are greater than among the general population. **Structural abnormalities** in the brain linked to schizophrenia are enlarged ventricles and diminished hippocampus, amygdala, and globus pallidus. **Functional abnormalities** in the brain linked to schizophrenia are hypofrontality and diminished activity in the prefrontal cortex. An abnormally large number of the people with schizophrenia in the Northern Hemisphere were born in the late winter or early spring. There is speculation that this may be because of a link between prenatal exposure to influenza and schizophrenia.

### SCHIZOPHRENIA AND DOPAMINE

For many years, the professional consensus was that schizophrenia was caused by either an excess of the neurotransmitter **dopamine** or oversensitive **dopamine receptors**. The **dopamine hypothesis** was supported by the fact that antipsychotic medications that block dopamine receptors had some success in treating schizophrenia, and by the fact that dopamine-elevating amphetamines amplified the frequency of delusions. The dopamine hypothesis has been somewhat undermined, however, by research that found elevated levels of norepinephrine and serotonin, as well as low levels of GABA and glutamate in schizophrenics. Some studies have shown that clozapine and other atypical antipsychotics are effective in treating schizophrenia, even though they block serotonin rather than dopamine receptors.

## POSITIVE SYMPTOMS

The symptoms of schizophrenia may be **positive, negative,** or **disorganized**. Positive symptoms are **delusions** and **hallucinations**. Delusions are false beliefs that are held despite clear evidence to the contrary. The delusions suffered by a schizophrenic usually fall into one of three categories:

- **Persecutory**, in which the person believes that someone or something is out to get him or her.
- **Referential**, in which the person believes that messages in the public domain (like song lyrics or newspaper articles) are specifically directed at him or her.
- **Bizarre**, in which the person imagines that something impossible has happened.

The most common sensory mode for hallucinations is sound, specifically the audition of voices.

## DISORGANIZED AND NEGATIVE SYMPTOMS

For many psychologists, the classic characteristic of schizophrenia is **disorganized speech**. Disorganized speech manifests as:

- Incoherence
- Free associations that make little sense
- Random responses to direct questions

**Disorganized behavior** manifests as:

- Shabby or unkempt appearance
- Inappropriate sexual behavior
- Unpredictable agitation
- Catatonia and decreased motor activity

**Negative symptoms** of schizophrenia include:

- Restricted range of emotions
- Reduced body language
- Lack of facial expression
- Lack of coherent thoughts
- Inability to make conversation
- Avolition (the inability to set goals or to work in a rational, programmatic manner)

### CATATONIA

**Criteria** for catatonia includes at least three of the following:

- Catalepsy
- Defying or refusing to acknowledge instruction
- Echolalia
- Echopraxia
- Little to no verbal response
- Grimacing
- Agitation
- Semi-consciousness
- Waxy flexibility
- Posturing
- Mannerism
- Stereotypy

### ASSOCIATED FEATURES

Features commonly associated with schizophrenia are:

- Inappropriate affect
- Anhedonia (loss of pleasure)
- Dysphoric mood
- Abnormalities in motor behavior
- Somatic complaints

One of the more troublesome aspects of schizophrenia is that the afflicted individual rarely has any insight into his or her own condition and so is unlikely to **comply** with treatment. People with schizophrenia often develop substance dependencies, especially to nicotine. Though many people believe that those with schizophrenia are more likely to be violent or aggressive than individuals in the general population, there is no statistical information to support this assertion. The onset of schizophrenia is typically during the ages of 18-25 for males and 25-35 for females. Males are slightly more likely to develop the disorder.

### PROGNOSIS AND DIFFERENTIAL DIAGNOSIS

Individuals typically develop schizophrenia as a **chronic condition**, with very little chance of full remission. Positive symptoms of schizophrenia tend to decrease in later life, though the negative symptoms may remain. The following factors tend to **improve prognosis**:

- Good premorbid adjustment
- Acute and late onset
- Female gender
- Presence of a precipitating event
- Brief duration of active-phase symptoms
- Insight into the illness
- Family history of mood disorder
- No family history of schizophrenia

**Differential diagnoses** for schizophrenia include bipolar and depressive disorders with psychotic features, schizoaffective disorder, and the effects of prolonged and large-scale use of amphetamines or cocaine.

## TREATMENT

Treatment for schizophrenia begins with the administration of **antipsychotic medication**. Antipsychotics are very effective at diminishing the positive symptoms of schizophrenia, though their results vary from person to person. Antipsychotics have strong side effects, however, including tardive dyskinesia. Medication is more effective when it is taken in combination with psychosocial intervention. Many people with schizophrenia are prone to relapse if they receive a great deal of criticism from family members, so it may be a good idea to initiate **family therapy** in which the level of expressed emotion in the family is discussed. Those who are recovering from schizophrenia also benefit from **social skills training** and **help with employment**.

## SCHIZOAFFECTIVE DISORDER

The **criteria** for schizoaffective disorder are as follows:

| Criteria A | For diagnosis the individual must have at least two of the following symptoms, one being a core positive symptom. The individual will experience the symptoms during a continuous period of illness during which there will also be a significant manic or depressive mood episode. <br>• Hallucinations (known as a core positive symptom) <br>• Delusions (known as a core positive symptom) <br>• Disorganized speech (known as a core positive symptom) <br>• Severely disorganized or catatonic behavior <br>• Negative Symptoms (such as avolition or diminished expression) |
|---|---|
| Criteria B | Individual experiences hallucinations or delusions for at least two weeks during illness that do not occur during a significant depressive or manic mood episode. |
| Criteria C | The individual experiences significant depressive or manic mood symptoms for most of the time of the illness. |
| Criteria D | The symptoms cannot be attributed to another medical condition or a substance. |

## SCHIZOPHRENIFORM DISORDER

The **criteria** for schizophreniform disorder are as follows:

| Criteria A | Diagnosis requires at least two of the following symptoms, one being a core positive symptom: <br>• Hallucinations (known as a core positive symptom) <br>• Delusions (known as a core positive symptom) <br>• Disorganized speech (known as a core positive symptom) <br>• Severely disorganized or catatonic behavior <br>• Negative Symptoms (such as avolition or diminished expression) |
|---|---|
| Criteria B | An illness of at least one month but less than six months duration. |
| Criteria C | Depressive disorder, bipolar disorder, and schizoaffective disorder have been ruled out. |
| Criteria D | The symptoms cannot be attributed to another medical condition or a substance. |

## BRIEF PSYCHOTIC DISORDER

Brief psychotic disorder is characterized as a delusion that has sudden onset and lasts less than one month. Brief psychotic disorder is a classification of the schizophrenia spectrum and other psychotic disorders.

| Criteria A | At least one of the following symptoms: delusions, hallucinations, disorganized speech, or catatonic behavior. |
|---|---|
| Criteria B | The symptoms last more than one day but less than one month. The individual does eventually return to baseline functioning. |
| Criteria C | The disorder cannot be attributed to another psychotic or depressive disorder. |

## DELUSIONAL DISORDER

Delusional disorder is typified by the presence of a persistent delusion. Delusion may be persecutory type, jealous type, erotomanic type (that someone is in love with delusional person), somatic type (that one has physical defect or disease), grandiose type, or mixed.

The following are the **criteria** for delusional disorder:

| Criteria A | The individual experiences at least one delusion for at least one month or longer. |
|---|---|
| Criteria B | The individual does not meet criteria for schizophrenia. |
| Criteria C | Functioning is not significantly impaired, and behavior except dealing specifically with delusion is not bizarre. |
| Criteria D | Any manic or depressive episodes are brief. |
| Criteria E | The symptoms cannot be attributed to another medical condition or a substance. |

It should be specified if the delusions are bizarre. Severity is rated by the quantitative assessment measure "Clinician-Rated Dimensions of Psychosis Symptom Severity."

## BIPOLAR DISORDERS

### DOCUMENTATION AND GENDER INFLUENCES

Bipolar disorders should be documented with current (or most recent) features, whether manic, hypomanic, or major depressive episode noted. The current severity of mild, moderate, or severe should also be noted as well as any applicable specifiers. Partial or full remission should be noted when applicable. Example: bipolar I disorder, current episode manic, moderate severity, with anxious distress. Bipolar **specifiers** include:

- With anxious distress
- With melancholic features
- With peripartum onset
- With seasonal pattern
- With psychotic features
- With catatonia
- With atypical features
- With mixed features
- With rapid cycling

Bipolar II is distinguished from Bipolar I by the fact that the individual has never had either a manic or a mixed episode. Males and females develop Bipolar I disorder equally, but Bipolar II is much more common for females. On average, the age of onset for the first manic episode is the early 20s.

## ETIOLOGY AND TREATMENT

Among all mental disorders, Bipolar I and II disorders are the most clearly linked to **genetic factors**. Identical twins are overwhelmingly more likely to develop the disease than are fraternal twins. Research suggests a traumatic event may precipitate the first manic episode, although later manic episodes do not need to be preceded by a stressful episode. The most effective treatment for Bipolar I and II is **lithium**. Lithium reduces manic symptoms and eliminates mood swings for more than 50% of individuals. One major problem with lithium is that it works so well, many individuals consider themselves cured and stop taking it, causing a relapse. Pharmacotherapy is most effective when combined with psychotherapy. Individuals who do not respond to lithium treatment are given **anticonvulsants** like carbamazepine or divalproex sodium. Anticonvulsants are also used in lieu of lithium for individuals who have rapid cycling or dysphoric mania.

## BIPOLAR I DISORDERS

The **criteria** for bipolar I disorder are as follows:

| Criteria A | The individual must meet the criteria (listed below) for at least one manic episode. The manic episode is usually either proceeded or followed by an episode of major depression or hypomania. |
|---|---|
| Criteria B | The episode cannot be explained by schizophrenia spectrum and other psychotic disorders criteria. |

The manic episode **criteria** are as follows:

| Criteria A | An episode of significantly elevated, demonstrative, or irritable mood. There is significant goal-directed behaviors, activities, and an increase in the amount of energy the individual normally has. These symptoms are present for most of the day and last at least one week. |
|---|---|
| Criteria B | During the period described in criteria A, the individual will experience 3 of the following symptoms (if the individual presents with only an irritable mood, 4 of the following symptoms need to be present for diagnosis):<br>• Less need for sleep<br>• Excessive talking<br>• Inflated self-esteem<br>• Easily distracted<br>• Flight of ideas<br>• Engages in activities that have negative consequences<br>• Engages in either goal directed activity or purposeless activity |
| Criteria C | The episode causes significant impairment socially. |
| Criteria D | The symptoms cannot be attributed to a substance. |

131

## BIPOLAR II DISORDERS

The **criteria** for bipolar II disorder are as follows:

| | |
|---|---|
| **Criteria A** | The individual has had one or more major depressive episodes and one or more hypomanic episodes. |
| **Criteria B** | The individual has never experienced a manic episode. |
| **Criteria C** | The episode doesn't meet criteria for schizophrenia spectrum or other psychotic disorder. |
| **Criteria D** | The depressive episodes or alterations between the two moods cause significant impairment socially or functionally. |

A **hypomanic episode** is severe enough to be a clear departure from normal mood and functioning, but not severe enough to cause a marked impairment in functioning, or to require hospitalization. The **criteria** for hypomania are as follows:

| | |
|---|---|
| **Criteria A** | An episode of significantly elevated, demonstrative, or irritable mood. There are significant goal-directed behaviors, activities, and an increase in the amount of energy the individual normally has. These symptoms are present for most of the day and last at least 4 days. |
| **Criteria B** | During the period described in criteria A, the individual experiences 3 of the following symptoms (if the individual presents with only an irritable mood, 4 of the following symptoms need to be present for diagnosis): <br> • Less need for sleep <br> • Excessive talking <br> • Inflated self-esteem <br> • Easily distracted <br> • Flight of ideas <br> • Engages in activities that have negative consequences <br> • Engages in goal directed activity or purposeless activity |
| **Criteria C** | The episode causes a change in the functioning of the individual. |
| **Criteria D** | The episode causes changes noticeable by others. |
| **Criteria E** | The episode does not cause social impairments. |
| **Criteria F** | The symptoms cannot be attributed to a substance. |

## CYCLOTHYMIC DISORDER

Cyclothymic disorder is characterized by chronic, fluctuating mood with many hypomanic and depressive symptoms, which are not as severe as either bipolar I or bipolar II. The **criteria** are as follows:

| Criteria A | The individual experiences a considerable number of hypomania symptoms without meeting all the criteria for hypomanic episodes and experiences depressive symptoms that do not meet the criteria for major depressive episode for two years or more (can be for one year or more in <18 years of age). |
|---|---|
| Criteria B | During the above time period, the individual exhibits the symptoms more than half of the time and they are never symptom free for more than two months at a time. |
| Criteria C | The individual has not met the criteria for manic, hypomanic, or major depressive episodes. |
| Criteria D | The episode doesn't meet criteria for schizophrenia spectrum or other psychotic disorder. |
| Criteria E | The symptoms cannot be attributed to a substance. |
| Criteria F | The episodes cause significant impairment socially or functionally. |

## MAJOR DEPRESSIVE DISORDER

### MAJOR DEPRESSIVE EPISODE

The **criteria** for a major depressive episode are as follows:

| Criteria A | The individual experiences 5 or more of the following symptoms during 2 consecutive weeks. These symptoms are associated with a change in their normal functioning. (Note: Of the presenting symptoms, either depressed mood or loss of ability to feel pleasure must be included to make this diagnosis.):<br>• Depressed mood<br>• Loss of ability to feel pleasure or have interest in normal activities<br>• Decreased aptitude for thinking<br>• Thoughts of death<br>• Fatigue (daily)<br>• Inappropriate guilt or feelings of worthlessness<br>• Observable motor agitation or psychomotor retardation<br>• Weight loss or gain of more than 5% in one month<br>• Hypersomnia or Insomnia (almost daily) |
|---|---|
| Criteria B | The episode causes distress or social or functional impairment. |
| Criteria C | The symptoms cannot be attributed to a substance or another condition or disease. |
| Criteria D | The episode does not meet the criteria for schizophrenia spectrum or other psychotic disorder. |
| Criteria E | The individual does not meet criteria for manic episode or a hypomanic episode. |

133

## DIAGNOSIS AND GENDER

Major depressive disorder is diagnosed when an individual has one or more major depressive episodes without having a history of manic, hypomanic, or mixed episodes. There are a few different **specifiers** (categories of associated features) for major depressive disorder issued by the DSM-5:

- With anxious distress
- With melancholic features
- With peripartum onset
- With seasonal pattern
- With psychotic features
- With catatonia
- With atypical features
- With mixed features

Some studies estimate that 20% of women will have symptoms worthy of a diagnosis of major depressive disorder after giving birth.

From the beginning of adolescence on, the rate of major depressive disorder is about twice as great for females as for males. Before adolescence, the rates are about the same. Most major depressive disorders occur in the mid-twenties.

## COGNITIVE-BEHAVIORAL ETIOLOGIES

Three major cognitive-behavioral etiologies have been offered for major depressive disorder:

- The **learned helplessness model** proposed by Seligman suggests afflicted individuals have been exposed to uncontrollable negative events in the past and have a tendency to attribute negative events to internal, stable, and global factors.
- **Rehm's self-control model** suggests depression occurs in individuals who obsess over negative outcomes, set extremely high standards for themselves, blame all of their problems on internal failures, and have low rates of self-reinforcement coupled with high rates of self-punishment.
- **Beck's cognitive theory** suggests depression is the result of negative and irrational thought and beliefs about the depressive cognitive triad (the self, the world, and the future).

## PROGNOSIS AND CATECHOLAMINE HYPOTHESIS

The severity and duration of a major depressive episode varies from case to case, but symptoms usually last about six months before remission to full function. 20-30% of individuals have lingering symptoms for months or years. About 50% of individuals experience more than one episode of major depression. Oftentimes, multiple episodes are precipitated by some severe psychological trauma. The **catecholamine hypothesis** suggests major depressive episodes are due to a deficiency of the neurotransmitter norepinephrine. The **indolamine hypothesis** proposes that depression is caused by inferior levels of serotonin.

## ETIOLOGY

Besides the catecholamine and indolamine hypotheses, there are a few other proposed ideas for the etiology of major depressive disorder. Some researchers speculate depression is caused by **hormonal disturbances**, like an increased level of cortisol. Cortisol is one of the stress hormones secreted by the adrenal cortex. Other researchers speculate there is a connection between depression and diminished new cell growth in certain regions of the brain, particularly the subgenual prefrontal cortex and hippocampus. The **subgenual prefrontal cortex** is the part of the brain associated with the formation of positive emotions. Many antidepressant drugs seem to stimulate new growth in the **hippocampus**.

## SYMPTOMS

Symptoms of major depressive disorder vary with age. For **children**, common symptoms are:

- Somatic complaints
- Irritability
- Social withdrawal

**Male preadolescents** often display aggressive and destructive behavior. When **elderly** individuals develop a major depressive disorder, it manifests as memory loss, distractibility, disorientation, and other cognitive problems. Many major depressive episodes are misdiagnosed as major neurocognitive disorder (formerly dementia). It is very common in non-Anglo cultures for the symptoms of depression to be described solely in terms of their somatic content. Latinos, for instance, frequently complain of jitteriness or headaches, while Asians commonly complain of tiredness or weakness.

## TREATMENT

The typical treatment program for major depressive disorder combines antidepressant drugs and psychotherapy. Three classes of **antidepressant medication** are commonly prescribed:

- **Selective serotonin reuptake inhibitors (SSRIs)** are prescribed for melancholic depressives; they have a lower incidence of serious adverse side effects than do tricyclics.
- **Tricyclics (TCAs)**, are prescribed for classic depression, involving vegetative bodily symptoms, a worsening of symptoms in the morning, acute onset, and short duration of moderate symptoms.
- **Monoamine oxidase inhibitors** are prescribed as a last resort for individuals who have an unorthodox depression that includes phobias, panic attacks, increased appetite, hypersomnia, and a mood that worsens as the day goes on.

## DEPRESSIVE DISORDER WITH SEASONAL PATTERN

Depressive disorder with seasonal pattern, formerly called seasonal affective disorder (SAD), is a depressive disorder that afflicts people in the Northern Hemisphere from October to April. Symptoms of this disorder are hypersomnia, increased appetite, weight gain, and an increased desire for carbohydrates. Research suggests this disorder is caused by circadian and seasonal increases in the level of melatonin production by the pineal gland from lack of sunlight. Affected individuals are treated with phototherapy (exposure to full-spectrum white light for several hours each day), aerobic exercise, and SSRIs.

## PERSISTENT DEPRESSIVE DISORDER

The **criteria** for persistent depressive disorder are the following:

| Criteria A | For at least two years, the individual experiences for most of a day, more days than they don't experience it, a depressed mood. |
|---|---|
| Criteria B | The individual experiences 2 or more of the following when depressed:<br>• Low self-esteem<br>• Decreased appetite or overeating<br>• A feeling of hopelessness<br>• Fatigue<br>• Difficulty concentrating<br>• Insomnia or hypersomnia |
| Criteria C | During the episode the individual has not had relief from symptoms for longer than 2 months at once. |
| Criteria D | The individual may have met the criteria for a major depressive disorder. |
| Criteria E | The individual does not meet criteria for cyclothymic disorder, manic episode, or hypomanic episode. |
| Criteria F | The episode does not meet the criteria for schizophrenia spectrum or other psychotic disorder. |
| Criteria G | The symptoms cannot be attributed to a substance. |
| Criteria H | The symptoms cause distress or impairment socially or functionally. |

Of those with persistent depressive disorder, 25-50% of individuals show sleep EEG abnormalities. Women are 2-3 times more likely to suffer from persistent depressive disorder than men. Around 75% of individuals with persistent depressive disorder develop major depressive disorder within 5 years. First degree relatives are likely to also suffer major depression or persistent depressive disorder. Treatment programs for persistent depressive disorder usually include a combination of **antidepressant drugs** (especially fluoxetine) and either **cognitive-behavioral therapy or interpersonal therapy**.

## SUICIDE STATISTICS AND CORRELATES

### GENDER, RACE, AND MARITAL STATUS

Statistics indicate that 4-5 times as many males as females successfully commit **suicide**. However, females attempt suicide about 3 times as often as males. The reason for this disparity is that men tend to employ more violent means of self-destruction, including guns, hanging, and carbon monoxide poisoning. Among racial and ethnic groups, the suicide rate is highest among whites. The exception is **American Indian** and **Alaskan Natives** aged 15-34, for whom suicide is the second leading cause of death. As for **marital status**, the highest rates of suicide are among divorced, separated, or widowed people. The suicide rate for single people trails that of those groups, but it remains higher than the suicide rate for married people.

### HISTORY, AGE, AND DRUGS OF CHOICE

Suicide is the eighth leading cause of death for **males** in the United States, and sixteenth for **females**. Indicators that a person is at risk for a suicide attempt include:

• Previous suicide attempt in 60-80% of cases
• Warning issued by the prospective suicide in 80% of cases

**Drug suicides** are the most common (>70% annually). In order of preference, suicides use: Sedatives (especially benzodiazepines), antidepressants, opiates, prescription analgesics, and carbon monoxide from car exhaust. The most likely persona to commit a successful suicide is a male, Caucasian, 45-49 years of age. Women are more likely to be saved from an attempted suicide through treatment at an Emergency Department. The average age of those saved is 15-19. A sharp increase in suicides aged 10-19 may be due to the increased use of antidepressants, which now carry an FDA black box warning. Around 25% of suicide attempts by seniors over age 65 are successful.

## PSYCHIATRIC DISORDERS AND BIOLOGICAL CORRELATES

Most of those who commit suicide are suffering from some mental disorder, most commonly **major depressive disorder** or **bipolar disorder**. Suicide associated with depression is most likely to occur within three months after the symptoms of depression have begun to improve. The risk of suicide among adolescents with depression increases greatly if the adolescent also has conduct disorder, ADHD, or is a substance abuser, particularly of inhaled solvents. As for biological correlates, people who commit suicide have been found to have low levels of **serotonin** and **5HIAA** (a serotonin metabolite). Individuals at risk for suicide need immediate psychological intervention and a 24-hour suicide watch.

## COGNITIVE CORRELATES AND LIFE STRESS

Research into suicide has indicated that **hopelessness** is the most common predictor of an inclination to self-destruction. It is a more accurate predictor even than the intensity of depressive symptoms. **Self-assigned or society-assigned perfectionism** has also been blamed for suicide. Many suicides are preceded by some **traumatic life event**, like the end of a romantic relationship or the death of a loved one. For adolescents, the most common precipitant of suicide is an **argument with a parent or rejection by a boyfriend or girlfriend**. Among adolescents, the common warning signs of suicide are talking about death, giving away possessions, and talking about a reunion with a deceased individual.

# FACTITIOUS DISORDER

An individual diagnosed with factitious disorder (FD) intentionally manifests physical or psychological symptoms to satisfy an intrapsychic need to fill the role of a sick person. The individual with FD presents the illness in an exaggerated manner and avoids interrogation that might expose the falsity. These individuals may undergo multiple surgeries and invasive medical procedures. They often hide insurance claims and hospital discharge forms. A disturbing variation of FD is **factitious disorder imposed on another** (sometimes referred to as Munchausen's syndrome by proxy), in which a caregiver intentionally produces symptoms in another individual. Usually, a mother makes her young child ill.

## MALINGERING VS. FACTITIOUS DISORDER

**Malingering** is feigning physical symptoms to avoid something specific, like going to work, or to gain a specific reward. Consider malingering as a possibility when:

- A person obtains a medical evaluation for legal reasons or to apply for insurance compensation.
- There is marked inconsistency between the individual's complaint and the objective findings, or if the individual does not cooperate with a diagnostic evaluation or prescribed treatment.
- The individual has an antisocial personality disorder.

Malingering contrasts with factitious disorder because in FD the individual does not feign physical symptoms for personal gain or to avoid an adverse event, but does it with no obvious external rewards.

## DISSOCIATIVE DISORDERS

Dissociative disorders are a disruption in consciousness, identity, memory, or perception of the environment that is not due to the effects of a substance or a general medical condition. These are all characterized by a disturbance in the normally integrative functions of identity, memory, consciousness, or environmental perception.

| Dissociative identity disorder (previously multiple personality disorder) | Two or more personalities exist within one person, with each personality dominant at a particular time. |
| --- | --- |
| Dissociative amnesia | Inability to recall important personal data, more than forgetfulness. It is not due to organic causes and comes on suddenly. |
| Depersonalization/derealization disorder | Feeling detached from one's mental processes or body, as if one is an observer. |

**Cultural influences** can cause or amplify some of the symptoms of dissociative disorders, so take these into account when making a diagnosis. For instance, many religious ceremonies try to foster a dissociative psychological experience; individuals participating in such a ceremony may display symptoms of dissociative disorder without requiring treatment.

### DISSOCIATIVE AMNESIA

Individuals may be diagnosed with dissociative amnesia if they have more than one episode in which they are unable to remember important personal information, and this memory loss cannot be attributed to ordinary forgetfulness. The gaps in the individual's memory are likely to be related to a traumatic event. The three most common patterns of dissociative amnesia are:

- **Localized**, in which the individual is unable to remember all events around a defined period
- **Selective**, in which the individual cannot recall some events pertaining to a circumscribed period
- **Generalized**, in which memory loss spans the individual's entire life

It should be specified if this is with dissociative fugue, a subtype of dissociative amnesia, which is a purposeful travel that is associated with amnesia.

### DISSOCIATIVE FUGUE AND DEPERSONALIZATION DISORDER

A **dissociative fugue** is a subtype of dissociative amnesia and is an abrupt, unexpected, purposeful flight from home, or another stressful location, coupled with an inability to remember the past. The individual is unable to remember his or her identity and assumes a new identity. Fugues are psychological protection against extreme stressors like bankruptcy, divorce, separation, suicidal or homicidal ideation, and rejection. Fugues happen in wars, natural disasters, and severe accidents. Fugues affect 2 in every 1,000 Americans. There will be no recollection of events that occur during the fugue. Individuals in a fugue state may seem normal to strangers. Dissociative fugue is a specifier that can be used with dissociative amnesia.

**Depersonalization/derealization disorder** is diagnosed when an individual has recurrent episodes in which he or she feels detached from his or her own mental processes or body or to the surroundings. In order to be diagnosed, this condition must be intense enough to cause significant distress or functional impairment.

## SEXUAL DYSFUNCTIONS

A sexual dysfunction is any condition in which the sexual response cycle is disturbed or there is pain during sexual intercourse, and this causes distress or interpersonal difficulty. **Types** of sexual dysfunctions:

- Delayed ejaculation
- Erectile disorder
- Female orgasmic disorder
- Female sexual interest/arousal disorder
- Genito-pelvic pain/penetration disorder
- Male hypoactive sexual desire disorder
- Premature ejaculation
- Substance-induced sexual dysfunction

**Male erectile disorder** is the inability to attain or maintain an erection. This condition is linked to diabetes, liver and kidney disease, multiple sclerosis, and the use of antipsychotic, antidepressant, and hypertensive drugs. **Orgasmic disorders** are any delay or absence of orgasm after the normal sexual excitement phase. Premature ejaculation is orgasm that occurs with a minimum of stimulation and before the person desires it. Premature ejaculation may be in part due to deficiencies in serotonin.

### PHYSICAL AND PSYCHOLOGICAL COMPONENTS AND TREATMENTS

Any individual with sexual dysfunction should be given a medical evaluation for diabetes, pelvic scars, kidney disease, hypertension, and drug interactions. Use sleep studies to determine if an impotent male gets an erection at night, and determine whether the cause of impotence is physical or psychological. **Psychological impotence** can be treated with cognitive-behavioral therapy. Sex therapy is most helpful in treating premature ejaculation. Sensate focus is used to reduce performance anxiety and increase sexual excitement. Kegel exercises, which strengthen the pubococcygeus muscle, can improve sexual pleasure. As for pharmacotherapy, Viagra is helpful in attaining and maintaining erections.

### GENITO-PELVIC PAIN/PENETRATION DISORDER AND CATEGORIES OF SEXUAL DYSFUNCTIONS

**Genito-pelvic pain/penetration disorder** is persistent difficulty with genital pain associated with sexual intercourse or involuntary spasms in the pubococcygeus muscle in the vagina, which make it difficult to have sexual intercourse, or fear or anxiety related to anticipation of pain during intercourse. Sexual dysfunctions are categorized as lifelong or acquired, and generalized or situational, depending on their cause. **Generalized dysfunctions** occur with every sexual partner in all circumstances. **Situational dysfunctions** only occur under certain circumstances. The cause may be psychological, physical, or both.

## PARAPHILIC DISORDERS

Paraphilic disorders are intense, recurrent sexual urges or behaviors involving either nonhuman objects, non-consenting partners (including children), or the suffering or humiliation of oneself or one's partner. **Common paraphilias** include:

- Fetishistic disorder
- Transvestic disorder
- Pedophilic disorder
- Exhibitionistic disorder
- Voyeuristic disorder
- Sexual masochism disorder
- Sexual sadism disorder
- Frotteuristic disorder (rubbing against a non-consenting person)

The most common **treatment** for paraphilia was previously in vivo aversion therapy, but now it is more common for treatment to include covert sensitization, in which the imagination is given aversion therapy. The medication Depo-Provera has been found to relieve paraphiliac symptoms for many men, although this relief ceases as soon as the man stops taking the drug.

## GENDER DYSPHORIA

DSM-5 defines gender dysphoria (formerly gender identity disorder) as a marked incongruence between one's expressed gender and assigned gender that causes significant distress or impairment over a period of at least 6 months. Informally, gender dysphoria is used to describe a person's persistent discomfort and disagreement with their assigned gender. DSM-5 criteria for diagnosis in **children** include:

- Strong desire to be of the other gender or insistence that one is the other gender
- Strong preference for clothing typically associated with the other gender
- Strong preference for playing cross-gender roles
- Strong preference for activities stereotypical of the other gender and rejection of those activities stereotypical of one's assigned gender
- Strong preference for playmates of the other gender
- Strong dislike of one's own sexual anatomy
- Strong desire for the sex characteristics that match one's expressed gender

DSM-5 criteria for diagnosis in **adolescents and adults** include:

- Marked incongruence between expressed gender and one's existing primary and secondary sex characteristics
- Strong desire to rid oneself of these sex characteristics for this reason
- Strong desire for the sex characteristics of the other gender
- Strong desire to be of the other gender and to be treated as such
- Strong conviction that one's feelings and reactions are typical of the other gender

## SLEEP-WAKE DISORDERS

Sleep-wake disorders include the following:

| | |
|---|---|
| **Insomnia disorders** | Difficulty falling asleep, staying asleep, or early rising without being able to go back to sleep. |
| **Hypersomnolence disorder** | Sleepiness despite getting at least 7 hours with difficulty feeling awake when suddenly awoke, lapses of sleep in the day, feeling unrested after long periods of sleep. |
| **Narcolepsy** | Uncontrollable lapses into sleep, occurring at least three times each week for at least 3 months. |
| **Obstructive sleep apnea hypopnea** | Breathing related sleep disorder with obstructive apneas or hypopneas. |
| **Central sleep apnea** | Breathing related sleep disorder with central apnea. |
| **Sleep-related hypoventilation** | Breathing related sleep disorder with evidence of decreased respiratory rate and increased $CO_2$ level. |
| **Circadian rhythm sleep-wake disorder** | Sleep wake disorder caused by a mismatch between the circadian rhythm and sleep required by person. |
| **Non-rapid eye movement sleep arousal disorder** | Awakening during the first third of the night associated with sleep walking or sleep terrors. |
| **Nightmare disorder** | Recurring distressing dreams that are well remembered and cause distress. |
| **Rapid eye movement sleep behavior disorder** | Arousal during REM sleep associated with motor movements and vocalizing. |
| **Restless legs syndrome** | The need to move legs due to uncomfortable sensations, usually relieved by activity. |

> **Review Video: Chronic Insomnia**
> Visit mometrix.com/academy and enter code: 293232

## ADJUSTMENT DISORDERS

Adjustment disorders appear as maladaptive reactions to one or more identifiable psychosocial stressors. In order to make the diagnosis, the onset of symptoms must be within three months of the stressor, and the condition must cause impairments in social, occupational, or academic performance. The symptoms do not align with normal grief or bereavement. Symptoms remit within six months after the termination of the stressor or its consequences. The adjustment disorder should be specified with at least one of the following:

- Depressed mood
- Anxiety
- Mixed anxiety and depressed mood
- Disturbance of conduct
- Mixed disturbance of emotions and conduct

## PERSONALITY DISORDERS

Personality disorders occur when an individual has developed personality traits so maladaptive and entrenched that they cause personal distress or interfere significantly with functioning.

The DSM-5 lists five **traits** involved in personality disorders:

- Neuroticism
- Extraversion/introversion
- Openness to experience
- Agreeableness/antagonism
- Conscientiousness

The following are the **criteria** for personality disorders:

| Criteria A | Long-term pattern of maladaptive personality traits and behaviors that do not align with the individual's culture. These traits and behaviors will be found in at least two areas: <br> • Impulse control <br> • Inappropriate emotional intensity or responses <br> • Inappropriately interpreting people, events, and self <br> • Inappropriate social functioning |
|---|---|
| Criteria B | The traits and behaviors are inflexible and exist despite changing social situations. |
| Criteria C | The traits and behaviors cause distress and impair functioning. |
| Criteria D | Onset was adolescence or early adulthood and has been enduring. |
| Criteria E | The behaviors and traits are not due to another mental disorder. |
| Criteria F | The behaviors and traits are not due to a substance. |

## CLUSTER A, B, AND C PERSONALITY DISORDERS

Personality disorders are **clustered** into three groups:

| Cluster A (eccentric or odd disorders) | Cluster B (dramatic or excessively emotional disorders) | Cluster C (fear- or anxiety-based disorders) |
|---|---|---|
| Paranoid | Antisocial | Avoidant |
| Schizoid | Borderline | Dependent |
| Schizotypal | Histrionic | Obsessive-Compulsive |
| | Narcissistic | |

## PARANOID PERSONALITY DISORDER

Paranoid personality disorder is a pervasive pattern of distrust and suspiciousness that involves believing the actions and thoughts of other people to be directed antagonistically against oneself. In order to make the diagnosis, the individual must have at least four of the following **symptoms**:

- Suspects that others are somehow harming him or her
- Doubts the trustworthiness of others
- Reluctant to confide in others
- Suspicious without justification about fidelity of one's partner
- Reads hidden meaning into remarks or events
- Consistently has grudges
- Believes there are attacks on his or her character that others present do not perceive

## SCHIZOID PERSONALITY DISORDER

Schizoid personality disorder is characterized by a pervasive lack of interest in relationships with others and limited range of emotional expression in contacts with others. Four of these **symptoms** must be present:

- Avoidance of or displeasure in close relationships
- Always chooses solitude
- Little interest in sexual relationships
- Takes pleasure in few activities
- Indifference to praise or criticism
- Emotional coldness or detachment
- Lacks close friends except first-degree relatives

## SCHIZOTYPAL PERSONALITY DISORDER

Schizotypal personality disorder is characterized by pervasive social deficits, oddities of cognition, perception, or behavior. Diagnosis requires five of the following:

- Ideas of reference
- Odd beliefs or magical thinking
- Lack of close friends except first-degree relatives
- Bodily illusions
- Suspiciousness
- Social anxiety (excessive)
- Inappropriate or constricted affect
- Peculiarities in behavior or appearance

## ANTISOCIAL PERSONALITY DISORDER

Antisocial personality disorder is a general lack of concern for the rights and feelings of others. In order to receive a diagnosis of antisocial personality disorder, the individual must:

- Be at least 18
- Have had a history of conduct disorder before age 15
- Have shown *at least three* of the following symptoms before the age of 15:
  o Failure to conform to social laws and norms
  o Deceitfulness
  o Impulsivity
  o Reckless disregard for the safety of self and others
  o Consistent irresponsibility
  o Lack of remorse
  o Irritability or aggressiveness

Antisocial personality disorder may also include an inflated opinion of self, superficial charm, and a lack of empathy for others.

## BORDERLINE PERSONALITY DISORDER

Borderline personality disorder is a pervasive pattern of instability in social relationships, self-image, and affect, coupled with marked impulsivity. A diagnosis of borderline personality disorder requires five of the following **symptoms**:

- Frantic efforts to avoid being abandoned
- A pattern of unstable and intense personal relationships, in which there is alternation between idealization and devaluation
- Instability of self-image
- Potentially self-destructive impulsivity in at least two areas
- Recurrent suicide threats or gestures
- Affective instability
- Chronic feelings of emptiness
- Inappropriate anger
- Paranoid ideation or dissociative symptoms

The changes in self-identity may manifest as shifts in career goals and sexual identity; impulsivity may manifest as unsafe sex, reckless driving practices, and substance abuse.

Borderline personality disorder is most common in people between the ages of 19 and 34. Most individuals see substantial improvement over a period of 15 years. Impulsive symptoms are the first to recede.

> **Review Video: Borderline Personality Disorder**
> Visit mometrix.com/academy and enter code: 550801

**Dialectical behavior therapy (DBT)** is often used to treat borderline personality disorder; it combines cognitive-behavioral therapy with the assumption of Rogers that the individual must accept his or her problem before any progress can be made. There are three basic strategies associated with dialectical behavior therapy:

- Group skills training
- Individual outpatient therapy
- Telephone consultations

Regular DBT has reduced the number of suicides and violent acts committed by individuals with borderline personality disorder.

## HISTRIONIC PERSONALITY DISORDER

Histrionic personality disorder is excessive emotionality and attention-seeking behavior. Five **symptoms** from the following list must be present:

- Annoyance or discomfort when not receiving attention
- Inappropriate sexual provocation
- Rapidly shifting and shallow emotions
- Vague and impressionistic speech
- Exaggerated expression of emotion
- Easily influenced by others
- Believes relationships are more intimate than they actually are
- Uses physical appearance to draw attention to self

## NARCISSISTIC PERSONALITY DISORDER

Narcissistic personality disorder is grandiose behavior along with a lack of empathy and a need for admiration. The individual must exhibit five of these **symptoms** for diagnosis:

- Grandiose sense of self-importance
- Fantasies of own power and beauty
- Belief in personal uniqueness
- Need for excessive admiration
- Sense of entitlement
- Exploitation of others
- Lack of empathy
- Envious of others or believes other envy him or her
- Arrogant behaviors

## AVOIDANT PERSONALITY DISORDER

Avoidant personality disorder is a pervasive pattern of social inhibition, feelings of inadequacy, and hypersensitivity to negative evaluation. A person with avoidant personality disorder exhibits at least four of these **symptoms**:

- Avoiding work or school activities that involve interpersonal contact
- Unwillingness to associate with any person who may withhold approval
- Preoccupation with concerns about being criticized or rejected
- Conception of self as socially inept, inferior, or unappealing to others
- General reluctance to take personal risks or engage in dangerous behavior
- Does not reveal self in intimate relationships, due to fear of shame
- Not able to excel in new situations due to fear of inadequacy

## DEPENDENT PERSONALITY DISORDER

Dependent personality disorder is excessive reliance on others. A diagnosis of dependent personality disorder requires five of these **symptoms**:

- Difficulty making decisions without advice
- Need for others to assume responsibility for one's actions
- Fear of disagreeing with others
- Difficulty self-initiating projects
- Feelings of helplessness or discomfort when alone
- Goes to great lengths to get support from others
- Seeks new relationships when an old one ends
- Preoccupied with the thought of having to care for self

## OBSESSIVE-COMPULSIVE PERSONALITY DISORDER

Obsessive-compulsive personality disorder is a persistent preoccupation with organization and mental or interpersonal control. Four of these **symptoms** are required for the diagnosis of obsessive-compulsive personality disorder:

- Preoccupation with rules and details
- Perfectionism that interferes with progress
- Excessive devotion to work
- Counterproductive rigidity about beliefs and morality
- Inability to throw away old objects
- Reluctance to delegate authority to others
- Rigid or stubborn
- Hoards money without spending

## BEHAVIORAL PEDIATRICS

### DISCLOSURE

Behavioral pediatrics, otherwise known as pediatric psychology, has become a more popular field because research revealed that many psychological disorders originate in childhood. For the most part, a pediatric mental health provider should be open with the child about his or her condition. Children may need some psychological help if they are to undergo any major medical procedures. Providers must relay any information related to the mental or medical condition in language the child can understand. **Multicomponent cognitive-behavioral interventions**, in which the child is given information about his or her condition and armed with some coping strategies, are especially helpful.

### HOSPITALIZATION, COMPLIANCE, AND SCHOOL ADJUSTMENT

Children who need to be **hospitalized** for a significant period of time are especially at risk of developing psychological problems, in large part because they have been separated from their families. Children and adolescents are generally less **compliant** with medical regimens. This may be because of poor communication, parent-child problems, or a general lack of skill. For adolescents, peer pressure and the desire for social acceptance may motivate noncompliance with potentially embarrassing medical programs. Children with serious medical conditions are more likely to have trouble **adjusting to school**. Problems may be caused by the illness itself, by the frequent absences it necessitates, or by the social stigma of illness. Some treatments, like chemotherapy, are associated with deficits in neurocognitive functioning and greater risk of learning disabilities.

# Substance Abuse

## HISTORY OF SUBSTANCE USE AND ABUSE IN THE UNITED STATES

### SCOPE OF ADDICTIONS ASSOCIATED WITH DRUG AND ALCOHOL USE

According to the National Institute of Alcohol Abuse and Alcoholism, 85.6% of Americans reported drinking alcohol at some point in their life, almost 70% reporting that they drank in the last year (2019). Around 50% of Americans drink **alcohol** as part of their daily routine; 10% of these routine drinkers will fall into addictive, habitual use. Statistics show that approximately 2% of the American population is addicted to **illegal drugs**, despite the *Harrison Narcotic Act of 1914,* the first legislation to ban the use of illegal drugs. Emergency rooms have exponentially increased their caseloads of patients who are drug abusers that accidentally overdose, take poisonous drug substitutes, or try to commit suicide. ER caseloads of drug casualties have also increased to include date-rape victims, drug mules whose ingested containers of smuggled drugs broke, drunk or impaired driving victims, and children who are accidentally poisoned by eating their parents' stash or absorbing toxins from growing operations. Alcohol and drugs are linked to thefts and domestic violence. Children who observe their intoxicated parents may come to accept addiction and suffer similar problems later in life.

> **Review Video: <u>Addictions</u>**
> Visit mometrix.com/academy and enter code: 460412

### EVOLUTION OF DRUG USE IN THE US FROM 1960'S TO PRESENT

In the 1960's, a substantial portion of the US population turned to **gateway drugs** like marijuana, then **hallucinogens**, and then to hardcore, **addictive drugs**. Society witnessed the use of drugs first on college campuses, then in high schools, in the workplace, and even within the military. Vietnam War veterans returned with addictions to heroin. By the 1980's, cocaine use mushroomed to include much of middle-class America. Texas and New York gave convicted criminals a life sentence for possession of marijuana. Hardcore drugs like heroin are still popular. However, designer drugs like China White, Ecstasy, Cat, Aminorex, and gamma-Butyrolactone are more prevalent than heroin now because they are very cheap to produce but can be sold at an astronomical profit. The most common **drugs of abuse** are alcohol, amphetamines, cocaine, codeine, heroin, and other opioids (morphine, hydromorphone, fentanyl, and methadone), hypnotics (meprobamate, methaqualone), PCP, sedatives (barbiturates and benzodiazepine), and THC.

### HISTORICAL COCAINE USE IN THE US

The first recorded use of **cocaine** was as a medicinal tea in 1596 by the Spaniards. France exported cocaine-laced wine to the US in 1863. Surgeons and psychiatrists touted cocaine as a cure-all and anesthetic in the 1880's. John Stith Pemberton patented Coca-Cola in 1886 as a commercial tonic for the elderly and debilitated. Many over-the-counter products contained cocaine until the *Harrison Narcotic Act of 1914* limited it for medical use only. *1970's Controlled Substances Act* also prohibited cocaine manufacturing, production, and distribution except for medical use as a Schedule II drug.

### PROHIBITION

Temperance and religious groups tried to stop the sale, manufacturing, transportation, and distribution of alcoholic drinks during **prohibition** from 1920-1933 through the 18th Constitutional Amendment of 1919. Crime syndicates flourished. In 1933, the 21st Amendment was passed to repeal the 18th Amendment. This was the only time in America's history that an amendment was rescinded.

## THEORETICAL APPROACHES TO ADDICTION

### OBJECT-RELATIONS THEORY

The object-relations theory holds that the alcoholic or drug addict is trying to deal with negative feelings about failed relationships. Resulting from these failures, the addict may experience depression, anxiety, anger, aggression, insularity, negativity, atypicality, and/or post-traumatic stress disorder (PTSD). Victims of child sexual abuse (CSA), neglect, or physical abuse as a child often turn to alcohol or drugs to deal with the memories of abuse that were suppressed as a survival mechanism and festered untreated in the person's mind. The addict may also have residual physical damage, such as improper development from malnutrition that leads to poor academic and intellectual functioning. The addict tries to assuage the pain with a chemical that blunts it temporarily. Alcohol, legally prescribed drugs, toxic herbs, or street drugs are methods of self-medication to decrease the pain by obscuring memories and altering consciousness.

### PSYCHOANALYTIC MODEL OF ADDICTION

The psychoanalytic model of addiction states the use of alcohol or drugs is the way a person has chosen to cope with anxiety or unconscious conflicts within his or her mind. The psychoanalytic model is directly related to the work of Sigmund Freud, who coined the term id to describe instinctual urgings. He believed that id instincts are seen in the libido and in aggressive acts. The superego tries to control the instinctive urges of the id. This is where internal conflict develops and is displayed in the ego, which exhibits states of anxiety. Defense mechanisms take the form of denial, projection, or redirecting the unacceptable impulses. Conflicted people use drugs and alcohol to disguise emotions that are too painful to confront. Addiction is a form of self-medication.

> **Review Video: Psychoanalytic Approach**
> Visit mometrix.com/academy and enter code: 162594

### SOCIAL LEARNING THEORY AND ADDICTION

In 1977, Albert Bandura developed the social learning theory to describe the relationship of a person to his or her environment. Bandura theorized that people learn from watching other people. He believed people self-regulate and manage their behaviors based on their established principles and inner values (standards). Inner values are not influenced unduly by external rewards or retributions. An inner value that does not oppose drinking to excess contributes to a person's alcoholic behavior. An inner value that opposes drinking to excess means the person has a restrictive view of drinking and will self-regulate by stopping before he or she is intoxicated. The person who experiences a distinct difference between values and behaviors finds it necessary to change one or the other so that the values win out over the undesired behavior. This leads to a change of behavior that befits the person's set of values.

### CLASSICAL CONDITIONING AND OPERANT CONDITIONING THEORY MODELS

**Classical conditioning theory** was developed by Russian Ivan Pavlov in the 1890's. Pavlov's experiments were based on the reflexive reactions of dogs that had been conditioned to salivate (the conditioned response) at the sound of a bell (the conditioned stimulus) that meant they would be fed soon. Addicts have a conditioned response associated with circumstances where drugs or alcohol were used. The conditioned response can be psychological (craving the drug or alcohol), or physical. The circumstance or environment is the conditioned stimulus.

**Operant conditioning** was developed by American B.F. Skinner in the 1930's using rats and pigeons. It describes responses of the conditioned individual to negative or positive reinforcers. Negative reinforcers are the addict's withdrawal signs and symptoms. The positive reinforcer is relieving the withdrawal symptoms by taking the drug or alcohol. Addictive behaviors can be switched off by removing the reinforcers.

## DISEASE MODEL OF ALCOHOLISM

The disease model is accepted by self-help organizations such as Alcoholics Anonymous (AA). The **disease model** contends that alcoholism is chronic (an unremitting, gradual disease that becomes more severe over time) and requires treatment. Alcoholism likely has a genetic root. Persons predisposed to the disease of alcoholism have genetic markers for lowered levels of platelet MAO activity, serotonin function, prolactin, adenylate cyclase, and ALDH2. Other theorists believe alcoholism is a learned behavior, rather than genetic. Research in this area is inconclusive. In 1956, E. M. Jellinek endorsed the American Medical Association's adoption of alcoholism as a disease. He described alcoholism as an infirmity with four stages of progression: Pre-alcoholic, prodromal, crucial, and chronic. Jellinek believed that alcoholics suffered from chemical dependencies that became relentless cravings for alcohol.

## STAGES OF PROGRESSION IN DRUG AND ALCOHOL USE

Not everyone who has used drugs or alcohol has a problem with addiction. The counselor must determine if the client has a pathological addiction or just engages in experimental use. The first step is to grade the client on the continuum of drug use, based on a five-stage progression.

| | |
|---|---|
| **Stage 1: Abstinence** | The client who is abstinent or involved in self-denial of use. Abstinence may allow for an occasional glass of wine. However, the person who chooses this route probably was heavily addicted to alcohol in the past, and completely abstains now to keep from falling back into old, addictive ways. Twelve step programs like AA and Narcotics Anonymous advocate complete abstinence. Self-help groups like these are complementary reinforcement for formal therapy because meetings are held daily in most metropolitan areas, and peer pressure can prevent a relapse. The therapeutic role in cases of past addictions is to help them stay "on the wagon" of abstinence. Even one drink can be detrimental to an alcoholic because it can trigger a drinking binge. |
| **Stage 2: Experimental Use** | Teens and young adults partake of a chemical to find out what it feels like. It is an expected rite of passage for many segments of our culture. Problems with experimentation include drunk driving and date rape. GHB is dissolved in alcohol at raves because it enhances the libido and lowers inhibitions. Victims enter a dream state and act drunk. They relax, sometimes to the point of unconsciousness, have problems seeing clearly, are confused, and have no recall of events or the passage of time while drugged. |
| **Stage 3: Social Use** | The test to determine if a person is a social user or addicted is whether or not the person can stop drug use. For example, a social drinker can drink a controlled amount and doesn't need it to function as a normal human being. But if a person needs alcohol or a drug to satisfy cravings, prevent unpleasant withdrawal symptoms, or as a means of coping with daily life, then it is considered an addiction. Counseling involves an educational group to develop coping skills and relationship skills with peers. |

| Stage 4: Abuse | The client's problem can be physiological or psychological in nature, or both. The addiction is detrimental to personal safety, family relationships, academic life, and work functions. Spousal and child abuse often coincide with drug abuse. Drunk driving and theft to support a habit are societal problems resulting from addictive behavior. Friends and associates are probably uncomfortable around the abuser by the time the addiction is visibly evident. At this point, the employer can insist the abuser get help on a professional level through employee assistance or public programs as a condition of continued employment. Abusers benefit from psychological counseling on a weekly basis and an intervention program to stop the alcohol or drug abuse. Antabuse (disulfiram), methadone, levo-alpha-acetylmethadol (LAAM), buprenorphine, and naltrexone are useful adjuncts to counseling to wean the abuser off the drug. Intensive outpatient programs may be sufficient for recovery. |
|---|---|
| Stage 5: Chemical Dependency | The addict experiences withdrawal symptoms when the drug or alcohol is not available for consumption. The addict builds up a tolerance to the drug to the point that more and more is needed just to keep from experiencing physical withdrawal. The high is harder and harder to reach. The addict is now at increased risk for unintentional overdose, because street drugs have inconsistent strengths. The addict is also on the verge of failing in marriage, academics, and work. The addict experiences serious medical issues like ventricular tachycardia and atrial fibrillation, and more powerful drugs like clonidine (Catapres patches or tablets) are used to prevent death. Permanent damage from Korsakoff's syndrome or Wernicke's encephalopathy may result from a poor diet lacking in vitamins. Long-term, inpatient rehabilitation programs are crucial in most cases. Intensive outpatient programs may be sufficient for a minority. |

## SCREENING AND ASSESSMENT

### QUESTIONS ASKED IN A CLINICAL INTERVIEW

12 questions to ask a client in a clinical interview as a means of screening for drug/alcohol abuse include the following:

- **Question 1**: Find out the client's motivation for getting a mental health referral.
- **Question 2**: Obtain historical background about the beginning and severity of the client's drug and alcohol use. Discuss changes or deterioration in the client's behavior from the alcohol and drug use.
- **Question 3**: Determine the longest length of time that the client has stayed sober. Delve into the reasons why this period of sobriety ended.
- **Question 4**: Ask about the intoxication level that the client reaches when drinking or using drugs. Are there blackouts? Violent incidents? Is it harder to get a high now than when the client first started using drugs?
- **Question 5**: Find out the arrest record of the client. Pay particular attention to impaired driving (DUI) and domestic violence charges resulting from chemical abuse.
- **Question 6**: Find out about military service where drug or alcohol use was part of the client's service time.
- **Question 7**: Discuss addictive cycles of abuse found in the client's family. Note psychological disorders in family members and dysfunctional family relationships.
- **Question 8**: Find out the psychiatric history of the client.

- **Question 9**: Ask the client about his or her educational and work experience, including any drug or alcohol activities at school or in the workplace.
- **Question 10**: Get the medical and substance use history of the client. Note chronic pain treated with OxyContin or other pain relievers, which subsequently led to addiction.
- **Question 11**: Ask about prior drug and alcohol abuse treatment programs in which the client participated. Is the client a recidivist? If so, use a different treatment technique.
- **Question 12**: Discuss drug and/or alcohol levels revealed by the client's latest toxicology screen.

The answers gleaned in the clinical interview should correspond with other data collected from various sources. If there is a discrepancy, determine the truth of the situation.

## MAST AND DAST ASSESSMENT TOOLS

The **Michigan Alcohol Screening Test (MAST)** was developed in 1971. The original assessment consisted of 25 yes or no questions with a complex grading system in which each question carried different weight when scoring. In the most recently revised version of this screening tool, the client must answer yes or no to 22 questions, which are then scored with a 0 or 1 based on the answer. Clients who score 0-2 have no alcohol problem. Clients who score 3-5 are early to middle problem drinkers. Clients who score 6 or more are problem drinkers. This test is accurate with a 0.05 level of confidence, according to the National Council on Alcoholism and Drug Dependence. Some research indicates that the 6-point cut-off for labeling an alcoholic should be raised to 10 points.

The **Drug Abuse Screening Test (DAST)** is the non-alcoholic counterpart to the MAST. If either the MAST or DAST is positive for addiction, then use the **Addiction Severity Index (ASI)** to determine in what areas the drug use has been the most invasive. The areas assessed include medical, legal, familial, social, employment, psychological, and psychiatric. The ASI test is longer, covering 180 items.

## SASSI

The **Substance Abuse Subtle Screening Inventory (SASSI-4)** was first developed in 1988 to help identify covert abusers. Multiple revisions have occurred since. Typically, abusers hide their drug problems with lies, subterfuge, and defensive responses because they are:

- Unwilling to accept responsibility
- Hesitant to confront bad feelings and pain
- Afraid of the consequences (incarceration or rehabilitation programs)
- Conflicted (have mixed feelings) about quitting use of the chemical

The counselor uses the SASSI-4 to determine the truth, produce profiles useful for treatment planning, and understand the client. It can be administered as a one-page paper and pencil test, a computerized test with automated scoring, or an audio tape test. SASSI-4 takes 15 minutes to complete and 5 minutes to score. The adult version has an overall accuracy of 93%. The Adolescent SASSI-A3 has an overall accuracy of 94%. They both contain face-valid and subtle items, which do not tackle drug abuse in a directly apparent way.

## TREATMENT

### SUBSTANCE USE TREATMENT PROGRAMS

Substance abusers do best when they abstain from drug and alcohol use entirely during their **treatment**. Relapses in the client's use interfere with treatment. Try not to conduct a session with an intoxicated client. Encourage the client to reschedule his or her session should intoxication be suspected. Make travel arrangements to ensure the client does not operate a vehicle on the way home while in an intoxicated state. Encourage the client to stay out of old hangouts where alcohol or drugs were used, and to discard drug paraphernalia and t-shirts associated with drugs or alcohol because they can evoke a conditioned response. Teach clients relaxation and imagery exercises to help them curb their urges and anxiety. Use operant conditioning to help clients tone down euphoric memories. Clients need reminders of negative consequences of addiction such as divorce, arrest, hangover, loss of income, or loss of health.

## METHADONE THERAPY FOR OPIATE ADDICTION

Methadone, an opioid itself, is used as pharmacotherapy to treat opioid use disorder, most commonly in the case of heroin addiction. Because it acts as an opioid agonist, it binds to the same mu-receptors as heroin (and other narcotics), but has less dangerous side-effects and can be administered orally, essentially eliminating the risks associated with intravenous opioid administration commonly experienced by opioid abusers. Methadone is commonly prescribed to help individuals addicted to opiates through their initial withdrawal from the addictive substance, and then the dose is tapered to help the individual achieve a drug-free state. In addition to preventing withdrawal symptoms, methadone also decreases cravings for opioids and mutes the high that was achieved by the addictive substance by building the individual's tolerance to opioids. Methadone therapy has proven particularly helpful in treating pregnant women with opioid addiction due to its ability to prevent cravings while having a less damaging impact on the fetus. It also helps the mother attain a more sober state, which facilitates healthier decision-making and a higher likelihood of participation in recommended prenatal care.

Methadone therapy may only be prescribed by a physician who has been specifically approved by the FDA to prescribe methadone treatments. While it is outside of the scope of the counselor to prescribe methadone therapy, the counselor must be aware of the possibility that a client with opioid use disorder is on methadone therapy, or be prepared to refer clients with opioid addiction to a physician that may be able to oversee this therapy if it is indicated.

## ALCOHOLICS ANONYMOUS

Alcoholics Anonymous (AA) is a 12-step self-help program that relies on comradery and accountability, with many locations throughout the United States. Meetings are held in church halls, libraries, and clubs. AA should be offered along with appropriate counseling by a therapist, because the meetings are not considered psychological therapy. The benefit of an AA meeting to the client is the reinforcement of the coping skills taught in counseling sessions and access to a peer group that is supportive. The group provides a sponsor (usually of the same sex) to help the client have a role model who has enjoyed a long period of sobriety. The alcoholic develops a more positive outlook of the self and a sense of unity with the group, so feelings of isolation are removed. The client gains a sense of hope about his or her future and comes to recognize that the substance use is out of control. Alcoholics are encouraged to seek God or a higher power of authority for outside help.

### AA RELAPSE PREVENTION CARD AND OTHER COPING STRATEGIES

The alcoholic participating in AA carries an AA relapse prevention card. The client is given this card to help him or her find alternative activities that do not include drugs or alcohol. The card contains instructions to communicate his or her feelings to a trusted AA member and phone numbers for the sponsor and the client's spouse or parents. The card may also instruct the client in relaxation techniques or imagery to get through the cravings. A client may find it beneficial to write down his or her feelings in a journal and bring it to the counseling sessions. Teach the client assertiveness techniques to stand up to his or her AA peers if they make inappropriate suggestions.

## STRATEGIES TO PREVENT RELAPSE

Strategies to prevent relapse include the following:

- Clients find it beneficial to get a reward when they have abstained from drugs or alcohol successfully, as a positive reinforcement. This strategy is known as a **contingency management or contractual agreement**. The reward should be one that the client wants, otherwise it will be an ineffective reward.
- **Cognitive therapy** is marked by replacing negative thought patterns with positive self-talk. Thought patterns that are automatically negative may trigger the client to relapse. When negative thought patterns happen, the client should replace them with a more functional action. Some techniques for reducing negative self-talk include free association, dream interpretation, and memory techniques. The client may rely on drugs to replace relationships.
- A new approach, called **motivational enhancement therapy**, uses role playing to teach the client how to communicate goals and feelings.

# Indicators of Substance Abuse

## GENERAL INDICATORS OF SUBSTANCE ABUSE

Many people with substance abuse (alcohol or drugs) are reluctant to disclose this information, but there are a number of indicators that are suggestive of substance abuse:

**Physical signs** include:

- Burns on fingers or lips
- Pupils abnormally dilated or constricted; eyes watery
- Slurring of speech or slow speech
- Lack of coordination, instability of gait, or tremors
- Sniffing repeatedly, nasal irritation, persistent cough
- Weight loss
- Dysrhythmias
- Pallor, puffiness of face
- Needle tracks on arms or legs

**Behavioral signs** include:

- Odor of alcohol or marijuana on clothing or breath
- Labile emotions, including mood swings, agitation, and anger
- Inappropriate, impulsive, or risky behavior
- Missing appointments
- Difficulty concentrating, short term memory loss, blackouts
- Insomnia or excessive sleeping
- Disorientation or confusion
- Lack of personal hygiene

## ALCOHOL

Alcohol is described as follows:

- A liquid distilled product of fermented fruits, grains, and vegetables
- Can be used as a solvent, an antiseptic, and a sedative
- Has a high potential for abuse
- Small-to-moderate amounts taken over extended periods of time may have positive effects on health

## *POSSIBLE EFFECTS OF ALCOHOL*

The following are **possible effects of alcohol use**:

- Intoxication
- Sensory alteration
- Reduction in anxiety

## PARTICULAR CHALLENGES OF DIAGNOSIS AND TREATMENT OF ALCOHOL ABUSE

Challenges in **diagnostics and treatment of alcohol abuse** include the following:

- Alcohol is the most available and widely used substance.
- Progression of alcohol dependence often occurs over an extended period of time, unlike some other substances whose progression can be quite rapid. Because of this slow progression, individuals can deny their dependence and hide it from employers for long periods.
- Most alcohol-dependent individuals have gainful employment, live with families, and are given little attention until their dependence crosses a threshold, at which time the individual fails in their familial, social, or employment roles.
- Misuse of alcohol represents a difficult diagnostic problem as it is a legal substance. Clients, their families, and even clinicians can claim that the client's alcohol use is normative.
- After friends, family members, or employers tire of maintaining the fiction that the individual's alcohol use is normative, the individual will be more motivated to begin the process of accepting treatment.

## ALCOHOL USE ASSESSMENT TOOLS

The **CAGE tool** is used as a quick assessment to identify problem drinkers. Moderate drinking, (1-2 drinks daily or one drink a day for older adults) is usually not harmful to people in the absence of other medical conditions. However, drinking more can lead to serious psychosocial and physical problems. One drink is defined as 12 ounces of beer/wine cooler, 5 ounces of wine, or 1.5 ounces of liquor.

- **C** – *Cutting down*: "Do you think about trying to cut down on drinking?"
- **A** – *Annoyed at criticism*: Are people starting to criticize your drinking?
- **G** – *Guilty feeling*: "Do you feel guilty or try to hide your drinking?"
- **E** – *Eye opener*: "Do you increasingly need a drink earlier in the day?"

"Yes" on one question suggests the possibility of a drinking problem. "Yes" on ≥2 indicates a drinking problem.

The **Clinical Instrument for Withdrawal for Alcohol (CIWA)** is a tool used to assess the severity of alcohol withdrawal. Each category is scored 0-7 points based on the severity of symptoms, except #10, which is scored 0-4. A score <5 indicates mild withdrawal without need for medications; for scores ranging 5-15, benzodiazepines are indicated to manage symptoms. A score >15 indicates severe withdrawal and the need for admission to the unit.

1. Nausea/Vomiting
2. Tremor
3. Paroxysmal Sweats
4. Anxiety
5. Agitation
6. Tactile Disturbances
7. Auditory Disturbances
8. Visual Disturbances
9. Headache
10. Disorientation or Clouding of Sensorium

## ALCOHOL OVERDOSE

Symptoms of alcohol overdose include the following:

- Staggering
- Odor of alcohol on breath
- Loss of coordination
- Dilated pupils
- Slurred speech
- Coma
- Respiratory failure
- Nerve damage
- Liver damage
- Fetal alcohol syndrome (in babies born to alcohol abusers)

## ALCOHOL WITHDRAWAL AND TREATMENT

Chronic abuse of ethanol (alcoholism) can lead to physical dependency. Sudden cessation of drinking, which often happens in the inpatient setting, is associated with **alcohol withdrawal syndrome**. It may be precipitated by trauma or infection and has a high mortality rate, 5-15% with treatment and 35% without treatment.

**Signs and symptoms**: Anxiety, tachycardia, headache, diaphoresis, progressing to severe agitation, hallucinations, auditory/tactile disturbances, and psychotic behavior (delirium tremens).

**Diagnosis**: Physical assessment, blood alcohol levels (on admission).

**Treatment** includes:

- **Medication**: IV benzodiazepines to manage symptoms; electrolyte and nutritional replacement, especially magnesium and thiamine.
- Use the **CIWA scale** to measure symptoms of withdrawal; treat as indicated.
- Provide an **environment** with minimal sensory stimulus (lower lights, close blinds) and implement fall and seizure precautions.
- **Prevention**: Screen all clients for alcohol/substance abuse, using CAGE or other assessment tool. Remember to express support and comfort to client; wait until withdrawal symptoms are subsiding to educate about alcohol use and moderation.

## PSYCHOSOCIAL TREATMENTS FOR ALCOHOL ABUSE

The following are psychosocial treatments for alcohol abuse:

- Cognitive behavioral therapies
- Behavioral therapies
- Psychodynamic/interpersonal therapies
- Group and family therapies
- Participation in self-help groups

## CANNABIS

Cannabis is the hemp plant from which marijuana (a tobacco-like substance) and hashish (resinous secretions of the cannabis plant) are produced.

## Possible Effects

Effects of cannabis include:

- Euphoria followed by relaxation
- Impaired memory, concentration, and knowledge retention
- Loss of coordination
- Increased sense of taste, sight, smell, hearing
- Irritation to lungs and respiratory system
- Cancer
- With stronger doses: Fluctuating emotions, fragmentary thoughts, disoriented behavior

## Overdose and Misuse

Symptoms of cannabis **overdose** include:

- Fatigue
- Lack of coordination
- Paranoia

Cannabis **misuse** indications are as follows:

- Animated behavior and loud talking, followed by sleepiness
- Dilated pupils
- Bloodshot eyes
- Distortions in perception
- Hallucinations
- Distortions in depth and time perception
- Loss of coordination

# Narcotics

Narcotics are drugs used medicinally to relieve pain. They have a high potential for abuse because they cause relaxation with an immediate rush. Possible effects include restlessness, nausea, euphoria, drowsiness, respiratory depression, and constricted pupils.

## Misuse and Symptoms of Overdose

Indications of possible **misuse** are as follows:

- Scars (tracks) caused by injections
- Constricted pupils
- Loss of appetite
- Sniffles
- Watery eyes
- Cough
- Nausea
- Lethargy
- Drowsiness
- Nodding
- Syringes, bent spoons, needles, etc.
- Weight loss or anorexia

Symptoms of narcotic **overdose** include:

- Slow, shallow breathing
- Clammy skin
- Convulsions, coma, and possible death

### WITHDRAWAL SYNDROME FOR NARCOTICS

The symptoms of narcotic **withdrawal** are as follows:

- Watery eyes
- Runny nose
- Yawning
- Cramps
- Loss of appetite
- Irritability
- Nausea
- Tremors
- Panic
- Chills
- Sweating

## DEPRESSANTS

Depressants are described below:

- Drugs used medicinally to relieve anxiety, irritability, or tension.
- They have a high potential for abuse and development of tolerance.
- They produce a state of intoxication similar to that of alcohol.
- When combined with alcohol, their effects increase and their risks are multiplied.

### POSSIBLE EFFECTS

Possible effects of depressant use are as follows:

- Sensory alteration, reduction in anxiety, intoxication
- In small amounts, relaxed muscles, and calmness
- In larger amounts, slurred speech, impaired judgment, loss of motor coordination
- In very large doses, respiratory depression, coma, death

Newborn babies of abusers may exhibit dependence, withdrawal symptoms, behavioral problems, and birth defects.

### MISUSE, OVERDOSE, AND WITHDRAWAL

The following are indications of possible depressant **misuse**:

- Behavior similar to alcohol intoxication (without the odor of alcohol)
- Staggering, stumbling, lack of coordination
- Slurred speech
- Falling asleep while at work
- Difficulty concentrating
- Dilated pupils

Symptoms of an **overdose** of depressants include:

- Shallow respiration
- Clammy skin
- Dilated pupils
- Weak and rapid pulse
- Coma or death

**Withdrawal syndrome** may include the following:

- Anxiety
- Insomnia
- Muscle tremors
- Loss of appetite

Abrupt cessation or a greatly reduced dosage may cause convulsions, delirium, or death.

## STIMULANTS

Stimulants are drugs used to increase alertness, relieve fatigue, feel stronger and more decisive, achieve feelings of euphoria, or counteract the down feeling of depressants or alcohol.

### POSSIBLE EFFECTS

Possible effects include:

- Increased heart rate
- Increased respiratory rate
- Elevated blood pressure
- Dilated pupils
- Decreased appetite

Effects with high doses include:

- Rapid or irregular heartbeat
- Loss of coordination
- Collapse
- Perspiration
- Blurred vision
- Dizziness
- Feelings of restlessness, anxiety, delusions

### MISUSE, OVERDOSE, AND WITHDRAWAL

Stimulant **misuse** is indicated by the following:

- Excessive activity, talkativeness, irritability, argumentativeness, nervousness
- Increased blood pressure or pulse rate, dilated pupils
- Long periods without sleeping or eating
- Euphoria

Symptoms of stimulant **overdose** include:

- Agitated behavior
- Increase in body temperature
- Hallucinations
- Convulsions
- Possible death

**Withdrawal** from stimulants may cause:

- Apathy
- Long periods of sleep
- Irritability
- Depression
- Disorientation

## HALLUCINOGENS

Hallucinogens are described below:

- Drugs that cause behavioral changes that are often multiple and dramatic.
- No known medical use, but some block sensation to pain and their use may result in self-inflicted injuries.
- "Designer drugs," which are made to imitate certain illegal drugs, can be many times stronger than the drugs they imitate.

### POSSIBLE EFFECTS

Possible effects of use:

- Rapidly changing mood or feelings, both immediately and long after use
- Hallucinations, illusions, dizziness, confusion, suspicion, anxiety, loss of control
- **Chronic use**: Depression, violent behavior, anxiety, distorted perception of time
- **Large doses**: convulsions, coma, heart/lung failure, ruptured blood vessels in the brain
- **Delayed effects**: flashbacks occurring long after use
- **Designer drugs**: possible irreversible brain damage

### MISUSE AND OVERDOSE

The following are indications of hallucinogen **misuse**:

- Extreme changes in behavior and mood
- Sitting or reclining in a trance-like state
- Individual may appear fearful
- Chills, irregular breathing, sweating, trembling hands
- Changes in sensitivity to light, hearing, touch, smell, and time
- Increased blood pressure, heart rate, blood sugar

Symptoms of hallucinogen **overdose** include:

- Longer, more intense episodes
- Psychosis
- Coma
- Death

## STEROIDS

Steroids are synthetic compounds closely related to the male sex hormone testosterone and are available both legally and illegally. They have a moderate potential for abuse, particularly among young males.

### POSSIBLE EFFECTS

Effects include:

- Increase in body weight
- Increase in muscle mass and strength
- Improved athletic performance
- Improved physical endurance

### MISUSE AND OVERDOSE

The following are indications of possible **misuse** of steroids:

- Rapid gains in weight and muscle
- Extremely aggressive behavior
- Severe skin rashes
- Impotence, reduced sexual drive
- In female users, development of irreversible masculine traits

**Overdose** of steroids includes the following:

- Increased aggressiveness
- Increased combativeness
- Jaundice
- Purple or red spots on the body
- Unexplained darkness of skin
- Unpleasant and persistent breath odor
- Swelling of feet, lower legs

### WITHDRAWAL SYNDROME

Withdrawal syndrome may include the following:

- Considerable weight loss
- Depression
- Behavioral changes
- Trembling

# Discrimination

## SYSTEMIC/INSTITUTIONALIZED DISCRIMINATION

Systemic or institutionalized discrimination is the unfair and unjust treatment of populations because of race, gender, sexual orientation, religion, disability, or any other perceived difference by society in general and by the institutions of society.

| Institution | Evidence of racism, sexism, or ageism |
|---|---|
| Healthcare | Provision and access to care may be unequal. People often lack insurance or depend on Medicaid, which limits access. Lack of prenatal care results in higher rates of infant morbidity/mortality. People often develop chronic illnesses because of poor preventive care. |
| Employment | Discriminatory hiring practices limit employment and advancement opportunities, resulting in unemployment or low income, which can result in homelessness, substance abuse, or criminal activity. |
| Finances/Housing | People may be denied loans or face high interest rates, limiting their ability to buy homes, pay for education, and start businesses or resulting in high rates of debt. Low-cost housing is often in areas of high crime and gang activity, which is especially a risk for adolescents and the elderly. |
| Education | Children may attend substandard schools with few enrichment programs, putting them at a disadvantage as they progress through school and into job market or advanced education programs. Many students graduate without adequate skills or drop out. |
| Criminal justice | People of color are more likely to be arrested and to receive longer sentences for crimes. |

## EFFECTS OF DISCRIMINATION ON BEHAVIOR

Discrimination can result in significant effects, primarily negative, on its subjects:

- **Health problems**: Individuals may suffer from increased stress, anxiety, sadness, and depression. Individuals may develop stress-related disorders, such as hypertension or eating disorders. Individuals may not have access to adequate healthcare or insurance and often delay seeking medical help.
- **Substance abuse**: Individuals may seek relief from the stress of discriminatory actions by resorting to the use of alcohol or drugs in order to dull their feelings.
- **Violence/Conflict/Antisocial behavior**: Individuals may respond with anger and seek vengeance against perpetrators of discrimination (or entire groups representing these perpetrators). Adolescents, for example, may join gangs so that they feel accepted. Some individuals may resort to criminal activity, such as robbery.
- **Withdrawal**: Some individuals begin to pull inward and withdraw from social activities or engagement in work or school, leading to increasing failure and even further discrimination. Discrimination in employment and housing may lead to high rates of unemployment and homelessness.
- **Disenfranchisement**: Individuals may feel that they have no voice and may avoid voting or face obstacles to voting, such as lack of proper identification or transportation.

## AGEISM AND STEREOTYPES OF THE ELDERLY

Ageism is an attitude toward the capabilities and experiences of old age which leads to devaluation and disenfranchisement. Some **stereotypes of the elderly** include the assumptions that all elderly individuals are:

- Asexual
- Rigid
- Impaired (psychologically)
- Incapable of change

## IMPLICATIONS OF BIAS IN HUMAN SERVICE CLINICAL WORK

Health and mental health services express the ideology of the culture at large (dominant culture). This may cause harm to clients or reinforce **cultural stereotypes**. Examples of this include:

- **Minorities and women** often receive more severe diagnoses and some diagnoses are associated with gender.
- **African-Americans** are at greater risk for involuntary commitment.
- **Gay and lesbian people** are sometimes treated with ethically questionable techniques in attempts to reorient their sexuality.

## IMMIGRANT CLIENTS

### STRESSES ASSOCIATED WITH IMMIGRATION

The process of **immigration introduces many stresses** that must be managed. They include the following:

- Gaining entry into and understanding a foreign culture
- Difficulties with language acquisition
- Immigrants who are educated often cannot find equivalent employment
- Distance from family, friends, and familiar surroundings

### CONSIDERATION WHEN ASSESSING IMMIGRANT CLIENTS' NEEDS

The following are considerations when assessing an immigrant's needs:

- Why and how did the client immigrate?
- Social supports the client has or lacks (community/relatives)
- The client's education/literacy in language of origin and in English
- Economic and housing resources (including number of people in home, availability of utilities)
- Employment history and the ability to find/obtain work
- The client's ability to find and use institutional/governmental supports
- Health status/resources (pre- and post-immigration)
- Social networks (pre- and post-immigration)
- Life control: Degree to which the individual experiences personal power and the ability to make choices

## KEY CONCEPTS OF DIVERSITY AND DISCRIMINATION

Key concepts of diversity and discrimination include the following:

| | |
|---|---|
| **Race** | The concept of race first appeared in the English language just 300 years ago. Race has great social and political significance. It can be defined as a subgroup that possesses a definite combination of characteristics of a genetic origin. |
| **Ethnicity** | Ethnicity is a group classification in which members share a unique social and cultural heritage that is passed on from one generation to the next. It is not the same as race, though the two terms are used interchangeably at times. |
| **Worldview** | Worldview is an integral concept in the assessment of the client's experience. This can be defined as a way that individuals perceive their relationship to nature, institutions, and other people and objects. This comprises a psychological orientation to life as seen in how individuals think, behave, make decisions, and understand phenomena. It provides crucial information in the assessment of mental health status, assisting in assessment and diagnosis, and in designing treatment programs. |
| **Acculturation** | Acculturation is the process of learning and adopting the dominant culture through adaptation and assimilation. |
| **Ethnic identity** | Ethnic identity is a sense of belonging to an identifiable group and having historical continuity, in addition to a sense of common customs and mores transmitted over generations. |
| **Social identity** | Social identity describes how the dominant culture establishes criteria for categorizing individuals and the normal and ordinary characteristics believed to be natural and usual for members of the society. |
| **Virtual/actual social identity** | Virtual social identity is the set of attributes ascribed to persons based on appearances, dialect, social setting, and material features. Actual social identity is the set of characteristics a person actually demonstrates. |
| **Stigma** | Stigma is a characteristic that makes an individual different from the group, and is perceived to be an intensely discreditable trait. |
| **Normalization** | Normalization describes treating the stigmatized person as if he or she does not have a stigma. |
| **Socioeconomic status** | Socioeconomic status is determined by occupation, education, and income of the head of a household. |
| **Prejudice** | Prejudice is bias or judgment based on value judgment, personal history, inferences about others, and application of normative judgments. |
| **Discrimination** | Discrimination is the act of expressing prejudice with immediate and serious social and economic consequences. |
| **Stereotypes** | Stereotypes are amplified distorted beliefs about an ethnicity, gender, or other group, often employed to justify discriminatory conduct. |
| **Oppressed minority** | A group differentiated from others in society because of physical or cultural characteristics. The group receives unequal treatment and views itself as an object of collective discrimination. |
| **Privilege** | Advantages or benefits that the dominant group has. These have been given unintentionally, unconsciously, and automatically. |
| **Racism** | Generalizations, institutionalization, and assignment of values to real or imaginary differences between individuals to justify privilege, aggression, or violence. These societal patterns have the cumulative effect of inflicting oppressive or other negative conditions against identifiable groups based on race or ethnicity. |

# Exploitation

## CHARACTERISTICS OF PERPETRATORS OF EXPLOITATION

Characteristics of perpetrators of exploitation may vary widely, depending on the type of exploitation, making them difficult to identify.

- Many of those that are involved in **sex trafficking** are part of large criminal enterprises or have a history of criminal acts and antisocial behavior. The perpetrator may exhibit a domineering attitude, speaking for the victims and never leaving the victim unattended.
- Perpetrators of **elder exploitation** are usually family members or caregivers who take advantage of the victims financially. These perpetrators may appear as loving and caring or sometimes abusive. Business people may take advantage of the elderly by overcharging for goods and services, and some people use scams to get victims to pay or invest money.
- Those involved in **exploitation of child labor** are often in agriculture, working children (most often immigrants) for long hours in the fields at low wages.
- Perpetrators of **slavery/involuntary servitude** may come from cultures with different values, or may be individuals with personal values that allow them to take advantage of others.

## SEXUAL TRAFFICKING

Risk factors for sexual trafficking include being homeless or a runaway, being part of the LGBTQ community, being African American or Latino, having involvement in the child welfare system, having a substance use disorder, and being an illegal immigrant. **Sexual trafficking** may include the following:

- **Children**: Children may be bought or sold for sexual use or forced by family members, even parents, into sex trafficking. Runaways are often picked up on the street and offered shelter, and some children are lured through internet postings. Children who resist may be beaten or even killed. Young girls especially may serve in prostitution rings or be forced to participate in pornography. Many turn to substance abuse.
- **Adults**: Many adult victims begin as victims of sexual trafficking during childhood and continue into adulthood as part of prostitution rings or the pornography industry which they are afraid of or too dependent on to try to escape. Substance abuse is common, often used to self-treat depression or other mental health conditions. Physical abuse is common, as are high rates of STDs and HIV. Forced abortions are also common.

## FINANCIAL EXPLOITATION

Individuals (especially the elderly and disabled) who become unable to manage their own financial affairs become increasingly vulnerable to **financial exploitation**, especially if they have cognitive impairment or physical impairments that impair their mobility. Financial exploitation includes any of the following:

- Outright stealing of property or persuading individuals to give away possessions
- Forcing individuals to sign away property
- Emptying bank and savings accounts
- Using stolen credit cards
- Convincing the individual to invest money in fraudulent schemes
- Taking money for home renovations that are not done

Indications of financial abuse may be unpaid bills, unusual activity at ATMs or with credit cards, inadequate funds to meet needs, disappearance of items in the home, change in the provision of a will, and deferring to caregivers regarding financial affairs. Family or caregivers may move permanently into the client's home and take over without sharing costs. Clients may be unable to recoup losses and forced to live with reduced means and may exhibit shame or confusion about loss.

## EXPLOITATION OF IMMIGRATION STATUS

People whose immigration status is illegal are especially at risk of exploitation because they have little recourse to legal assistance that doesn't increase the risk of deportation. Many have paid a high price to "coyotes" to smuggle them into the country and may have been robbed or sexually abused with impunity. Once in the United States, they are often hired at substandard wages and without benefits, including insurance. Many have little access to health care and may suffer from dental and health problems. Housing is often inadequate, and children may drop out of school or have poor attendance because parents move from place to place. Immigrants are often fearful of authorities. Mental health problems, such as depression and substance abuse, are common, but little treatment is available, and many immigrants come from cultures that consider mental illness a cause for shame. Legal immigrants who qualify for assistance may face similar problems, especially related to employment and housing, because of poor language skills and societal discrimination.

# Globalization and Institutionalism

## GLOBALIZATION

Globalization refers to the international integration and interaction of multiple systems, such as economics, communications, and trade. Considerations include the following:

- **International integration**: This term most often refers to financial and business affairs related to trade and investments. For example, one company may manufacture in the United States, Europe, and China and do business throughout the world. International integration is most successful when tariffs and quotas are eliminated or restricted in order to allow the free flow of goods. International integration may affect the cost of items to the client and may affect job opportunities.
- **Financial crisis**: Because of international integration, a financial crisis (devaluing currency, recession, inflation) in one country can have a profound effect on other countries. For example, the financial crisis that occurred in 2008-2009 resulted in high rates of unemployment and increased homelessness worldwide. The unemployed were unable to afford goods, causing businesses to fold or suffer losses, increasing unemployment, and increasing prices to the consumer.
- **Interrelatedness of systems**: Something that affects one system is likely to have an effect on other systems. For example, if a person works in a US factory that manufacturers equipment and a disaster occurs in the country from which the factory obtains materials, production may slow down and profits decrease, making it difficult for the company to obtain loans needed to finance operations, and the client may be laid off. Because the person has little or no income, they may be unable to make mortgage payments, resulting in the bank foreclosing, and the person becoming homeless.
- **Technology**: Knowledge flows with technology, and those countries with the most technological progress tend to have stronger economies and higher standards of living. Technology transfers have facilitated international integration and allowed instant sharing of information around the world, making inventory control, manufacturing, and delivery (shipping, ground, and air transport) more efficient.

## IMPACT OF GLOBALIZATION ON ENVIRONMENTAL CRISES AND EPIDEMICS

Globalization may have a profound effect on the following crises:

- **Environmental crises**: As industrialization moves into developing countries, pollution and stripping of natural resources follows. The increased worldwide demand for goods means that countries are motivated more by monetary gain than environmental concerns. Forests are decimated, water and air polluted, but the global community has been unable to reach a worldwide agreement on environmental planning, resulting in increasingly common environmental problems.
- **Pandemics**: Because of the rapid increase in international marketing and travel, it is now almost impossible to completely contain an outbreak that at one time may have been local, such as Ebola (which has killed over 11,000 people), HIV (which has killed over 35 million people), and most recently, the COVID-19 pandemic which is still active worldwide, killing half a million Americans in its first year. Additionally, health laws and practices vary widely, so not all populations have adequate preventive care or treatment. Thus, any outbreak can pose a worldwide threat. Viruses especially pose a grave threat because they readily mutate and treatment may be unavailable or inadequate.

## PROBLEMS OF GLOBALIZATION CREATED BY MODERNIZATION

Based on the idea that agrarian and impoverished countries would be improved by industrialization, **modernization** has been criticized for contributing to the problems of globalization. In globalization, multinational corporations have relocated their operations and jobs to less-developed regions where poverty remains the norm and average wages are extremely low. These corporations make higher profits, whereas workers in more-developed countries lose their jobs to workers in less-developed countries. Although the merits of this process in regard to workers in the less-developed countries can be debated, the effects on the previously employed workers in the more-developed countries are undeniably negative.

## INSTITUTIONALISM

Institutionalism is the idea that social interventions should be state run, and planning should be centralized in government. Reform is initiated through the electoral process, and a benevolent state would oversee reform efforts. Social services would be provided by the state as well. Critiques would include the assumption of a paternalistic and helpful state, run by individuals uninterested in personal power and gain at the expense of others. However, a counterargument may be the success of countries of northern Europe (e.g., Sweden, Denmark, and Norway) where institutionalism provides citizens with health care, free education, employment, childcare, and housing benefits.

# Social and Economic Justice

## CHILDREN
### CHILDREN IN POVERTY IN THE US

The following are basic facts/statistics relating to children in poverty in the US:

- Almost **one in six** children lives in poverty.
- **Minority** children under age six are much more likely than white children of the same age to live in poverty.
- Many of these children in poverty are **homeless** or are in the **child welfare system**.
- Fewer than one-third of all poor children below age six live solely on **welfare**.
- More than half of children in poverty have at least one **working parent**.
- Children of **single mothers** are more likely to live in poverty.
- Poor children have increased risk of **health impairment**.

### CHILDREN IN THE FOSTER CARE SYSTEM

The following are some barriers that children in the foster care system face in this country:

- Children in foster care often go through frequent **relocations** due to rejection by foster families, changes in the family situation, returns to biological families and later returns to foster care, agency procedures, and decisions of the court. Additionally, many foster children experience **sexual and physical abuse** within the foster care system.
- Due to frequent changes in their situation, children in foster care may **change schools** multiple times, which can have an adverse impact on their academic achievement.
- Many youths age out of the foster care system at age 18; this can abruptly **end the relationships** with foster families and other supportive structures.
- Compared with children raised with their own families, children who have been through the foster care system have a higher incidence of **behavioral problems**, increased **substance abuse**, and greater probability of entering the **criminal justice system**.

## SOCIAL WELFARE ORGANIZATIONS
### APPROACHES TO SOCIAL WELFARE POLICY MAKING

The **rational approach to social welfare policy making** is an idealized and structured approach. It includes identifying and understanding a social problem, identifying alternative solutions and their consequences for consumers and society, and rationally choosing the best alternatives. The rational approach minimizes ideological issues.

The political approach recognizes the importance of compromise, power, competing interests, and partial solutions. Those who are most affected by social policies often have the least amount of political power to promote change. Those who have political power are often influenced by interests that are seeking to protect their own position. Policy makers are often concerned with retaining privilege and power. Without aggressive advocacy, the needs of the disadvantaged can become marginalized.

## ADMINISTRATIVE CHALLENGES

Administrative challenges unique to social welfare organizations include the following:

- Clinical services can be difficult to assess objectively.
- It is difficult to evaluate prevention programs, as few techniques are able to measure events that have not occurred.
- Staff turnover is high due to low salary and burnout.
- Programs are often dependent on the political environment for funding.
- It can be difficult to implement systematization or routine work due to the flexibility often required when dealing with human problems.

## LESSER ELIGIBILITY

This concept of lesser eligibility asserts that welfare payments should not be higher than the lowest paying job in society and derives from Elizabethan Poor Law. It suggests that economic and wage issues underlie the size of benefits and the availability of welfare. Some believe it is a way to control labor and maintain incentives for workers to accept low-paying or undesirable jobs that they might otherwise reject.

## CHALLENGES FOR PROGRAMS FOR POOR AND HOMELESS PEOPLE

One criticism of program development supposedly targeting homeless and poor people is that whereas programs affecting the middle class, such as Individual Development Accounts (IDAs), are put into operation upon conception, programs for poor people are first put through testing phases, with implementation taking years, if it happens at all. In program development for the poor, policies at the level of government may be at odds with actually implementing and carrying out a program.

## CRIMINAL JUSTICE SYSTEM

The criminal justice system includes agencies and processes involved in apprehending, prosecuting and defending, reaching a verdict, sentencing, and punishing offenders:

- **Law enforcement agencies**: These may include police, sheriffs, highway patrol, US Marshal service, FBI, DEA, ICE, and ATF. Law enforcement agencies may be local, state, or federal. Their purpose is to investigate and apprehend criminals.
- **Court system**: Prosecutors provide evidence against an individual, and defense attorneys attempt to discredit the evidence or otherwise provide a defense against the charges brought. Judges preside over court cases and may, in some cases, determine the verdict and sentence. In some states, judges determine if probable cause for arrest exists (preliminary hearing). A grand jury may meet in other state and federal cases to determine whether the evidence indicates probable cause.
- **Jail/prison systems**: Individuals may be incarcerated in local jails or state or federal prisons for varying duration of sentences.
- **Probation system**: Some individuals may receive probation instead of jail or prison time but must report regularly to probation officers and may have other requirements, such as attending rehab programs. Individuals released from jail or prison on parole may also enter the probation system for a specified period of time.

## CRIMINAL JUSTICE PROCESS

The criminal justice process includes the following:

- **Investigation** of a crime by law enforcement officers.
- **Probable cause** of a crime must be established in order to obtain a search warrant unless exigent circumstances exist.
- **Interrogation** may be carried out to obtain information on the suspect after the suspect receives the Miranda warning.
- An **arrest** may be made with or without a warrant in public places and with a warrant in private. After an arrest, the person must be charged or released within 24-48 hours (state laws vary).
- With federal cases and in some states, a grand jury decides whether **evidence supports probable cause**. In some states, this decision is made by a judge in a preliminary hearing.
- **Arraignment** involves presenting the charge in court and reading the charges to the individual.
- **Bail** may be set to allow the individual to remain out of jail.
- The case may be resolved by a **plea bargain or a trial** in which the evidence is presented, a **verdict** reached, and sentence determined.
- The individual may be eligible for **appeal** if found guilty.

## IMPACT OF EARLY EXPERIENCE WITHIN THE CRIMINAL JUSTICE SYSTEM

Early experience within the criminal justice system depends to some degree on the action taken. For example, an adolescent arrested for delinquent acts is more likely to reoffend if the sentence is punitive than if it is more lenient. Additionally, the child or adolescent may develop negative attitudes toward law enforcement and authority in general, and is more likely to commit crimes as an adult. Those who are incarcerated in juvenile facilities may suffer bullying and abuse from others, resulting in emotional and physical problems, and may receive inadequate education, limiting future educational and employment opportunities. Children in the juvenile justice system have high rates of depression, but mental health care and rehabilitation programs are often very limited. Children charged as adults may spend many years in juvenile facilities and then prison, and youth incarceration is one of the highest predictors of recidivism. Many youths are in juvenile detention because of non-violent offenses (such as drug use) but may be exposed to and influenced by more serious offenders.

# Out-of-Home Placement and Displacement

## OUT-OF-HOME DISPLACEMENT

Out-of-home displacement may have varying effects on clients and client systems:

- **Natural disasters***:* Some clients may develop PTSD and have recurring nightmares or fears regarding the disaster, especially if it was particularly frightening or the individual or family members experienced injuries. Some may experience depression and withdrawal. Living situations may change if the home was damaged or destroyed, sometimes forcing clients into sharing homes with others, living in substandard housing, or being homeless. Some may have to move away from schools, neighborhoods, and friends.
- **Homelessness**: Many clients that are homeless develop depression and low self-esteem and may engage in substance abuse. Children may attend school irregularly, have difficulty studying, and lack adequate clothing and nutrition. They may be bullied by other children aware of their circumstances. Families may be separated and children placed in separate shelters or foster care. Risk of injuries and chronic disease increases.

## OUT-OF-HOME PLACEMENT

Out-of-home placements may have varying effects on clients and client systems, depending on the age, duration, and reason:

- **Hospitalization**: Both children and adults may feel fearful and anxious. Children, especially, may feel abandoned or rejected and may regress (bed wetting, thumb sucking). Children may be compliant out of fear when alone but cry and express feelings when parents or other caregivers are present. Adolescents may resent the lack of privacy, isolation, and loss of control. Adults may be concerned about the family unit and loss of income.
- **Foster care**: Children may have difficulty attaching and may become depressed or exhibit behavioral issues (anger or aggression). Developmental delays are common, and children often have poor educational backgrounds, resist studying, get low grades, or must repeat grades. Children may act out or become withdrawn after family visits.
- **Residential care**: Those in residential care may suffer from abuse or molestation because of inadequate supervision. Adults may have an increased risk of falls and injuries. Clients of all ages may become withdrawn and regress because of a lack of personal attention and caring. Small children, especially, may exhibit growth and developmental delays.

## FOLLOW-UP AFTER PLACING CHILD IN OUT-OF-HOME PLACEMENT

Follow-up after placing a child in out-of-home placement may vary according to the state regulations, age of the child, type of placement, and the child's specific plan of care, but common **follow-up activities** include:

- Making regularly scheduled visits to observe the child and caregivers in the home environment
- Ensuring that the child's special needs, such as for medical care or counseling, are met
- Assessing the caregiver's communication with the child, disciplinary actions, and attention to special needs, such as giving medications and providing a special diet
- Recording compliance with court ordered actions required of the child (such as rehabilitation for an adolescent drug abuser) or the parents (such as attendance at child development or anger management classes or testing free of alcohol and drugs)
- Monitoring health and education, including school records of grades and attendance
- Ensuring that support services are provided to the caregivers as needed
- Sending periodic reports to the court

## PERMANENCY PLANNING

Permanency planning for permanent placement should begin when the child is admitted to the care of child protective services (CPS) and the initial plan of care is developed. Permanent placement may include reunification, foster care, kinship placement, adoption, residential care facility, group home, or transition to adult living. **Elements of permanency planning** include:

- Assessing the child and the child's needs as well as those of the potential caregivers
- Reviewing any previous CPS records
- Noting any previous history with the juvenile justice system and reviewing records
- Preparing the child by engaging them in the process as appropriate for their age through explaining options, showing photographs, and asking for the child's input
- Reviewing health and education records (including lists of schools attended and grades) to ascertain the child's needs and the need for interventions or support services
- Establishing permanency goals and target dates
- Attending permanency hearings and providing justification for termination of parental rights when appropriate

# Sexual Orientation

## SEXUALITY

Sexuality is an integral part of each individual's personality and refers to all aspects of being a sexual human. It is more than just the act of physical intercourse. A person's sexuality is often apparent in what they do, in their appearance, and in how they interact with others. There are four main aspects of sexuality:

- **Genetic identity** or one's chromosomal gender
- **Gender identification** or how one perceives oneself with regard to male or female
- **Gender role** or the attributes of one's cultural role
- **Sexual orientation** or the gender to which one is attracted

Assessing and attempting to conceptualize a person's sexuality will lead to a broader understanding of the client's beliefs and allow for a more holistic approach to providing care.

## GENDER IDENTITY

Gender identity is the gender to which the individual identifies, which may or may not be the gender of birth (natal gender). Most children begin to express identification and behaviors associated with gender between ages 2 and 4. The degree to which this identification is influenced by genetics and environment is an ongoing debate because, for example, female children are often socialized toward female roles (dresses, dolls, pink items). Societal pressure to conform to gender stereotypes is strong, so gender dysphoria, which is less common in early childhood than later, may be suppressed. At the onset of puberty, sexual attraction may further complicate gender identity although those with gender dysphoria most often have sexual attraction to those of the same natal gender, so a natal boy who identifies as a girl is more likely to be sexually attracted to boys than to girls. Later in adolescence, individuals generally experiment with sexual behavior and solidify their gender identity.

## INFLUENCE OF SEXUAL ORIENTATION ON BEHAVIORS

The degree to which sexual orientation influences behavior may vary widely depending on the individual. For example, some gay males may be indistinguishable in appearance and general behavior from heterosexual males while others may behave in a stereotypically flamboyant manner. The same holds true for lesbians, with some typically feminine in appearance and behavior and others preferring a more masculine appearance. The typical heterosexual model (two people in a stable relationship) is increasingly practiced by homosexual couples while others prefer less traditional practices. Depending on the degree of acceptance that LGBTQ individuals encounter, they may hide their sexual orientation or maintain a heterosexual relationship in order to appear straight. LGBTQ individuals are at higher risk of depression and suicide, especially if they experience rejection because of their sexual orientation or have been taught that it is sinful. LGBTQ individuals with multiple sexual partners (especially males) are at increased risk for STDs, including HIV/AIDS.

## COMING OUT PROCESS

The coming out process is the act of revealing LGBTQ sexual orientation to family and friends. This generally occurs during adolescence or early adulthood although some may delay coming out for decades or never do so. Individuals may come out to select groups of people. For example, friends may be aware of an individual's orientation but not family or co-workers. Coming out can be frightening for many people, especially if they have reason to fear rejection or fear for their safety. Stages in coming out typically progress in the following order:

| Stage | Actions and feelings involved |
|---|---|
| Confusion | The individual may be unsure of feelings or be in denial. |
| Exploration | The individual begins to question orientation and wonder about LGBTQ people. |
| Breakthrough | The individual accepts the likelihood of being LGBTQ and seeks others of the same orientation. |
| Acceptance | The individual accepts orientation and begins to explore and read about the LGBTQ culture. |
| Pride | The individual begins to exhibit pride in orientation and may reject straight culture or exhibit stereotypically LGBTQ behaviors. |
| Synthesis | The individual comes to terms with the reality of the LGBTQ orientation, is at peace with their identity, and is generally out to family, friends, and co-workers. |

## PRACTICE ISSUES WHEN WORKING WITH LGBTQ CLIENTS

Possible practice issues with LGBTQ clients include, but are not limited to, the following:

- Stigmatization and violence
- Internalized homophobia
- Coming out
- AIDS
- Limited civil rights
- Orientation vs. preference (biology vs. choice)

**Problematic treatment models** for treating gay and lesbian people include the following:

- The moral model for treatment is religiously oriented and views homosexuality as sinful.
- Reparative or conversion psychotherapy focuses on changing a person's sexual orientation to heterosexual. Traditional mental health disciplines view this type of treatment as unethical and as having no empirical base.

# Self-Image

## FACTORS INFLUENCING SELF-IMAGE

Factors influencing self-image include the following:

- **Spirituality**: Religious or spiritual beliefs may affect how individuals see their place in the world and their self-confidence. Individuals may gain self-esteem through secure beliefs and membership in a like group, but belief systems with a strong emphasis on sin may impair self-image.
- **Culture**: Individuals are affected (negatively and positively) by cultural expectations, especially if they feel outside of the norm.
- **Ethnicity**: Whether or not the individual is part of the dominant ethnic group may have a profound effect on self-image. Minority groups often suffer discrimination that reinforces the idea that they are less valuable than others.
- **Education**: Those with higher levels of education tend to have a better self-image than those without, sometimes because of greater unemployment and fewer opportunities associated with low education.
- **Gender**: Society often reinforces the value of males (straight) over females and LGBTQ individuals.
- **Abuse**: Those who are abused may often develop a poor self-image, believing they are deserving of abuse.
- **Media**: The media reinforces stereotypes and presents unrealistic (and unattainable) images, affecting self-image.

## BODY IMAGE

Body image is the perception individuals have of their own bodies, positive or negative. An altered body image may result in a number of responses, most often beginning during adolescence but sometimes during childhood:

- **Obesity**: Some may be unhappy with their body image and overeat as a response, often increasing their discontent.
- **Eating disorders**: Some may react to being overweight or to the cultural ideal by developing anorexia or bulimia in an attempt to achieve the idealized body image they seek. They may persist even though they put their lives at risk. Their body image may be so distorted that they believe they are fat even when emaciated.
- **Body dysmorphic disorder**: Some may develop a preoccupation with perceived defects in their body image, such as a nose that is too big or breasts or penis that is too small. Individuals may become obsessed to the point that they avoid social contact with others, stop participating in sports, get poor grades, stop working, or seek repeated plastic surgery.

# Grief

## IMPACT OF GRIEF ON THE INDIVIDUAL

**Grief** is an emotional response to loss that begins at the time a loss is anticipated and continues on an individual timetable. While there are identifiable stages of grief, it is not an orderly and predictable process. It involves overcoming anger, disbelief, guilt, and a myriad of related emotions. The grieving individual may move back and forth between stages or experience several emotions at any given time. Each person's grief response is unique to their own coping patterns, stress levels, age, gender, belief system, and previous experiences with loss.

## KUBLER-ROSS'S FIVE STAGES OF GRIEF

Kubler-Ross taught the medical community that the dying person and their family welcome open, honest discussion of the dying process. She believed that there were certain stages that people go through while experiencing grief. The stages may not occur in order; they may occur out of order, some may be skipped, and some may occur more than once. **Kubler Ross's stages of grief** include the following:

- **Denial**: The person denies the loss and tries to pretend it isn't true. During this time, the person may seek a second opinion or alternative therapies (in the case of a terminal diagnosis) or act as though the loss never occurred. They may use denial until they are better able to emotionally cope with the reality of the loss or changes that need to be made.
- **Anger**: The person is angry about the situation and may focus that rage on anyone or anything.
- **Bargaining**: The person attempts to make deals with a higher power to secure a better outcome to their situation.
- **Depression**: The person anticipates the loss and the changes it will bring with a sense of sadness and grief.
- **Acceptance**: The person accepts the loss and is ready to face it. They may begin to withdraw from interests and family.

> **Review Video: The Five Stages of Grief**
> Visit mometrix.com/academy and enter code: 648794

## ANTICIPATORY GRIEF

Anticipatory grief is the mental, social, and somatic reactions of an individual as they prepare themselves for a perceived future loss. The individual experiences a process of intellectual, emotional, and behavioral responses in order to modify their self-concept, based on their perception of what the potential loss will mean in their life. This process often takes place ahead of the actual loss, from the time the loss is first perceived until it is resolved as a reality for the individual. This process can also blend with past loss experiences. It is associated with the individual's perception of how life will be affected by the particular diagnosis as well as the impending death. Acknowledging this anticipatory grief allows family members to begin looking toward a changed future. Suppressing this anticipatory process may inhibit relationships with the ill individual and contribute to a more difficult grieving process at a later time. However, appropriate anticipatory grieving does not take the place of grief during the actual time of death.

## DISENFRANCHISED GRIEF

Disenfranchised grief occurs when the loss being experienced cannot be openly acknowledged, publicly mourned, or socially supported. Society and culture are partly responsible for an individual's response to a loss. There is a social context to grief. If a person incurring the loss will be putting himself or herself at risk by expressing grief, disenfranchised grief occurs. The risk for disenfranchised grief is greatest among those whose relationship with the thing they lost was not known or regarded as significant. This is also the situation found among bereaved persons who are not recognized by society as capable of grief, such as young children, or needing to mourn, such as an ex-spouse or secret lover.

## GRIEF VS. DEPRESSION

Normal grief is self-limiting to the loss itself. Emotional responses will vary and may include open expressions of anger. The individual may experience difficulty sleeping or vivid dreams, a lack of energy, and weight loss. Crying is evident and provides some relief of extreme emotions. The individual remains socially responsive and seeks reassurance from others.

By contrast, **depression** is marked by extensive periods of sadness and preoccupation often extending beyond two months. It is not limited to the single event. There is an absence of pleasure or anger and isolation from previous social support systems. The individual can experience extreme lethargy, weight loss, insomnia, or hypersomnia. Crying is absent or persistent and provides no relief of emotions. Professional intervention is often required to relieve depression.

# Domestic Violence

## ABUSIVE BEHAVIORS ASSOCIATED WITH DOMESTIC VIOLENCE

Abusive behaviors often occur in a series of escalating degrees.

1. The series begins with **verbal abuse** in the form of mocking comments, put-downs, name-calling, or abusive language.
2. The next degree is **emotional abuse** in the form of rejecting, degrading, terrorizing, isolating, corrupting, financially exploiting, and denying emotional responsiveness.
3. **Physical abuse** is next on the continuum in the form of restraining, slapping, beating, biting, burning, striking with an object, strangulation, and the use of weapons with the intent of wounding or causing death.

According to the CDC, 1 in 4 women and 1 in 10 men have experienced some form of intimate partner violence.

> **Review Video: <u>Domestic Abuse</u>**
> Visit mometrix.com/academy and enter code: 530581

## SOCIETAL COST OF ABUSE

Abuse costs Americans over $4 billion dollars per year for:

- Physical injuries treated by medical practitioners
- Psychological injuries treated by mental health professionals
- Violence prevention campaigns
- Police and judiciary costs
- Emergency housing
- Social services costs

There are also hidden costs from **eroded social capital** like:

- Increased morbidity from stress
- Lost pay from work absences
- Low productivity from worry at work and painful movement
- Lower earnings and savings
- Increased mortality from suicide through depression
- Poor school performance by traumatized children
- Increased mortality from murder

Victims can be either a member of an intimate relationship, or children in violent homes, which are often neglected or abused. Victims of childhood abuse often become the perpetrators of violence in later life. Many suffer from poor self-esteem that undermines their job choices and social interactions.

## VIOLENCE AGAINST WOMEN ACT OF 1994

President Bill Clinton signed the Violence Against Women Act of 1994, a law based on zero tolerance for violence. **Zero tolerance** means no reported abuse will be ignored; the perpetrator always faces stiff penalties. The Violence Against Women Act was not a productive deterrent from abuse because the stiff penalties caused women to withdraw from legal protection. Abused women feared:

- Police would take their children away from the violence
- Their husbands or significant others would retaliate after release from jail
- They would be unable to cope financially without their husband's or significant other's income to help support the family
- Taking on the fees charged by lawyers, bondsmen, and the courts

Women are frequent targets for abuse because they are often:

- Untrained in self-defense
- Small enough to wound and intimidate easily
- Socialized not to leave a relationship except under extreme duress

## WOMEN IN ABUSIVE RELATIONSHIPS

Women tend to stay in abusive relationships for many reasons, including:

- Abuse being normalized from watching their parents participate in similarly dysfunctional relationships
- Being concerned that their children will have no traditional nurturer if they leave
- Feeling a social responsibility to keep up the facade of a happy home
- Early training from childhood that they are inferior and deserve abuse

**Abuse screening tools** have been implemented in doctors' and mental health providers' offices in an effort to identify abused women who do not spontaneously disclose. The woman is asked:

- Whether or not she has been physically struck over the last year
- About the safety of her present relationship
- About past relationships that may threaten her present safety

## COMMON PROBLEMS THAT CHILDREN OF ABUSE MAY DEVELOP

Physical and mental issues often develop in a **child from an abusive home** that follows him or her into adulthood. Some common behavior and social problems include:

- Deficient social skills
- Inadequate problem-solving skills; aggressiveness
- Delinquency
- Oppositional behaviors
- Attention deficit/hyperactivity disorder (ADHD)
- Obsessive-compulsive disorders (OCD)
- Suicidal tendencies
- Drug and alcohol abuse
- Social disengagement
- Denial
- Anxiety and depression
- Social withdrawal
- Avoidance of problems
- Excessive self-criticism

These social, behavioral, and intimacy problems are very prevalent and costly to our society, and degrade the children's quality of life.

## CHARACTERISTICS OF ABUSERS

Abusers of either sex have various unmet psychological needs or motivations. Common **types of abusers** include the following:

- A person who assaults his or her victims in the **home setting** and has a strong need to dominate relationships with his or her intimate partners.
- The abuser who is suffering from significant **psychological issues**, like antisocial personality disorder, who is a convicted criminal, or who has past assault and battery charges (often dropped by intimidated victims).
- The person who works through a **continuum of abusive behaviors**. These often begin with verbal and emotional abuses, which lead to throwing objects at the victim, intimidation, and an effort to dominate the relationship by withholding money or restraining movement and social access. Violence can escalate, followed by feelings of remorse. The pattern can become part of a never-ending cycle of behavior.

### MALE ABUSERS

Male abusers were usually abused as children, watched their mothers being abused, or saw abuse perpetrated by male friends (e.g., gang rapes as initiation rites). The **male abuser** often displays one or several of the following qualities:

- He has a **disproportionate sense of entitlement** that he has the right to hurt others, especially females. He truly believes he has the right to hit a woman if she is unfaithful or withholding sex from him.
- He usually **does not have a good opinion of women** because that is the way he has been socialized.
- He often justifies his behavior by stating he was **drunk or high on drugs** at the time of an attack.
- He may have a **psychological problem** such as post-traumatic stress disorder (PTSD), a delayed reaction caused by trauma or witnessing an event that caused him a great deal of suffering. Other psychological problems common to abusers are depression, poor self-esteem, personality disorders, and psychopathy.

Male abusers may have been abandoned as children. **Abandonment** leads to a state of rage in the adult male. Be alert to three states of child abuse that commonly have detrimental effects on the future adult male:

- The father or an adult male authority figure inflicts physical abuse on a male child.
- The father inflicts emotional abuse by rejecting and humiliating his son.
- The mother does not form a maternal bond with her son.

Anger is part of the attachment process. The attachment object may be the victim of the violence as the male abuser takes out his feelings of jealousy or rejection. The male's veneer of icy indifference conceals a strong emotional dependency on the significant other or wife.

## RECOMMENDED TREATMENT APPROPRIATE FOR ABUSERS

The first step is to determine if abuse actually exists and to diagnose the type of abuser. Rule out addiction to drugs or alcohol. If the abuser is an addict, refer the abuser to a separate drug or alcohol intervention program, in conjunction with treatment. Next, determine the severity of past abuse perpetrated on the abuser when he or she was a child. The abuse need not have been directed at the child. It is sufficient that he or she witnessed violence being perpetrated on other family members. Evaluate the abuser for borderline personality disorder and post-traumatic stress disorder. Provide the abuser with anger management training in a group setting. Anger management involves discussions of dominant and controlling behaviors, and the development of personal responsibility. The abuser needs to control his own or her own behavior.

The male abuser should be **counseled** regarding the abuse that was perpetrated on him as a child. The male adult should understand that he was a victim himself, and is not to be blamed for the past abuse perpetrated upon him as a child. He is not the one that caused others to hurt him. Bring to light his wrong assumptions. Try to develop his understanding of the root of his self-esteem issues. The male needs to develop a healthier self-view and learn thought patterns that lead to appropriate behavior. Encourage him to discuss and deal with internal conflicts and the internalized pain of his past. Use a motivational approach to help the male client gain a healthy perspective on his behavior. Base the approach on cognitive, emotional, and behavioral conflicts in the client's life.

Avoid **jointly counseling** a couple in an abusive relationship, as this can lead to further abuse. Assess the clients individually, followed by group therapy. The small group of 6-8 members should be led either by a sole male counselor, or male and female co-counselors to help the clients see positive interaction between a male and female. The co-leader relationship must be evenly balanced in power and control of the group. The focus of the group is self-improvement. Each individual in the group examines his or her emotional responses that are reflected in angry behaviors. The **emotions** behind the anger are usually sadness, pain, rejection, and humiliation. Turn angry behavior to the appropriate expression of emotion. Discuss families and relationships. Relate childhood experiences to present attitudes and behaviors.

## COMPONENTS OF A 20-WEEK ANGER MANAGEMENT GROUP OUTLINE

**Anger management group therapy** can be accomplished in 20 weeks with one session per week. The anger management treatment group should consist of 6-8 male members. Here is a suggested outline for discussion topics:

- **Week 1**: The group makes a participation agreement. Each individual shares their personal violence statement.
- **Week 2**: Clients learn to take a time-out from anger. Discuss other anger management principles. Provide some stress management skill instructions.
- **Week 3**: Each client participates in a discussion on issues they face in their daily life that they can or cannot control. Follow this discussion with another discussion on conflict, emotions, and actions. Encourage clients to practice the use of "I" messages to communicate their feelings. Help clients to gain insight into assertive requests and refusals.
- **Week 4**: Involve clients in an examination of values and discuss the clients' reactions.
- **Week 5**: Discuss the continuum of abuse and the power wheel.
- **Week 6**: Discuss childhood experiences, especially the parental relationship that the child witnessed, and parenting styles.
- **Week 7**: Discuss how abuse of the child is reflected in the life of the adult. The resulting conversation will deal with emotions that this discussion conjures up.
- **Week 8**: Clients discuss the difference between punishment and discipline.
- **Week 9**: Clients discuss praise and respect.
- **Week 10**: Discuss self-talk and its impact, and examine scripts.
- **Week 11**: Discuss the abuse cycle along with a conversation regarding communication.
- **Week 12**: Incorporate empathy, listening, and reflection.
- **Week 13**: Discuss assertiveness.
- **Week 14**: Summarize and consolidate the communication skills taught in the first 13 weeks.
- **Week 15**: Review the power wheel and include a practice exercise.
- **Week 16**: Discuss intimacy.
- **Week 17**: Give empathy exercises.
- **Week 18**: Follow-up on the empathy exercises.
- **Week 19**: Outline a relapse prevention plan.
- **Week 20**: Summarize and reinforce what was learned in the previous 19 weeks. In ending conversation, discuss ways to implement the relapse prevention plan in case a problem develops.

## POSSIBLE ISSUES RESULTING FROM TREATMENT

Treatment that involves discussing the client's abusive relationship with others may unearth feelings that are uncomfortable for both the client and the counselor. The client may want to place the blame for his or her violent actions on the client's spouse or significant other. Help the client to understand the motivations behind those actions and the desire to place the blame elsewhere. Understanding helps the client to establish a closer relationship with his or her spouse. Do not force the client to take responsibility for his or her behavior, or criticize the client, as this will likely cause the client to become defensive. Do not force a confrontation that could turn into an aggressive act. Confrontations increase the sense of humiliation the client is feeling. Humiliation will lead the client to express feelings of blame and anger.

# Stress, Crisis, and Trauma

## STRESS

### RELATIONSHIP BETWEEN STRESS AND DISEASE

Stress causes a number of physical and psychological changes within the body, including the following:

- Cortisol levels increase
- Digestion is hindered and the colon stimulated
- Heart rate increases
- Perspiration increases
- Anxiety and depression occur and can result in insomnia, anorexia or weight gain, and suicide
- Immune response decreases, making the person more vulnerable to infections
- Autoimmune reaction may increase, leading to autoimmune diseases

The body's **compensatory mechanisms** try to restore homeostasis. When these mechanisms are overwhelmed, pathophysiological injury to the cells of the body result. When this injury begins to interfere with the function of the organs or systems in the body, symptoms of dysfunction will occur. If the conditions are not corrected, the body changes the structure or function of the affected organs or systems.

### PSYCHOLOGICAL RESPONSE TO STRESS

When stress is encountered, a person responds according to the threat perceived in order to compensate. The threat is evaluated as to the amount of harm or loss that has occurred or is possible. If the stress is benign (typical day-to-day burdens or life transitions) then a challenge is present that demands change. Once the threat or challenge is defined, the person can gather information, resources, and support to make the changes needed to resolve the stress to the greatest degree possible. Immediate psychological response to stress may include shock, anger, fear, or excitement. Over time, people may develop chronic anxiety, depression, flashbacks, thought disturbances, and sleep disturbances. Changes may occur in emotions and thinking, in behavior, or in the person's environment. People may be more able to adapt to stress if they have many varied experiences, good self-esteem, and a support network to help as needed. A healthy lifestyle and philosophical beliefs, including religion, may give a person more reserve to cope with stress.

### IMPACT OF DIFFERENT KINDS OF STRESS

Everyone encounters stress in life and it impacts each person differently. There are the small daily hassles, major traumatic events, and the periodic stressful events of marriage, birth, divorce, and death. Of these stressors, the daily stress that a person encounters is the one that changes the health status over time. Stressors that occur suddenly are the hardest to overcome and result in the greatest tension. The length of time that a stressor is present also affects its impact, with long-term, relentless stress, such as that generated by poverty or disability, resulting in disease more often. If there is **ineffective coping**, a person will suffer greater changes resulting in even more stress. The solution is to help clients to recognize those things that induce stress in their lives, find ways to reduce stress when possible, and teach effective coping skills and problem-management.

# CRISIS
## CHARACTERISTICS OF A CRISIS

A crisis occurs when a person is faced with a highly stressful event and their usual problem solving and coping skills fail to be effective in resolving the situation. This event usually leads to increased levels of anxiety and can bring about a physical and psychological response. The problem is usually an acute event that can be identified. It may have occurred a few weeks or even months before or immediately prior to the crisis and can be an actual event or a potential event. The crisis state usually lasts less than six weeks with the individual then becoming able to utilize problem solving skills to cope effectively. A person in crisis mode does not always have a mental disorder. However, during the acute crisis their social functioning and decision-making abilities may be impaired.

## TYPES OF CRISES
### DEVELOPMENTAL

There are basically two different types of crises. These types include developmental or maturational crisis and situational crisis. A **developmental crisis** can occur during maturation when an individual must take on a new life role. This crisis can be a normal part of the developmental process. A youth may need to face and resolve crisis to be able to move on to the next developmental stage. This may occur during the process of moving from adolescence to adulthood. Examples of situations that could lead to this type of crisis include graduating from school, going away to college, or moving out on their own. These situations would cause the individual to face a maturing event that requires the development of new coping skills.

### SITUATIONAL

The second type of crisis is the **situational crisis**. This type of crisis can occur at any time in life. There is usually an event or problem that occurs, which leads to a disruption in normal psychological functioning. These types of events are often unplanned and can occur with or without warning. Some examples that may lead to a situational crisis include the death of a loved one, divorce, unplanned or unwanted pregnancy, onset or change in a physical disease process, job loss, or being the victim of a violent act. Events that affect an entire community can also cause an individual situational crisis. Terrorist attacks or weather-related disasters are examples of events that can affect an entire community.

## COLLECTING A TRAUMA HISTORY

A trauma history should be collected from any client with a known history of physical/emotional abuse, accident involvement, or signs/symptoms of PTSD from known or unknown events. There are several methods of trauma history collection:

- **Trauma History Screen (THS)**: The client self-reports (via questionnaire) by responding with "Yes" or "No" to 14 event types and includes the number of times the event occurred. These events include abuse, accidents/natural disasters, military service, loss of loved ones, and life crises/transitions. Next, the client is prompted to respond to the question, "Did any of these things really bother you emotionally?" If the client responds with "Yes," they are then instructed to provide details about every event that bothered them.
- **Trauma History Questionnaire (THQ)**: Similar to the THS, this questionnaire requires the client to self-report experiences with 24 potentially traumatic events, and then to provide the frequency and details of each experience.

# Terrorism and Natural Disasters

## IMPACT OF TERRORISM ON THE AMERICAN POPULATION

The **September 11 attacks** are the most prominent example of foreign terrorism against the United States in recent decades. On 9/11/2001, Al-Qaeda terrorists used hijacked passenger aircraft to attack the World Trade Center buildings in New York City and the Pentagon, and were believed to be targeting the US Capitol building with another hijacked plane that was brought down in Pennsylvania before reaching its intended destination. Around 3,000 people were killed in the attacks. Media coverage was extensive and continuous, which was unusual at that time, and it contributed to varying degrees of psychological trauma for people across the nation.

In more recent years, the United States has experienced **domestic terrorism** and **independent acts of violence** that have also pervaded the American psyche. Mass shootings occurring in public places previously thought of as places of safety (e.g., schools, churches, shopping centers) have led to efforts to prepare children and adults alike for future attacks in their schools or workplaces through the use of mandatory drills and efforts such as the Run-Hide-Fight campaign. These practices, combined with the now-standard extensive media coverage of any mass casualty incident, can create an underlying and pervasive fear that impacts the worldview of Americans today.

## IMPACT OF TERRORISM ON VICTIMS

Terrorism can lead victims to lose the safe assumptions they made about the world around them. Loss of assumption means the **terror victim** loses their trust in mankind's ability to perform good or charitable acts. The terror victim may question the significance and meaning of humanity's existence. Loss of assumption leads to a form of post-traumatic stress disorder (PTSD) in terror victims. Terrorists typically use bombs, acts of violence, or intimidation. The **psychological problem** occurs when the victim is faced with the motivations and antisocial logic that cause the actions of the terrorist. A severe, violent terrorism event can cause temporary mental disturbance, such as in Stockholm syndrome, where the victims bond with their captors and defend them against police. Other terms for Stockholm syndrome are Bonding-to-the-Perpetrator and Trauma-Bonding, seen in domestic abuse where the battered spouse and children refuse to leave their abuser.

## IMPACT OF TERRORISM ON THE PSYCHOLOGICAL STATE OF THE VICTIM

There are multiple immediate and long-term **psychological effects** of terrorism on its victims:

- The terror victim loses positive assumptions about the world by experiencing great fear and loss of his or her sense of personal invulnerability.
- The victim may lose sight of meaningful interpretations of mankind's position in the world.
- The victim may lose confidence in that which was previously within his or her control.
- The victim may be overwrought and afraid of future possible acts of terrorism.
- Fear invades the victim's daily life and routines, causing a state of incapacitating and irrational apprehension.
- The victim finds that his or her self-image has changed from confident to unsure and is full of self-doubts.

## VICARIOUS IMPACT OF TERRORISM ON VICTIM'S LOVED ONES AND COMMUNITY MEMBERS

Terrorism has a vicarious effect on those associated with the victim. **Vicarious traumatization** is experienced by members of a community that has been subject to bombings or deliberate acts of terrorism. Many in the United States experienced vicarious trauma after the fall of the World Trade Center buildings and the Oklahoma City bombing. Members of the media added to the vicarious trauma by broadcasting these events to the general public. The unintended effect of this exposure caused adults and children to suffer from post-traumatic stress disorder. PTSD clients suffer depression, apprehension, and are more susceptible to alcohol or substance abuse.

## STAGES EXPERIENCED IN AFTERMATH OF DISASTER

The survivors of a disaster go through a series of emotional and psychological stages.

- In the first stage, the survivor sees himself or herself as a **hero** and acts out these heroic thoughts by helping to save someone else or their property.
- These altruistic feelings of individual heroism are followed by a **honeymoon period,** in which the whole neighborhood joins together to work as one unit to save others.
- The honeymoon period is followed by the **disillusionment stage**, which comes as a result of the postponement of help from others. The person feels let down by others.
- The final stage involves the **reconstruction period**. The survivor no longer looks for help from others, but instead takes control and responsibility for his or her situation, and works to resolve the problem.

## COGNITIVE APPRAISAL OF TERRORISM

The person who adopts a **positive cognitive appraisal** of the terrorist act develops coping styles to deal with the event. Those who take on a **negative cognitive appraisal** find they feel out of control of the situation and that there is nothing they can do to prevent future acts of terror from being directed against them. This feeling of helplessness is especially concentrated in members of the community who lived or worked near the disaster site. The negative individual may have sustained injuries as a result of the terrorists' actions, or lost people they knew and cared about, and is extremely likely to suffer from PTSD.

## ROLE OF MENTAL HEALTH PROVIDER IN AFTERMATH OF TRAUMATIC EVENTS

An act of terror or a natural disaster will likely increase demand on the mental health provider to provide services in the field.

- As a **first responder**, provide psychological first aid by letting victims know they have reached safety.
- The **secondary response** should be one of direction by setting up triage. Provide workers and bereaved priority care. Stabilize the survivors.
- The **third response** should be one of connection. Rescue workers need to be connected to support systems that give them the psychoeducational support they need to complete the tasks at hand. Follow up with acute care treatment.
- The **final response** is consultation or referral to other specialized service providers.

## MENTAL HEALTH INTERVENTIONS TO ESTABLISH IN A DISASTER

Mental health interventions are critical responsibilities of the counselor in times of crisis. Help the victim to cope by re-establishing feelings of well-being, predictability, and stability. Let the victim see that social support is available and that the counselors assigned are caring and kind. Next, help the victim grasp the meaning of the traumatic event and adapt to changes in worldview and loss of assumption. This can involve the development of an appreciation for life. The victim may find that his or her priorities have changed as a result of the trauma and require direction in order to formulate new priorities and positive expectations. Help the victim find outlets that can produce feelings of good will and help build confidence. Suggest that the victim help others to partake in the heroic actions of the community.

## THREE-PHASE FRAMEWORK OF CRISIS INTERVENTION

The three-phase framework of intervention for a crisis are as follows:

- In the **pre-attack phase**, threat assessment and prevention are performed by law enforcement, military, and the intelligence resources available. The therapist gives pre-incident resiliency training to emergency response teams.
- In the **acute event management phase**, the mental health therapist provides continuing psychological support and encouragement to the emergency response teams and seeks to provide the victims and the community with factual, age-appropriate information.
- In the **reconstruction phase**, the counselor instructs people on coping strategies and communication skills, reassures the victims, and helps them feel safe by reconnecting them to their normal routines and schedules. Specifically, the counselor tries to help the victim adjust to a loss of assumption and change in worldview.

## FIVE-PHASE FRAMEWORK OF CRISIS INTERVENTION

The five-phase framework of crisis intervention is as follows:

- The **pre-incident phase** entails the preparation involved in anticipation of an incident, often applicable in the case of forecasted natural disasters, but also in training efforts.
- The **impact phase** lasts for the first 48 hours following the crisis. Basic needs are the priority. The counselor tends to the psychological first aid required in this period.
- The **rescue phase** lasts from after the first 48 hours through the first week. A needs assessment is performed, crisis counseling is initiated, and information is disseminated.
- The **recovery phase** lasts from the end of week 1 through week 4, during which crisis counseling is ongoing and the recovery status is monitored.
- The **return to life phase** lasts for the next 2 years. More long-term counseling may be required for some victims as they are supported to a return to life (career, family life, mental health) after the trauma.

### PRE-INCIDENT PHASE OF INTERVENTION

The goals of the pre-incident phase include preparation, set-up, and improving coping skills by training first responders. The counselor works in partnership to shape policy and inform others. The counselor sets up and organizes structures that are capable of providing swift assistance.

### IMPACT PHASE OF INTERVENTION

The goals of the impact phase include survival and communication techniques during the 48 hours following the event. The survivor may be in denial at this point, or may display fight-or-flight reactions. They may appear unable to respond, as if frozen in an admission of defeat. The first responder's job is to rescue and protect the victim. The counselor seeks to provide four types of services to the victim and first responders:

- Basic needs
- Psychological first aid
- Assessment of the impact on the environment
- Technical assistance, consultation, and training opportunities

During the impact phase of disaster intervention, the counselor uses keen observation to triage the victims with the most severe symptoms for priority treatment. The counselor keeps check on factors that may introduce further stress to the situation. The counselor also provides technical assistance, consultation, and training to the victims and the first responders to re-establish

community structures. Families may require some grief counseling and training on how to cope with their feelings that are a result of the disaster. Organizations may need the counselor's help to connect the appropriate service to the caregivers, first responders, and leaders within the community. The counselor can improve the organization's ability to provide care to survivors.

## IMMEDIATE POST-IMPACT STAGE

The immediate post-impact stage lasts **up to 48 hours after a traumatic event**. This is the stage where mental health providers give psychological first aid to the victims to stabilize them. The Critical Incident Stress Management (CISM) system is designed to reduce negative psychological reactions to trauma. Disaster survivors and rescue workers are given the opportunity to discuss the trauma and its resulting conditions by defusing in one-hour long conversations with a counselor. During this phase, the counselor must support and encourage the participants to calm them. Debriefing is a two-hour long meeting to provide information to the rescue workers about the survivors and how to best meet their needs. Psychoeducational debriefings are designed to provide assistance and direction to those suffering from post-traumatic stress disorder (PTSD).

## DEBRIEFINGS AFTER DISASTERS

The **communal debriefing** is given to victims who have endured an experience that caused them to feel marked as socially unacceptable in some manner. Do not conduct a communal debriefing before giving pre- and post-intervention assessments to the group members individually. The victims have experienced an emotional shock, producing extreme, acute traumatic symptoms, such as suicidal ideation, severe disassociations, and substance abuse. Survivors with any of these symptoms should be referred for specialized, higher level treatments as soon as they become available. Exclude victims who are acutely bereaved by the death of a loved one from psychological debriefing, because research indicates that debriefing is a leading contributor to PTSD in some survivors. The American Red Cross and the Federal Emergency Management Agency (FEMA) both employ debriefing practices as part of their standard intervention procedures.

## RESCUE PHASE OF INTERVENTION

The rescue phase occurs within the **first week of the disaster**. This stage has adjustment goals. The survivor may be resilient or exhausted in this stage. The first responders are assisted by other helpers who seek to orient the survivors and provide secondary assistance. The counselor's role in the rescue stage is to perform a needs assessment to determine the status of the survivor and to ensure that his or her needs are being met. The counselor establishes a recovery environment, where he or she can assess the needs of various groups and individuals. The counselor performs a walk-through to determine if everyone has gained the assistance that is needed, because some are unwilling or unable to seek out help on their own. A clinical assessment is performed in the triage stage. Survivors may be referred to other specialists, or hospitalized. High risk individuals are targeted for immediate treatment.

## OUTREACH AND INFORMATION ELEMENT OF INTERVENTION

In the outreach and information distribution element of the rescue phase of disaster intervention, the counselor seeks to inform those in need of the services that are available. Information can be shared through websites, community structures, bulletin boards, runners, word of mouth, or fliers. The counselor works to re-establish social interaction. The survivor may need instruction in coping strategies, and the caregivers need education about stress responses found in survivors, including triggers that can cause the victim to experience traumatic flashbacks. Caregivers should be aware of risk factors, services that are available, and the difference between normal and abnormal functioning levels. The counselor also provides family and group support systems and spiritual support. The counselor fosters natural social supports and helps care for those suffering with bereavement. The counselor participates in debriefings as part of the rescue operations.

## RECOVERY AND RETURN TO LIFE PHASES OF INTERVENTION

The recovery stage extends from **one to four weeks after the disaster**. The recovery phase goals involve planning and appraisal. Survivors are grieving, and some have intrusive memories. Teach caregivers to be sensitive in response to the survivors. Monitor the recovery process and the environment. Watch and listen to traumatized survivors. Look for toxins or physical dangers that could be present at the site. Watch for potential threats that may become an issue. Examine and observe the services that are provided to the surviving community.

The return-to-work phase occurs from **two weeks to two years following the disaster**, and its goal is regeneration. Try to reduce or alleviate psychological symptoms by offering more long-term psychotherapy to individuals, families, or groups. If the client's trauma is still not responding to psychotherapy, refer him or her to a psychiatrist for pharmacotherapy, and perhaps hospitalization.

### COGNITIVE-BEHAVIORAL INTERVENTION IN LATER PHASE TREATMENTS

Cognitive-behavioral intervention (CBI) is for those victims who have shattered basic assumptions. Class size should ideally be 8-10 people but definitely no more than 15. Deliver 15 lessons, 2-3 times per week, for 90 minutes each. Two instructors are required to address stress and anxiety in traumatized victims. Teach victims how to identify and modify disturbing thoughts and how to independently employ relaxation techniques when anxious or stressful reactions are triggered.

The survivors that should **not** use this technique include the following:

- The bereaved
- Survivors who suffer from intense, intrusive fear or panic attacks
- Survivors with an IQ below 80
- Those who cannot engage in abstract reasoning
- Those adults who do not have at least a 5th grade education
- Clients with cardiovascular disease, such as uncontrolled arrhythmias
- Survivors who disassociate should not perform deep relaxation strategies that could produce trance-like states. Instead, incorporate breathing exercises into their treatment therapy.

### EXPOSURE STRATEGIES AND EYE MOVEMENT DESENSITIZATION AND REPROCESSING (EMDR)

**Exposure strategies** are part of the cognitive-behavioral intervention (CBI) for treating survivors of traumatic events. The survivor re-exposes himself or herself to an imaginary traumatic place that resembles the initial trauma scene. Alternatively, the survivor may choose to revisit the actual trauma scene.

**Eye Movement Desensitization and Reprocessing (EMDR)** is a treatment successfully used with Vietnam War veterans who suffer from post-traumatic stress disorder (PTSD) from wartime assignments. EMDR joins two interventions, exposure strategies and cognitive-restructuring, into one procedure. Doctors Silver and Rogers support EMDR in their Humanitarian Assistance Program that helps victims around the world.

## GRIEF COUNSELING

**Bereavement** is the physical, psychological, social, and spiritual grief response of family members and close friends to a loved one's death. In 1991, William Worden distinguished grief counseling from grief therapy:

- **Grief counseling** facilitates the normal, uncomplicated response to death in a reasonable amount of time.
- **Grief therapy** uses special techniques to end abnormal, complicated grief that is prolonged, produces somatic symptoms or behavioral derangement, or is exaggerated.

Worden said the counselor should attempt to change the subjective experience and behavior of the bereaved and provide symptomatic relief. Treat the bereaved in a private area. Conduct one-hour sessions for individuals, and 90-minute sessions for groups. Sessions can be closed (registration is required, and the number of treatment sessions is limited), or open (no registration is required, and treatment sessions are ongoing). Get referrals from crisis intervention hotlines. Utilize the "empty chair" Gestalt technique, art and music therapy, journaling, meditation, role playing, and reviewing photos or personal possessions of the dead to relieve grief.

### CONSTRUCTIVIST INTERVENTION

Constructivist intervention is underpinned by the ideas that the loss of one human being affects us all, and every human needs to express grief when they experience loss. Grievers may find meaning through allegorical reflections that allow them the opportunity to carefully consider the traumatic events that resulted in loss. Many people find comfort in formal rituals, like memorial services, which bring survivors together to act as a single entity. Community-wide memorial services help affected neighborhoods to reconstruct meaning and redefine their life roles for the future. Informal family rituals help the survivors to honor the loved one who died, privately. Verbal expression of grief is also therapeutic. Additionally, both local and national communities can be comforted and supplied with hope by watching or reading about the humanitarian efforts of rescuers and donors.

## TRAUMA'S EFFECT ON CHILDREN

Children who are subjected to trauma and terrorism are either not psychologically mature enough to cope with the event or have not reached the developmental age to understand what has actually happened. Assess for the following **signs and symptoms of trauma in children**:

- Depression
- Anxiety
- Behavioral changes
- Aggression
- Dissociative responses
- Helplessness
- Generalized fear
- Heightened arousal
- Nightmares or sleep disturbances
- Acting out the trauma in a repetitive play scenario
- School avoidance
- Preoccupation with danger and the parents' concerns and fears
- Rebelliousness
- Social withdrawal and attempts to distance themselves from others
- Recklessness and excessive risk-taking

## NEEDS OF CHILDREN AFTER TRAUMA

The child has specific counseling needs after a traumatic event:

- Make conversations age-appropriate and talk to the child in a language that he or she understands well.
- Present opportunities for the child to demonstrate tenderness and love for the surviving parent (in the case of losing a parent/loved one) and continue to develop their relationship.
- Ensure surroundings are safe and healthy to restore feelings of security and place in the world.
- Plan opportunities for play and enjoyable activities to build his or her confidence.
- Find a way for the child to contribute to the solutions of problems.
- Tell the child the truth, but omit unnecessary details, because they may overwhelm the child.
- Allow the child to express concerns about the traumatic event in ways that help him or her develop understanding.

## ROLE OF COUNSELOR IN HELPING A CHILD AFTER TRAUMATIC EVENT

The counselor plays a specific role in supporting a child through a traumatic event. The following are important considerations:

- Do not provide cognitive-based interventions (CBI) to children under 7, because they do not develop self-talk until age 5 or 6, and have not yet mastered it.
- Do not minimize the danger that caused the trauma, or encourage the child to delve too deeply into negative emotions. Instead, help the child to develop a story that relates the factual events of what happened.
- Many young children are not equipped to express their emotions because they lack the correct vocabulary. Nonverbal communications help children who cannot accurately express their emotions.
- Play therapy helps the child deal with anxiety over a traumatic event. Try re-enactments, role-plays, or art forms.
- If the child has obsessive thoughts, sleep disturbances or bedwetting, or behavioral problems for more than a few days after the traumatic incident, then refer the child to a psychiatrist for further assessment. The child may require drug therapy or more intensive psychotherapy.

## PLAY THERAPY TREATMENTS

Play helps children communicate and understand traumatic events, even if they do not have good language skills. For example, child survivors of 9/11 re-enacted the crash using blocks and toy planes, and role-played firemen and other helpers in this scenario. Role-play allows the child to attach a deeper meaning to tragic events. Creative art therapists use an art form as a play therapy intervention. Art provides the child with a safe environment to explore feelings about the traumatic event. **Play therapy** for children impacted by 9/11 related to the following:

- The concept of immediate death
- Disability from inhaled particles
- Victims' bodies that could not be recovered from the rubble of the twin towers
- Loss of privacy through media attention
- Disenfranchised grief, because certain deaths were trumpeted as heroic, while others went unacknowledged

- Botched efforts to break the news to children who lost a parent
- Doubts over the memorial service, because victims' status depended on whether they were civilians or public service members
- Loss of control over the memorial service
- Intrusive media presence at the memorial service

Play therapy was also utilized after the mass shooting at Sandy Hook Elementary School in Connecticut in 2012, resulting in the deaths of 20 children and 6 adults. Crisis intervention involved the use of play therapy, along with music and art therapy, to help the children to feel safe within the walls of their school again.

## IMPACT OF TRAUMA ON THE COUNSELOR

**Secondary traumatic stress disorder (STSD)** appears when a counselor ignores his or her physical and emotional symptoms of distress and burnout. Sometimes, **countertransference** reactions occur in mental health providers, making their reactions appear under-responsive or over-responsive.

- **Under-responsive reactions** indicate that the counselor has ceased to be affected by the pain and suffering of the survivor.
- **Over-responsive reactions** indicate that the counselor has lost the ability to remain emotionally detached from the survivor's pain.

Either reaction is inappropriate and can lead to a serious problem for both the counselor and the survivor. Counselors should be able to access help for themselves from other mental health providers. Counselors require adequate rest, physical and mental breaks or vacations, relaxation and recreation, and social support systems. Use these strategies to help maintain a balanced state.

## VICARIOUS TRAUMATIZATION, COMPASSION FATIGUE, AND BURNOUT

Disaster and terrorism counselors must constantly evaluate self-care areas. The counselor must not become so caught up in the victim's suffering that **vicarious traumatization** occurs, in which the counselor absorbs the negative psychological consequences of the trauma that occurred to their client. The counselor must also avoid reaching a state of **compassion fatigue**. These two conditions are a direct result of a long-term commitment to care. The counselor becomes so caught up in the pain that he or she witnesses in the survivors that prolonged stress leads to **burnout**. Burnout appears as a variety of disturbances, including the following:

- Sleep disturbances
- Backaches
- Fatigue
- Headaches
- Irritability
- Mental confusion
- Cynicism
- Depression
- Intense vulnerability

## AMERICAN RED CROSS RESPONSE SYSTEM

The American Red Cross founded a system that organized volunteers to respond to disasters systematically.

- The Red Cross first responds with the **damage assessment team**, who evaluate what is needed.
- The **disaster action team** then provides food and medical supplies to the first responders and survivors.
- **Disaster response human resources** includes **disaster mental health (DMH) services**, consisting of licensed and trained volunteers who provide psychological assistance to the survivors. DMH services delivers an organized response and assures quality control during a disaster.

The Red Cross requires their mental health counselors obtain Red Cross licensed training. Psychologists, psychiatrists, social workers, marriage and family therapists, and psychiatric nurses are eligible to receive DMHS-certified training.

### ARC CERTIFICATION FOR MENTAL HEALTH PROVIDERS WORKING IN DISASTER RELIEF SITUATIONS

The American Red Cross (ARC) has developed a **certification procedure** to ensure that mental health providers are trained to be **disaster responders**. Mental health providers who wish to receive ARC-certified training can find it from the Red Cross's website. The events of 9/11 caused many anxious moments and a great deal of unorganized response. Counselors who responded to the 9/11 crisis found out after the fact that they were ill-prepared to meet the needs of the survivors. This awareness resulted in a substantial increase in responders taking **Red Cross DMH training courses** in 2002. 9/11 responders wanted to be adequately prepared for the next disaster and to prevent future problems in caring for survivors. Before seeking DMH certification, the mental health provider must have these prerequisites:

- A Master's degree in the mental health field
- Work experience in the mental health field
- Licensure by applicable boards

After receiving their DMH certification, counselors should become standing members of the Red Cross chapter nearest to their homes, and make prior arrangements with their employers allowing them to take necessary time off from work to assist in a disaster.

### RED CROSS SERVICE DELIVERY GIVEN TO SURVIVORS AT DISASTER SITES

The professionals working in **Red Cross' disaster mental health (DMH) services** provide psychological assistance to the survivors at the **disaster site**. Service given is in an interventional format. The client may be seeking food, medical care, or information. Confidentiality is difficult in this setting. The counselor either gives interventions to a small collection of survivors, or to a large group of people, such as family and friends awaiting casualty lists. The counselor may supply information to the media to reach a wide audience. Many interventions are based on a single point of contact where the counselor tries to keep survivors occupied or entertained (e.g., the counselor asks clients to help with clean up and issues cleaning supplies or distributes reading material, coloring books, and toys to children). Counselors assess survivors for sound mental health and stability during casual conversation and observation.

## RESOURCES
## NCCEV, NACCT, AND NMHA

The **National Center for Children Exposed to Violence (NCCEV)** is located at Yale University's Child Studies Center. NCCEV publishes materials for mental health providers working with children who have been subjected to acts of terror or natural disasters. The center makes a strong distinction between how to respond to natural disasters versus how to respond to acts of terror.

The **National Advisory Committee on Children and Terrorism (NACCT)** suggests that early intervention is critical in helping a child develop resiliency after a traumatic event. NACCT's material makes distinctions between age groups and cultural diversities for counselors.

**Mental Health America (MHA)** also produces materials that can be found on their website.

## THE FAMILY READINESS KIT

The Family Readiness Kit is a tool that parents can use to prepare their families for emergency situations. This disaster plan was created by the American Academy of Pediatrics. The plan involves listing emergency contacts and other pertinent information. Children are taught to keep their identification and cards listing medical needs with them in an emergency. The family designates meeting points in case of a disaster. These meeting points include a destination nearby home, a family member's or trusted friend's home in another town, and the children's school plan and meeting location. Families who evacuate their homes must shut off all utility, fuel, and water supplies, circumstances permitting. It is recommended that the family also leave a note stating their destination. The **Family Readiness Kit** can be found on the AAP's website.

## NASP RESOURCES AND ARC

The **National Association of School Psychologists (NASP)** has prepared a publication that adults can use with children subjected to terrorism. The leaflet, *A National Tragedy, Helping Children Cope: Tips for Parents and Teachers* is available on the NASP website. A trusted adult uses it as a guideline to help the child regain feelings of safety and security, and to cope with the changes in his or her world following a catastrophic event.

The **American Red Cross (ARC)** recommends that families create a four-step Family Disaster Plan before an impending natural disaster or if Homeland Security anticipates terrorism. ARC states that making children part of disaster planning relieves their anxiety and feelings of helplessness during an actual event. ARC also offers a financial plan for emergency preparedness, explains how to stock an emergency supplies kit, and explains how to take care of pets in a disaster.

# Career Counseling

## HISTORICAL DEVELOPMENT OF CAREER COUNSELING FROM POST WWI

After World War I, the works of Frank Parson were incorporated into **career counseling efforts**. Interest inventories, such as those created by E. K. Strong in 1927, became more popular. In 1939, G. Frederick Kuder created his own version of interest inventories. In 1962, many counselors adopted the popular Myers-Briggs Type Indicator (MBTI) inventory. In 1973, John Holland developed a theory that led to the establishment of the Self-Directed Search, the Harrington-O'Shea Career Decision-Making System, and the Interest Finder. In 1990, Donald Super expanded the narrow ideas found in interest inventories by adding a values-based approach and an examination of personality types. The Strong Interest Inventory was revised in 1994 and 2004. Resultingly, modern and comprehensive career counseling includes the consideration of personality types, values, and interests.

## VALUES-BASED APPROACH FOUND IN CAREER COUNSELING

The value-based career theory (Brown, 2002) posited that central to career counseling is an understanding of the client's underlying values. According to this model, goal-directed behavior is stimulated by values. Values are an incentive. Therefore, the client gains satisfaction when he or she reaches a value-based goal. When the client does not reach a value-based goal successfully, disappointment and dejection are the likely outcome. Value-based goals can be well defined or based on a crystallized priority ranking. According to Brown's model, the three types of values are **cultural**, **work**, and **life values**.

Cultural values are further divided into social relations, time, and relationship to nature, activity, and self-control. Social relations are then further divided into individualism, collateralism, and hierarchy. (Collateralism's motto is: "Over and above one's basic needs, to each one according to one's needs, and from each one proportionate to one's collateral.") The values-based approach attempts to define motivating factors in order to develop a holistic lifestyle plan for the client.

### CULTURAL VALUES
#### SELF-CONTROL AND TIME

Self-control is derived from cultural values and is defined as the client's control over his or her thought patterns, emotions, and actions. The client may have some reservations, especially if the client is of certain cultures where this characteristic is prevalent (Asian American or American Indian descent). Do not alienate the reserved client by asking questions that are too personal.

**Time perspectives** are cultural values separated into future, past-future, present, and circular.

- **Future perspective clients** are unconcerned with past events.
- **Past-future perspective clients** use past events as background to learn from while developing future plans.
- **Present perspective clients** are not worried about the future and live only in the now.
- **Circular perspective clients** see time as part of nature and are unconcerned with time schedules.

Problems occur when future time perspective employers hire workers with circular time or present time perspectives, who do not understand stringent emphasis on deadlines, timeliness, and punctuality.

## SOCIAL RELATIONS

Social relations are derived from cultural values. **Social relations** are divided into individualism, collateralism, and hierarchy.

- Persons who prioritize **individualism** place a high level of importance on making independent decisions.
- Persons who prioritize **collateralism** place a high level of importance on making decisions that reflect positively on their peers or family members.
- Persons who prioritize **hierarchy** place a high level of importance on making a decision that will be approved of by the leader of their peer group or family. This is the alpha male in the patriarchal family and the alpha female in the matriarchal family.

Understanding the underlying influences that affect a client's career decision may change the delivery of career counseling to include a member of the client's social relations group.

## ACTIVITY VALUES

Activity values are derived from cultural values, and are the client's response to a dilemma that necessitates an action of some kind. In Western European cultures, the response is to do something to alleviate the problem, which is termed a **doing activity**. Persons who hold this stance may act for personal gain. Some cultures respond by waiting to see what happens next, which is termed a **being activity**. Others respond with a **being-in-becoming activity**, which is deliberating in a controlled manner before commencing action in a calm and regulated manner. Activity values define how the client may respond to a work problem. Therefore, a career counselor must determine the client's activity value to find a good job fit.

## RELATIONSHIP TO NATURE VALUES AND LIFE VALUES

Typically, persons with a strong belief in the **controlling power of nature** also hold fatalistic viewpoints. Fatalistic viewpoints define problem solving as a useless task. Some cultures hold that **people have controlling power** over nature and their environments and believe that there is every reason to problem solve.

**Life values** are classified into two groups: work and leisure. Three scales can be used to determine a client's work satisfaction. These three scales are the Values Scale, the Minnesota Importance Questionnaire, and the Life Values Inventory. The values and relationships involved in each are measured to determine levels of satisfaction felt by the client.

## *WORK VALUES*

Twenty-one work values were defined under the **Values Scale (VS)** published by Super and Nevill in 1986 as part of the Work Importance Study (WIS). These include: Ability utilization, achievement, advancement, prestige, economic security, autonomy, working conditions, authority, economic rewards, aesthetics, creativity, physical activity, social interaction, variety, social relations, altruism, cultural identity, physical prowess, personal development, risk, and lifestyle. In 1975, Weiss, Dawis, and Lofquist presented a list of needs that can be combined with the Values Scale to help determine a client's work values.

There are twenty values listed under the **MIQ or Minnesota Importance Questionnaire**, including ability utilization, achievement, social status, security, independence, working conditions, authority, activity, coworkers, compensation, creativity, variety, social service, responsibility, recognition, supervision-technical, supervision-human relationships, advancement, moral values, and company policies and practices. Clients expect fulfillment in these areas for work satisfaction.

## LIFE VALUES

The **Life Values Inventory (LVI)** was created in 1996 by Crace and Brown. They categorized values under five life spectra: Work, leisure, spirituality, citizen, and relationships to significant others. Career planning cannot be made without regard to all spectra if the client is to reach fulfillment. The client is asked to grade value statements on a scale of 1-5 based on how strongly each value guides their behavior. The values can be contained within the following categories:

- **Achievement** contains social status, advancement, and authority.
- **Belonging** contains co-workers, social interaction, and working conditions.
- **Concern for the environment** contains altruism.
- **Concern for others** contains altruism and social service.
- **Creativity** contains aesthetics.
- **Financial prosperity** contains compensation, economic rewards, security, and prestige.
- **Humility, Objective Analysis, and Interdependence** stand-alone and are not further categorized.
- **Health and activity** contain activity and physical prowess.
- **Independence** contains autonomy, variety, cultural identity, and ability utilization.
- **Responsibility** contains supervision-technical, supervision-human relationships, and composing policies and practices.
- **Privacy** contains absence of co-workers.
- **Scientific Understanding** contains knowledge of science and scientific progress.
- **Spirituality** contains moral values and altruism.

## CAREER COUNSELING PROCESS

The career counselor's role is one of **facilitator** who assists the client in coming to a decision on his or her occupational choices and in making other role choices. Collateral and hierarchical social values are of primary concern to some clients. Food and shelter are high priority for individuals who cannot find positions that meet their qualifications. This client may be forced to take on a pot-boiler job (low-paying, difficult hours, or hard labor positions taken on in order to provide life's necessities for oneself and the family). The career counselor should consider working for necessities as a short-term solution only, and encourage the client to keep looking for a long-term solution. Geography, family obligations, and disabilities affect a person's ability to gain a desired position that is satisfying. When this happens, the counselor should seek to help the client determine life roles that can bring satisfaction.

## PRIORITIES

The career counselor can understand the **client's priorities** through the following considerations:

- The career counselor must take note of the **activity values** of a client. Clients who have a future or past-future perspective on time with a doing activity value should find the decision-making process easy.
- A client who has a very strong preference for either a **collateral or hierarchical social value** may have more difficulty deciding which career or life role to take on, as opposed to the client who prioritizes individualism.
- Use an additional list of priorities to determine **job satisfaction**. Persons who value their individualism also find it important to gain direct feedback in order to feel satisfaction. Persons who have a collateral value thrive on indirect, positive feedback from family and social groups.
- The career counselor should also make note of **job requirements** as determined by the prospective supervisor, such as job-related skills, aptitude for the work, interpersonal skills, and good work habits. The client will be evaluated against the job requirements, so these should be a prominent component of the client assessment.
- Identify the **client's values as distinct** from interested family members' who attend the counseling session. Some families make known exactly what is required of the person making a career choice, and other families are less clear about the choice that should be made. This can make it difficult to define the expectations of the family or leader of the family. Regardless, the client's values and interests should be investigated as independently as possible.

## CLIENT CULTURAL IDENTIFICATION

The first step of client cultural identification is determining through a series of questions if collateral social relations exist that will play a part in the client's decision-making process. These questions will help the counselor to avoid a stance that may seem culturally insensitive or biased towards individualism. The client should be the one to determine who is involved in his or her choice. It is not up to the counselor to make this determination. Adhere to verbal and nonverbal communications in accordance with cultural expectations. The following elements of communication mean different things to different cultures and should be used with care:

- Eye contact
- Interpersonal space
- Handshakes
- Facial expressions
- Verbal expressions that involve self-disclosure
- Volume
- Rapid speech
- Interruptions of others' speech
- Pauses
- Direct communications

Avoid elevated levels of self-disclosure. Avoid probing questions that might be perceived as rude.

## FIRST STAGE OF ASSESSMENT

The first stage of a career counseling assessment requires the counselor to assess the client for mental health problems that have not been previously identified and treated. Record problems already being treated in the client's profile. Persons with multiple disabilities may need a specialist in vocational assessment, so it may be appropriate to refer the client on to a specialist. Assess clients who do not have mental health issues according to their culture, work, and life values. The goal in this assessment is to help the client reveal his or her core values and to sort out those values according to priorities. Educate the client about how his or her values influence motivation. Help the client to understand the process involved in goal setting and self-evaluation. The client can expect to be apprised of life roles that do not directly involve an occupational choice, but may provide satisfaction and fulfillment in agreement with the client's life plan.

## GOAL SETTING AND ASSESSMENT

Goal setting and assessment should occur after the client states his or her expectations, desired outcomes, and motivation. The client's **goal**:

- Does not need to be obtainable at this point
- May or may not confirm previous choice decisions
- May not meet the client's needs for life's necessities
- May not be compatible with the client's current relationships
- May require the client to change jobs
- May not meet the geographical criteria
- May not be the final product

However, if following the assessment regulations according to Brown's values-based career theory, the refinements will make the client's goal obtainable and fitting for the client's lifestyle plan.

## END RESULTS OF ASSESSMENT

The end result of the assessment process will likely produce multiple employment options for the client. Use a balance sheet tool, such as that developed by Janis and Mann in 1977, to help the client narrow down the options further. Originally, this tool was intended to help students select a college. However, the counselor can adapt the balance sheet for career occupational choices. Instruct the client on how to check O*NET (the Occupational Information Network) for up-to-date occupational data. Encourage the client to seek out professionals who are experienced in their field of interest and request informational interviews. Clients must develop employment skills, a resume, job search skills, and job interview skills. The culmination is the review of the expected outcomes discussed in the first session. Inform the client that he or she can return for further assistance.

# Areas of Clinical Focus Chapter Quiz

**1. Which of the following chromosome pairs are affected in cases of Down syndrome?**

   a. 12
   b. 13
   c. 19
   d. 21

**2. Which of the following is NOT a type of value according to Brown's value-based career theory (2002)?**

   a. Moral
   b. Cultural
   c. Work
   d. Life

**3. Which of the following medicines would you NOT expect to be involved in treatment for a patient with Tourette's syndrome?**

   a. Methylphenidate
   b. Haloperidol
   c. Pimozide
   d. Clonidine

**4. What is the earliest a child can be diagnosed with encopresis per DSM-5 criteria?**

   a. 7 years old
   b. 6 years old
   c. 5 years old
   d. 4 years old

**5. Which of the following is NOT a subtype of specific phobia?**

   a. Animal
   b. Natural environment
   c. Irrational
   d. Blood-injection-injury

**6. Which of the following is considered the best treatment for a specific phobia?**

   a. Psychopharmacology
   b. In vivo exposure
   c. Multicomponent cognitive-behavioral therapy
   d. Hypnosis

**7. An Amytal interview would have most likely been used to treat which of the following disorders?**

   a. Motor disorder
   b. Conduct disorder
   c. Conversion disorder
   d. Adjustment disorder

**8. Which of the following is considered a Cluster C personality disorder?**
   a. Obsessive-compulsive
   b. Schizoid
   c. Antisocial
   d. Histrionic

**9. According to the National Institute of Alcohol Abuse and Alcoholism, what percentage of Americans drink alcohol as part of their daily routine?**
   a. 35%
   b. 50%
   c. 75%
   d. 85%

**10. All of the following are stages experienced by survivors in the aftermath of a disaster EXCEPT?**
   a. Villain stage
   b. Honeymoon period
   c. Disillusionment stage
   d. Reconstruction period

# Treatment Planning

## Theoretical Frameworks

### THEORIES OF CARL JUNG

**Jung's archetypes** are the images and concepts that develop the collective unconscious of humanity. The main archetypes are:

- **The Way**: The image of a journey or voyage through life
- **The Self**: The aspect of the mind that unifies and orders experience
- **Animus and Anima**: The image of gender
- **Rebirth**: The concept of being reborn, resurrected or reincarnated
- **Persona**: The role or mask one shows to others
- **Shadow**: The dark side of one's personality
- **Stock characters**: Dramatic roles that appear over and over in folktales
- **The Hero**: The character who vanquishes evil and rescues the downtrodden
- **The Trickster**: The character who plays pranks or works magic spells
- **The Sage**: The wise old person
- **Power**: A symbol such as the eagle or the sword
- **Number**: Certain numbers appear throughout history and across cultures

The two **attitudinal types** according to Jung are:

- **Introvert**: One oriented toward the inner, subjective world
- **Extrovert**: One oriented toward the outer, external world

The four **functional types** according to Jung are:

- **Thinking**: An intellectual process involving ideas
- **Feeling**: An evaluative function involving value or worth
- **Sensing**: A function involving recognition that something exists, without categorizing or evaluating it
- **Intuiting**: A function involving creative inspiration without having all the facts

### THEORIES OF SIGMUND FREUD
#### PSYCHOANALYTIC/PSYCHODYNAMIC PERSONALITY THEORY

**Sigmund Freud**, commonly known as the father of psychoanalysis, based his practice on **psychoanalytic and psychodynamic personality theories**. The foundations of these theories are based on the following concepts.

**Levels of awareness**:

- **Conscious**: Thoughts, feelings, desires of which a person is aware and able to control.
- **Preconscious**: Thoughts, feelings, desires not in immediate awareness but can be recalled to consciousness.
- **Unconscious**: Thoughts, feelings, desires not available to the conscious mind

**Stages of development**: Each person passes through stages of psychosexual development (can become trapped in any stage):

- **Oral**: Focus on sucking and swallowing
- **Anal**: Focus on spontaneous bowel movements or control over impulses
- **Phallic**: Focus on genital region, and identification with parent of same gender
- **Latency**: Sexual impulses are dormant, focus on coping with the environment
- **Genital**: Focus on erotic and genital behavior, leading to development of mature sexual and emotional relationships

**Personality structure**: The personality has three main components:

- **Id**: Unconscious pleasure principle, manifest by a desire for immediate and complete satisfaction with disregard for others
- **Ego**: Rational and conscious reality principle, which weighs actions and consequences
- **Superego**: Conscious and unconscious censoring force of the personality, which evaluates and judges behavior

Common **Freudian psychiatric terms** include:

- **Oedipus Complex or Electra Conflict**: At the age of four or five, the child falls in love with the parent of the opposite sex and feels hostility toward the parent of the same sex.
- **Defense mechanisms**: Conscious or unconscious actions or thoughts designed to protect the ego from anxiety.
- **Freudian slips**: Also known as parapraxes, these are overt actions with unconscious meanings.
- **Free association**: A method designed to discover the contents of the unconscious by associating words with other words or emotions.
- **Transference**: Transference takes place when feelings, attitudes and/or wishes linked with a significant figure in one's early life, which are projected onto others in one's current life.
- **Counter-transference**: This happens when the feelings and attitudes of the therapist that are projected onto the client inappropriately.
- **Resistance**: Resistance is anything that prohibits a person from retrieving information from the unconscious.
- **Fixation**: Someone who is bogged-down in one stage of development has a fixation.

> **Review Video: Who was Sigmund Freud?**
> Visit mometrix.com/academy and enter code: 473747

### FREUD'S CONCEPT OF SUPEREGO

Freud coined the word *superego* to make sense out of the rules imposed upon us by our parents. Rules involving parents, family, religion, and culture contribute to our sense of right and wrong. The problem arises whenever a rule has been imposed that is unrelenting and harsh. Freud linked this to his interview of female clients. Victorian women had difficulty accepting their sexual urges as a natural occurrence. This conflict of right and wrong caused the females to experience hysterical paralysis and other notable anxiety disorders. However, symptoms were alleviated when the clients gained insight and emotional release from their inner turmoil. **Free association** is the client's expression concerning secretive and painful thoughts, feelings, and memories in a non-judgmental

therapy session. The therapeutic bond or relationship is imperative in this technique. Free association used in this way can still be beneficial today.

> **Review Video: How do the Id, Ego, and Superego Interact?**
> Visit mometrix.com/academy and enter code: 690435

## FREUD'S CONCEPT OF TRANSFERENCE

Freud's concept of **transference** can be applied to the exchanges that take place between the modern client and the mental health care provider. The client's propensity is to behave toward the provider as one would a key authority figure. The provider can help the client understand this propensity and work to help the client alter this unconscious transference to other people. Awareness of transference must become a part of the client's conscious thought. The client must be aware when this has happened and seek to change the behavior on a conscious level. Cognitive rethinking techniques and behavioristic role plays enable the provider's efforts to get the client to work through a maladaptive behavior. The provider can also use a variety of techniques to help the client internalize positive feelings and thought patterns.

## UNCONSCIOUS MIND IN CONJUNCTION WITH PSYCHODYNAMIC THEORIES

Sigmund Freud's theories involve getting at **unconscious thoughts** that cause behaviors. The client must come to terms with unconscious thoughts rather than bottle up those feelings, and thus deal with issues in a more functional manner. **Psychodynamic theorists** of today try to help the client make a connection between the past and existing problems. However, a cognitive-behavioral approach may need to be supplemented with in-depth counseling. Some topics that may require further investigation are the client's family and parental interactions, unresolved issues, unconscious practices, and defensive mechanisms. Freud believed pathological thinking was at odds with the id instincts of Eros and Thanatos. Eros stands for the life processes involving love and relationships. Thanatos stands for death processes involving negative emotions and the fighting response. The mind is trying to manage these forces, which causes anxiety and the client forms phobias or conversion disorders.

## OBJECT-RELATIONS SCHOOL

The **Object-Relations School** looks at the primary caregiver relationship in a child's early years of growth. A positive parental relationship leads the infant to understand about safety, security, self-worth, nurturance, and caring. The infant grows into a child with a positive self-identity and is better able to form healthy relationships with others. Those infants that have a negative parental relationship feel unloved, detested, valueless, insignificant, inferior, and shamed. These images form the person's personality and behaviors. The inner belief system is referred to as the schema in the cognitive therapy model. It is known as the **incorporated object relation** in the psychodynamic model. Object-relations take into account the Freudian theories regarding instinctive urges. These urges are the driving force to form either loving or destructive relationships. The client explores the repressed feelings in front of a provider who has created a safe and trusted setting.

## ALFRED ALDER'S THEORY OF INDIVIDUAL PSYCHOLOGY

Alder's **key concepts** include:

- Inferiority feelings are the source of all human striving.
- Personal growth results from one's attempts to compensate for this inferiority.

Two types of **complexes** exist:

- **Inferiority**: An inability to solve life's problems
- **Superiority**: An exaggerated opinion of one's abilities and accomplishments in an attempt to compensate for an inferiority complex

The goal of life is to strive for superiority. Lifestyle is the unique set of behaviors created to compensate for inferiority and to achieve superiority.

Alder also theorized that **birth order** affects personality:

- **First born**: Happy, secure, and the center of attention until dethroned by the second child; interested in authority and organization
- **Second born**: Born into a more relaxed atmosphere and has the first-born as a model; interested in competition
- **Youngest child**: Pet of the family and may retain a sense of dependency

## FRITZ PERLS' GESTALT THERAPY

The removal of masks and facades is the goal of Gestalt therapy, according to Perls. A creative interaction needs to be developed so the client can gain an ongoing awareness of what is being felt, sensed, and thought. **Boundary disturbances** (lack of awareness of the immediate environment) may occur:

- **Projection**: Fantasy of what another person is experiencing
- **Introjection**: Accepting the beliefs and opinions of others without question
- **Retroflection**: Turning back on oneself that which is meant for someone else
- **Confluence**: Merging with the environment
- **Deflection**: Interfering with contact, used by receivers and senders of messages

**Goal of therapy** is integration of self and world awareness. **Techniques** of therapy include:

- **Playing the projection**: Taking on and experiencing the role of another person
- **Making the rounds**: Speaking or doing something to other group members to experiment with new behavior
- **Sentence completion**: "I take responsibility for…"
- **Exaggeration** of a feeling or action to clarify the purpose or intent
- **Empty chair dialogue**: Having an interaction with an imaginary provocateur
- **Dream world**: Explored by describing and playing parts of a dream

## CARL ROGERS' CLIENT CENTERED THEORY

Key concepts in **Carl Rogers' client centered theory** include:

- The **attributes** of the therapist
- **Congruence**: inner feelings match outer actions
- **Unconditional positive regard**: therapist sees the client as a person of intrinsic worth and treats the client non-judgmentally
- **Empathic understanding**: therapist is a sensitive listener

The **goal of therapy** is helping the client become a fully functioning person, achieving this goal by:

- Relinquishing facades
- Banishing "oughts"
- Becoming a non-conformist by moving away from cultural expectations
- Becoming self-directed as opposed to pleasing others
- Dropping defenses
- Trusting one's own intuition
- Accepting others

## NEUROLINGUISTIC PROGRAMMING

The major concepts of **neurolinguistic programming (NLP)** according to Bandler and Grinder include:

- **Representational Systems**: Sensory models through which people access information, such as audio, visual and kinesthetic models. Cues to representational systems are patterns which can be heard or observed.
  - Preferred predicates: a "view" that suggests a visual system
  - Eye-Accessing cues: looking upward suggests a visual system
  - Hand movements: pointing toward the ear suggests an auditory system
  - Breathing patterns: suggest a kinesthetic system
  - Speech pattern/tone: suggests an auditory system
- **Language structure**:
  - Surface structure: sentences that native speakers of a language speak and write
  - Deep structure: the linguistic representations from which the surface structures of a language are derived
  - Ambiguity: a surface language may represent more than one deep structure
- **Human modeling**: The process of representing something through language
  - Generalization: specific experiences that come to represent the entire category of which they are a member
  - Deletion: selected portions of the world are excluded from the representation created by an individual
  - Distortion: the relationship among the parts of the model which differ from the relationships they were supposed to represent

## JOHN HATTIE'S THEORY OF SELF CONCEPT

The major concepts of **Hattie's theory of self-concep**t include:

- A cognitive appraisal consisting of beliefs about the self
- Expectations from self and others: High expectations can lead to low self-esteem and vice versa

**Descriptions of oneself** are:

- **Hierarchical**: From a description of simple or isolated characteristics to an all-inclusive description of the self
- **Multifaceted**: Having numerous dimensions

Methods of **integration** across dimensions include:

- **Self-verification**: Soliciting feedback to confirm the anticipated view of the self
- **Self-consistency**: Internal harmony among opinions, attitudes, and values
- **Self-complexity**: Viewing the self as complex and multifaceted
- **Self-enhancement**: Viewing the self's positive qualities as more important than the self's negative qualities

## NEUROBIOLOGICAL THEORIES

The general features and findings foundational to **neurobiological theories** include:

- Cognitive and emotional dysfunctions may result from any insult that affects the brain's neurotransmitters, such as genetic anomalies, infection, and nutrition.
- Neurotransmitters, such as acetylcholine, are chemical substances found in the nervous system that carry messages from the axon of one neuron to the receptor site on another. In the brain, these neurotransmitters may affect cognitive, emotional, and behavioral functioning. After utilization, neurotransmitters are either inactivated by enzymatic degradation (such as a cholinesterase) or are drawn back into the presynaptic neuron.
- Psychotherapeutic drugs are prescribed to influence the process of neurotransmitter production and absorption in an attempt to establish a "normal" neurochemical balance.

## THEORIES OF EMOTION

Cross-cultural research has distinguished six basic **universal human emotions**: Fear, anger, happiness, disgust, surprise, and sadness. The **James-Lange theory** of emotion asserts that emotions are the body's reaction to changes in the autonomic nervous system caused by external stimuli. This theory is supported by the fact that quadriplegics report feeling less-intense emotions. The **Cannon-Bard theory** of emotion proposes that the body and emotions react to stimuli based on thalamic stimulation of the cortex and peripheral nervous system. The **two-factor theory of Schachter and Singer** proposes that emotions are the result of arousal, the cognitive interpretation of that arousal, and the environment in which the arousal occurs.

## CHANGE THEORIES

### TRANSTHEORETICAL MODEL

The **transtheoretical model** focuses on changes in behavior based on the individual's decisions (not on society's decisions or others' decisions) and is used to develop strategies to promote changes in health behavior. This model outlines stages people go through when changing problem behavior and trying to have a positive attitude about change. Stages of change include the following:

- **Precontemplation**: The person is either unaware or under-informed about consequences of a problem behavior and has no intention of changing behavior within the next 6 months.
- **Contemplation**: The person is aware of costs and benefits of changing behavior and intends to change within the next 6 months but is procrastinating and not ready for action.
- **Preparation**: The person has a plan and intends to initiate change in the near future (≤1 month) and is ready for action plans.
- **Action**: The person is modifying behavior change occurs only if behavior meets a set criterion (such as complete abstinence from drinking).
- **Maintenance**: The person works to maintain changes and gains confidence that he or she will not relapse.

## MOTIVATIONAL INTERVIEWING

**Motivational interviewing** (Miller, 1983) aims to help people identify and resolve issues regarding ambivalence about change and focuses on the role of motivation to bring about change. MI is a collaborative approach in which the interviewer assesses the individual's readiness to accept change and identifies strategies that may be effective with the individual.

| Elements | Principles | Strategies |
|---|---|---|
| **Collaboration** rather than confrontation in resolving issues<br>**Evocation** (drawing out) of the individual's ideas about change rather than imposition of the interviewer's ideas<br>**Autonomy** of the individual in making changes | **Expression of empathy**: Showing understanding of individual's perceptions<br>**Support of self-efficacy**: Helping individuals realize they are capable of change<br>**Acceptance of resistance**: Avoiding struggles/conflicts with client<br>**Examination of discrepancies**: Helping individuals see discrepancy between their behavior and goals | **Avoiding Yes/No questions**: Asking informational questions<br>**Providing affirmations**: Indicating areas of strength<br>**Providing reflective listening**: Responding to statements<br>**Providing summaries**: Recapping important points of discussion<br>**Encouraging change talk**: Including desire, ability, reason, and need |

## RESISTANCE TO ORGANIZATIONAL CHANGE

Performance improvement processes cannot occur without organizational change, and **resistance to change** is common for many people, so coordinating collaborative processes requires anticipating resistance and taking steps to achieve cooperation. Resistance often relates to concerns about job loss, increased responsibilities, and general denial or lack of understanding and frustration. Leaders can prepare others involved in the process of change by taking these steps:

- Be honest, informative, and tactful, giving people thorough information about anticipated changes and how the changes will affect them, including positives.
- Be patient in allowing people the time they need to contemplate changes and express anger or disagreement.
- Be empathetic in listening carefully to the concerns of others.
- Encourage participation, allowing staff to propose methods of implementing change so they feel some sense of ownership.
- Establish a climate in which all staff members are encouraged to identify the need for change on an ongoing basis.
- Present further ideas for change to management.

# Theory Development

## PHILOSOPHICAL FOUNDATIONS OF COUNSELING

The philosophical foundations of counseling are based on various theoretical approaches to human nature, behavior, and interactions:

- **Immanuel Kant** held the assumption that reality is based on subjective observations drawn from a person's objective reality or environmental events. Kant's theories are based on interactionism.
- **Sigmund Freud** found Kant's interactionism offered a starting point for his psychoanalytical work.
- **Gottfried Leibniz** was a philosopher who believed in personology, which states that a person can change when his or her perceptual awareness is changed. Leibniz's **theory of mind** is based on subjective reality—how a person perceives things to be within his or her own mind. Leibniz's **theory of personology** evolved into humanistic psychology, resulting in a counseling model known as **Rogers' person-centered psychotherapy**.
- **John Locke** held a more empiricist viewpoint, believing the human brain absorbs environmental events and sensory inputs from its surroundings in an effort to form meaning and knowledge, so studying only nature and the environment unlocks a person's mental health needs. Locke's empiric theories evolved into behavior therapy and behavioral counseling.

Despite the differences in philosophies, the goal of each of these psychotherapy models is the same. Each works to transform a person's thought patterns to affect the way that person handles emotional responses and behaves.

## STAGES OF THEORY DEVELOPMENT

The stages of theory development can be divided into five paradigms:

| Stage | Paradigm | Theorists |
|-------|----------|-----------|
| 1 | Original Paradigm | Freud's psychoanalysis, client-centered therapy, and behavior therapy |
| 2 | Paradigm Modification | Jung, Adler, Patterson, Bandura |
| 3 | Paradigm Specificity | Berne, Jourard, Genlin, Bech, and Krumboltz |
| 4 | Paradigm Experimentation | Strupp, Mitchell and Aron, Ellis, Beutler, Wexler, and Lazarus |
| 5 | Paradigm Consolidation | Lazarus, Seay, and Beutler |

In the **paradigm modification stage**, Jung, Adler, Patterson, and Bandura adapted Freud's **original paradigm** (which was the foundation for psychoanalysis, client-centered therapy, and behavior therapy). Adaptation was necessary because the original paradigm of development theory did not adequately answer all of the questions these theorists raised. Jung had a more restrained viewpoint regarding Freud's bisexual theories. Adler had a more social viewpoint regarding Freud's theories. Modification stage theorists worked to add to the developing paradigm without making revolutionary changes.

In the **paradigm specificity stage**, changes to counseling tactics were initiated by theorists Berne, Jourard, Genlin, Beck, and Krumboltz. Berne replaced Freud's superego, id, and ego with adapted terms referring to the parent, child, and adult. Berne's new nomenclature allowed Freud's work to remain intact, except for minor alterations in terminology.

In the **paradigm experimentation stage**, Strupp, Mitchell, Aron, Ellis, Beutler, Wexler, and Lazarus initiated changes to the rules for conducting counseling sessions. Experimentation stage theorists began making abstract structures, practices, and paradigm-linked procedures. Stages 1-3 of theory development were greatly altered. Old parameters were disregarded by radical behaviorists who accepted more humanistic, cognitive processing theories. Humanists adopted relaxation techniques common to the behaviorist theories. The models found in stage 4 are inconsistent, without the foundational supports of previous paradigms, and are not reconciled with a philosophy.

Stage 5, **paradigm consolidation**, is in its infancy, started by the continued exploration of Lazarus, Seay, and Beutler. There are more developments along its horizon.

## MOTIVES FOR PSYCHOTHERAPY

According to Joseph Rychlak, psychotherapy can be broken down into three basic motives that correspond with learning, ethics, and healing.

- **Scholarly motive** corresponds with learning. Rychlak believed this rationale for performing psychotherapy was best characterized in the works of Freud, where the psychotherapist is a scientist who records the inner workings of the mind, instinctive drives, and actions, and then analyzes the data collected.
- **Ethical motive** refers to the counselor's desire to help the client grow and express strong feelings and opinions about his or her life problems.
- **Curative motive** is when the psychotherapist wants to initiate the healing process for the client by engaging in such a way as to help modify those behaviors detrimental to the client's success in society.

## THEORIES THAT VIOLATE PARADIGM PARAMETERS

There are various theories that violate basic paradigm parameters. Examples include the following:

- Cognitive-behavioral theory operates on a person's interaction with his or her surroundings. Environmental interaction is based on the person's cognitive abilities to organize information. Cognitive-behavioral theory violates the paradigm parameters found in Lockean philosophy.
- Robert Carkhuff violated Leibniz' theories in his affective-behavioral approach therapy that reinterpreted Carl Rogers' work.

Non-conformity or violation is known as **technical eclecticism**. Technical eclecticism is designed to improve the therapist's ability to select the best treatment for the client, based on validated procedures, strategies, and applied techniques. Therapists choose a treatment focus and specific strategies that are consistent with the client's coping style, resistance level, and emotional arousal.

## DE-EMPHASIS ON THEORETICAL DEPENDENCY

Thomas Kuhn (1962) suggested that psychotherapists adopt a single paradigm instead of the many paradigms already in place. Kuhn's suggestion was embraced in Lazarus' technical eclecticism, which allows more freedom of selection in choosing preferred or best theoretical models. Eclectic approaches allow for a mixture of different models. One example is to mix Freud's psychoanalytic approaches with Beck's cognitive theory. Another example is models that are founded on phenomenological knowledge structures, which incorporate Rogers' person-centered therapy. Some combine Wolpe's behavior therapy and behavior modification strategies. Model lines become indistinguishable when combinations of theoretical models cease to follow more structured guidelines. Abbreviations that demonstrate this blending are as follows: CB is a mixture of cognitive and behavioral standards, CA is a mixture of information processing structures with affective models, AB is a mixture of affective models with behavioral standards, and CAB is a combination of all three.

# Treatment Planning Chapter Quiz

**1. Stage 2 of theory development is:**

   a. The original paradigm
   b. Paradigm modification
   c. Paradigm experimentation
   d. Paradigm consolidation

**2. The unconscious motivation ruled by the pleasure principle is known as the:**

   a. Ego
   b. Id
   c. Superego
   d. Shadow

**3. Which of the following is one of Jung's archetypes?**

   a. The World
   b. The King
   c. The Hero
   d. The Villain

**4. Who developed Gestalt therapy?**

   a. Alder
   b. Rogers
   c. Perls
   d. Hattie

**5. Which of the following is NOT a basic universal emotion?**

   a. Fear
   b. Anger
   c. Surprise
   d. Guilt

**6. Which of the following lists the stages of change of the transtheoretical model from FIRST to LAST?**

   a. Precontemplation, Contemplation, Preparation, Action, Maintenance
   b. Preparation, Precontemplation, Contemplation, Action, Maintenance
   c. Precontemplation, Contemplation, Maintenance, Preparation, Action
   d. Preparation, Action, Maintenance, Precontemplation, Contemplation

**7. Who developed the theory of personology?**

   a. Leibniz
   b. Rogers
   c. Locke
   d. Kant

**8. Which of the following is NOT one of Rychlak's three basic motives?**

   a. Scholarly motive
   b. Ethical motive
   c. Curative motive
   d. Carnal motive

**9. Which of the following is NOT a strategy employed in motivational interviewing?**

    a. Providing affirmations
    b. Avoiding Yes/No questions
    c. Providing reflective listening
    d. Discouraging change talk

**10. Freudian slips are overt actions with unconscious meanings, also known as which of the following?**

    a. Dormant impulses
    b. Parapraxes
    c. Cathexis
    d. Anti-cathexis

# Counseling Skills and Interventions

## Therapeutic Frameworks

### HISTORICAL IMPACT ON THERAPEUTIC INTERVENTIONS

**Therapeutic interventions** require the use of foundational models incorporating philosophy, theory, and practice methodologies. The disadvantage of applying past solutions is their tendency to hinder the application of unconventional solutions not found in old psychotherapy treatment manuals. Unconventional solutions may work for the individual who has not had success with a conventional method, though it may have previously worked for another client. Mental health care has undergone a progressive development throughout time. Therapeutic trends have become part of the accepted model for mental health care. Institutions of the past have been replaced with community treatment centers that have had an innovative impact on mental health. Treatments have become more **psychologically based** as clients' surroundings have become a factor. Psychologically-trained and educationally-trained counselors have begun to specialize.

### COUNSELING VS. PSYCHOTHERAPY

Some practitioners use the terms counseling and psychotherapy interchangeably to indicate the same service. However, those practitioners who believe these terms are not identical state the difference lies in the class of client that receives treatment. Other substantive differences in terminology include: the kind of therapy received, degree and nature of illness, clinical work setting or environment in which treatment is received, and the training received by the therapist. **Counseling** is a treatment that allows the client to express emotions while the therapist provides support, education, and feedback. However, **psychotherapy** is a remediation process that involves getting to the root cause of the problem. Neither counselor nor psychotherapist can make these divisions in treatment, as there is a distinctive overlap when talking with the client.

### COGNITIVE-BEHAVIORAL THERAPY

**Cognitive-behavioral therapy (CBT)** focuses on the impact that thoughts have on behavior and feelings and encourages the individual to use the power of **rational thought** to alter perceptions and behavior. This approach to counseling is usually short-term, about twelve to twenty sessions, with the first sessions used to obtain a history, the middle sessions used to focus on problems, and last sessions used to review and reinforce. Individuals are assigned "homework" during the sessions to practice new ways of thinking and to develop new coping strategies. The therapist helps the individual identify **goals** and then find ways to achieve those goals. CBT acknowledges that all problems cannot be resolved, but one can deal differently with problems. The therapist asks many questions to determine the individual's areas of concern and encourages the individual to question his or her own motivations and needs. CBT is goal-centered so each counseling session is structured toward a particular goal, such as coping techniques. CBT centers on the concept of unlearning previous behaviors and learning new ones, questioning behaviors, and doing homework. Different approaches to CBT include Aaron Beck's cognitive therapy, rational emotive behavior therapy, and dialectic behavior therapy.

#### COGNITIVE-BEHAVIORAL GROUP THERAPY FOR SOCIAL PHOBIAS

**Cognitive-behavioral group therapy (CBGT) for social phobias** is a form of **exposure therapy** done in a group environment, usually limited to about six clients with one or (preferably) two therapists to monitor and guide group exercises. Having an equal mix of men and women is preferred because social phobias often involve male-female interactions. Clients with different

215

types of fears are appropriate for the group because they complement each other during therapy. The initial sessions involve psychoeducation about phobias and basic instruction in cognitive restructuring, including identifying automatic thoughts and discussing how they are errors in thinking. During exercises, such as speaking in front of the group, clients are asked to express their automatic thoughts and discuss them. The **subjective units of distress rating scale** (0–10 scale of distress) is used throughout exercises with clients giving their score every minute. Each client is provided with individualized homework. Sessions are usually weekly for 2–3 hours for 12–24 weeks.

### PERSONAL SCIENCE

**Personal Science** was developed in 1977 by Michael Mahoney, based on the cognitive-behavioral (CB) approach. The acronym SCIENCE is used to explain the sequential steps through which the therapist guides the client to solve a problem:

- **S** for *specification* of the problem
- **C** for *collection* of data or facts
- **I** for *identification* of patterns or reasons for existing behaviors
- **E** for *examination* of choices that can be used to modify behavior
- **N** for *narrowing* the options and experimenting with possible modifications
- **C** for *comparing* data or facts
- **E** for *expanding*, modifying, or substituting unwanted behaviors

### PSYCHOBEHAVIORAL THERAPY AND COGNITIVE-CLIENT THERAPY

**Psychobehavioral therapy** was developed in 1971 by George E. Woody. This is simply a combination of two psychoanalytic and behavioral techniques with a variety of eclectic approaches. Psychobehavioral therapy is based on the cognitive-behavioral (CB) approach.

**Cognitive-client therapy** was a cognitive-affective (CA) model designed by David Wexler in 1974. He used **information processing theory** as the foundation for his beliefs concerning cognitive roles. Wexler postulated that client-centered therapy was better established by combining affective experience with cognitive thoughts. Wexler's belief was similar to those of the cognitive-behaviorists. He believed that the client could gain control over his or her behavior through cognitive deliberations. Wexler also believed that emotional experiencing could not be accomplished without a forerunner of cognitive thought processes.

### ACCEPTANCE COMMITMENT THERAPY

**Acceptance commitment therapy (ACT)** approaches behavioral change from a different perspective than conventional CBT. Clients are encouraged to examine their thought processes (**cognitive defusion**) when undergoing episodes of anxiety or depression. They identify a thought, such as "People think I am ugly," and then analyze whether or not this is true, listing evidence, and then evaluating whether or not the anxiety is decreased after this evaluation process. Eventually, this process becomes automatic, eliminating the need to write everything down. Mindfulness is a basic concept of ACT, and clients are encouraged to examine their values and control those things that are under their control, such as their facial expression or actions. ACT represents:

- **A**: Accepting reactions
- **C**: Choosing a direction
- **T**: Taking action to effect change.

## Aaron Beck's Cognitive Therapy

Aaron Beck discovered that during psychotherapy clients often had a second set of thoughts while undergoing "free association." Beck called these **automatic thoughts**, which were labeled and interpreted, according to a personal set of rules. Beck called dysfunctional automatic thoughts **cognitive disorders**. Beck identified a triad of negative thoughts regarding the self, the environment, and the world. The key concepts in **Aaron Beck's cognitive therapy** include the following:

- **Therapist/client relationship**: Therapy is a collaborative partnership. The goal of therapy is determined together. The therapist encourages the client to disagree when appropriate.
- **Process of therapy**: The therapist explains the following: the perception of reality is not reality. The interpretation of sensory input depends on cognitive processes. The client is taught to recognize maladaptive ideation, identifying observable behavior, underlying motivation, and his or her thoughts and beliefs. The client practices distancing the maladaptive thoughts, explores his or her conclusions, and tests them against reality.
- **Conclusions**: The client makes the rules less extreme and absolute, drops false rules, and substitutes adaptive rules.

## Eric Berne's Transactional Analysis

The major concepts of **transactional analysis** according to Eric Berne are:

- **Ego State**: One's personal frame of mind
- **Parent**: Parents who exhibit feelings/behaviors learned from their parents, which may be nurturing or critical
- **Adult**: An individual who exhibits feelings/behaviors of a mature adult
- **Child**: An individual who exhibits feelings/behaviors natural to children under seven years old
- **Transaction**: Verbal and nonverbal communication between two people
- **Complementary transactions**: A message sent from the ego state of Person A which is responded to in that same ego state, or a message sent to the ego state of Person B which is responded to in that same ego state
- **Crossed transactions**: A message sent from the ego state of Person A which is responded to in another ego state, or a message sent to the ego state of Person B which is responded to from another ego state
- **Ulterior transactions**: messages that occur on two levels, the social or overt level and the hidden or psychological level

## Behaviorism

Behaviorists anticipate that the client can unlearn dysfunctional behaviors. Pavlov cultivated his theories from experiments where he conditioned dogs to salivate to different stimuli. Watson and Rayner experimented on a young boy by conditioning his response to white, furry animals, causing the boy to develop a phobia. This can be related to a person's development of a phobia after a negative experience. Some people become afraid of the water after a near drowning experience. Addictive cravings, anxieties, insomnia, and pain management may be improved with relaxation training and methodical desensitization techniques. B. F. Skinner's experiments involved operant conditioning, where he proposed that feelings and actions are reinforced and rewarded. Therefore, the way to stop a behavior is to take away the reinforcement. For example, a child who exhibits misbehaviors in school may be doing so to gain the teacher's attention.

## OPERANT CONDITIONING

**Operant conditioning** is based on feelings and actions that are reinforced and rewarded. The way to stop the behavior is to take away the reinforcement. An explanation for a client's pathological behavior is that it was reinforced. Behaviorists look for rewards that may cause their client to act out inappropriately. For example, a person who feels isolated may experience health problems out of a need to gain attention from hospital staff and or family. Token economy and contingency contractual agreements are the result of operant conditioning. Albert Bandura created **social learning theory** in 1969, based on people learning from watching others. Violence on television has been linked to real life violent acts by social learning theory. Proponents say a more functional TV model should be presented to replace the pathological behavior. Behaviorists use relaxation techniques, imagery, systematic desensitization, reinforcement contingencies, positive role modeling, and token economies.

## ALBERT ELLIS'S RATIONAL EMOTIVE THERAPY

Key concepts of **Albert Ellis's rational emotive therapy** include the idea that people control their own destinies and interpret events, according to their own values and beliefs.

**Forms of irrational beliefs** include:

- Something is awful or terrible
- One cannot tolerate something
- Something or someone is damned or cursed

**"Musturbatory" ideologies** have three forms:

- I must do well and win approval or I am a rotten person.
- You must act kindly toward me or you are a rotten person.
- My life must remain comfortable or life hardly seems worth living.

**Therapy** consists of detecting and eradicating irrational beliefs, as follows:

- **Disputing**: Detecting irrationalities, debating them, discriminating between logical and illogical thinking, and defining what helps create new beliefs
- **Debating**: Questioning and disputing the irrational beliefs
- **Discriminating**: Distinguishing between wants and needs, desires and demands, and rational and irrational ideas
- **Defining**: Defining words and redefining beliefs

## RATIONAL BEHAVIOR THERAPY

**Rational behavior therapy** was developed in 1977 by Maxie C. Maultsby, Jr. It is a more direct method of dealing with a client's emotional state than Ellis' rational emotive therapy from the mid-1950's. Maultsby was Albert Ellis' student. Rational behavior is based on the cognitive-behavioral (CB) approach and has five steps, known as **emotional re-education**:

1. **Self-analysis** using rational thought helps the client to gain intellectual insights.
2. **Changing actions** or behaviors to reflect newly gained intellectual insights.
3. **Cognitive emotive dissonance** is a refocus of attention that helps the client bring feelings and thought patterns into alignment with each other.
4. **Rationalized feelings** promote cohesive thought patterns through consistent emotional insights.
5. **Habitual practice** of newly gained insights develops new personality traits in the client.

## Multimodal Behavior Therapy

**Multimodal Behavior Therapy** was invented in 1971 by Arnold Lazarus. This is a complex system that mingles client-conceptualization theories into all the human modalities of cognition, affect, and behavior that cannot be excluded from a client's everyday life. Lazarus believed that there were exactly seven modalities. He used the acronym **BASIC ID** to explain each one:

- **B** for *behavior*
- **A** for *affect*
- **S** for *sensory*
- **I** for *imagery*
- **C** for *cognition*
- **I** for *intrapersonal*
- **D** for *drugs*

**Multimodal Behavior Therapy** has no guide for which technique to choose for treatment, no set therapy process, or sequential steps to take. Multimodal Behavior Therapy identifies a theme, and then the therapist utilizes the BASIC ID techniques for treating the client.

> **Review Video: <u>Multimodal Behavior Therapy</u>**
> Visit mometrix.com/academy and enter code: 813824

## RECOVERY MODEL

The recovery model approach to mental health **shifts control** of treatment options to the client rather than the provider deciding the plan of care. This has been effective in those clients who have the capacity to make decisions to allow them to be more independent and take a more active role in the decision-making regarding their treatment plan. The goal of this model is to allow the client to be more **autonomous** so that they may achieve the ultimate goals of finding employment and housing and living independently. The more independent the client can become, the more they progress to making independent decisions about the treatment of their mental health issues. This model is not appropriate for those clients who are so incapacitated by their illness that they do not understand they are ill. The amount of independence and decision-making that is turned over to the client should increase as they become more stable.

## PHYSIOLOGICAL FOUNDATION FOR PSYCHOTHERAPY

The **physiological foundation for psychotherapy** is gaining momentum as research in this area advances. Biopsychological research is based on the notion that biological systems in the body are linked to human behaviors. Prescription drugs are used to alter brain chemistry to help the client cope with imbalances in their biological systems. An alternative or supplement to drug therapy is exercise that releases endorphins and helps the client to decrease feelings of depression. In the past, the person receiving psychological treatment was treated more like a casualty who was responsible for his or her own injured state. The mental health provider held to the belief that the client's mental state, shortfalls involving relationships, and maladaptive behaviors were at the root of the client's mental disorder.

## ORGANIZATIONAL MODELS FOR PSYCHOECOLOGICAL DELIVERY

The **organizational models for psychoecological delivery** were identified by Seay in 1983. Care can be delivered through direct preventive interventions, remedial, or aftercare systems.

- **Direct preventive interventions** are the primary delivery target.
- **Remedial care** is the secondary delivery target.
- **Aftercare** is tertiary prevention.

These five areas are addressed:

- Residential
- Community
- Educational
- Business and political arenas
- The private sector

Services offered include:

- Individual psychotherapy
- Group psychotherapy
- Family psychotherapy
- Educational courses
- Synchronization of services
- Restructuring the client's surroundings
- Making contacts within the community
- Advocacy
- Referral
- Ongoing professional instruction and training
- Psychodiagnostics
- Research and assessment
- Financial support

The model contains:

- Counseling/psychotherapy
- Marriage counseling services
- Family counseling services
- Drug and alcohol therapy
- Environmental restructuring
- Funding
- Community health centers
- Other approaches

This model should correct some of the organization deficiencies that are currently part of the mental health provider system.

## TRAUMA-INFORMED CARE

**Trauma-informed care** acts on the premise that many individuals have experienced some sort of trauma, and therefore every client should be approached with sensitivity and care. Traumatic events are deeply individualized, and what may have been traumatic to one individual, may not be to the next. Withholding judgment of what qualifies as trauma is imperative for the psychiatric-mental health professional.

The five elements of trauma-informed care include the following:

- **Safety**: Ensuring that the client feels emotionally and physically safe must be the first priority in order to create a conducive environment for treatment.
- **Choice**: Treatment cannot be forced and must honor the individual's right to choose.
- **Collaboration**: The client and the provider must work collaboratively through shared decision-making.
- **Trustworthiness**: The client must trust the provider in order for treatment to be effective. Trustworthiness can be established by communicating what is happening and what will happen next to the client.
- **Empowerment**: Empower the client with tools to cope on their own so that their recovery extends outside the walls of treatment.

## PARENT-CHILD INTERACTION THERAPY

**Parent-child interaction therapy (PCIT)** is designed for preschool children with conduct disorder or oppositional defiant disorder. Sessions are usually 1 hour a week for 10–16 weeks. The therapist observes the parent-child interaction from outside the room (usually with a two-way mirror) and provides feedback. PCIT has two phases:

- **Child-directed interaction:** Parents learn specific skills to use when engaging children in free play, including reflecting a child's statements and describing and praising appropriate behavior while ignoring undesirable behavior. The goal is to strengthen the parent–child bond and eliminate undesirable behavior.
- **Parent-directed interaction:** During this phase, positive behaviors are increased and undesirable behaviors are decreased. Parents learn to give clear commands, provide consistent reinforcement, and use time out for noncompliance.

## INCREDIBLE YEARS PROGRAM

The **Incredible Years program** for conduct disorder and oppositional defiant disorder has both a child (ages 4–7) and a parent component:

- **Child**: "Dinosaur school" is a group of children (about six children) who attend 2-hour weekly sessions for about 17 weeks. Videos and life-sized puppets are used to demonstrate ways of dealing with interpersonal problems, such as making friends, empathizing, coping with teasing, and resolving conflicts. Children practice social skills and are rewarded for positive social skills. Parents receive weekly updates and are asked to reward children for positive social skills.
- **Parent**: Parents meet in groups (about ten parents) for 2-hour sessions for 22 weeks. Parents view seventeen videos modeling appropriate methods for dealing with problem behavior and discuss them in the group. Parents learn to initiate nonthreatening play sessions, use positive reinforcement and consistent limit-setting, and learn strategies for dealing with problem behavior, such as time-outs.

## PSST AND PMT

**Problem-solving skills training (PSST)** is designed for children 7-13 years old to address antisocial behavior, conduct disorder, and oppositional defiant disorder. Parents of these children can take a **parent management training (PMT)** course simultaneously.

- **PSST**: Children attend 50-minute individual weekly sessions for 25 weeks. The therapist presents problem situations similar to those faced by the child and then helps the child to evaluate the situation, develop goals, and alternate goals for dealing with these situations. As homework, children are assigned "super solver" tasks in which they use skills learned in therapy in real-life situations. Parents learn to assist the child in using new strategies.
- **PMT**: Parents attend a total of 16 sessions of 2 hours each over a period of 6-8 months. Parents learn techniques for managing their child's behavior, such as reinforcement, shaping, and time-outs. The therapist uses a variety of teaching methods, including instruction, modeling, and role-playing.

## CONDITION-SPECIFIC THERAPEUTIC APPROACHES
### HABIT REVERSAL THERAPY FOR IMPULSE CONTROL DISORDERS

**Habit reversal therapy (HRT)**, a form of cognitive-behavioral therapy, is used to help people with tic disorders and for those with impulse control disorders, such as trichotillomania. A number of steps are involved, which are listed below.

- **Awareness**: The client must pay attention, as behaviors are often unconscious. This often involves keeping a detailed log of the behavior, including time, duration, activity during the episode, and emotional state before, during, and after these behaviors.
- **Identification of Triggers**: The log and client interviews help to identify triggers to help clients understand when they are at risk of the behavior and how to use stimulus control to prevent the behavior or to avoid triggers.
- **Assessment**: The client begins to identify feelings (negative or positive) associated with the behavior and the reason for it.
- **Competitive response**: The client carries out another action to compete with the urge to carry out the behavior, thereby preventing it.
- **Assessment of Rationalizations**: The client must confront the rationalizations used to allow the behavior to continue.
- **Mindfulness**: The client learns that it is not necessary to give in to the urge to carry out the behavior as urges often are of short duration.

### THERAPY OPTIONS FOR OBSESSIVE-COMPULSIVE DISORDER

**Therapy for obsessive-compulsive disorder** aims to develop expression of thoughts and impulses in a manner that is appropriate:

**Behavioral therapy** (most successful):

- Combined exposure with training to delay obsessive responses; best used in conjunction with pharmacotherapy
- Steady decrease of rituals by exposure to anxiety-producing situations until client has learned to control the related obsessive compulsion
- Reduction of obsessive thoughts by the use of reminders or noxious stimuli to stop chain-of-thought patterns, such as snapping a rubber band on the wrist when obsessive thoughts occur

**Family therapy** (primary issues):

- Helping the family to avoid situations that trigger OCD response
- Pointing out the tendency of family members to reassure the client, which is apt to support the obsession
- Introducing family strategies, which involve the following:
  - Remaining neutral and not reinforcing through encouragement
  - Avoiding trying to reason logically with the client

**Pharmacologic therapy** (FDA-approved medications for OCD):

- Clomipramine (Anafranil)
- Sertraline (Zoloft)
- Paroxetine (Paxil)
- Fluoxetine (Prozac)
- Fluvoxamine (Luvox)

## EXPOSURE AND RESPONSE/RITUAL PREVENTION

**Exposure and response/ritual prevention (ERP)** is a type of therapy used to treat obsessive-compulsive disorder (OCD). ERP helps the client learn to reduce anxiety by not performing ritualistic behavior. The goal is to habituate the person to the anxiety associated with an act so that it lessens and the ritual stops. Steps include the following:

1. **Psychoeducation**: ERP begins with education about the nature of OCD and ritualistic behavior.
2. **Ritual/fear analysis**: Fact-finding may be carried out in one or two sessions, during which a fear hierarchy is outlined regarding obsessional material starting with those that cause low anxiety and building to those that cause extremely high anxiety.
3. **Exposure and response/ritual prevention**: Exposure begins with small steps. For example, if a person is obsessed with germs, a first step might be to touch a tissue that touched a toothpick that touched a dirty tissue. The response/ritual prevention part is to avoid washing hands after touching the tissue. This may be done repeatedly to desensitize the person before moving to a high-anxiety item on the fear hierarchy.

## THERAPY FOR PTSD

Individuals with **post-traumatic stress disorder (PTSD)** are usually treated with antidepressants, mood stabilizers, or antipsychotic drugs, depending on their symptoms, but one of the following therapies is essential:

- **Cognitive-behavioral therapy (CBT)**: Individuals learn to confront trauma through psychoeducation, breathing, imaginary reliving, and writing; they are taught to recognize thoughts related to their trauma and attempt a method of coping, such as distraction and self-soothing.
- **Eye-movement desensitization and reprocessing**: This form of CBT requires the individual to talk about the experience of trauma while keeping the eyes and attention focused on the therapist's rapidly moving finger. (There is no clear evidence this is more effective than standard CBT.)

- **Family therapy**: PTSD impacts the entire family, so counseling and classes in anger management, parenting, and conflict resolution may help reduce family conflict related to the PTSD.
- **Sleep therapy**: Individuals may fear sleeping because of severe nightmares. Sleep therapy teaches methods to cope with nightmares through imagery rehearsal therapy and relaxation techniques.

## PSYCHOEDUCATION FOR BIPOLAR DISORDER AND SCHIZOPHRENIA

**Psychoeducation**, often part of cognitive-behavioral therapy, involves teaching individuals about their disease to help them manage symptoms and behavior.

- **Bipolar disorder**: Individuals are taught to understand the patterns of their disease and the triggers of mood changes so they can seek appropriate medical help. Additionally, they are taught to use self-monitoring tools, such as a daily record, to determine patterns of activity, such as sleeping, so they can maintain as consistent a schedule of eating, sleeping, and engaging in physical activities as possible; consistency tends to reduce unstable mood swings.
- **Schizophrenia**: Individuals must be taught about their disease and the effects of medications. Because medication may not eliminate all symptoms, such as hearing voices, individuals are taught methods to test reality to determine if their perceptions are correct.

## DIALECTICAL BEHAVIORAL THERAPY FOR BORDERLINE PERSONALITY DISORDER

**Dialectical behavioral therapy** was developed for the treatment of clients with **borderline personality disorder (BPD)**. In therapy, the mental health professional helps clients to change behavior by replacing **dichotomous thinking** that paints the world as black or white with rational (dialectical) thinking. This therapy is based on the premise that clients with BPD lack the ability to self-regulate, have a low tolerance for stress, and encounter social and environmental factors that impact their behavioral skills. Therapy includes the following:

- **Cognitive-behavioral therapy** (once a week) focuses on adaptive behaviors that help the client to deal with stress or trauma. Therapy focuses on a prioritized list of problems: suicidal behavior, behavior that interferes with therapy, quality of life issues, post-traumatic stress response, respect for self, acquisition of behavioral skills, and client goals.
- **Group therapy** (2.5 hours a week) helps the client learn behavioral skills, such as self-distracting and soothing.

## MOTIVATIONAL ENHANCEMENT THERAPY FOR SUBSTANCE ABUSE

**Motivational enhancement therapy (MET)** is a nonconfrontational, structured approach to treatment for substance abuse that is usually done in four sessions. MET helps motivate the client to change, accept responsibility for change, and remain committed to change. The MET therapist guides the client through different stages of change:

1. **Pre-contemplation**: Client does not wish to change behavior.
2. **Contemplation**: Client considers positive and negative aspects of drug or alcohol use.
3. **Determination**: Client makes a decision to change.
4. **Action**: Client begins to modify behavior over time (2–6 months).
5. **Maintenance**: Client remains abstinent.
6. **Relapse**: Client begins the cycle again. Relapses are common.

The therapist questions, compliments, and supports the client but avoids criticizing, labeling, or directly advising the client. Clients, especially those who have failed previous attempts to stop using, require much encouragement. A pretreatment assessment is completed, and the client is provided with a written report at the first meeting. The therapist uses eight strategies during sessions:

- Eliciting statements of self-motivation
- Listening empathetically
- Questioning
- Providing feedback
- Providing affirmation
- Handling or preventing resistance by reflecting, amplifying, or changing focus
- Reframing
- Summarizing

## VISUALIZATION TO TREAT ANXIETY DISORDERS

**Visualization (therapeutic imagery)** is used to treat **anxiety disorders** primarily for relaxation, stress reduction, and performance improvement. Visualization may be used in conjunction with many other types of therapy, such as exposure therapy, which can be very stressful for some people. Visualization strives to create a visual image of a desired outcome in the mind of the client when he or she imagines himself or herself in that place or situation. Intense concentration helps to block feelings of anxiety. For example, if the focus is on reducing anxiety, the mind focuses on that goal of therapy. All of the senses (e.g., looks, smells, feelings, sounds) may be used to imagine the feeling of relaxation in a certain place.

## SINGLE-SESSION THERAPY

**Single-session therapy** is the **most frequent form of counseling** because individuals often attend only one session for various reasons even if more are advised. Individuals may not have insurance or believe that one session is sufficient. Sessions typically last 1 hour. The goal is to identify a problem and reach a solution in one session. The therapist serves as a facilitator to motivate the individual to view the problem as part of a pattern that can be changed and to identify a solution. The therapist may use a wide range of techniques that culminates in a **plan for the individual** (e.g., homework exercises) so the individual can begin to make changes.

## SOLUTION-FOCUSED THERAPY

**Solution-focused therapy** aims to differentiate methods that are effective from those that are not, and to identify areas of strengths so they can be used in problem solving. The premise of solution-focused therapy is that change is possible but that the individual must identify problems and deal with them in the real world. This therapy is based on questioning to help the individual establish goals and find solutions to problems:

- **Pre-session**: The client is asked about any differences he or she noted after making the appointment and coming to the first session.
- **Miracle**: The client is asked if any "miracles" occurred or if any problems were solved, including what, if anything, was different and how this difference affected relationships.
- **Exception**: The client is asked if any small changes were noted and if there were any problems that no longer seemed problematic and how that manifested.
- **Scaling**: The client is asked to evaluate the problem on a 1-10 scale and then to determine how to increase the rating.
- **Coping**: The client is asked about how he or she is managing.

225

# Counseling Techniques

## Open vs. Closed Questioning in Counseling

**Open questioning** asks for general information about a topic ("Can you tell me about your childhood?") and cannot be answered with a simple "yes" or "no." Open questioning is used to encourage the client to talk about issues and is often used at the beginning of a discussion to help put the client at ease and to gain information that the counselor expects the client knows about and can share. Open questions are less threatening than closed (more specific) questions because the client can choose how much to disclose.

**Closed questions** ask for specific factual information ("Did your father physically abuse you?") and are often asked as follow-up questions to the initial open questions. Because closed questions often require a short answer ("yes" or "no"), the closed question is often followed by another open question to allow the client to expound ("Can you tell me more about that?").

## Proxemics

Proxemics is the study of personal space and the distance between individuals at which people feel comfortable or uncomfortable. **Proxemics** vary according to culture, and the counselor should assess the client's personal space of comfort and avoid violating that space or communicating the wrong message. In the United States, distances are classified as the following:

- **Intimate** (0-2 feet): Reserved for those in very close relationships, such as mother-child, person-partner, spouse-spouse. However, some clients, such as some with autism, may feel uncomfortable at intimate distance with anyone.
- **Personal** (2-4 feet): This distance ("arm's length") is commonly used for conversations with friends and associates. Generally, the closer the relationship, the closer the distance.
- **Social** (4-12 feet): A broader distance is maintained between strangers and acquaintances, especially in public spaces such as a store or at formal social gatherings.
- **Public** (greater than 12 feet): Interactions in public, such as a public speaking event, are often at a far distance, and people may feel comfortable moving about and avoiding eye contact.

## Enhancing the Client's Coping Methods

Professional counselors help their clients adjust and function in their everyday surroundings. Environments consist of work, school, home, and neighborhood communities. Professional counselors help individual clients gain better awareness of personal growth and self-development. The progression of this awareness is directed in care that helps the client cope with crises and issues in everyday life situations. The client is directed to develop appropriate **coping methods**. The client may also be referred for other health care services when the client has more complex needs or stresses that are not handled within the professional counselor's scope. The counselor educates the client in coping strategies for particular situations.

## Utilizing the Developmental Preventive Model

The mental health counselor helps the client handle life stresses by applying developed skills. The counselor also helps the client to evaluate his or her own character strengths. The counselor operates on a **developmental preventive model**. This positive approach model concentrates on the client's normalcy and the client's ability to obtain wellness. The counselor attempts to prevent relapses of the mental illness or disorder, and to keep new illnesses from developing. The model recognizes that each person will go through certain crises in life. The way a person deals with the

crises constitutes normal development. The developmental preventive model allows for a more natural way to view and accept needed mental health services.

## APPLYING SELF-AWARENESS TO THE COUNSELOR-CLIENT RELATIONSHIP

**Self-awareness** helps a counselor to provide foundational therapeutic benefits. The counselor comes with his or her own experiences that provide a good backdrop for relating to others. The counselor allows the client to explore his or her own thought patterns, wishes, wants, and goals in a session. The counselor may discuss his or her own comparative experiences in the session while giving the client feedback about an incident. This approach can be seen in the work of Carl Rogers, who believed in promoting an atmosphere of therapy that provided a sense of self-respect and honor for others. Roger's approach is contrary to the long-established, more analytical therapeutic method found in the works of Freud. Self-awareness is one attribute that put professional counselors in a distinctive class not commonly found in other vocations.

## PRIORITIZING COUNSELOR SELF-CARE

Important in the list of techniques utilized by the counselor is also the ability to conduct **self-care**. The mental health counselor should take care of his or her own needs, to ensure an ongoing ability to do the job. Self-care should be attended to on a daily basis. The counselor should seek out psychotherapy, coaching, exercise, meditation, hobbies, and healthy relationships with others.

- **Psychotherapy** is useful in helping the counselor realize areas in which he or she may be deficient. Training may be needed in a specific area. Psychotherapy can help the counselor to target character issues that can have a negative impact on virtue ethics.
- **Coaching** is useful in helping the counselor target career or family goals. Coaching can be achieved via the phone or secure internet connections.
- **Exercise programs** are beneficial but should be scheduled as a fun and rewarding part of the day.
- **Meditation** can be utilized, in the form of transcendental meditation, yoga, or breathing exercises.

The counselor should develop **hobbies** and **healthy relationships** with others. Hobbies and a wide range of interests help the counselor to remain stimulated on an intellectual and emotional level. These activities can give the counselor a zest for life and help them to refocus their attention. Family and friends provide the counselor with social and emotional outlets. These outlets can help the counselor reduce feelings of isolation that can lead to burnout. Peers or colleagues can be supportive in the work environment. These supportive groups can provide needed opportunities for socialization in the work setting. Overall, the counselor should approach self-care needs as priorities in their daily life.

# Family Therapy

## GOALS OF FAMILY THERAPY

Family therapy is a therapeutic modality theorizing that a client's psychiatric symptoms are a result of **pathology within the client's family unit**. This dysfunction is due to problems within the system, usually arising from conflict between marital partners. Psychiatric problems result from these behaviors. This conflict is expressed by:

- **Triangulation**, which manifests itself by the attempt of using another family member to stabilize the emotional process
- **Scapegoating**, which occurs when blaming is used to shift focus to another family member

The **goals** of family therapy are:

- To allow family members to recognize and **communicate their feelings**
- To determine the **reasons for problems** between marital partners and to **resolve** them
- To assist parents in **working together** and to strengthen their **parental authority**
- To help define and clarify **family expectations and roles**
- To learn more and different **positive techniques for interacting**
- To achieve **positive homeostasis** within the family
  - Homeostasis means remaining the same, or maintaining a functional balance. Homeostasis can occur to maintain a dysfunctional status as well.
- To enhance the family's **adaptability**
  - Adaptability is maintaining a balanced, positive stability in the family. A prerequisite for balanced stability, and a basic goal of family therapy, is to help the client family develop strategies for dealing with life's inevitable changes. Morphogenesis is the medical term often applied to a family's ability to react functionally and appropriately to changes.

## THEORETICAL APPROACHES TO FAMILY THERAPY

Four theoretical approaches to family therapy are **strategic**, **behavioral**, **psychodynamic**, and **object relations** theories:

- A **strategic approach** to family therapy was proposed by Jay Haley. Haley tried to map out a different strategic plan for each type of psychological issue addressed. With this approach, there is a special treatment strategy for each malady.
- A **behavioral approach** uses traditional behavior-modification techniques to address issues. This approach relies heavily on reinforcement strategies. B.F. Skinner is perhaps the most famous behaviorist. This approach relies on conditioning and often desensitizing as well.
- The **psychodynamic approach** attempts to create understanding and insight on the part of the client. Strategies may be diverse, but in all of them the therapist acts as an emotional guide, leading the client to a better understanding of mental and emotional mechanisms. One common example is Gestalt therapy.
- **Object relations theory** asserts that the ego develops attachment relationships with external and internal objects. A person's early relationships to objects (which can include people) may result in frustration or rejection, which forms the basis of personality.

## STRATEGIC FAMILY THERAPY

Strategic family therapy (Haley, 1976) is based on the following concepts:

- This therapy seeks to learn what **function** the symptom serves in the family (i.e., what payoff is there for the system in allowing the symptom to continue?).
- **Focuses**: Problem-focused behavioral change, emphasis of parental power and hierarchical family relationships, and the role of symptoms as an attribute of the family's organization.
- Helplessness, incompetence, and illness all provide **power positions** within the family. The child uses symptoms to change the behavior of parents.

Jay Haley tried to develop a strategy for each issue faced by a client. Problems are isolated and treated in different ways. A family plagued by alcoholism might require a different treatment strategy than a family undermined by sexual infidelity. Haley was unusual in that he held degrees in the arts and communication rather than in psychology. Haley's strategies involved the use of directives (direct instructions). After outlining a problem, Haley would tell the family members exactly what to do. If John would bang his head against the wall when he was made to do his homework, Haley might tell a parent to work with him and to be there while he did his homework.

## VIRGINIA SATIR AND THE ESALEN INSTITUTE'S EXPERIENTIAL FAMILY THERAPY

Virginia Satir and the Esalen Institute's experiential family therapy draws on sociology, ego concepts, and communication theory to form **role theory concepts**. Satir examined the roles of "rescuer" and "placatory" that constrain relationships and interactions in families. This perspective seeks to increase intimacy in the family and improve the self-esteem of family members by using awareness and the communication of feelings. Emphasis is on individual growth in order to change family members and deal with developmental delays. Particular importance is given to marital partners and on changing verbal and nonverbal communication patterns that lower self-esteem.

### SATIR'S COMMUNICATION IMPEDIMENTS

Satir described four issues that impede communication between family members under stress. Placating, blaming, being overly reasonable, and being irrelevant are the **four issues which blocked family communication**, according to Virginia Satir:

- **Placating** is the role played by some people in reaction to threat or stress in the family. The placating person reacts to internal stresses by trying to please others, often in irrational ways. A mother might try to placate her disobedient and rude child by offering food, candy, or other presents on the condition that he stop a certain behavior.
- **Blaming** is the act of pointing outwards when an issue creates stress. The blamer thinks, "I'm very angry, but it's your fault. If I've wrecked the car, it's because you made me upset when I left home this morning."
- **Irrelevance** is a behavior wherein a person displaces the potential problem and substitutes another unrelated activity. A mother who engages in too much social drinking frequently discusses her split ends whenever the topic of alcoholism is brought up by her spouse.
- Being overly reasonable, also known as being a **responsible analyzer** is when a person keeps his or her emotions in check and functions with the precision and monotony of a machine.

229

### MURRAY BOWEN'S FAMILY SYSTEMS THEORY

Bowen's family systems theory focuses on the following concepts:

- The role of **thinking versus feeling/reactivity** in relationship/family systems.
- Role of **emotional triangles**: The three-person system or triangle is viewed as the smallest stable relationship system and forms when a two-person system experiences tension.
- **Generationally repeating family issues**: Parents transmit emotional problems to a child. (Example: The parents fear something is wrong with a child and treat the child as if something is wrong, interpreting the child's behavior as confirmation.)
- **Undifferentiated family ego mass**: This refers to a family's lack of separateness. There is a fixed cluster of egos of individual family members as if all have a common ego boundary.
- **Emotional cutoff**: A way of managing emotional issues with family members (cutting off emotional contact).
- Consideration of thoughts and feelings of **each individual family member** as well as seeking to understand the family network.

> **Review Video: Bowen Family Systems**
> Visit mometrix.com/academy and enter code: 591496

### FAMILY SYSTEM THEORY ASSUMPTIONS ABOUT HUMAN BEHAVIOR

Family systems theory makes several basic assumptions:

- Change in one part of the family system brings about change in other parts of the system.
- The family provides the following to its members: unity, individuation, security, comfort, nurturance, warmth, affection, and reciprocal need satisfaction.
- Where family pathology is present, the individual is socially and individually disadvantaged.
- Behavioral problems are a reflection of communication problems in the family system.
- Treatment focuses on the family unity; changing family interactions is the key to behavioral change.

### MOTIVATIONS FOR CHANGE AND MEANS THROUGH WHICH CHANGE OCCURS

The **motivations for change** according to Bowen's family systems theory are as follows:

- **Disequilibrium** of the normal family homeostasis is the primary motivation for change according to this perspective.
- The family system is made up of three subsystems: the marital relationship, the parent-child relationship, and the sibling relationship. **Dysfunction** that occurs in any of these subsystems will likely cause dysfunction in the others.

The **means for change** in the family systems theory approach is the family as an interactional system.

### CONTRIBUTIONS TO FAMILY SYSTEMS THEORY

The **psychodynamic theory** emphasizes multi-generational family history. Earlier family relations and patterns determine current ones. Distorted relations in childhood lead to patterns of miscommunication and behavioral problems. Interpersonal and intrapersonal conflict beneath apparent family unity results in psychopathology. Social role functioning is influenced by heredity and environment.

Don Jackson, a major contributor to family therapy, focuses on **power relationships**. He developed a theory of double-bind communication in families. Double-bind communication occurs when two conflicting messages communicated simultaneously create or maintain a no-win pathological symptom.

## ASSESSMENT AND TREATMENT PLANNING IN THE FAMILY SYSTEMS THEORY

**Assessment** in family systems theory includes the following:

- Acknowledgement of **dysfunction** in the family system
- **Family hierarchy**: Who is in charge? Who has responsibility? Who has authority? Who has power?
- Evaluation of **boundaries** (around subsystems, between family and larger environment): Are they permeable or impermeable? Flexible or rigid?
- How does the **symptom** function in the family system?

**Treatment planning** is as follows:

- The therapist creates a mutually satisfactory contract with the family to establish service boundaries.
- Bowenian family therapy's goal is the differentiation of the individual from the strong influence of the family.

## SAL MINUCHIN'S STRUCTURAL FAMILY THERAPY

Sal Minuchin's structural family therapy seeks to strengthen boundaries when family subsystems are enmeshed, or seeks to increase flexibility when these systems are overly rigid. Minuchin emphasizes that the family structure should be hierarchical and that the parents should be at the top of the hierarchy.

Joining, enactment, boundary making, and mimesis are four techniques used by Salvador Minuchin in structural family therapy:

- **Joining** is the therapist's attempt at greeting and bonding with members of the family. Bonding is important when obtaining cooperation and input.
- Minuchin often had his clients enact the various scenarios which led to disagreements and conflicts within families. The **enactment** of an unhealthy family dynamic would allow the therapist to better understand the behavior and allow the family members to gain insight.
- **Boundary making** is important to structural family therapies administered by Salvador Minuchin, because many family conflicts arise from confusion about each person's role. Minuchin believed that family harmony was best achieved when people were free to be themselves yet knew that they must not invade the areas of other family members.
- **Mimesis** is a process in which the therapist mimics the positive and negative behavior patterns of different family members.

## THERAPEUTIC METHODS EMPLOYED BY CARL WHITAKER

Carl Whitaker, known as the dean of family therapy, developed **experiential symbolic family therapy**. Whitaker would freely interact with other family members and often played the part of family members who were important to the dynamic. He felt that experience, not information and education, had the power to change family dynamics.

Whitaker believed that in family therapy, theory was also less important than experience and that co-therapists were a great aid to successful counseling. Co-therapists freed one of the counselors to

231

participate more fully in the counseling sessions. One counselor might direct the flow of activity while the other participated in role playing. The "psychotherapy of the absurd" is a Whitaker innovation which was influenced by the "theatre of the absurd," a popular existential art form at the time. In this context, the absurd is the unreasonable exaggeration of an idea, to the point of underscoring the underlying meaninglessness of much of human interaction. A person who repeated a neurotic or destructive behavior, for example, was being absurd. The **psychotherapy of the absurd**, as Whitaker saw it, was a method for bringing out repeated and meaningless absurdities. A person pushing against an immovable brick wall, for example, might eventually understand the psychological analogy to some problem behavior.

## THEORIES OF CAUSALITY

Multiple theories of causality exist in the interpretation of family dynamics, which are then applied to the selection of therapeutic interventions. While linear causality (the concept that one cause equals one effect) uses a direct line of reasoning and is commonly used in individual counseling, **circular/reciprocal causality** is often used in family therapy and refers to the dynamic interactions between family members. Think of a situation in which one member of a family (a father, perhaps) has a severe emotional problem accompanied by violent and angry outbursts. The father periodically assaults his teenage son. Reciprocal or circular causality would apply in this family situation, since the father's angry behavior resonates throughout the family, causing different problems for each person. The spouse might feel inadequate to protect her son and sink into a depression. The other children would suffer, too, from anxiety and fear that the same treatment would befall them. Owing to circular causality, a single cause can have many effects.

## PARADOXICAL INTERVENTION STRATEGIES

Paradoxical intervention strategies involve the use of the client's disruptive behavior as a treatment itself, requiring the client to put the behavior in the spotlight to then motivate change. This technique tries to accomplish the opposite of what it suggests on the surface. Interventions include the following:

- **Restraining** is advising that a negative behavior not be changed or be changed only slightly or slowly. This can be effectively used in the context of couples therapy when a couple is struggling with intimacy issues. The therapist may challenge the couple to refrain from sexual intimacy for a period of time, thus removing certain stressors from that dynamic, possibly resulting in a positive intimate experience that occurs naturally and spontaneously.
- **Positioning** is characterizing a negative behavior in an even more negative light through the use of exaggeration. "David, do you feel you are not terrifying your family enough with your reckless driving or that you ought to drive faster in order to make them worry more about your wellbeing? Perhaps that way you will know that they care about you," says the therapist using positioning as a technique. It is important that this technique be used only with great care, as it can be harmful to clients with a negative self-image. It is generally used in situations where the client is behaving in a certain negative way in order to seek affirmation or attention.

- **Prescribing the symptom** is another paradoxical technique used by therapists to obtain an enlightened reaction from a client. A therapist using this technique directs the client to activate the negative behavior in terms that are absurd and clearly objectionable. 'John, I want you to go out to that sidewalk overpass above the freeway and yell as loud as you can at the cars passing below you. Do it for at least four hours." The therapist prescribes this activity to cure his client's dangerous tendency toward road rage.
- **Relabeling** is recasting a negative behavior in a positive light in order to get an emotional response from the client. "Perhaps your wife yells at you when you drink because she finds this behavior attractive and wants your attention," the therapist might say. The therapist might even support that obviously illogical and paradoxical argument by pointing out invented statistics, which support the ridiculous assertion.

## EXTINCTION, TIME OUT, AND THOUGHT STOPPING

**Behavior modification** is a term used in facilities like schools and jails to bring behavior into line with societal or family rules:

- **Extinction** is the process of causing a behavior to disappear by providing little or no reinforcement. It is different from punishment, which is negative reinforcement rather than no reinforcement at all. Very often, a student will be removed from the general population and made to sit alone in a quiet room. In schools, this goes by various names, but is often called in-school suspension (ISS). It is hoped that, through lack of reinforcement and response from outside, the offensive behavior will become extinct.
- **Time out** is another extinction technique, generally applied to very young children. A disobedient child will be isolated for a specified, usually short time whenever he or she misbehaves. The method's operant mechanism assumes that we are all social animals and require the reinforcement of the outside world. Deprived of this, we adapt by altering our behavior.
- **Thought stopping** is a learned response which requires the participation and cooperation of the client to change a negative behavior. When it is successful, the client actively forbids negative thoughts from entering his or her mind.

## SPECIFIC FAMILY THERAPY INTERVENTIONS
### FAMILY THERAPY INTERVENTIONS USED WITH OCD

Family therapy interventions used to treat individuals with **obsessive-compulsive disorder (OCD)** include therapy oriented to develop expression of thoughts and impulses in a manner that is appropriate. This approach assumes that family members often:

- Attempt to avoid situations that trigger OCD responses
- Constantly reassure the individual (which often enables the obsession)

Family therapy to address these issues involves:

- Remaining neutral and not reinforcing through encouragement
- Avoiding attempts to reason logically with individual

### FAMILY THERAPY INTERVENTIONS FOR PANIC DISORDERS

Family dynamics and therapy interventions for **panic disorders** include:

- Individuals with agoraphobia may require the presence of family members to be constantly in close proximity, resulting in marital stress and over-reliance on the children.
- Altered role performance of the afflicted member results in family and social situations that increase the responsibility of other family members.
- The family must be educated about the source and treatment of the disorder.
- The goal of family therapy is to reorganize responsibilities to support family change.

### FUNCTIONAL FAMILY THERAPY FOR ADOLESCENTS WITH ANTISOCIAL BEHAVIOR

Functional family therapy (FFT) is designed for adolescents (11–17 years of age) with **antisocial behavior**. FFT uses the principles of family systems theory and cognitive-behavioral therapy and provides intervention and prevention services. While the therapy has changed somewhat over the past 30 years, current FTT usually includes three phases:

1. **Engagement/motivation**: The therapist works with the family to identify maladaptive beliefs to increase expectations for change, reduce negativity and blaming, and increase respect for differences. Goals are to reduce dropout rates and establish alliances.
2. **Behavior change**: The therapist guides the parents in using behavioral interventions to improve family functioning, parenting, and conflict management. Goals are to prevent delinquent behavior and build better communication and interpersonal skills.
3. **Generalization**: The family learns to use new skills to influence the systems in which they are involved, such as school, church, or the juvenile justice system. Community resources are mobilized to prevent relapses.

### MULTISYSTEMIC THERAPY FOR ADOLESCENTS WITH ANTISOCIAL BEHAVIOR

Multisystemic therapy (MST) is a **family-focused program** designed for adolescents (11–17 years of age) with antisocial and delinquent behaviors. The primary goal is **collaboration** with the family to develop strategies for dealing with the child's behavioral problems. Services are delivered in the family's natural environment rather than at a clinic or office with frequent home visits, usually totaling 40–60 hours over the course of treatment. Sessions are daily initially and then decrease in frequency. A variety of different therapies may be used, including family therapy, parent training, and individual therapy. Therapists use different approaches but adhere to basic principles, including focusing on the strength of the systems, delivering appropriate treatment for developmental level, and improving family functioning. The goals of therapy are to improve family relations and parenting skills, to engage the child in activities with nondelinquent peers, and to improve the child's grades and participation in activities, such as sports.

### THERAPEUTIC METHODS FOR COUNSELING AN ADOLESCENT WITH BEHAVIORAL PROBLEMS

When an **adolescent's behavior** is a problem, some parents have him or her sign an agreement to perform in a specified manner. The agreement may state that a reward will be provided to the adolescent so long as the contract is upheld. The therapist can help parents and children write an effective contract. Another time-honored method of behavior conditioning is the withholding of leisure activity until chores are done. In a family therapy session, the therapist might advise stating the case like this: "Your television has a parental guide lock which will not be turned on unless you can demonstrate that all your homework is complete."

## ROLE OF THE THERAPIST

The role of the therapist in family therapy is to interact in the here and now with the family in relation to current problems. The therapist is a consultant to the family. Some aspects of the therapist's role differ according to school of thought:

- **Structural**: The therapist actively challenges dysfunctional interaction.
- **Strategic and Systemic**: The therapist is very active.
- **Milan School**: Male/female clinicians are co-therapists; a team observes from behind a one-way mirror and consults and directs the co-therapists with the clients.
- **Psychodynamic**: The therapist facilitates self-reflection and understanding of multi-generational dynamics and conflicts.
- **Satir**: The therapist models caring, acceptance, love, compassion, nurturance in order to help clients face fears and increase openness.

## KEY CONCEPTS OF FAMILY THERAPY

Key **concepts of family therapy** include the following:

| Behavior modeling | The manner in which a child bases his or her own behavior on the behavior of his or her parents and other people. In other words, a child will usually learn to identify acceptable behaviors by mimicking the behavior of others. Some children may have more difficulty with behavior modeling than others. |
|---|---|
| Boundaries | The means of organization through which system parts can be differentiated both from their environment and from each other. They protect and improve the differentiation and integrity of the family, subsystems, and individual family members. |
| Collaborative therapy | Therapy in which a different therapist sees each spouse or member of the family. |
| Complementary family interaction | A type of family relationship in which members present opposite behaviors that supply needs or lacks in the other family member. |
| Complementarity of needs | Circular support system of a family, in which reciprocity is found in meeting needs; can be adaptive or maladaptive. |
| Double-bind communication | Communication in which two contradictory messages are conveyed concurrently, leading to a no-win situation. |
| Family of origin | The family into which one is born. |
| Family of procreation | The family which one forms with a mate and one's own children. |
| Enmeshment | Obscuring of boundaries in which differentiation of family subsystems and individual autonomy are lost. Similar to Bowen's "undifferentiated family ego mass." Characterized by "mind reading" (partners speak for each other, complete each other's sentences). |
| Heritage | The set of customs, traditions, physical characteristics, and other cultural artifacts that a person inherits from his or her ancestors. |
| Homeostasis | A state of systemic balance (of relationships, alliances, power, authority). |
| Identified patient | The "symptom bearer" in the family. |
| Multiple family therapy | Therapy in which three or more families form a group with one or more clinicians to discuss common problems. Group support is given and problems are universalized. |
| Scapegoating | Unconscious, irrational election of one family member for a negative, demeaned, or outsider role. |

# Group Work

## COUNSELING VALUES IN GROUP PRACTICE

The underlying values of group counseling include:

- Every individual has dignity and worth.
- All people have a right and a need to realize their full potential.
- Every individual has basic rights and responsibilities.
- The group acts out democratic values and promotes shared decision-making.
- Every individual has the right of self-determination in both setting and achieving goals.
- Positive change is made possible by honest, open, and meaningful interaction.

## PURPOSES AND GOALS OF GROUP PRACTICE

Group practice takes a multiple-goal perspective to solving individual and social problems and is based on the recognition that group experiences have many important functions and can be designed to achieve any or all of the following:

- Provide restorative, remedial, or rehabilitative experiences
- Help prevent personal and social distress or breakdown
- Facilitate normal growth and development, especially during stressful times in the life cycle
- Achieve a greater degree of self-fulfillment and personal enhancement
- Help individuals become active, responsible participants in society through group associations

## ADVANTAGES OF GROUP WORK

Advantages of group work include the following:

- Members can help and identify with others dealing with similar issues and situations.
- Sometimes people can more easily accept help from peers than from professionals.
- Through consensual validation, members feel less violated and more reassured as they discover that their problems are similar to those of others.
- Groups give opportunities to members to experiment with and test new social identities and roles.
- Group practice is not a replacement for individual treatment. Group work is an essential tool for many counselors and can be the method of choice for some problems.
- Group practice can complement other practice techniques.

> **Review Video: Group Work and its Benefits**
> Visit mometrix.com/academy and enter code: 375134

## IMPORTANCE OF RELATIONSHIPS IN GROUP WORK

Establishing meaningful, effective relationships in group work is essential, and its importance cannot be overemphasized. The counselor will form multiple changing relationships with individual group members, with sub-groups, and with the group as a whole. There are multiple other parties who have a stake in members' experiences, such as colleagues of the counselor, agency representatives, relatives, friends, and others. The counselor will relate differentially to all of those individuals.

## TYPES OF COUNSELING GROUPS

The different types of counseling groups are as follows:

- **Educational groups**, which focus on helping members learn new information and skills.
- **Growth groups**, which provide opportunities for members to develop a deeper awareness of their own thoughts, feelings, and behavior, as well as develop their individual potentialities (i.e., values clarification, consciousness-raising, etc.).
- **Therapy groups**, which are designed to help members change their behavior by learning to cope with and improve personal problems and to deal with physical, psychological, or social trauma.
- **Socialization groups**, which help members learn social skills and socially acceptable behaviors and help members function more effectively in the community.
- **Task groups**, which are formed to meet organizational, client, and community needs and functions.

## GROUP STRUCTURE AND GROUP PROPERTIES

**Group structure** refers to the patterned interactions, network of roles and statuses, communications, leadership, and power relationships that distinguish a group at any point in time.

**Group properties** are attributes that characterize a group at any point in time. They include:

- Formal vs. informal structure
- Primary group (tight-knit family, friends, neighbor)
- Secondary relationships (task centered)
- Open vs. closed
- Duration of membership
- Autonomy
- Acceptance-rejection ties
- Social differentiation and degrees of stratification
- Morale, conformity, cohesion, contagion, etc.

## CLOSED GROUPS VS. OPEN GROUPS

Groups can be either closed or open, serving different functions and purposes:

| Closed Groups | Open Groups |
|---|---|
| • Convened by counselors. <br> • Members begin the experience together, navigate it together, and end it together at a predetermined time (set number of sessions). <br> • Closed groups afford better opportunities than open groups for members to identify with each other. <br> • Closed groups provide greater stability to the helping situation, and they allow the stages of group development progress more powerfully. <br> • Closed groups provide a greater amount and intensity of commitment due to the same participants being counted on for their presence. | • Open groups allow participants to enter and leave according to their choice. <br> • A continuous group can exist, depending on the frequency and rate of membership changes. <br> • The focus shifts somewhat from the whole group process to individual members' processes. <br> • With membership shifts, opportunities to use the group's social forces to help individuals may be reduced. The group will be less cohesive, and therefore less available as a therapeutic instrument. <br> • The counselor is kept in a highly central position throughout the life of the group, as he or she provides continuity in an open structure. |

## SHORT-TERM GROUPS AND FORMED GROUPS

Some circumstances call for the formation of short-term and/or formed groups:

| Short-Term Groups | Formed Groups |
|---|---|
| • Short-term groups are formed around a particular theme or in order to deal with a crisis. <br> • Limitations of time preclude working through complex needs or adapting to a variety of themes or issues. <br> • The counselor is in the central position in a short-term group. | • Deliberately developed to support mutually agreed-upon purposes. <br> • Organization of the group begins with the realization of a need for group services. <br> • The purpose is established by an identification of common needs among individuals in an agency or counselor caseload. <br> • The group is counselor-guided in interventions and timing by an understanding of individual and interpersonal behavior related to the group's purpose. <br> • It is advisable to have screening, assessment, and preparation of group members in formed groups. <br> • Different practice requirements for voluntary and non-voluntary groups exist, as members will respond differently to each. |

## SMALL GROUP THEORY

### SYSTEM ANALYSIS AND INTERACTIONAL THEORY OF SMALL GROUPS

**The system analysis and interactional theory of small groups** is a broadly used framework for understanding small groups. In this framework, small groups are living systems that consist of interacting elements that function as a whole. In this framework, a social system is a structure of relationships or a set of patterned interactions. System concepts help maintain a focus on the whole group, and explain how a group and its sub-groups relate functionally to larger environments. This framework describes how interaction affects status, roles, group emotions, power, and values.

## SOCIAL SYSTEM CONCEPTS AND GENERAL SYSTEMS CONCEPTS

The following are **social system concepts** used in the system analysis and interactional theory of small group work:

- **Boundary maintenance**: Maintaining group identities and separateness
- **System linkages**: Two or more elements combine to act as one
- **Equilibrium**: Maintaining a balance of forces within the group

**General systems concepts** used in the system analysis and interactional theory of small group work are as follows:

- **Steady state**: The tendency of an open system to remain constant but in continuous exchange
- **Equifinality**: The final state of a system that can be reached from different initial conditions
- **Entropy**: The tendency of a system to wear down and move toward disorder

## SYMBOLIC INTERACTIONISM

Symbolic interactionism is characterized by the following:

- Emphasizes the **symbolic nature** of people's relationships with others and the external world versus a social system analysis that emphasizes form, structures, and functions.
- Group members play a part in determining their own actions by recognizing symbols and **interpreting meaning**.
- Human action is accomplished mainly through the process of **defining and interpreting situations** in which people act. The counselor uses such concepts to explain how individuals interact with others, and to understand the following:
    - The role of the individual as the primary resource in causing change
    - The significance of social relationships
    - The importance of self-concept, identification, and role identity in group behavior
    - The meanings and symbols attributed to group interactions

## GESTALT ORIENTATIONS AND FIELD THEORY

**Gestalt psychology** played a major part in the development of group dynamics. Contrasting with earlier psychologies that stressed elementary sensations and associations, Gestalt theorists viewed experiences not in isolation, but as perpetually organized and part of a **field** comprised of a system of co-existing, interdependent factors. Group dynamics produced a plethora of concepts and variables:

- Goal formation
- Cohesion
- Group identification and uniformity
- Mutual dependency
- Influences and power
- Cooperation and competition
- Productivity

Group dynamics (or group processes) provide a helpful framework of carefully defined and operationalized relevant group concepts.

## SOCIOMETRY

Sociometry, inspired by the work of J. L. Moreno, is both a general theory of human relations and a specific set of practice techniques (psychodrama, sociodrama, role playing).

- Sociometric tests are devised to measure the affectivity factor in groups.
- Quality of interpersonal attraction in groups is a powerful force in rallying group members, creating feelings of belonging, and making groups sensitive to member needs.

## COGNITIVE CONSISTENCY THEORY AND BALANCE THEORY

The basic assumption of **cognitive consistency theory** is that individuals need to organize their perceptions in ways that are consistent and comfortable. Beliefs and attitudes are not randomly distributed but rather reflect an underlying coherent system within the individual that governs conscious processes and maintains internal and psychosocial consistency.

According to the balance theory, processes are balanced when they are consistent with the individual's beliefs and perceptions. Inconsistency causes imbalance, tension, and stress, and leads to changing perceptions and judgments which restore consistency and balance. The counselor incorporates varying ideas from these orientations. Some stress the need for the group to be self-conscious and to study its own processes, emphasizing that cognition is apparent in contracting, building group consciousness, pinpointing or eliminating obstacles, and sharing data.

## SOCIAL REINFORCEMENT AND EXCHANGE THEORY

The **social reinforcement and exchange theory** in regard to group work is summarized as follows:

- Social exchange theorists propose that members of groups are motivated to seek **profit** in their interactions with others (i.e., to maximize rewards and minimize costs).
- Analysis of interactions within groups is done in terms of a series of **exchanges or tradeoffs** group members make with each other.
- The individual member is the **primary unit of analysis**. Many of the core concepts of this theory are merely transferred to the group situation and do not further the understanding of group processes.

## GROUP FORMATION

### ELEMENTS IN THE GROUP FORMATION PROCESS

The key elements in the group formation process include the following:

- The counselor makes a clear and uncomplicated statement of purpose that includes both the members' stakes in coming together and the agency's (and others') stakes in serving them.
- The counselor's part should be described in as simple terms as possible.
- Identify the members' reactions to the counselor's statement of purpose and how the counselor's statement connects to the members' expectations.
- The counselor helps members do the work necessary to develop a working consensus about the contract.
- Recognize goals and motivations, both manifested and latent, stated and unstated.
- Recontract as needed.

### COUNSELOR'S ROLE IN GROUP MEMBER SELECTION

The counselor's process of selecting members for a group is as follows:

- The counselor explains **reasons** for meeting with group applicants.
- The counselor elicits applicants' **reactions** to group participation.
- The counselor assesses applicants' **situations** by engaging them in expressing their views of the situation and goals in joining the group.
- The counselor determines **appropriateness** of applicants for the group, accepts their rights to refuse membership, and provides orientation upon acceptance into the group.

### HETEROGENEITY VS. HOMOGENEITY IN GROUP FORMATION

Issues of heterogeneous vs. homogenous group formation include the following:

- A group ought to have sufficient homogeneity to provide stability and generate vitality.
- Groups that focus on socialization and developmental issues or on learning new tasks are more likely to be homogeneous.
- Groups that focus on disciplinary issues or deviance are more likely to be heterogeneous.
- The composition and purposes of groups are ultimately influenced or determined by agency goals.

## BEGINNING PHASE OF GROUP PROCESS

### INTERVENTION SKILLS

Intervention skills of the counselor that are used in the **beginning phase** of group process include the following:

- The counselor must tune into the needs and concerns of the members. Member cues may be subtle and difficult to detect.
- The counselor must seek members' commitment to participate through engagement with members.
- The counselor must continually assess the following:
  o Members' needs/concerns
  o Any ambivalence/resistance to work
  o Group processes
  o Emerging group structures
  o Individual patterns of interaction
- The counselor must facilitate the group's work.

### FACILITATING THE GROUP'S WORK

The counselor's role in facilitating group process is as follows:

- Promote **member participation and interaction**.
- Bring up **real concerns** in order to begin the work.
- Help the group keep its **focus**.
- Reinforce observance of **rules** of the group.
- Facilitate **cohesiveness** and focus the work by **identifying emerging themes**.
- Establish counselor **identity** in relation to group's readiness.
- **Listen** empathically, **support** initial structure and rules of the group, and **evaluate** initial group achievements.
- Suggest **ongoing tasks or themes** for the subsequent meeting.

## STRESSORS

The following are stressors that the counselor might experience in the beginning phase of group process:

- Anxiety regarding gaining acceptance by the group
- Integrating group self-determination with an active leadership role
- Fear of creating dependency and self-consciousness in group members which would deter spontaneity
- Difficulty observing and relating to multiple interactions
- Uncertainty about the counselor's own role

## MIDDLE PHASE OF GROUP PROCESS

Intervention skills of the counselor used in the **middle phase** of group process include the following:

- Judge when work is being avoided
- Reach for opposites, ambiguities, and what is happening in the group when good and bad feelings are expressed
- Support different ways in which members help each other
- Partialize larger problems into more manageable parts
- Generalize and find connections between small pieces of group expression and experience
- Facilitate purposeful communication that is invested with feelings
- Identify and communicate the need to work and recognize when work is being accomplished by the group

## ONGOING GROUP DEVELOPMENT

Group development refers to the ongoing group processes that influence the progress of a group, or any of its sub-groups, over time. Group development typically involves changing structures and group properties that alter the quality of relationships as groups achieve their goals. Understanding group development gives counselors a blueprint for interventions that aid the group's progression toward attaining goals. A danger in using development models is in the counselor forcing the group to fit the model, rather than adapting interventions for what is occurring in the group. A complex set of properties, structures, and ongoing processes influence group development. Through processes that are repeated, fused with others, modified, and reinforced, movement occurs.

## MODELS OF GROUP PRACTICE

### LINEAR STAGE MODELS OF GROUP DEVELOPMENT

There are many models of group development, often describing the group's process through a series of **linear stages** in which the group progresses predictably from one to another.

**Tuckman's** five stages of group development are as follows:

1. **Form**: Group comes together, rules are established and agreed upon, and members are relatively subdued and hesitant.
2. **Storm**: Expression of feelings begins by the members who still feel individual versus members of the group; there may be resistance to cues by the counselor or signs of cynicism.

3. **Norm**: A sense of unity and teamwork prevails; members begin to interact with and encourage one another.
4. **Perform**: A sense of hierarchy dissipates as the member take control of the group process and feel empowered in an open and trusting team environment.
5. **Adjourn**: The team recognizes time for closure, some members may mourn the loss of the group and need guidance and support for next steps, and reflection on progress and celebration of accomplishments occur.

The **Boston Model** (Garland, Jones, & Kolodny) of group development is as follows:

1. **Preaffiliation stage**: Consists of regulation by the counselor, expressions of concern or anxiety, heavy dependence on the counselor, hesitant disclosure of personal goals, clarification of purpose, timeline, and roles
2. **Power and control stage**: Consists of limit setting, clarification, and the use of the program
3. **Intimacy stage**: Consists of handling transference, rivalries, and a degree of uncovering
4. **Differentiation stages**: Consist of clarification of differential and cohesive processes, and group autonomy
5. **Separation**: Consists of a focus on evaluation, handling ambivalence, and incorporating new resources

The **Relational Model**, developed by Schiller, in regard to group development in groups of women, is as follows:

- Preaffiliation
- Establishing a relational base
- Mutuality and interpersonal empathy
- Challenge and change
- Separation and termination

## SOCIAL GOALS MODEL
The social goals model of group practice is as follows:

- The primary focus is to influence a wide range of small group experiences, to facilitate members' identifying and achieving of their own goals, and to increase social consciousness and social responsibility.
- It assumes a rough unity between involvement in social action and the psychological health of the individual. Early group work was concerned with immigrant socialization and emphasized principles of democratic decision making, in addition to tolerance for difference.
- The methodology is focused on establishing positive relationships with groups and members, using group processes in doing with the group rather than for the group, identification of common needs and group goals, stimulation of democratic group participation, and providing authentic group programs stemming from natural types of group living.

## REMEDIAL/REHABILITATIVE MODEL

The remedial/rehabilitative model of group practice is as follows:

- It uses a medical model and the counselor is focused primarily on **individual change**.
- This model includes **structured** program activities and exercises.
- It is more commonly found in organizations concerned with **socialization**, such as schools, and in those concerned with treatment and social control (inpatient mental health treatment, etc.).
- Practice techniques in this model focus on **stages** of treatment.
  - **Beginning**: Intake, group selection, diagnosis of each member, and setting specific goals.
  - **Middle**: Planned interventions. Counselor is central figure and uses direct means to influence group and members. Counselor is spokesperson for group values and emotions. Counselor motivates and stimulates members to achieve goals.
  - **Ending**: Group members have achieved maximum gains. Counselor helps clients deal with feelings about ending. Evaluation of work, possible renegotiation of contract.

## RECIPROCAL INTERACTIONAL OR MEDIATING MODEL

The reciprocal interactional or mediating model of group practice can be summarized as follows:

- The counselor is referred to as a **mediator** and participates in a network of reciprocal relationships. Goals are developed mutually through contracting process. The interaction and insight of group members is the primary force for change in what is seen as a "mutual aid" society.
- **Counselor's task**: Help search for common ground between group members and the social demands they experience, help clients in their relationships with their own social systems, detect and challenge obstacles to clients' work, and contribute data.
- **Phases** of intervention:
  - **Tuning in or preparation for entry**: The counselor helps the group envision future work, but makes no diagnosis. The counselor is also sensitive to members' feelings.
  - **Beginning**: The counselor engages group in contracting process, and the group establishes clear expectations.
  - **Middle**: The middle phase consists of searching for common ground, discovering/challenging obstacles, data contribution, sharing work visions, and defining limits/requirements
  - **Ending**: Finally, the counselor is sensitive to his or her own reactions and members' reactions and helps members evaluate the experience and consider new beginnings.

## FREUDIAN/NEO-FREUDIAN APPROACH

The Freudian/Neo-Freudian approach to group practice is as follows:

- Groups consist of 8-10 members.
- Interaction is mainly through discussion.
- Group members explore feelings and behavior, and interpret unconscious processes.
- The counselor uses interpretation, dream analysis, free association, transference relations, and working through.
- This approach aims to help group members re-experience early family relationships, uncover deep-rooted feelings, and gain insight into the origins of faulty psychological development.

## TAVISTICK GROUP-CENTERED MODELS

The Tavistick "group as a whole" group-centered model for group practice is as follows:

- This approach derives from Wilfred Bion's work with leaderless groups. Bion developed analytic approaches that focused on the **group as a whole**.
- Latent group feelings are represented through the group's prevailing emotional states or **basic assumption cultures**.
- The therapist is referred to as a **consultant**. The consultant does not suggest an agenda, establishes no rules and procedures, but instead acts as an observer. A major role of the consultant is to alert members to ongoing group processes and to encourage study of these processes.
- The consultant encourages members to explore their experiences as group members through **interaction**.

## GROUP THERAPY METHODS

### PROCESS GROUPS

Irvin Yalom's "here-and-now" or process groups are characterized by the following:

- Yalom stressed using clients' **immediate reactions** and discussing members' **affective experiences** in the group.
- Process groups have relatively unstructured and spontaneous sessions.
- Process groups emphasize **therapeutic activities**, like imparting information, or instilling hope, universality, and altruism.
- The group can provide a **rehabilitative narrative** of primary family group development, offer socializing techniques, provide behavior models to imitate, offer interpersonal learning, and offer an example of group cohesiveness and catharsis.

### MORENO'S PSYCHODRAMA GROUP THERAPY

Moreno's psychodrama group therapy is summarized as follows:

- **Spontaneous drama techniques** contribute to powerful therapy to aid in the release of pent-up feelings and to provide insight and catharsis to help participants develop new and more effective behaviors.
- The five **primary instruments** used are the stage, the client or protagonist, the director or therapist, the staff of therapeutic aides or auxiliary egos, and the audience.
- Psychodrama group therapy can begin with a **warm-up**. The warm-up uses an assortment of techniques such as self-presentations, interviews, interaction in the role of the self and others, soliloquies, role reversals, doubling techniques, auxiliary egos, mirroring, multiple doubles, life rehearsals, and exercises.

### BEHAVIORAL GROUP THERAPIES

Behavioral group therapies are characterized by the following:

- The **main goals** are to help group members eliminate maladaptive behaviors and learn new behaviors that are more effective. Behavioral groups are not focused on gaining insight into the past, but rather on current interactions with the environment.
- It is one of the few research-based approaches.
- The counselor utilizes **directive techniques**, provides information, and teaches coping skills and methods of changing behavior.
- The counselor arranges **structured activities**. The primary techniques used include restructuring, systematic desensitization, implosive therapies, assertion training, aversion techniques, operant-conditioning, self-help reinforcement and support, behavioral research, coaching, modeling, feedback, and procedures for challenging and changing conditions.

### INFLUENCING THE GROUP PROCESS

Influencing group process in group work methodology can be done through the following:

- The counselor's ability to recognize, analyze, understand, and influence group process is necessary and vital. The group is a system of relationships rather than a collection of individuals. This system is formed through associations with a unique and changing quality and character (this is known as group structures and processes).
- Processes that the counselor will be dealing with include understanding group structures, value systems, group emotions, decision-making, communication/interaction, and group development (formation, movement, termination).

### EXTERNALIZING

The counselor must be prepared to help individual members profit from their experiences in and through the group. Ultimately, what happens to group members and how they are influenced by the group's processes determines the success of any group experience, not how the group itself functions as an entity. The counselor should give attention to helping members relate beyond the group (**externalizing**), to encouraging active participation and involvement with others in increasingly wider spheres of social living. This should occur even when the group is relatively autonomous.

### PROGRAMMING

The importance of programming in group work methodology is as follows:

- The counselor uses activities, discussion topics, task-centered activities, exercises, and games as a part of a planned, conscious process to address individual and group needs while achieving group purposes and goals.
- Programming should build on the needs, interests, and abilities of group members and should not necessitate a search for the unusual, esoteric, or melodramatic.
- Counseling skills used in implementing programs include the following: initiating and modifying program plans to respond to group interests, self-direction, responsibility, drawing creatively upon program resources in the agency and environment, and developing sequences of activities with specific long-range goals.
- Using program activities is an important feature of group practice.

## CONTRACTING WORKING AGREEMENTS IN GROUP WORK

Only if group members are involved in clarifying and setting their own personal and common group goals can they be expected to be active participants on their own behalf. **Working agreements** consider not only counselor-member relationships, but also others with a direct or indirect stake in the group's process. Examples would be agency sponsorship, collaborating staff, referral and funding sources, families, caretakers, and other interested parties in the public at large.

The following are the **counselor's role in contracting**:

- Setting goals
- Determining membership
- Establishing initial group structures and formats

All three of these elements require skillful management by the counselor.

## ANALYZING GROUP PROCESSES

The following are categories for analyzing group work:

- Communication processes
- Power and influence
- Leadership
- Group norms and values
- Group emotion
- Group deliberation and problem solving

## GROUP PRACTICE WITH SPECIAL POPULATIONS

### GROUPS FOR SERIOUS MENTAL ILLNESS

Group work with clients who have serious mental illness should include the following elements:

- **Clearly defined programs** that use psychosocial rehabilitation approaches (not psychotherapeutic).
- Focus on making each group session **productive and rewarding** for group members.
- **Themes** addressed include dealing with stigma, coping with symptoms, adjusting to medication side effects, dealing with problems (family, relationships, housing, employment, education, etc.), and real and imagined complaints about mental health treatment organizations.
- Many groups in community-based settings focus on helping members learn **social skills** for individuals with limited or ineffective coping strategies.
- Mandated groups in **forensic settings** are highly structured and focus on basic topics such as respect for others, responsibility for one's behavior, or staying focused.

### CHEMICAL DEPENDENCY GROUPS

Group work for chemical dependency focuses on the following:

- Group work is the treatment of choice for **substance use disorder**.
- Guidelines for these groups include maintaining confidentiality, using "I" statements, speaking directly to others, never speaking for others, awareness of one's own thoughts and feelings, honesty about thoughts and feelings, and taking responsibility for one's own behavior.
- Types of groups used include:
  - **Orientation groups** that give information regarding treatment philosophy/protocols.
  - **Spiritual groups** that incorporate spirituality into recovery.
  - **Relapse prevention groups** that focus on understanding and dealing with behaviors and situations that trigger relapse.
  - **AA and NA self-help groups** utilize the principles and philosophies of 12-step programs. For family and friends, **Nar-Anon** and **Al-Anon groups** provide support.

### PARENT EDUCATION GROUPS

Parent education groups are used in social agencies, hospitals, and clinics. They are often labeled as psycho-ed groups or parent training groups and use a cognitive-behavioral approach to improve the parent-child relationship. Parent education groups are often structured to follow manuals or curricula. Their main focus is helping parents improve parent-child interactions, parent attitudes, and child behaviors.

### ABUSED WOMEN'S GROUPS

Abused women's groups can be described as follows:

- Provide a warm, accepting, and caring environment in which members can feel secure.
- Structured for consciousness raising, dispelling false perceptions, and resource information.
- Common themes these groups explore include the use of power which derives from the freedom to choose, the need for safety, the exploration of resources, the right to protection under the law, and the need for mutual aid.
- Basic principles of these groups include respect for women, active listening and validation of members' stories, ensuring self-determination and individualization, and promoting group programs that members can use to demonstrate their own strength and achieve empowerment.
- For post-group support, groups typically seek to utilize natural supports in the community.

### GROUPS FOR SPOUSE ABUSERS

Groups for spouse abusers (perpetrators of domestic violence) are explained below:

- Work with this population is typified by resistance and denial.
- Clients have difficulty processing guilt, shame, or abandonment anxiety and tend to convert these feelings into anger.
- These clients have difficulties with intimacy, trust, mutuality, and struggle with fear of abandonment and diminished self-worth.
- Mandatory group treatment is structured. It is designed to challenge male bonding that often occurs in such groups.
- Including spouses/victims in these groups is quite controversial in clinical literature.

## GROUPS FOR SEX OFFENDERS

Groups for sex offenders are summarized below:

- Typically, membership in these groups is ordered by the court. There is no assurance of confidentiality, as counselors may have to provide reports to the courts, parole officers, or other officials.
- Clients typically deny wrongdoing, test counselors, and are often resistant.
- In groups with voluntary membership, confidentiality is extremely important, as group members often express extreme fear of exposure.
- Prominent themes include denial, victim-blaming, blaming behavior on substances, blaming behavior on uncontrollable sex drives/needs.
- Treatment emphasizes the importance of conscious control over drives/needs, regardless of their strength or if they are natural.
- A culture of victimization is strongly discouraged.

## GROUPS FOR CHILDREN OF ALCOHOLICS

Groups for children of alcoholics are discussed below:

- Individuals who grow up with parents who abuse alcohol and/or drugs often learn to distrust others as a survival strategy. They become used to living with chaos and uncertainty and with shame and hopelessness.
- These individuals commonly experience denial, secrecy, and embarrassment.
- They may have a general sense of fearfulness, especially if they faced threats of violence, and tend to have rigid role attachment.
- Treatment in these groups requires careful planning, programming, and mutual aid in the form of alliances with parental figures and other related parties in order to create a healthy environment that increases the individual's safety and ability to rely on self and others.

## GROUPS FOR SEXUALLY ABUSED CHILDREN

Groups for sexually abused children are summarized below:

- The counselor must pay particular attention to her or his own attitudes toward sexuality and the sexual abuse of children.
- Important in these groups are contracting, consistent attendance, and clearly defined rules and expectations.
- Clients may display control issues and may challenge the counselor's authority.
- Confidentiality is not guaranteed.
- Termination can be a particularly difficult process.
- Common themes that come up include fear, anger, guilt, depression, anxiety, inability to trust, and delayed developmental/socialization skills.
- Programming can include ice breaking games, art, body drawings, letter writing, and role playing.

## TERMINATION OF GROUP PROCESS

Group members' experience of termination and the counselor's role in helping group members to cope with the ending of the group are discussed below:

- Group members may have feelings of loss and may desire to minimize the painful feelings they are experiencing.
- Members may experience ambivalence about ending.
- The counselor will:
  o Examine her or his own feelings about termination
  o Focus the group on discussing ending
  o Help individuals express their feelings of loss, relief, ambivalence, etc.
  o Review achievements of the group and members
  o Help members prepare to cope with next steps
  o Assess members' and group's needs for continued services
  o Help members with transition to other services

## METHODS OF FORESTALLING OR DEALING WITH TERMINATION

The following are group members' methods of forestalling or dealing with termination:

- **Simple denial**: A member may forget ending, act surprised, or feel "tricked" by termination.
- **Clustering**: Members may physically draw together, also called super-cohesion.
- **Regression**: Reaction can be simple-to-complex. Earlier responses reemerge, outbursts of anger, recurrence of previous conflicts, fantasies of wanting to begin again, attempts to coerce the leader to remain, etc.
- **Nihilistic flight**: Members may reject and perform rejection-provoking behavior.
- **Reenactment and review**: Members begin recounting or reviewing earlier experiences in detail or actually repeating those experiences.
- **Evaluation**: Members assess meaning and worth of former experiences.
- **Positive flight**: There is a constructive movement toward self-weaning. Members find new groups, etc.

# Using Humor in the Counseling Process

## THERAPEUTIC HUMOR

The American Association of Therapeutic Humor defines **therapeutic humor** as an intervention. An intervention is an action that seeks to stop something from happening that may be undesirable. The intervention of therapeutic humor can be an expression of laughter that can stimulate playful discovery about a problem that the client may be experiencing. Some therapeutic benefits are found in humorous expressions or in the appreciation of such expressions. Humor can help people deal with absurd, bizarre, or out of the ordinary life events in a healthy manner. This therapeutic result can lead to an increase in work performance. Likewise, humor can be used to reinforce learning. Another benefit can be found in improving the person's sense of well-being. Humor can help treat persons with an illness of emotional, cognitive, spiritual, social, or physical origin.

## HISTORICAL USE OF HUMOR IN PSYCHOTHERAPY

In 1951, Carl Rogers promoted the **therapeutic relationship** that could be gained through bonding between the counselor and the client. Humor can be used to improve this bond, promote trust, make important interpersonal connections, and help the clients deal with subjects that make them anxious. Social interaction can increase dialogue. Studies indicate people are more likely to trust someone who is amusing over someone who appears sober-minded. Humor may indicate to the client that the counselor shares his or her world view. Freud proposed that humor indicates the client and counselor have reached an agreement of some kind.

## CORRELATES OF HUMOR

The correlates of humor are what make it successful in producing an amusing result. There are three **correlates of humor**:

- The **suddenness** of the punch line or surprising conclusion gives the audience the opportunity to laugh at the unexpected twist.
- **Optimal arousal** is derived from an appropriate level of intellectual, emotional, or physical stimulation (e.g., adults find it difficult to laugh at childish jokes that have ceased to be of interest).
- **Play frame** is setting up the joke or story to be non-threatening for the listener. Some jokes may be too intense for the individual's comfort level. Play frame involves cueing the listener through facial expressions or vocal tones that intend a time for play.

## CATEGORIES OF HUMOR

Humor can be separated into three categories:

- **Incongruity** is depicted in humorous jokes, stories, or scenes that create one set of expectations for an outcome, which are altered in the punch line to produce a totally different outcome than first expected.
- **Release** is a humorous way to let off pent-up, negative emotions that have aggressive or sexual undertones. Sarcasm is a form of release. Sometimes, pent-up emotions are released after a physical event that was particularly stressful.
- **Superiority** is humor exercised at the expense of another, as in slapstick humor.

## PHYSICAL SYMPTOMS THAT CAN BE RELIEVED USING HUMOR

Physical symptoms that may be relieved through the use of humor include the following:

- Reduction of pain
- An increased immune system response, particularly immunoglobin A, a disease-fighting antibody found in mucous membranes that repels attacks by viruses and bacteria.
- Improved mental functions
- Muscle exercise and relaxation
- Improved respiration
- Stimulated circulation
- Decreased stress hormones
- Decreased blood pressure

## PSYCHOTHERAPEUTIC BENEFITS OF HUMOR

Tensions, aggression, and negative feelings can be released by humor. This translated into **psychotherapeutic studies and applications of humor**:

- In 1942, Obrdlik studied a group of citizens who used humor to relieve the tensions of being in a town occupied by Nazi soldiers.
- In 1959, Coser studied patients using humor during their hospital confinements.
- In 1960, Frankl proposed exaggerating to make the patient laugh at absurd solutions to a problem.
- In 1977, Albert Ellis explored expressive therapy.
- In 1985, Murstein and Brust explored humor linking romantic couples.
- In 1994, Minden used humor to treat military veterans suffering with depression. Six sessions produced a reduction in their anxieties.
- In 2004, Berk declared humor helps the client to gain a new perspective on problems.

The counselor should apply these perspectives to the counseling relationship by encouraging the client to express his or her negative feelings and explaining that expression is much healthier than repression, which leads to physical health problems.

## POSSIBLE HARMFUL EFFECTS OF HUMOR

In 1994, Brooks warned counselors to ensure that their relationships with clients are stable and conducive before making attempts to incorporate humor. Without a foundation of trust, the use of humor may have counterproductive results. Brooks outlined the following areas of sensitivity to be considered when using humor:

- Do not make the client the target of humor or ridicule the client.
- Do not fall back on humor to relieve one's own inner tensions about a subject. The session is not for the counselor's benefit. The client's needs are paramount.
- Avoid humor when there is any hint of negative personal feelings about the client.
- Do not allow the client to use humor as a defense mechanism to avoid painful topics.
- Only apply humor when a substantial time has passed after a crisis.

## Counseling Skills and Interventions Chapter Quiz

**1. Morphogenesis is:**

   a. An adaptability skill a family may use in handling change.
   b. An adaptability skill a family may use in balancing stability.
   c. An adaptability skill a family may use when having a new child.
   d. An adaptability skill a family may use when experiencing extreme stress.

**2. Mahoney developed which acronym based on the cognitive behavioral approach?**

   a. NARROW
   b. SCIENCE
   c. EXAMINE
   d. BRAIN

**3. The idea that people control their own destinies and interpret events according to their own values and beliefs is a key concept of which of the following?**

   a. Acceptance commitment therapy
   b. Rational emotive therapy
   c. Rational behavior therapy
   d. Solution-focused therapy

**4. Yalom's process groups are characterized by all of the following EXCEPT?**

   a. Utilizing delayed and thoughtful responses
   b. Emphasizing therapeutic activities
   c. Providing a rehabilitative narrative of primary family group development
   d. Discussing members' affective experiences

**5. Which of the following is the study of personal space and the distance between individuals at which people feel comfortable or uncomfortable?**

   a. Proxemics
   b. Contiguity
   c. Juxtapology
   d. Vicinics

**6. Using blame to shift focus to another family member is known as:**

   a. Intellectualization
   b. Justification
   c. Rationalization
   d. Scapegoating

**7. Which of the following is NOT one of the four communication impediments described by Satir?**

   a. Placating
   b. Unresponsive
   c. Irrelevance
   d. Being overly reasonable

**8. The idea that one cause equals one effect is called**

    a. Reciprocal determinism
    b. Linear causality
    c. Circular causality
    d. Relational causality

**9. Which of the following theories posits that members of groups are motivated to seek profit in their interactions with others?**

    a. Assimilation-contrast theory
    b. Balance theory
    c. Social exchange theory
    d. Transactional analysis theory

**10. How many correlates of humor are there?**

    a. Six
    b. Five
    c. Four
    d. Three

# Core Counseling Attributes

## Therapeutic Environment

### THERAPEUTIC MILIEU

The **therapeutic milieu** is a stable environment provided by an organization to assist in a **treatment plan**. The main purposes of a milieu are to teach individuals certain social skills and to provide a **structured environment** that promotes interactions and personal growth along with attempting to control many types of deviant or destructive behaviors. There are **five main components** that the milieu should include in therapy. These components include containment, structure, support, involvement, and validation. Through the use of these components, the therapeutic milieu can help the individuals achieve their highest level of functioning.

### CONTAINMENT COMPONENT

The **containment component** in a milieu involves the actual **physical safety** of the participants. It provides a **safe clean physical environment** as well as providing food and some medical care. The actual environment will often be very comfortable with colorful walls, pictures, and comfortable chairs and couches. Participants are allowed a certain freedom of movement throughout this environment. Many times, the participants will work to help maintain a clean and functioning environment. They may perform certain tasks or chores to help with the upkeep of the milieu. This containment will provide a feeling of safety and trust for the individual.

### STRUCTURED COMPONENT

The **structured component** in the milieu lies hand in hand with **consistency**. The milieu provides a place with consistent staff members, consistent physical surroundings, and limits on behavior. This predictability allows the participants to feel safe and secure and to know what to expect. This environment also provides **structure** through providing an environment where the participants can interact with a purpose. These purposes can range from daily tasks and chores to the different roles they may assume within various meetings. Through acceptance of this consistent and structured environment, the individual can begin to achieve some level of self-responsibility and consequences for their actions.

### SUPPORT COMPONENT

The **support component** in a milieu comes directly from the staff members involved in the milieu. Their goal is to help the participants have increased **self-esteem** through creating an environment of acceptance for all individuals. They provide a safe and comfortable atmosphere, therefore decreasing anxiety levels. Encouragement, empathy, nurturing, reassurance, and providing physical wellbeing for participants will help increase their feelings of self-worth. Consistency in attitudes and actions by all staff members are very important in the success of this setting. By providing this type of environment, the milieu will assist clients in their abilities to gain new healthy relationships and appropriate interactions with others.

### INVOLVEMENT COMPONENT

The **involvement component** of the milieu is the development of a sense of **open involvement** for each client from the staff members. The staff should convey their desire to be personally involved with each client through both their actions and attitudes. They should encourage the clients to **communicate** with them openly about feelings and experiences. This sense of individual interest and involvement will help to increase the client's sense of self-worth and self-esteem. The staff

255

members should encourage client involvement through encouraging client-lead group sessions and activities. By becoming involved, the clients have opportunities to practice new social skills, such as working together with others, learning to compromise, and dealing with conflict. The hope of involvement is to achieve the goal of appropriate social interactions for each client.

## VALIDATION COMPONENT

The **validation component** of the milieu is the recognition of each client as an **individual**. The staff members should convey **respect and consideration** for each and every client. This respect and consideration should be shown through acts of kindness, empathy, nonjudgmental attitude, and acceptance of each individual for who they are. In a milieu, each client contributes through responsibilities and involvement in many decision-making processes. Through these actions, the clients should begin to feel some self-responsibility and with this new sense of responsibility comes validation for their individuality and humanity.

## CHARACTERISTICS OF A SUCCESSFUL MILIEU

The characteristics of a **successful milieu** include:

- Successful communication between and among staff and clients
- Standards that provide consistency and security
- Client government using the democratic process
- Client responsibility for his or her own treatment
- Encouraging self-perception and change
- Acknowledging and positively dealing with destructive behavior and poor judgment

## CONFLICT RESOLUTION

When attempting to **resolve conflict** between two or more individuals, the desired outcome is a feeling by each party of getting what they wanted out of the situation. Resolving conflict should include the following steps:

1. **Problem Identification**: The parties are each allowed their opportunity to discuss what they think is wrong. This portion of the resolution process may become emotional and involve angry outbursts.
2. **Ascertain Expectations**: Each party identifies exactly what they want. With the disclosure of these expectations, a sense of trust can begin to evolve. The mental health professional will need to remain objective and respectful to everyone involved during this phase.
3. **Identify Special Interest**: Determine if anyone has unspoken objectives or interests that could slow down the resolution progress. Everyone needs to be honest about what they want and need.
4. **Brainstorm Resolution Ideas**: Assist the parties with creating ideas to help resolve the conflict.
5. **Reach a Resolution**: Assist the parties in bringing together a situation where everyone can feel happy about the outcome.

## CLIENT-PROVIDER RELATIONSHIP

### INTRODUCTORY PHASE

The first thing the mental health care provider should do when meeting a client is to find out **why** they are there. This **initial phase** provides a time for the provider and client to get to know each other. There is no definite time frame and this phase can last for a few minutes to a few months. There are certain goals that should be accomplished during this time. The provider and client should develop a mutual sense of trust, acceptance, and understanding. They may enter into a contract with each other. They will need to determine expectations, goals, boundaries, and ending criteria for the contract. This initial phase often involves obtaining the client's history, his or her account of the problems, and developing a general understanding of the client.

## WORKING PHASE

The second phase of the client-provider relationship is the **working phase**. During this time the client will identify and evaluate specific problems through the development of insight and learn ways to effectively **adapt their behaviors**. The provider will assist the client in working through feelings of fear and anxiety. They will also foster new levels of self-responsibility and coping mechanisms. The development of new and successful ways of approaching problems is the goal of this phase. The provider may often face resistance by the client to move through this phase, and by utilizing different communication techniques may help to assist the client in moving forward.

## TERMINATION PHASE

The final stage of the client-provider relationship is the **termination or resolution phase**. This phase begins from the time the problems are actually solved to the actual **ending of the relationship**. This phase can be very difficult for both the client and the provider. The client must now focus on continuing without the guiding assistance of the therapy. The client will need to utilize their newfound approaches and behaviors. This time may be one of varying emotions for the client and they may be reluctant to end the relationship. They may experience anxiety, anger, or sadness. The provider may need to guide the client in utilizing their newfound strategies in dealing with their feelings about the termination of the relationship. Focus should be placed on the future.

## THERAPEUTIC COMMUNICATION
### VERBAL COMMUNICATION

**Verbal communication** is achieved through spoken or written words. This form of communication represents a very small fraction of communication as a whole. Much information achieved verbally may be **factual** in nature. Communication occurs along a two-way path between the client and the provider. One limitation of verbal communication can be **different meanings of words** in different ethnic and cultural populations. The meanings may differ in denotative, actual meaning, and/or connotative, implied meaning, of the words. The use of words may differ depending upon personal experiences. The client may assume the provider understands their particular meaning of the word.

### EMPATHY

**Empathy** is perhaps one of the most important concepts in establishing a therapeutic relationship with a client, and it is associated with **positive client outcomes**. It is the ability of one person to put themselves in the shoes of another. Empathy is more than just knowing what the other person means. The provider should seek to imagine the **feelings** associated with the other person's experience without having had this experience themselves and then communicate this understanding to the client. Empathy should not be confused with sympathy, which is feeling sorry for someone. The provider should also be aware of any social or cultural differences that could inhibit the conveyance of empathy.

### OPEN-ENDED STATEMENTS AND REFLECTION

Broad **open-ended statements** allow the client the opportunity to expand on an idea or select a topic for discussion. This type of communication allows the client to feel like the provider is actually listening and interested in what they have to say. It also helps the client gain insight into his or her emotions or situations.

**Reflection** conveys interest and understanding to the client. It can also allow for a time of validation so the provider can show that they are actually listening and understanding the shared information. It involves some minimal repetition of ideas or summing up a situation. These ideas or summaries are directed back to the client often in the form of a question.

### RESTATING AND CLARIFICATION

Restating and clarification are verbal communication techniques that the provider may use as part of therapeutic communication. **Restating** involves the repetition of the main points of what the client expressed. Many times, the provider will not restate everything but narrow the focus to the main point. This technique can achieve both clarification of a point and confirmation that what the client said was heard.

**Clarification** involves the provider attempting to understand and verbalize a vague situation. Many times, a client's emotional explanations can be difficult to clearly understand and the provider must try to narrow down what the client is trying to say.

### SILENCE AND LISTENING

Silence and listening are very effective during verbal communication.

- **Silence** allows the client time to think and formulate ideas and responses. It is an intentional lull in the conversation to give the client time to reflect.
- **Listening** is more active in nature. When listening, the provider lends attention to what the client is communicating. There are two different types of listening.
  - **Passive listening** allows the client to speak without direction or guidance from the provider. This form of listening does not usually advance the client's therapy.
  - **Active listening** occurs when the provider focuses on what is said in order to respond and then encourage a response from the client.

### RAPPORT AND VALIDATION

Communication between the mental health care provider and the client can be improved by establishing rapport and validating certain information. **Establishing rapport** with a client involves achieving a certain level of harmony between the provider and the client. This is often achieved through the establishment of trust through conveying respect, nonbiased views, and understanding. By establishing rapport, the provider helps the client feel more comfortable about sharing information.

**Validation** requires the provider to use the word "I" when talking with the client. It evaluates one's own thoughts or observations against another person's and often requires feedback in the form of confirmation.

### USE OF THERAPEUTIC COMMUNICATION WITH GROUPS

A **group** is a gathering of interactive individuals who have commonalities. Interventions through **group sessions** can provide an effective treatment opportunity to allow for growth and self-development of the client. This setting allows the clients to interact with each other. This allows the clients to see the emotions of others, such as joy, sorrow, or anger, and to receive as well as participate in feedback from others in the group. The group can be very supportive and thrive in both inpatient and outpatient settings. The one thing the group cannot lack is definite **leadership and guidance** from the health care provider. The provider must guide the members of the group in facilitating therapeutic communications.

## NONVERBAL COMMUNICATION IN THE THERAPEUTIC RELATIONSHIP

**Nonverbal communication** occurs in the form of expressions, gestures, body positioning or movement, voice levels, and information gathered from the five senses. The **nonverbal message** is usually more accurate in conveying the client's feeling than the **verbal message**. Many clients will say something quite different than what their nonverbal communication indicates. Nonverbal communication may also vary by cultural influences. The mental health care provider must be aware of these cultural differences and respect their place within the therapy. The provider should utilize positive, respectful, non-threatening body language. A relaxed, slightly forward posture with uncrossed arms and legs may encourage communication.

## VOCAL CUES, ACTION CUES, AND OBJECT CUES AS FORMS OF NONVERBAL BEHAVIORS

There are many different types of nonverbal behaviors. There are five main areas of **nonverbal communication**. They include vocal cues, action cues, object cues, space, and touch.

- **Vocal cues** can involve the qualities of speech, such as tone and rate. Laughing, groaning, or sounds of hesitation can also convey important communication.
- **Action cues** involve bodily movements. They can include things such as mannerisms, gestures, facial expressions, or any body movements. These types of movements can be good indicators of mood or emotion.
- **Object cues** include the use of objects. The client may not even be aware that they are moving these objects. Other times the client may choose a particular object to indicate a specific communication. This intentional use of an object can be less valuable than other forms of nonverbal communication.

Space and touch as nonverbal forms of communication can vary greatly depending upon social or cultural norms.

- **Space** can provide information about a relationship between the client and someone else. Most people living in the United States have four different areas of space. **Intimate space** is less than 1.5 feet, **personal space** is 1.5-4 feet, **social-consultative space** is 9-12 feet, and **public space** is 12 feet or more. Observations concerning space and the client's physical placement in a setting can give a great deal of insight into different interpersonal relationships.
- **Touch** includes personal or intimate space with an action involved. This fundamental form of communication can send very personal information and communicate feelings such as concern or caring.

## NON-THERAPEUTIC COMMUNICATION

Techniques that are detrimental to establishing a trusting therapeutic relationship include giving advice, challenging the client's communications, or indicating disapproval. **Giving advice** includes telling the client what they should do in a particular situation. This does not allow the client to develop the ability to solve their own problems and may not always be the right answer. **Challenging** occurs when the client's thoughts are disputed by the provider. This communication only serves to lower the client's self-esteem and create an environment of distrust between the client and the mental health care provider. **Disapproval** occurs when the provider negatively judges the client's beliefs or actions. This again serves to lower client self-esteem and does not foster their ability to solve their own problems or create new coping abilities.

## CLIENT SAFETY ISSUES

### PROFESSIONAL ASSAULT RESPONSE

A protocol for a **professional assault response** should be established at all mental health facilities because statistics show that 75% of mental health staff experience a **physical assault**. Most injuries are incurred by nursing staff caring for violent clients. Assaults may occur in both psychiatric units and emergency departments, where security staff may also be assaulted. Additionally, clients may be victims. Common injuries include fractures, lacerations, contusions, and unconsciousness from head injuries. Victims are at risk for psychological distress and post-traumatic stress syndrome, so a prompt response is critical. The assault response should include the following:

- Routine assessment of clients for violent or aggressive tendencies
- Protocol for managing violent or aggressive clients
- Physical assessment and medical treatment as needed for injuries
- Completion of an incident report by those who were involved or who observed the incident

Psychological intervention, including individual counseling sessions and critical incident stress management, require a response team that includes staff members who are trained to deal with crisis intervention (e.g., psychologists, psychiatrists, nurses, peer counselors, social workers).

### CONTRABAND AND UNSAFE ITEMS

State regulations identify **contraband and unsafe items** that are prohibited from mental health and correctional facilities; however, each facility must develop site-specific restrictions and protocols for responding to contraband and unsafe items. **Contraband** may include the following:

- Alcohol or products (mouthwash) that contain alcohol
- Drugs, including prescription, over-the-counter, and illicit drugs
- Poisonous and toxic substances
- Pornographic or sexually explicit material
- Food (hoarded or excessive)

Depending on the type of facility or clients, a wide range of items may be considered **unsafe**. These often include the following:

- Knives, scissors, sharp instruments, and razor blades
- Flammable materials, such as lighter fluid and matches
- Breakable items, such as glass and mirrors
- Dangerous materials (which might be used for a suicide attempt), such as belts (over 2 in wide), large buckles, rope, electrical cords (i.e., over 6 feet in length), and wire
- Potential weapons, such as pens (except felt point), pencils, and plastic bags
- Electrical equipment, such as fans and recording devices

# Therapeutic Relationships and Communication

## CONDITIONS REQUIRED FOR A POSITIVE THERAPEUTIC RELATIONSHIP

In order for a counselor to establish a positive therapeutic relationship, he or she must express non-possessive warmth and concern, genuineness, appropriate empathy, nonjudgmental acceptance, optimism regarding prospects for change, objectivity, professional competence, ability to communicate with a client, and self-awareness. Self-disclosure should be used only purposefully and for the client's benefit.

For clients to contribute to a positive therapeutic environment, they must have hope and courage to undertake change processes, be motivated to change, and trust in the counselor's interest and skill. They must also be dealt with as an individual and not a case, personality type, or category. Clients must be able to express themselves, to make their own choices, and to change at their own pace.

## PROFESSIONAL OBJECTIVITY IN COUNSELOR-CLIENT RELATIONSHIP

Objectivity requires remaining neutral when making judgements. Because of the nature of counseling, a large part of evaluation tends to be subjective and not easily quantified, but these evaluations can then reflect the counselor and the counselor's biases. The goal should be to make objective observations as much as possible—reporting what is seen and heard rather than the subjective opinion about those things. In order to ensure that opinions are objective, specific parameters should be developed for decision making. For example, when evaluating a client's socioeconomic status, judging by language and appearance may produce one opinion while judging according to occupation and income may produce another (and probably more accurate) opinion. The way a counselor measures may also reflect biases. For example, measuring gender by male and female only suggests a subjective rejection of other choices, such as non-binary or transgender.

## PRINCIPLES OF COMMUNICATION

Communication involves the conveying of information, whether verbally or nonverbally, between individuals and has two key aspects: sending and receiving information. Each of these requires unique skills, and effective communication requires proficiency in both. **Essential principles of communication** include:

- All aspects of communication must be considered and interpreted in any exchange.
- Communication may be written, verbally spoken, or nonverbally delivered via body language, gestures, and expressions.
- Not all communication is intentional, as unintentional information may also be conveyed.
- All forms of communication have limits, further imposed by issues of perception, unique experiences, and interpretation.
- Quality communication accounts for issues of age, gender, ethnicity/culture, intellect, education, primary language, emotional state, and belief systems.
- Optimum communication is active (or reflective), using strategies such as furthering responses (nodding, etc.), paraphrasing, rephrasing, clarification, encouragement ("tell me more"), partialization (reducing long ideas into manageable parts), summarization, feelings reflection, exploring silence, and nonverbal support (eye contact, warm tone, neutral but warm expressions, etc.).

## QUALITY COMMUNICATION WITH CLIENTS

The following are key rules for quality communication with clients:

- Don't speak for the client; instead allow the client to fully express him or herself.
- Listen carefully and try diligently to understand.
- Don't talk when the client is speaking.
- Don't embellish; digest what the client has actually said, not what was presumed to be said.
- Don't interrupt, even if the process is slow or interspersed with long pauses.
- Don't judge, criticize, or intimidate when communicating.
- Facilitate communication with open-ended questions and a responsive and receptive posture.
- Avoid asking "why" questions, which can be perceived as judgmental.
- Communicate using orderly, well-planned ideas, as opposed to rushed statements.
- Moderate the pace of speech and adjust expressions to fit the client's education, intellect, and other unique features.
- Ask clarifying questions to enhance understanding.
- Attend to nonverbal communication (expression, body language, gestures, etc.).
- Limit closed-ended and leading questions.
- Avoid "stacked" (multi-part) questions that can be confusing.

## CONGRUENCE IN COMMUNICATION

Congruence in communication is consistently communicating the same message verbally and nonverbally. The individual's words, body language, and tone of voice should all convey the same message. If they do not, then the communication is incongruent, and the receiver cannot trust the communication. For example, if a person says, "I really want to help you," in a very harsh tone of voice and with an angry affect, the communication is incongruent, and the message may actually be perceived as the exact opposite of the words spoken. Communication is also incongruent if the individual gives a series of conflicting messages: "I'm going to get a job," "Why should I work?" "I know I need to work," "There's no point in taking a low-paying job." The counselor must be alert to the congruence of client communication in order to more accurately assess the client as well as be aware of personal congruence of communication when interacting with client. This helps to ensure that the counselor can cultivate a relationship built on trust.

## ACTIVE LISTENING

Active listening techniques include the use of paraphrasing in response, clarification of what was said by the client, encouragement ("tell me more"), etc. Key **overarching guidelines** include the following:

- Don't become preoccupied with specific active listening strategies; rather, concentrate on reducing client resistance to sharing, building trust, aiding the client in expanding his or her thoughts, and ensuring mutual understanding.
- The greatest success occurs when a variety of active listening techniques are used during any given client meeting.
- Focus on listening and finding ways to help the client to keep talking. Active listening skills will aid the client in expanding and clarifying his or her thoughts.
- Remember that asking questions can often mean interrupting. Avoid questioning the client when he or she is midstream in thought and is sharing, unless the questions will further expand the sharing process.

262

## ALLOWING CLIENTS UNINTERRUPTED OPPORTUNITIES TO SPEAK

There are many reasons to limit a client's opportunities to speak. Time may be inadequate, the workload may be impacted, the client may seem distracted or uninterested in sharing, etc. However, only by **allowing the client to divulge his or her true feelings** can the counselor actually know and understand what the client believes, thinks, feels, and desires.

**Barriers to client sharing** include the following:

- **Frequent interruptions**: Instead, the counselor might jot a short note to prompt a question later.
- **Supplying client words**: A client may seem to have great difficulty finding words to express his or her feelings and the counselor may be tempted to assist. However, this may entirely circumvent true expression, as the client may simply say, "Yes, that's it," rather than working harder to find his or her true feelings.
- **Filling silence**: Long pauses can be awkward. The counselor may wish to fill the silence, but in doing so, he or she may prevent the client from finding thoughts to share.

## UTILIZING NONVERBAL COMMUNICATION

To facilitate the sharing process it is important for a counselor to present as warm, receptive, caring, and accepting of the client. However, the counselor should also endeavor not to bias, lead, or repress client expressions by an inappropriate use of **nonverbal** cues. Frowning, smiling, vigorous nodding, etc., may all lead clients to respond to the counselor's reactions rather than to disclose their genuine feelings and thoughts. To this end, a counselor will endeavor to make good eye contact, use a soft tone of voice, present as interested and engaged, etc., but without marked expressions that can influence the dialogue process. Sitting and facing the client (ideally without a desk or other obstruction in between), being professionally dressed and groomed, sitting close enough to be engaging without invading the client's space, and using an open posture (arms comfortable in the lap or by the sides, rather than crossed over the chest) can all facilitate the communication process.

## LEADING QUESTIONS

Leading questions are those that predispose a particular response. For example, saying, "You know that it is okay to ask questions, don't you?" is a strongly leading question. While it may seem an innocuous way to ensure that someone feels free to ask questions, it may not succeed in actually eliciting questions. Instead, ask the client directly, "What questions do you have?" This way of asking not only reveals that questions are acceptable, but is much more likely to encourage the client to openly share any confusion he or she is having.

Even less forceful leading questions can induce a bias. For example, when a couple comes in for counseling, the counselor asking, "Would you like to sit over here?" could prevent the counselor from seeing how they elect to arrange themselves in relation to the counselor and to each other (a very revealing element in the relationship). Instead, the counselor might simply say, "Feel free to sit anywhere you'd like." Avoiding leading questions is an important skill in the communication process.

## OBTAINING SENSITIVE INFORMATION FROM CLIENTS

Sensitive information includes that involving sexual activity, abuse, intimate partner violence, substance abuse, and mental health issues. Clients are more likely to answer questions truthfully if they have developed a relationship of trust with the questioner. **Methods of obtaining sensitive information** include the following:

- Embedding the questions in a series of questions in context: "Do you spend time with your friends?" "Are your friends sexually active?" "Do you think you are more or less sexually active than your friends?" "How many sexual partners have you had?"
- Asking for facts and not opinions
- Using familiar language and terminology
- Asking for permission to question, "Do you mind if I ask you about…" and explaining the reason for questioning, "In order to plan for your medical care, I need to ask you about…"
- Using a scale (1 to 10) rather than asking for detailed information
- Explaining what kinds of information can remain confidential and what kinds cannot (such as child abuse)

# Multicultural Counseling

## DIVERSITY IN THE UNITED STATES

In recent years, the African American population has grown and many individuals in that population have moved to suburban areas and established more lucrative socioeconomic positions. The Latino population has also grown drastically, now outnumbering the African American population (18.5% to 13.4% according to the US Census of 2019). This growth has elevated the Latino population to the largest minority group in America. Native Americans (referred to as American Indians by the US Census) are one of the smallest minority groups in America (1.3%). However, this small group has had a lucrative experience in the operation of reservation-based casinos and other service-oriented businesses. The Native American population has also made economic gains from construction and retail. The counselor must be aware and cognizant of the **diverse mental health needs of the minority groups in America**. Competence in these areas include the following:

- Self-awareness about one's own prejudices and cultural backgrounds
- Knowledge about diverse populations
- Skills in treating diverse populations

## HISTORY OF MULTICULTURAL COUNSELING

The United States has a populace derived from a variety of different countries and cultures. The Association for Multicultural Counseling and Development publishes a guide to the culture, ethnicity, and race of individual groups of people served by mental health providers. The foundation for the association was laid by civil rights groups of the 1950s-1960s, renowned for their social justice reforms that addressed racial problems, discrimination issues, subtle biases, and segregation in schools and public places. **Multicultural counseling** promotes cultural competence as an ongoing training effort for counselors working in other disciplines. Cultural awareness outlines are used during multicultural counseling. Multicultural counselors must receive appropriate training and preparation that includes preventive care.

## ESSENTIAL ELEMENTS OF MULTICULTURAL COUNSELING

In 1990, Don C. Locke defined these **four elements** of the ever-changing role of multicultural counseling:

1. Multicultural counseling is aware of the cultural background, values, and world view of the client and the therapist.
2. Multicultural counseling makes note of socialization aspects in regard to race, ethnicity, and culture of the client.
3. Multicultural counseling makes every effort to see the individual within the group of people that he or she belongs.
4. Multicultural counseling does not label the person as deficient, but acknowledges that there can be a difference between the person as an individual and his or her group.

The differences in a person may need to be addressed to help the person come to terms with his or her own self-identity. The individual is also encouraged to value the racial or ethnic group of which he or she is a member.

> **Review Video: Multicultural Counseling**
> Visit mometrix.com/academy and enter code: 965442

## FRAMEWORK FOR CULTURAL UNDERSTANDING

The framework for cultural understanding is based on the diverse cultural backgrounds that exist between a client and a counselor. Personal experiences shape the counselor's and the client's worldview and impact behaviors of both. Areas in which different points of view surface include historical perspectives, social perspectives, economical perspectives, and political perspectives. Likewise, socialization and life experiences change the client's and counselor's worldviews and behaviors. Counseling sessions are impacted by differences between the counselor and the client because they can cause a lack of empathy and understanding in the client/counselor relationship. Prejudices and biases are detrimental to the counselor/client relationship. If one is considering becoming a counselor, they should expect to have their own belief system scrutinized, and to establish an operations framework where commonalities are first identified to achieve empathy and understanding.

## MULTICULTURAL AWARENESS CONTINUUM

The linear tool used to help a counselor gain cultural competence is the **Multicultural Awareness Continuum**. The counselor cannot expect to achieve mastery, as the continuum is designed to be ongoing and revisited throughout the career of the counselor. Progression allows the counselor to go on to the next level, but if the counselor is confronted by a deficiency in his or her awareness when treating a culturally diverse person, then the counselor returns to the previous level for insight into that aspect of the culture. Levels of cultural competence within the Multicultural Awareness Continuum include the following:

1. Self-awareness
2. Awareness of one's cultural groupings
3. Awareness of racism, sexism, and poverty in relation to cultural problems
4. Awareness of individual differences
5. Awareness of other groups of people and cultures
6. Awareness of diversity
7. Skills and techniques related to the multicultural counselor

### LEVELS OF THE MULTICULTURAL AWARENESS CONTINUUM

The first level of the Multicultural Awareness Continuum is a **high level of self-awareness**. This component is essential for the counselor to understand why he or she feels a certain way and to identify biases in his or her own thinking. It is imperative for a counselor to understand how he or she interacts with others. Likewise, the counselor needs to examine his or her beliefs, attitudes, opinions, and values. A multicultural counselor must spend time in introspection to determine areas in which he or she may have cultural biases.

The second level has to do with an **awareness of one's own culture**. Certain cultures may place values upon a person's name, its origin and cultural significance. Other cultures may place values upon birth order. Some cultures have naming ceremonies for infants. Language and its use can also play a significant part in the values placed upon a person through his or her culture.

The third level on the Multicultural Awareness Continuum is **awareness of racism, sexism, and poverty bias**. Counselors discover this awareness by looking closely at their own personal belief system. Sexism and racism are an entrenched part of cultural beliefs. Some counselors and clients may not have biases against token minority individuals whom they know personally, but may think of smaller cultures folded into the American melting pot as subtly inferior. Poverty touches everyone to some extent. Many have either experienced poverty directly, or have simply seen shocking evidence of its existence. The counselor must determine his or her own bias before helping others gain insights into a cultural belief system.

The counselor must not overgeneralize any culture. This lends itself to the fourth and fifth levels of multicultural awareness. The fourth level is an **awareness of individual differences**. Overgeneralization leads to misconceptions founded on observations of only a few members of a culture. To avoid misconceptions, treat the client first and foremost as an individual with his or her own set of unique needs and then as a member of his or her specific culture. Understand that the individual has to function both as a member of their own culture and in American society at large. Avoid projecting personal cultural beliefs on the client.

The fifth level is an **awareness of other cultures**. This begins with the client's language. A multicultural counselor does not need to learn a foreign language in its entirety, but just certain words that have significant meanings. In 1980, Hofstede researched 40 countries to determine identifiable differentiations in their various cultures. He determined the following characteristics are the most identifiable:

- Power distance
- Uncertainty avoidance
- Masculinity/femininity
- Individualism/collectivism

In 1961, Kluckhorn and Strodtbect determined the following characteristics are the most identifiable:

- Time
- View of human nature
- Importance of relationships
- Human activity
- View of the supernatural

In 2001, Gelso and Fretz exhibited a series of dimensions to describe the differences they found between ethnic groups within American society. Gelso and Fretz described five areas:

- Family relationships, and how the person perceived oneself in relation to family
- Value of self over value of family
- Value of individual success or value of combined success of the family
- Importance of the past versus importance of the present or future
- Concepts regarding focus of control over one's life choices and events

In each of these areas, the counselor must be able to understand and identify exactly what viewpoint the client holds. Out of this understanding, the counselor can provide explanations regarding the nature of the client's stress that will initiate a more trusted, shared view.

The sixth level of awareness is the **awareness of diversity**, which begins with a grasp of just how erroneous the idea is that America's cultures have joined to become one super-culture. There are marked differences in the cultures of various races, ethnicities, religious groups, and sexual orientations. In the melting pot theory, the differences in these cultures went undervalued and unrecognized. Immigrants and the poor were encouraged to buy into the values, beliefs, and attitudes of mainstream America. The melting pot theory is being replaced by the mosaic theory, and the terms "salad bowl" or "rainbow coalition." The salad bowl concept suggests a mix of ingredients that are best when the flavors are allowed to stand out and complement each other.

The final level on the Multicultural Awareness Continuum is the **necessary skills and techniques required to counsel diverse populations**. A prerequisite for beginning the multicultural process is the counselor's general competence in counseling. The counselor is required to complete each level of study successfully and satisfy internship requirements in order to achieve general competency. The counselor should be thoroughly educated in counseling theories, standards, and applications. The historical significance of the theory must be understood in context of the time period in which the theory was framed. The theorist's own cultural belief system should be noted, in conjunction with the theory he or she developed. By studying the theory in context, the counselor can better understand how to maintain the integrity of the theory when applying it to cultural groups. A counselor should perform within his or her own cultural sub-group before attempting to perform those same duties with clients of other cultural groups. There is no replacement for basic counseling skills.

## PREPARATIONS INVOLVED IN TRAINING MULTICULTURAL COUNSELORS

Since concepts of globalization are ever widening, it is imperative that a counselor maintains constant vigilance to **maintaining cultural competency**. The counselor should assume that training and education will be a life-long venture. Preparation methods should involve an all-inclusive educational program that takes into account the client's developmental capacities and a wide range of psychological theories and content available in colleges and institutions. The American Mental Health Counselors Association (AMHCA) stresses the importance of the counselor exploring his or her own cultural, ethnic, racial, and religious identity as the groundwork for this training. The counselor puts the client's needs first. To abide by AMHCA's code of ethics regarding diversity, the counselor must refer a client whenever an irresolvable conflict arises in the areas of culture, ethnicity, race, or religion.

## THE MULTICULTURAL COUNSELING FRAMEWORK

The **content of the framework** for multicultural counseling is communicative, collaborative, open to alteration or exchange, and open to quality improvement according to the client's needs. Consider the client's existing issues and incorporate up-to-date research that impacts these issues. Some core structures are required to provide consistency of care, including the following:

- Communication styles that involve an exchange of ideas and information
- Beliefs, opinions, and attitudes about psychological problems or issues
- Strategies or devised plans of action for handling and solving problems
- Counseling expectations of conduct and performance levels
- Racial identity development (the way someone absorbs cultural behavior and societal thinking from birth)
- The way the counselor sees people, events, and happenings in relation to their world view

Following this framework will help the counselor meet the needs of the client.

## PREVENTION AS PART OF MULTICULTURAL COUNSELING MODEL

Prevention is any practice that eliminates potential client suffering from psychological, emotional, and social distress. The Surgeon General reports one out of five Americans has a mental disorder but only a small portion seek out mental health services. *Mental Health: Culture, Race, and Ethnicity* (2001) is a supplement to the U.S. Department of Health and Human Services report on mental health, and addresses the issue that persons of diverse ethnic and racial backgrounds are highly

unlikely to access needed mental health services. Statistics would improve if **multicultural counseling** was available in areas not currently serviced. Ideally, at-risk groups should receive preventive care through schools, employers, social policy, vocational programs, and women and infant medical facilities. Communities can promote preventive care models through advocacy, outreach, psychoeducational interventions, and self-help groups.

## PRIMARY PREVENTION AND SYSTEMS APPROACH USED IN MULTICULTURAL COUNSELING MODELS

The multicultural mental health counselor uses his or her progressive insights and creativity to produce a positive result in helping clients. Different systems are incorporated within this task. Social justice and equity issues are a part of the lifestyle of the counselor. The counselor is willing to take preventive actions to make a difference for the client. The counselor works hard to gain cultural awareness and understanding by learning through experience, study, and training to acquire needed skills. A **systems approach** makes note of the following parameters:

- The client and existing issues
- Societal surroundings attributed to the existing issues
- The way that the person relates to issues within his or her surroundings

The counselor makes an initial assessment to determine the client's overall mental health status and how that is impacted by the issues at hand.

## SOCIAL JUSTICE AS PART OF THE MULTICULTURAL COUNSELING MODEL

Social justice is equated with problematic issues in racial conflicts, sexism, and sexual preferences. Discrimination and prejudice negatively impact quality of life for both individuals and groups. Changing discriminatory practices and prejudicial viewpoints is part of preventive mental health practices. Domestic violence, sexual attacks, child abuse, discriminatory educational and suspension practices, discriminatory employment and promotion procedures, and culturally insensitive managers and coworkers are just some possible areas where social justice should be applied. The counselor instructs the client in coping or empowerment skills that assist the client to overcome the detrimental effects of social injustice. The multicultural counselor works to change organizational, institutional, and societal thought patterns and actions of social injustice which have an adverse impact on a client's mental health status and general feeling of wellbeing.

## COMPONENTS THAT CAN IMPROVE MULTICULTURAL EDUCATIONAL COURSES

Multicultural educational courses can be improved with a broader scope on diverse populations. The United States has a diverse populace and the world at large is becoming one of mixed culture. The counselor should be apprised of issues that might arise in multiracial or multiethnic families. **Educational courses** include those that inform the counselor about religious factors, spiritual factors, gender factors, sexual orientation, disability issues, socioeconomic statures, age factors, and immigrant issues. The multicultural element may also be introduced across the curriculum in all areas of study. Counselor educators can promote multicultural competencies in educational courses. These competencies will influence the care the minority client receives by ensuring that the counselor is skilled in consultation, outreach, and advocacy.

## DETERMINING PERSONAL PREJUDICES AND ORGANIZATIONAL PREJUDICES

The danger of projecting a specific trait onto a whole group lies in a misconception about the client and leads to pathological labels that can be discriminatory. Contrarily, these misconceptions can produce guilt in the counselor who is trying to make up for the client's feeling of oppression. These misconceptions can get in the way of the counseling session. The counselor may choose to use a systems approach in exploring differences between **personal prejudices** that determine how an individual acts, and **organizational prejudices** that determine how an organization or institution acts. For example, discrepancies in behavior result when:

- The worker's personal beliefs conflict with official policies in the workplace.
- The congregation's beliefs do not follow the church's official policy.
- The electorate does not agree with government policy.

Therefore, the counselor must determine what beliefs and attitudes are promoted by those organizations in which the counselor is a member. A counselor may wish to apply a systems approach to his or her place of employment to find out if there are institutional prejudices present within.

# Core Counseling Attributes Chapter Quiz

**1. The stable environment provided by an organization to assist in a treatment plan is known as which of the following?**

    a. Safe space
    b. Therapeutic milieu
    c. Structural equanimity
    d. Integral environment

**2. How many main areas of nonverbal communication are there?**

    a. Six
    b. Five
    c. Four
    d. Three

**3. If someone is 10 feet away from someone else, they are in which category of space?**

    a. Intimate space
    b. Personal space
    c. Social-consultative space
    d. Public space

**4. What percentage of mental health staff experience physical assault at work?**

    a. 40%
    b. 50%
    c. 60%
    d. 75%

**5. All of the following are methods for obtaining sensitive information EXCEPT:**

    a. Embedding the questions in a series of questions in context
    b. Utilizing hypothetical questions instead of asking directly
    c. Using familiar rather than clinical language
    d. Using a scale (1 to 10) rather than asking for detailed information

**6. The melting pot theory of diversity in America is being replaced by which of the following theories?**

    a. River theory
    b. Mosaic theory
    c. Mainstream theory
    d. Demarcation theory

**7. The Surgeon General reports that roughly how many Americans have a mental disorder?**

    a. 1 in 20 (5%)
    b. 1 in 15 (7%)
    c. 1 in 10 (10%)
    d. 1 in 5 (20%)

**8. All of the following are non-therapeutic communication techniques EXCEPT:**

a. Clarification
b. Challenging
c. Disapproval
d. Giving advice

**9. Which of the following would NOT be considered unsafe or contraband items in a mental health facility?**

a. Alcohol
b. Over-the-counter medicine
c. Matches
d. Felt point pen

**10. Which of the following refers to consistently communicating the same message verbally and nonverbally?**

a. Rehearsed
b. Congruence
c. Moderation
d. Orchestration

# Chapter Quiz Answer Key

## Professional Practice and Ethics

**1. A:** Content validity, which can also be called rational validity or logical validity, is the reflection of the subject matter in the content of the test; for example, a math test will contain material covered in the specific math course.

**2. C:** Concurrent validity is the immediate comparison of test results with the results from other sources that measure the same factors in the same short time span.

**3. A:** There are nine steps used in the problem-solving model for ethical dilemmas designed by Koocher and Keith-Spiegel in 1998:

- Step 1: Determine the ethical problem.
- Step 2: Review the ethical guidelines available that pertain to the problem at hand, including possible solutions that have previously worked with other clients.
- Step 3: Peruse the impact that other sources may have on the decisions that should be made to resolve the problem.
- Step 4: Consult with trusted professionals about the problem and possible solutions.
- Step 5: Assess the human rights and civil liberties of the client, which may be impacted by the solution to the problem, and consider possible consequences of the solution for the problem at hand.
- Step 6: Create a number of avenues that may be explored in the solution to the problem.
- Step 7: Evaluate the possible consequences that can be the result of each solution applied to the problem at hand.
- Step 8: Make a decision about one solution to be implemented.
- Step 9: Follow through with the decision that was made.

**4. D:** Immanuel Kant is most commonly associated with the deontological view of ethics. One foundational philosophy developed by Kant was his categorical imperative. Deontological perspectives deal in universal truths, where everyone receives equal treatment. Therefore, when a counselor believes that privacy should be part of their service, then that privacy is applied to all clients in every situation. There is no room for exceptions to the rule. Likewise, there is no need to consider consequences in this philosophy, as all people are treated equally. The Golden Rule is at the heart of deontology ("Do unto others as you would have them do unto you").

**5. B:** John Stuart Mill proposed that the utilitarian should break confidentiality when it benefited the majority of the people. In 1976, a lawsuit was brought to the California Supreme Court to contest the deontological perspective against the utilitarian perspective. In the case of *Tarasoff versus the Board of Regents of the University of California*, the courts supported the utilitarian perspective on breaking confidentiality for the good of the majority. The court allowed that keeping confidentiality in this case could have caused injury to others. However, some counselors do tend to believe that confidentiality should be an absolute right of the client.

**6. B:** The most basic single system design is the A-B design. The baseline phase (A) has no intervention, followed by the intervention phase (B) with data collection. Typically, data are collected continuously through the intervention phase. Advantages of this design include the following:

- Versatility
- Adaptability to many settings, program styles, and problems
- Clear comparative information between phases

A significant limitation, however, is that causation cannot be demonstrated.

**7. C:** The key steps in the research process are as follows:

1. Problem or issue identification: Includes a literature review to further define the problem and to ensure that the problem has not already been studied
2. Hypothesis formulation: Creating a clear statement of the problem or concern, worded in a way that it can be operationalized and measured
3. Operationalization: Creating measurable variables that fully address the hypothesis
4. Study design selection: Choosing a study design that will allow for the proper analysis of the data to be collected

**8. B:** The three common study designs used in the research process include the following:

- An exploratory research design is common when little is known about a particular problem or issue. Its key feature is flexibility. The results comprise detailed descriptions of all observations made, arranged in some kind of order. Conclusions drawn include educated guesses or hypotheses.
- When the variables chosen have already been studied (e.g., in an exploratory study), further research requires a descriptive survey design. In this design, the variables are controlled partly by the situation and partly by the investigator, who chooses the sample. Proof of causality cannot be established, but the evidence may support causality.
- Experimental studies are highly controlled. Intervening and extraneous variables are eliminated, and independent variables are manipulated to measure effects in dependent variables (e.g., variables of interest)—either in the field or in a laboratory setting.

**9. C:** A population is the total set of subjects sought for measurement by a researcher.

**10. A:** Correlation refers to the strength of relatedness when a relationship exists between two or more numerical values, which, when assigned a numerical value, is the correlation coefficient ($r$). A perfect (1:1) correlation has an $r$ value of 1.0, with decimal values indicating a lesser correlation as the correlation coefficient moves away from 1.0. The correlation may be either positive (with the values increasing or decreasing together) or negative (if the values are inverse and move opposite to each other).

# Intake, Assessment, and Diagnosis

**1. B:** Freud's psychoanalytic theory postulates that behavior is influenced not only by environmental stimuli (i.e., physical influences) and external social constrains and constructs (i.e., taboos, rules, social expectations), but also by four specific unconscious elements as well. These elements exist only in the unconscious mind, and individuals remain substantively unaware of all the forces, motivations, and drives that shape their thoughts and behavioral decisions. The four elements are:

- Covert desires
- Defenses needed to protect, facilitate, and moderate behaviors
- Dreams
- Unconscious wishes

**2. D:** The Industry vs. inferiority stage occurs between 6 to 11 years of age:

- Same as Freud's latency stage.
- The need of the child is to make things well, to be a worker, and a potential provider.
- Developmental task is mastery over physical objects, self, social transaction, ideas, and concepts.
- School and peer groups are necessary for gaining and testing mastery.
- Psychological dangers include a sense of inferiority, incompetence, self-restraint, and conformity.

**3. A:** B. F. Skinner developed the empty organism concept, which proposes that an infant has the capacity for action built into his or her physical makeup. The infant also has reflexes and motivations that will set this capacity in random motion. Skinner asserted that the law of effect governs development. Behavior of children is shaped largely by adults. Behaviors that result in satisfying consequences are likely to be repeated under similar circumstances. Halting or discontinuing behavior is accomplished by denying satisfying rewards or through punishment.

**4. C:** The Luria-Nebraska neuropsychological battery (LNNB) contains 11 subtests that assess areas like rhythm, visual function, and writing. The examinee is given a score between 0 and 2, with 0 indicating normal function and 2 indicating brain damage.

**5. C:** The fourth edition of the Wechsler Adult Intelligence Scale (WAIS-IV, 2008) is used to measure the intellectual ability of late-adolescents and adults. This interrelationship between the various types of intelligence is described in the current test in terms of four index scores:

- Verbal Comprehension Index (VCI)
- Perceptual Reasoning Index (PRI)
- Working Memory Index (WMI)
- Processing Speed Index (PSI)

**6. B:** The developmental model of couples therapy (Bader & Pearson) accepts the inevitable change in relationships and focuses on both individual and couple growth and development. The goal is to assist the couple to recognize their stage of development and to gain the skills and insight needed to progress to the next stage. Problems may especially arise if members of the couple are at different stages.

**7. C:** The following are terms that pertain to Anna Freud's defense mechanisms:

- Splitting—Seeing external objects as either all good or all bad. Feelings may rapidly shift from one category to the other.

**8. D:** The following are terms that pertain to Anna Freud's defense mechanisms:

- Introjection—Absorbing an idea or image so that it becomes part of oneself.

**9. B:** One form of assessment involves nonstandard procedures that are used to provide individualized assessments. Nonstandard assessment procedures include observations of client behaviors and performance. There are three levels of observation techniques that can be applied:

- The first level is casual informational observation, where the counselor gleans information by watching the client during unstructured activities throughout the day.
- The second level is guided observation, an intentional style of direct observation accomplished with a checklist or rating scale to evaluate the performance or behavior seen.
- The third level is the clinical level, where observation is done in a controlled setting for a lengthy period of time. This is most often accomplished on the doctoral level with applied instrumentation. Clinical predictions are then based on the intuition and experience of the observing clinician.

**10. A:** Many different organizations, from schools to the armed forces, administer group intelligence tests:

- The Kuhlman-Anderson Test (KA) is for children in grades K-12; it measures verbal and quantitative intelligence. This test is unique in that it relies less on language than do other individual and group tests.
- The Woodcock Johnson IV consists of a test of cognitive abilities and a test of achievement; the latter of which measures oral language and academic achievement.
- The Wonderlic Personnel Test (WPT-R) takes about 12 minutes to fill out with paper and pencil; it purports to measure the mental ability of adults. The Wonderlic is a good predictor of performance, but some critics maintain that it unfairly discriminates against some cultural groups in certain jobs.

# Areas of Clinical Focus

**1. D:** Down syndrome (Trisomy 21) occurs when a person has three #21 chromosomes instead of two. Down syndrome causes 20-30% of all cases of moderate and severe intellectual disability (1:800 births). Around 80% of Trisomy 21 pregnancies end in miscarriage. Classic physical characteristics associated with Down syndrome are slanted, almond-shaped eyes with epicanthic folds; a large, protruding tongue; a short, bent fifth finger; and a simian fold across the palm.

**2. A:** The value-based career theory (Brown, 2002) posited that central to career counseling is an understanding of the client's underlying values. According to this model, goal-directed behavior is stimulated by values. Values are an incentive. Therefore, the client gains satisfaction when he or she reaches a value-based goal. When the client does not reach a value-based goal successfully, disappointment and dejection are the likely outcome. Value-based goals can be well defined or based on a crystallized priority ranking. According to Brown's model, the three types of values are cultural, work, and life values.

**3. A:** Most successful treatments for Tourette's syndrome include pharmacotherapy. The antipsychotics haloperidol (Haldol) and pimozide (Orap) are successful in relieving the symptoms of Tourette's syndrome because they inhibit the flow of dopamine in the brain; their success has led many scientists to speculate that Tourette's Disorder is caused by an excess of dopamine. In some cases, psychostimulant drugs amplify the tics displayed by the individual. In these cases, a doctor may treat the hyperactivity and inattention of Tourette's with clonidine or desipramine. The former of these is a drug usually used to treat hypertension, while the latter is typically used as an antidepressant.

**4. D:** Encopresis is the involuntary fecal soiling in children who have already been toilet trained. Encopresis diagnosis cannot be made until the child is at least 4 years of age per DSM-5 criteria.

**5. C:** Adults with a specific phobia should be able to recognize that their fear is irrational and excessive. The onset of a specific phobia is typically in childhood or in the mid-20s. According to the DSM-5, there are five subtypes of specific phobia:

- Animal
- Natural environment
- Situational
- Blood-injection-injury
- Other

**6. B:** As with panic disorder, in vivo exposure is considered the best treatment for a specific phobia. Relaxation and breathing techniques are also helpful in dispelling fear and controlling physical response.

**7. C:** The symptoms of a conversion disorder can often be removed with hypnosis or Amytal interview. Some researchers believe that simply suggesting that these symptoms will go away is the best way to relieve them. The individual can develop complications, like seizures, from disuse of body parts.

**8. A:** Personality disorders are clustered into three groups:

| Cluster A (eccentric or odd disorders) | Cluster B (dramatic or excessively emotional disorders) | Cluster C (fear- or anxiety-based disorders) |
| --- | --- | --- |
| Paranoid | Antisocial | Avoidant |
| Schizoid | Borderline | Dependent |
| Schizotypal | Histrionic | Obsessive-Compulsive |
| | Narcissistic | |

**9. B:** According to the National Institute of Alcohol Abuse and Alcoholism, 85.6% of Americans reported drinking alcohol at some point in their life, almost 70% reporting that they drank in the last year (2019). Around 50% of Americans drink alcohol as part of their daily routine; 10% of these routine drinkers will fall into addictive, habitual use.

**10. A:** The survivors of a disaster go through a series of emotional and psychological stages.

- In the first stage, the survivor sees himself or herself as a hero and acts out these heroic thoughts by helping to save someone else or their property.
- These altruistic feelings of individual heroism are followed by a honeymoon period, in which the whole neighborhood joins together to work as one unit to save others.
- The honeymoon period is followed by the disillusionment stage, which comes as a result of the postponement of help from others. The person feels let down by others.
- The final stage involves the reconstruction period. The survivor no longer looks for help from others, but instead takes control and responsibility for his or her situation, and works to resolve the problem.

# Treatment Planning

**1. B:** Stage 2 of theory development is paradigm modification by Jung, Adler, Patterson, and Bandura.

**2. B:** Personality structure: The personality has three main components:

- Id: Unconscious pleasure principle, manifest by a desire for immediate and complete satisfaction with disregard for others
- Ego: Rational and conscious reality principle, which weighs actions and consequences
- Superego: Conscious and unconscious censoring force of the personality, which evaluates and judges behavior

**3. C:** Jung's archetypes are the images and concepts that develop the collective unconscious of humanity. The main archetypes are:

- The Way: The image of a journey or voyage through life
- The Self: The aspect of the mind that unifies and orders experience
- Animus and Anima: The image of gender
- Rebirth: The concept of being reborn, resurrected or reincarnated
- Persona: The role or mask one shows to others
- Shadow: The dark side of one's personality
- Stock characters: Dramatic roles that appear over and over in folktales
- The Hero: The character who vanquishes evil and rescues the downtrodden
- The Trickster: The character who plays pranks or works magic spells
- The Sage: The wise old person
- Power: A symbol such as the eagle or the sword
- Number: Certain numbers appear throughout history and across cultures

**4. C:** The removal of masks and facades is the goal of Gestalt therapy, according to Perls. A creative interaction needs to be developed so the client can gain an ongoing awareness of what is being felt, sensed, and thought.

**5. D:** Cross-cultural research has distinguished six basic universal human emotions: Fear, anger, happiness, disgust, surprise, and sadness. The James-Lange theory of emotion asserts that emotions are the body's reaction to changes in the autonomic nervous system caused by external stimuli. This theory is supported by the fact that quadriplegics report feeling less-intense emotions.

**6. A:** The transtheoretical model focuses on changes in behavior based on the individual's decisions (not on society's decisions or others' decisions) and is used to develop strategies to promote changes in health behavior. This model outlines stages people go through when changing problem behavior and trying to have a positive attitude about change. Stages of change include the following:

- Precontemplation: The person is either unaware or under-informed about consequences of a problem behavior and has no intention of changing behavior within the next 6 months.
- Contemplation: The person is aware of costs and benefits of changing behavior and intends to change within the next 6 months but is procrastinating and not ready for action.
- Preparation: The person has a plan and intends to initiate change in the near future (≤1 month) and is ready for action plans.

- Action: The person is modifying behavior change occurs only if behavior meets a set criterion (such as complete abstinence from drinking).
- Maintenance: The person works to maintain changes and gains confidence that he or she will not relapse.

**7. A:** Gottfried Leibniz was a philosopher who believed in personology, which states that a person can change when his or her perceptual awareness is changed. Leibniz's theory of mind is based on subjective reality—how a person perceives things to be within his or her own mind. Leibniz's theory of personology evolved into humanistic psychology, resulting in a counseling model known as Rogers' person-centered psychotherapy.

**8. D:** According to Joseph Rychlak, psychotherapy can be broken down into three basic motives that correspond with learning, ethics, and healing.

- Scholarly motive corresponds with learning. Rychlak believed this rationale for performing psychotherapy was best characterized in the works of Freud, where the psychotherapist is a scientist who records the inner workings of the mind, instinctive drives, and actions, and then analyzes the data collected.
- Ethical motive refers to the counselor's desire to help the client grow and express strong feelings and opinions about his or her life problems.
- Curative motive is when the psychotherapist wants to initiate the healing process for the client by engaging in such a way as to help modify those behaviors detrimental to the client's success in society.

**9. D:** Motivational interviewing (Miller, 1983) aims to help people identify and resolve issues regarding ambivalence about change and focuses on the role of motivation to bring about change. MI is a collaborative approach in which the interviewer assesses the individual's readiness to accept change and identifies strategies that may be effective with the individual.

| Elements | Principles | Strategies |
|---|---|---|
| Collaboration rather than confrontation in resolving issues Evocation (drawing out) of the individual's ideas about change rather than imposition of the interviewer's ideas Autonomy of the individual in making changes | Expression of empathy: Showing understanding of individual's perceptions Support of self-efficacy: Helping individuals realize they are capable of change Acceptance of resistance: Avoiding struggles/conflicts with client Examination of discrepancies: Helping individuals see discrepancy between their behavior and goals | Avoiding Yes/No questions: Asking informational questions Providing affirmations: Indicating areas of strength Providing reflective listening: Responding to statements Providing summaries: Recapping important points of discussion Encouraging change talk: Including desire, ability, reason, and need |

**10. B:** Common Freudian psychiatric terms include:

- Freudian slips: Also known as parapraxes, these are overt actions with unconscious meanings.

# Counseling Skills and Interventions

**1. A:** Adaptability is maintaining a balanced, positive stability in the family. A prerequisite for balanced stability, and a basic goal of family therapy, is to help the client family develop strategies for dealing with life's inevitable changes. Morphogenesis is the medical term often applied to a family's ability to react functionally and appropriately to changes.

**2. B:** Personal Science was developed in 1977 by Michael Mahoney, based on the cognitive-behavioral (CB) approach. The acronym SCIENCE is used to explain the sequential steps through which the therapist guides the client to solve a problem:

- S for *specification* of the problem
- C for *collection* of data or facts
- I for *identification* of patterns or reasons for existing behaviors
- E for *examination* of choices that can be used to modify behavior
- N for *narrowing* the options and experimenting with possible modifications
- C for *comparing* data or facts
- E for *expanding*, modifying, or substituting unwanted behaviors

**3. B:** Key concepts of Albert Ellis's rational emotive therapy include the idea that people control their own destinies and interpret events, according to their own values and beliefs.

**4. A:** Irvin Yalom's "here-and-now" or process groups are characterized by the following:

- Yalom stressed using clients' immediate reactions and discussing members' affective experiences in the group.
- Process groups have relatively unstructured and spontaneous sessions.
- Process groups emphasize therapeutic activities, like imparting information, or instilling hope, universality, and altruism.
- The group can provide a rehabilitative narrative of primary family group development, offer socializing techniques, provide behavior models to imitate, offer interpersonal learning, and offer an example of group cohesiveness and catharsis.

**5. A:** Proxemics is the study of personal space and the distance between individuals at which people feel comfortable or uncomfortable. Proxemics vary according to culture, and the counselor should assess the client's personal space of comfort and avoid violating that space or communicating the wrong message.

**6. D:** Family therapy is a therapeutic modality theorizing that a client's psychiatric symptoms are a result of pathology within the client's family unit. This dysfunction is due to problems within the system, usually arising from conflict between marital partners. Psychiatric problems result from these behaviors. This conflict is expressed by:

- Triangulation, which manifests itself by the attempt of using another family member to stabilize the emotional process
- Scapegoating, which occurs when blaming is used to shift focus to another family member.

**7. B:** Satir described four issues that impede communication between family members under stress. Placating, blaming, being overly reasonable, and being irrelevant are the four issues which blocked family communication, according to Virginia Satir:

- Placating is the role played by some people in reaction to threat or stress in the family. The placating person reacts to internal stresses by trying to please others, often in irrational ways. A mother might try to placate her disobedient and rude child by offering food, candy, or other presents on the condition that he stop a certain behavior.
- Blaming is the act of pointing outwards when an issue creates stress. The blamer thinks, "I'm very angry, but it's your fault. If I've wrecked the car, it's because you made me upset when I left home this morning."
- Irrelevance is a behavior wherein a person displaces the potential problem and substitutes another unrelated activity. A mother who engages in too much social drinking frequently discusses her split ends whenever the topic of alcoholism is brought up by her spouse.
- Being overly reasonable, also known as being a responsible analyzer is when a person keeps his or her emotions in check and functions with the precision and monotony of a machine.

**8. B:** Multiple theories of causality exist in the interpretation of family dynamics, which are then applied to the selection of therapeutic interventions. While linear causality (the concept that one cause equals one effect) uses a direct line of reasoning and is commonly used in individual counseling, circular/reciprocal causality is often used in family therapy and refers to the dynamic interactions between family members.

**9. C:** The social reinforcement and exchange theory in regard to group work is summarized as follows:

- Social exchange theorists propose that members of groups are motivated to seek profit in their interactions with others (i.e., to maximize rewards and minimize costs).
- Analysis of interactions within groups is done in terms of a series of exchanges or tradeoffs group members make with each other.
- The individual member is the primary unit of analysis. Many of the core concepts of this theory are merely transferred to the group situation and do not further the understanding of group processes.

**10. D:** The correlates of humor are what make it successful in producing an amusing result. There are three correlates of humor:

- The suddenness of the punch line or surprising conclusion gives the audience the opportunity to laugh at the unexpected twist.
- Optimal arousal is derived from an appropriate level of intellectual, emotional, or physical stimulation (e.g., adults find it difficult to laugh at childish jokes that have ceased to be of interest).
- Play frame is setting up the joke or story to be non-threatening for the listener. Some jokes may be too intense for the individual's comfort level. Play frame involves cueing the listener through facial expressions or vocal tones that intend a time for play.

# Core Counseling Attributes

**1. B:** The therapeutic milieu is a stable environment provided by an organization to assist in a treatment plan. The main purposes of a milieu are to teach individuals certain social skills and to provide a structured environment that promotes interactions and personal growth along with attempting to control many types of deviant or destructive behaviors. There are five main components that the milieu should include in therapy. These components include containment, structure, support, involvement, and validation. Through the use of these components, the therapeutic milieu can help the individuals achieve their highest level of functioning.

**2. B:** There are many different types of nonverbal behaviors. There are five main areas of nonverbal communication. They include vocal cues, action cues, object cues, space, and touch.

**3. C:** Space can provide information about a relationship between the client and someone else. Most people living in the United States have four different areas of space. Intimate space is less than 1.5 feet, personal space is 1.5-4 feet, social-consultative space is 9-12 feet, and public space is 12 feet or more. Observations concerning space and the client's physical placement in a setting can give a great deal of insight into different interpersonal relationships.

**4. D:** A protocol for a professional assault response should be established at all mental health facilities because statistics show that 75% of mental health staff experience a physical assault. Most injuries are incurred by nursing staff caring for violent clients. Assaults may occur in both psychiatric units and emergency departments, where security staff may also be assaulted. Additionally, clients may be victims. Common injuries include fractures, lacerations, contusions, and unconsciousness from head injuries.

**5. B:** Sensitive information includes that involving sexual activity, abuse, intimate partner violence, substance abuse, and mental health issues. Clients are more likely to answer questions truthfully if they have developed a relationship of trust with the questioner. Methods of obtaining sensitive information include the following:

- Embedding the questions in a series of questions in context: "Do you spend time with your friends?" "Are your friends sexually active?" "Do you think you are more or less sexually active than your friends?" "How many sexual partners have you had?"
- Asking for facts and not opinions
- Using familiar language and terminology
- Asking for permission to question, "Do you mind if I ask you about…" and explaining the reason for questioning, "In order to plan for your medical care, I need to ask you about…"
- Using a scale (1 to 10) rather than asking for detailed information
- Explaining what kinds of information can remain confidential and what kinds cannot (such as child abuse)

**6. B:** The sixth level of awareness is the awareness of diversity, which begins with a grasp of just how erroneous the idea is that America's cultures have joined to become one super-culture. There are marked differences in the cultures of various races, ethnicities, religious groups, and sexual orientations. In the melting pot theory, the differences in these cultures went undervalued and unrecognized. Immigrants and the poor were encouraged to buy into the values, beliefs, and attitudes of mainstream America. The melting pot theory is being replaced by the mosaic theory, and the terms "salad bowl" or "rainbow coalition." The salad bowl concept suggests a mix of ingredients that are best when the flavors are allowed to stand out and complement each other.

**7. D:** The Surgeon General reports that approximately one out of five Americans has a mental disorder but only a small portion seek out mental health services. *Mental Health: Culture, Race, and Ethnicity* (2001) is a supplement to the U.S. Department of Health and Human Services report on mental health, and addresses the issue that persons of diverse ethnic and racial backgrounds are highly unlikely to access needed mental health services.

**8. A:** Techniques that are detrimental to establishing a trusting therapeutic relationship include giving advice, challenging the client's communications, or indicating disapproval. Giving advice includes telling the client what they should do in a particular situation. This does not allow the client to develop the ability to solve their own problems and may not always be the right answer. Challenging occurs when the client's thoughts are disputed by the provider. This communication only serves to lower the client's self-esteem and create an environment of distrust between the client and the mental health care provider. Disapproval occurs when the provider negatively judges the client's beliefs or actions. This again serves to lower client self-esteem and does not foster their ability to solve their own problems or create new coping abilities.

**9. D:** Depending on the type of facility or clients, a wide range of items may be considered unsafe. These often include the following:

- Potential weapons, such as pens (except felt point), pencils, and plastic bags

**10. B:** Congruence in communication is consistently communicating the same message verbally and nonverbally. The individual's words, body language, and tone of voice should all convey the same message. If they do not, then the communication is incongruent, and the receiver cannot trust the communication. For example, if a person says, "I really want to help you," in a very harsh tone of voice and with an angry affect, the communication is incongruent, and the message may actually be perceived as the exact opposite of the words spoken. Communication is also incongruent if the individual gives a series of conflicting messages: "I'm going to get a job," "Why should I work?" "I know I need to work," "There's no point in taking a low-paying job." Being alert to the congruence of client communication makes it possible to more accurately assess the client.

# NCE Practice Test #1

**1. A study measuring the IQ levels of a group of men, of differing ages, performed on a single day is most likely an example of:**

    a.  a cross-sectional study.
    b.  a longitudinal study.
    c.  a stratified sample study.
    d.  a systematic sample study.

**2. Which of the following is TRUE of testing people with disabilities?**

    a.  Test scores administered under standardized and modified conditions are typically equivalent.
    b.  General agreement exists on how tests should be modified for people with disabilities.
    c.  There exists a need for a growing body of research related to the equivalency between tests administered under standardized and under modified conditions.
    d.  The presence of disabilities should not impact test results.

**3. If a client with antisocial behavior begins to stroke the counselor's arm and hand suggestively during a session, which of the following is the most appropriate response?**

    a.  "Stop touching me this instance! You know very well that is inappropriate behavior."
    b.  "If you don't stop touching me immediately, you will lose all TV privileges."
    c.  "Why are you touching me? What exactly are you trying to prove?"
    d.  "Remove your hand. We are discussing your plan of care, and you don't need to touch me."

**4. Which of the following best describes norms?**

    a.  They give meaning to a behavior sample
    b.  They provide a parallel form for comparison
    c.  They indicate whether a test is reliable
    d.  They tell whether a distribution of scores is normally distributed

**5. Leisure activities are those activities that a professional career counselor:**

    a.  may also refer to as avocations.
    b.  never discusses with clients.
    c.  describes as relaxing and done at work.
    d.  describes as involving going on vacations.

**6. An individual is given the Wechsler Adult Intelligence Scales (WAIS-IV) by a psychologist. When showing the client the results, the tester compares the client's score on the vocabulary subtest to his score on the digit span subtest and his score on the block design subtest, etc. This type of assessment is:**

    a.  norm-referenced.
    b.  criterion-referenced.
    c.  ipsatively interpreted.
    d.  cohort-referenced.

**7. A counselor is asked to evaluate a client for possible intellectual disabilities. The client achieves a score of 50 on the WAIS-IV. According to the DSM, what range does this place her in?**

    a. Moderate to severe intellectual disabilities
    b. Mild to moderate intellectual disabilities
    c. Mild to profound intellectual disabilities
    d. Severe to profound intellectual disabilities

**8. Who developed the archway model of self-concept determinants?**

    a. John Holland
    b. Linda Gottfredson
    c. Donald Super
    d. John Krumboltz

**9. The treatment for a 26-year-old female client with bulimia nervosa sets limits regarding the client's eating habits. Which of the following limits is counterproductive?**

    a. Requiring the client to eat in the dining room
    b. Asking the client to keep a food diary
    c. Discussing reactions to different types of food
    d. Assigning daily "grades" for compliance with eating limits

**10. According to Carl Rogers, _____ is love and support given to another with no strings attached.**

    a. the condition of worth
    b. unconditional positive regard
    c. existentialism
    d. self-actualization

**11. Which term does NOT fall under the "appraisal" process?**

    a. Group testing
    b. Individual testing
    c. Clinical observation
    d. Clinical intervention

**12. A client who is devoutly religious and believes her disability is punishment for sins may benefit most from which of the following?**

    a. Self-help groups
    b. Pastoral counseling
    c. Self-help literature
    d. Psychotherapy

**13. A counselor wants to make sure that the test she is using provides the same scores for people when they retake the test a month later. What should the counselor look for when reviewing the test manual?**

    a. Alternate or parallel-forms reliability
    b. Split-half reliability
    c. Scorer reliability
    d. Test-retest reliability

**14. What is accreditation?**

    a. A process whereby a counselor becomes certified or licensed to practice therapy

    b. A process whereby a researcher receives credit for his or her work in a publication

    c. A process whereby an institution or program receives public recognition for meeting standards

    d. A process whereby a doctoral student is credited for earning a counseling degree

**15. A couple who each have children from previous marriages are planning to marry. During premarital counseling, which of the following statements is of most concern?**

    a. Male: "I've already told my children that they have a new mother and they are to call her 'Mom.'"

    b. Female: "All of the different custody agreements are going to be confusing at first."

    c. Male: "I don't think I can have the exact same feelings for a stepchild as I do a biological child."

    d. Female: "My children still love their father, so they may have some problem adjusting."

**16. When completing the client assessment and developing the plan of care with a client with an eating disorder, it is especially important to ask the client about which of the following?**

    a. Motivation to change behavior

    b. Self-injurious behavior

    c. Sexual dysfunction

    d. Goal for weight

**17. The counselor is conducting vocational assessment of a client with disabilities, beginning with the initial rehabilitation assessment. Which of the following should the counselor do next?**

    a. Workplace assessment

    b. Functional capacity evaluation

    c. Physical conditioning assessment

    d. Risk assessment

**18. The resolution of conflicts and breaking out of destructive habits are the primary goals of:**

    a. family therapy.

    b. existential therapy.

    c. psychodynamic therapy.

    d. couples therapy.

**19. What is the female version of Freud's Oedipus complex?**

    a. The Superego

    b. The Electra complex

    c. There isn't a female version

    d. The Id

**20. What is NOT true of HIPAA?**

    a. It is a law that varies from state to state

    b. It protects the privacy of patient records

    c. It regulates the sharing of information

    d. It regulates electronic insurance claims

**21. Regression is all of the following except:**

    a. A Freudian concept
    b. A defense mechanism
    c. A psychoanalytic concept
    d. A rational emotive therapy

**22. Who is best known for the terms "collective unconscious" and "archetypes?"**

    a. Alfred Adler
    b. Sigmund Freud
    c. Carl Jung
    d. Aaron Beck

**23. A depressed client continually refers to thoughts of being inferior and unworthy of love, and chooses self-destructive behavior as a result. The counselor believes that changing her thought process will alter or eliminate her depression. What type of therapy is being utilized?**

    a. Operant conditioning
    b. Psychoanalysis
    c. Rational-emotive therapy (RET)
    d. Aversive conditioning

**24. Arnold Gesell believed that:**

    a. development was genetically pre-ordained and realized via maturation.
    b. development was differentially influenced via environmental conditions.
    c. development resulted from a combination of genetics and environment.
    d. development could be realized via nature or nurture, depending on the individual.

**25. In an experiment, what is the "independent variable"?**

    a. The experimental factor
    b. The element that is measured and observed
    c. The variable that depends upon what happens to the experimental subjects
    d. The variable that determines causation

**26. What is empathy?**

    a. A type of projection
    b. A way to experience the world as the client does
    c. A way to feel what oneself would feel in the client's situation
    d. Feeling the same feelings that the client has

**27. The bond of confidence and mutual understanding established between therapist and client is called the:**

    a. therapeutic window.
    b. therapeutic alliance.
    c. clubhouse model.
    d. window of opportunity.

**28. Which of the following is NOT considered a specialty counseling certification from the National Board for Certified Counselors, Inc. (NBCC)?**

a. National Certified School Counselor (NCSC)
b. Certified Clinical Mental Health Counselor (CCMHC)
c. Master Addictions Counselor (MAC)
d. National Certified Counselor (NCC)

**29. Gilbert Wrenn's book *The Counselor in a Changing World* (1962) stressed the role of the counseling profession as being focused on:**

a. neurotic needs.
b. collective (group) needs.
c. developmental needs.
d. individual needs.

**30. What is proxemics?**

a. The idea that proximity impacts psychosis
b. The study of proximity
c. The ability of one individual to act as proxy for another
d. The study of conducive therapeutic environments

**31. What did passage of the Smith-Hughes Act accomplish?**

a. It provided money to fund the training of school counselors
b. It granted federal funds for vocational education and guidance
c. It required the licensure of marriage, family, and child counselors
d. It greatly expanded the counseling services to veterans in the VA

**32. Which of the following statements by a client in cognitive behavioral therapy for major depressive disorder suggests that the client, who is experiencing negative thoughts, is applying principles learned in therapy?"**

a. "I know I need to change because I feel so worthless all the time."
b. "I can't fix this situation, so I'm going to think about taking a vacation."
c. "I should have known better than to think I could fix this situation."
d. "I want to feel better about this situation."

**33. One of the differences between individual therapy and family therapy is that family therapists believe that:**

a. family members act entirely independently of one another.
b. problems typically involve only one person.
c. causality should be understood as a circular process rather than a linear one.
d. an individual should withdraw from the family dynamic before trying to address issues.

**34. Giving a negative consequence every time an unwanted behavior occurs could be considered all of the following EXCEPT:**

a. behavioral therapy.
b. operant conditioning.
c. punishment.
d. positive reinforcement.

**35. One of Meichenbaum's three stages of "stress inoculation" focuses on:**
   a.   the relationship between the client and meaningful work
   b.   mastering the hierarchy of needs
   c.   skills acquisition
   d.   the relationship between the client and their family

**36. Which of the following is correct regarding either norm-referenced tests or criterion-referenced tests?**
   a.   Norm-referenced tests show what knowledge an individual has
   b.   Criterion-referenced tests show an individual's rank in the group
   c.   Criterion-referenced tests compare an individual's score to others
   d.   Norm-referenced tests compare an individual's score to others

**37. Who established the very first psychological laboratory in history?**
   a.   Wilhelm Wundt
   b.   Sigmund Freud
   c.   Jesse Davis
   d.   Clifford Beers

**38. Which pair seems to go together?**
   a.   Roe and Holland
   b.   Holland and Krumboltz
   c.   Roe and Hoppock
   d.   Roe and Krumboltz

**39. Who developed transactional analysis (TA) and "life scripts"?**
   a.   Sigmund Freud
   b.   Eric Berne
   c.   Eric Erikson
   d.   Alfred Adler

**40. Which of the following are the four essential components of informed consent before a client can make a decision about care?**
   a.   Competence, disclosure, options, and voluntarism
   b.   Competence, comprehension, non-coercion, and disclosure
   c.   Voluntarism, competence, non-coercion, and disclosure
   d.   Voluntarism, competence, disclosure, and comprehension

**41. At a dinner party, the counselor encounters a client and, in the presence of four other guests at the party, the client tells the counselor that he feels guilty because he committed a serious crime. Which of the following best describes whether this is privileged communication or not?**
   a.   Yes, because they have a client-counselor relationship already established
   b.   No, because the communication was made in the presence of others
   c.   No, because the client committed a crime
   d.   Yes, because the client did not specifically say the communication was not privileged

42. Dr. Stanwyck has used two different counseling approaches with two different groups of college students. Both groups had similar scores on a pre-test of self-efficacy. He gives each group the same post-test to measure their self-efficacy levels following the course of counseling. What kind of test would he most likely use to see if there is a statistically significant difference between the two groups' post-test scores?

    a.  A t-test
    b.  A one-way ANOVA
    c.  A factorial ANOVA
    d.  A MANOVA

43. A client who has been in recovery from cocaine addiction is laughing and telling the counselor about the good times he had when he was using cocaine and how much better his social life was. Which of the following should the counselor suspect?

    a.  The client is in relapse
    b.  The client remains abstinent
    c.  The client thinks addiction is humorous
    d.  The client is no longer interested in using cocaine

44. Which of the following is an appropriate statement for a counselor to make on a social networking site about working with clients?

    a.  "I really like some of my clients, especially the older woman who calls me 'dear.'"
    b.  "I had a client today who threw a screaming fit at me."
    c.  No statement whatsoever about specific clients or workload.
    d.  "I have to see way too many clients in a day!"

45. When applying to graduate school, the admissions committee compares the candidate's scores on the GRE with the candidate's grade point average reported on the college transcripts. This is an example of:

    a.  construct validity.
    b.  content validity.
    c.  criterion-related validity.
    d.  concurrent validity.

46. The values clarification process has three steps: (1) choosing, (2) prizing, and (3) which of the following?

    a.  Evaluating
    b.  Assessing
    c.  Demonstrating
    d.  Acting

47. A counselor is asked to speak to a group of Junior Rangers about future career choices, and plan a presentation based upon knowledge of one of the members of the group. What type of reasoning is the counselor employing?

    a.  Operant rationalization
    b.  Deductive reasoning
    c.  Inductive reasoning
    d.  Constructive reasoning

**48. The James-Lange theory of arousal and emotion says that:**

   a.   a physiological response precedes emotion.
   b.   emotion precedes a physiological response.
   c.   emotion and physiological response occur together.
   d.   physiological response and emotion are not related.

**49. A counselor wants to measure happiness, and decides that he will keep track of how many times his subjects laugh in the course of a day. He writes down every detail of his study so it can be replicated, specifying the measurement of "smiles" as a way to determine happiness levels. What has the counselor provided?**

   a.   A research report
   b.   An operational definition
   c.   A replication report
   d.   An analogy

**50. If, in a support group, the counselor observes that one member routinely takes over the discussions and sometimes bullies others, this might be described as which of the following?**

   a.   Group theme
   b.   Group blocking
   c.   Group directing
   d.   Group pattern

**51. What branch of psychology deals primarily with groups and social factors?**

   a.   Behavioral Psychology
   b.   Cognitive-Behavioral Psychology
   c.   Psychoanalytic Psychology
   d.   Social Psychology

**52. A dog that has been trained to stop and stand at attention when she hears a duck call does not stop and stand at attention when she hears a goose call. This is an example of:**

   a.   stimulus generalization.
   b.   higher-order conditioning.
   c.   conditioned response.
   d.   stimulus discrimination.

**53. A researcher reports that $p < 0.05$ in his study. This means that:**

   a.   the probability that the results were obtained in error is less than 5%.
   b.   the probability that no relationship between the independent variable and the dependent variable exists is less than 5%.
   c.   the independent variable is responsible for more than 95% of the observed difference in the dependent variable.
   d.   the study is designed to produce an incorrect conclusion less than 5% of the time.

**54. Managing a counseling program may require skills in all of the following areas except:**

   a.   Program design and development
   b.   Marketing and public relations
   c.   Budgeting
   d.   Accounting

**55. Which of the following types of exercise may best reduce symptoms of anxiety and depression?**

a. Aerobic
b. Isometric
c. Stretching
d. Weight lifting

**56. During the orientation phase of building a therapeutic relationship, the counselor discovers that he had come to the first meeting with preconceptions about the client. Based on this, the counselor should do which of the following?**

a. Ask another counselor to work with the client
b. Apologize to the client
c. Spend extra time with the client
d. Recognize and set aside the preconceptions

**57. The key difference between ipsative scales and normative scales is that ipsative scales:**

a. allow the counselor to make comparisons among individuals.
b. provide information about an individual client.
c. include achievement and aptitude tests.
d. have been standardized and normed.

**58. Only _____ permits a researcher to identify cause and effect.**

a. a correlational study
b. an experiment
c. a survey
d. naturalistic observation

**59. An 18-year-old university student who attended an off-campus drinking party and was attacked and raped is having difficulty coping and tells the counselor, "I'm so stupid. It was my fault!! I shouldn't have gone to the party!" Which of the following is the best response?**

a. "It was a hard way to learn a lesson."
b. "You're not to blame for someone else's actions. It's not your fault."
c. "Yes, it was irresponsible, but you need to move forward now."
d. "Perhaps you were both too drunk to be responsible for your actions."

**60. Who developed the first intelligence test?**

a. Alfred Binet and Theophilus Simon
b. Sigmund Freud
c. David Wechsler
d. Stanford University and Alfred Binet

**61. In the Stanford prison study, what caused the guards to treat the prisoners harshly?**

a. Their instructions from the researchers
b. The uncooperative behavior of the prisoners
c. The social context
d. The pressure the guards got from one another

62. A researcher conducts a study in which she looks at the effects of using Nicorette gum on smoking cessation. Most likely, her statistical analysis will include:

    a. Pearson's r.
    b. a t-test.
    c. an ANOVA.
    d. a chi-square.

63. According to Linda Gottfredson, young children around age 6 tend to choose occupations based upon:

    a. their social values.
    b. their ability levels.
    c. their sex or gender.
    d. their personal traits.

64. Which of the following is the correct chronological order of the four career development stages identified by Linda Gottfredson?

    a. Orientation to size and power, orientation to sex roles, orientation to social valuation, orientation to the internal unique self
    b. Orientation to the internal unique self, orientation to sex roles, orientation to size and power, orientation to social valuation
    c. Orientation to sex roles, orientation to size and power, orientation to social valuation, orientation to the internal unique self
    d. Orientation to social valuation, orientation to the internal unique self, orientation to sex roles, orientation to size and power

65. Which of the following is true of electroconvulsive therapy (ECT):

    a. ECT is an incredibly dangerous therapy.
    b. ECT involves little discomfort.
    c. ECT is mostly used for schizophrenia.
    d. ECT is a common treatment for bipolar disorder.

66. In family therapy, the terms "enmeshed" and "disengaged" are most closely associated with:

    a. Adler.
    b. Minuchin.
    c. Ackerman.
    d. Haley.

67. The counselor who is taking the on-call services for the evening receives a call from an individual asking if her boyfriend is seeing a counselor at the clinic. The best course of action is to:

    a. get the phone number of the individual and call her back with the information.
    b. not acknowledge anything.
    c. suggest that she ask her boyfriend herself.
    d. provide her with the information she is asking for.

68. Juan is from a Hispanic culture and Mai is from an Asian culture. According to multicultural counseling theorists, they will have certain needs if seeking counseling. Of the following, which would likely be a more suitable counseling orientation for both of them?

    a. Traditional Freudian psychoanalysis
    b. Rogerian client-centered counseling
    c. Abraham Maslow's self-actualization
    d. Fritz Perls' Gestalt model of therapy

69. Which of the following best describes hypnosis?

    a. A drug-induced mental state
    b. A deep state of relaxation
    c. A meditative state
    d. A magician's trick

70. In Albert Bandura's cognitive behavioral therapeutic approach, ___is very important in developing adaptive behavior.

    a. aversive conditioning
    b. catharsis
    c. a token economy
    d. self-efficacy

71. John Watson is probably best known for his:

    a. Little Albert experiment.
    b. contributions to psychoanalytic theory.
    c. Bobo doll study.
    d. intuitive learning research.

72. According to Ginzberg, Ginsburg, Axelrad, and Herma's developmental theory, occupational choice passes through three periods. Which is NOT one of the main periods they identified?

    a. Fantasy
    b. Tentative
    c. Transition
    d. Realistic

73. One way to reduce Type I and Type II errors is to:

    a. increase sample size.
    b. decrease sample size.
    c. increase the level of significance.
    d. decrease the level of significance.

74. The SBIRT (Screening, Brief Intervention, Referral to Treatment) program is designed for which of the following?

    a. Adolescents engaging in substance abuse
    b. Older adults with addiction
    c. Substance abusers at risk but not yet dependent
    d. Substance abusers with long-time addiction

**75. The primary goal of _____ therapy is to find meaning in life.**

    a. rational-emotive
    b. reality
    c. existential
    d. transactional analysis

**76. When it comes to displaying aggression, girls more often engage in _____ aggression than boys.**

    a. hostile
    b. instrumental
    c. relational
    d. physical

**77. When compared to the past, modern-day careers tend to be viewed least as which of the following:**

    a. self-expression
    b. a status symbol
    c. a social expectation
    d. a means to earn money

**78. Which is NOT an example of resistive individual or group behavior that would impede progress in a therapy group?**

    a. Being unable to set goals
    b. Talking too much or too little
    c. Discussing members' problems
    d. Arriving late to group meetings

**79. Madelyn has been in a long-term psychotherapy group for the past five years, and the group's leader often encourages members to explore issues originating in their childhoods. According to Gerald Caplan's model, this would be an example of:**

    a. a primary therapy group.
    b. a secondary therapy group.
    c. a tertiary therapy group.
    d. a foundational therapy group.

**80. If a researcher who found a negative correlation between the amount of TV viewing done by children and academic performance were to graph her results, she would use a:**

    a. normal bell curve.
    b. positively skewed curve.
    c. scatterplot.
    d. negatively skewed curve.

**81. Which of the following is a myth about suicide in the United States?**

    a. Male suicide rates are four times higher than that among females
    b. It occurs in age groups of 90 years and up
    c. Psychiatrists, physicians, and dentists are most prone to suicide
    d. Asking someone about suicide may push that person over the edge

**82. What is "positive psychology?"**

    a. The study of the processes that contribute to optimal functioning
    b. A type of therapy that encourages positive thinking to overcome difficulties
    c. A discipline that analyzes developmental abnormalities
    d. A theory that eliminating negative behaviors leads to positive outcomes

**83. Logotherapy focuses on:**

    a. pleasure.
    b. power.
    c. human will.
    d. pain.

**84. The counselor is assessing an older adult who experienced an "accidental" overdose of drugs and alcohol for possible suicidal ideation. When assessing the client for depression, which of the following initial queries is most effective?**

    a. "What has changed in your life or health over the last 6-8 months?"
    b. "Have you been feeling depressed?"
    c. "What were you thinking when you took the drugs and alcohol?"
    d. "Why do you think the overdose occurred?"

**85. A researcher looks at one subject across time and takes numerous measurements throughout the process. This is known as a(n):**

    a. AB design.
    b. ABAB design.
    c. time-series or continuous measurement design.
    d. correlational design.

**86. A client has a drinking problem so the counselor starts him on medication that induces nausea whenever he drinks alcoholic beverages. What type of therapy is being utilized?**

    a. Rational-emotive therapy
    b. Operant conditioning
    c. Systematic desensitization
    d. Aversive conditioning

**87. Which of the following is true about Holland's RIASEC hexagon?**

    a. Pairs of types that are not on adjacent sides are more psychologically alike
    b. Pairs of types that are adjacent on the hexagon are less psychologically alike
    c. An individual's six-type profile may be differentiated or undifferentiated
    d. Congruence refers to similarity between pairs of types on different sides

**88. The counselor is administering the Digit Repetition Test to an older adult client. Which of the following is the primary purpose of administering this test?**

    a. Assess attention
    b. Assess depression
    c. Assess dementia
    d. Assess functional ability

89. A client has frequent panic attacks that have become debilitating and that prevent him from socializing with others despite his taking antianxiety medication. The initial intervention should be which of the following?

    a. Help the client recognize precipitating factors
    b. Provide instructions in relaxation exercises
    c. Assist the client to develop goals for recovery
    d. Assist the client to develop a plan to avoid panic attacks

90. Who first established the trait-factor guidance approach?

    a. Jesse Davis
    b. Frank Parsons
    c. E. G. Williamson
    d. Clifford Beers

91. An independent variable is the one the experimenter _____, while the dependent variable is the one the experimenter _____.

    a. manipulates; looks at for outcomes.
    b. looks at for outcomes; manipulates.
    c. leaves unattended; changes.
    d. changes; leaves unattended.

92. A counselor will be seeing a 15-year-old girl who has problems with anxiety. At the initial session, the counselor has her guardian complete the intake questionnaire and sign a permission form giving the counselor permission to treat the girl. The counselor will proceed with all of the following actions except:

    a. gets all the financial information so that the insurance company can be billed.
    b. discusses the limits of confidentiality with both the guardian and the teenager.
    c. has the adolescent sign the consent form as well.
    d. include the guardian in the first few sessions.

93. What is stratified sampling?

    a. This refers to selecting naturally occurring groups of individuals
    b. This refers to selecting samples of convenience or of volunteers
    c. This refers to selecting from major subgroups of the population
    d. This refers to selecting so that all individuals have equal chances

94. A client achieves a full-scale IQ of 100 on the WAIS-IV. What intellectual level does this put him at?

    a. Borderline
    b. Superior
    c. Average
    d. High average

**95. A client who has developed sudden onset of blindness with no identifiable physical cause seems completely unconcerned about the deficit. This suggests which of the following disorders?**

    a. Somatization disorder
    b. Pain disorder
    c. Conversion disorder
    d. Body dysmorphic disorder

**96. Psychosurgery is usually considered:**

    a. a last resort treatment.
    b. highly effective for many mental disorders.
    c. too recently developed to be reliable.
    d. a good choice as a treatment for schizophrenia.

**97. Which of these is an example of noninteractive research?**

    a. Historical analysis
    b. Ethnography
    c. Case study
    d. Dramaturgy

**98. What did Lev Vygotsky stress in his developmental theory?**

    a. Six particular stages of development
    b. Cultural context and language
    c. Independent thought
    d. The conditioning of aggressive tendencies

**99. A counselor wants to discuss the treatment of a particular client with the client's physician. Ethically, the counselor should:**

    a. call the physician on the telephone.
    b. send a letter of introduction to the physician.
    c. have the client sign a release-of-information consent form prior to any contact with the physician.
    d. have the client talk to her/his physician.

**100. A client is instructed in cognitive methods to reduce his high blood pressure. What treatment is he probably utilizing?**

    a. Transference
    b. Biofeedback
    c. Imagery therapy
    d. Pharmaceuticals

**101. One of the most criticized aspects of Sigmund Freud's theories is his view of:**

    a. defense mechanisms.
    b. dream interpretation.
    c. personality development.
    d. female sexuality.

**102. When engaging in psychoeducation with a client who has schizophrenia and the client's family, which of the following should the counselor include as an early sign of relapse?**

    a. Increased inhibition
    b. Impaired cause and effect reasoning
    c. Increased alertness/wakefulness
    d. Decreased negativity

**103. In Ellis' rational-emotive behavior therapy (REBT), what do the A, B, and C stand for in his A-B-C-D-E modalities' classification?**

    a. Action, belief, consequent affect
    b. Activity, behavior, consequences
    c. Alternatives, beginning, correction
    d. Avoidance, basis, conceptualizing

**104. In the Stanford prison simulation, male college students agreed to participate in an experiment to discover what would happen when they took on the roles of prisoners and guards. The researchers found that:**

    a. within a short time the students playing prisoners emulated the real prisoners, acting distressed and panicky, with accompanying emotional and physical ailments.
    b. a small percentage of the students playing guards became tyrannical and abusive in order to maintain the social structure of the prison.
    c. the "tough but fair" guards urged the tyrannical guards to lighten up on the prisoners.
    d. all of the prisoners and the guards became harsh and abusive.

**105. If one believes that the only behavior he can control is his own, and that "all we do is behave," he may be an advocate of which theorist?**

    a. B. F. Skinner
    b. Albert Ellis
    c. Sigmund Freud
    d. William Glasser

**106. Murray is a bright student, but he procrastinates. He puts off writing term papers and gets incompletes, which eventually become failing grades. Murray's therapist helps him establish small, specific goals rather than vague, long-range goals. The therapist also asks Murray to keep a diary of how he is spending his time when he is avoiding his studies. The method used to help Murray deal with his problem is:**

    a. psychodynamic therapy.
    b. behavioral therapy.
    c. Gestalt therapy.
    d. existential therapy.

**107. ___ men suffer from depression, and most are ___ likely to seek help for it.**

    a. Many, very
    b. Many, not
    c. Few, very
    d. Few, not

**108. The symptoms of schizophrenia can be categorized into three groups. What are they?**

   a. Good, bad, and neutral
   b. Evident, non-evident, and normal
   c. Active, inactive, and edifying
   d. Positive, negative, and disorganized

**109. If a therapist has a good ability to perceive and appreciate their client's subjective reality (i.e., emotions and cognitions), the therapist is said to have:**

   a. empathic understanding.
   b. congruence.
   c. unconditional positive regard.
   d. reflection.

**110. A Puerto Rican client almost always comes late to his therapy appointments. This is probably because of which of the following?**

   a. Lack of respect for therapist
   b. Passive-aggressive behavior
   c. Cultural ideas of time
   d. Poor time management

**111. Which of the following is an appropriate response when caring for a client who admits to being a victim of intimate partner violence?**

   a. "You should call the police."
   b. "Your partner is a thug."
   c. "I'm worried about your safety."
   d. "Don't worry. I'll take care of everything for you."

**112. A client is in a manic phase of bipolar disorder and is speaking very rapidly and incoherently. Which of the following is the most appropriate response?**

   a. "You are speaking too fast. You need to slow down."
   b. "Let's continue this conversation at a later time."
   c. "I'm having some trouble understanding. Could you speak more slowly."
   d. "You are not making any sense. Can you say that again more slowly?"

**113. A fellow counselor has begun coming to work inebriated on a regular basis. As his colleague, the first step of your ethical obligations is:**

   a. to confront him about his drinking problem and his impaired functioning.
   b. to report him to the police.
   c. to cover for him by seeing his clients as well as yours while he deals with his personal problems.
   d. report him to the licensing board.

**114. Which of these is true regarding the licensure of counselors?**

   a. Licensure can be at the state level or at the national level
   b. Licensure requirements are the same in every U.S. state
   c. Licensure is possible in several different states at once
   d. Licensure is portable from one U.S. state to another

**115. Which is correct regarding a type I (alpha) error or type II (beta) error?**

    a.  A type I error means accepting the null hypothesis when it is not true
    b.  A type II error means rejecting the null hypothesis when it is correct
    c.  A type I error means rejecting the null hypothesis when it is correct
    d.  A type II error means accepting the null hypothesis when it is correct

**116. Considering anticipatory guidance, at which of the following ages is it generally recommended that the parent and/or counselor should begin discussions about methods to avoid gangs, tobacco, drugs, alcohol, and abusive relationships?**

    a.  6-7
    b.  8-10
    c.  11-14
    d.  15-17

**117. A client who has perfectionist tendencies and unrealistic expectations of himself and others is experiencing severe stress and frustration over his inability to control all aspects of his life. A useful exercise is to ask the client to make a list of which of the following?**

    a.  Things within his control and things outside his control
    b.  Those things in his life that most stress him
    c.  Things he can modify in his life to reduce stress
    d.  Resources in his family and community that can assist him

**118. Intervention performed with three or more clients at a time is known as:**

    a.  group cohesion.
    b.  group practice.
    c.  group dynamics.
    d.  group therapy.

**119. In cognitive-behavioral therapy, behaviors are specifically related to:**

    a.  early childhood trauma.
    b.  thoughts and feelings.
    c.  conditioning.
    d.  reinforcement.

**120. A client with a history of substance abuse receives a coupon for a free meal at a local fast-food restaurant each time a urine test for drug use is negative. The type of therapy that the client is likely undergoing is which of the following?**

    a.  Cognitive behavioral therapy
    b.  Family behavior therapy
    c.  Matrix model
    d.  Motivational enhancement therapy

**121. If there is a 95% chance that an experiment's results are not due to chance, one might say that the experiment:**

    a.  has achieved reliability and validity.
    b.  would create a great scatter plot.
    c.  has a high correlation coefficient.
    d.  is statistically significant.

**122. An adolescent client with muscular dystrophy has become wheelchair bound but appears to be adjusting well and denies distress over the change in his mobility status although the counselor is concerned that the client is in denial. On which of the following should the counselor focus therapy?**

  a. Helping the client come to terms with denial
  b. Assisting the client to express feelings about his changing physical condition
  c. Discussing the stages of grief and normal responses
  d. Assisting the client to develop strategies for managing wheelchair use

**123. A client who has been diagnosed with bipolar disorder but has consistently refused to take medications or attend therapy, insisting that he has been misdiagnosed and has only "mild stress," is probably experiencing which of the following?**

  a. Dissociation
  b. Resistance
  c. Denial
  d. Suppression

**124. An adolescent hospitalized to receive chemotherapy for cancer treatment has been very resistant to treatment and pulled out his intravenous line during recent chemotherapy, resulting in tissue damage at the intravenous site. The counselor is meeting with the adolescent. Which of the following is the best initial approach?**

  a. "Why did you pull out your intravenous line?"
  b. "What do you think you can do to make these treatments easier for you?'
  c. "You must complete the treatments if you want to go into remission."
  d. "You should try to avoid getting so angry that you end up hurting yourself."

**125. Which of the following best represents the beliefs and practices of Carl Rogers?**

  a. The psychoanalyst is directive and in charge of giving advice, teaching, and interpreting
  b. The focus of counseling is based on the client's phenomenological world and feelings
  c. The therapeutic process is holistic, focused in the present, and it is existentially based
  d. The counseling process is focused upon helping clients to gain insights into themselves

**126. A counselor saw a client for a year and then terminated the treatment, as all goals were met. Six months later the counselor calls this client and asks her for a date. This is:**

  a. okay, since he terminated the counseling relationship six months ago.
  b. okay, since all treatment goals were met and none of them had to do with intimacy.
  c. unethical.
  d. not unethical but unacceptable.

**127. At a support group for caregivers of people with Alzheimer's disease, one of the group members reports that her mother, who has moderately severe Alzheimer's disease, has started to wander off during the night and has gotten lost three times and been brought back to the home by police. Which of the following is likely the best advice?**

  a. Place a latch at the top or bottom of outside doors
  b. Place a loud alarm on the door so it sounds when the door opens
  c. Place movement sensors about the house
  d. Lock the individual in her bedroom at night

**128. Which of the following tools is most appropriate for a client with cognitive impairment to assess the client's ability to function in the home environment?**

    a.  Mini-Mental State Exam (MMSE)
    b.  Memory Impairment Screen
    c.  Dementia Severity Rating Scale
    d.  Mini-Cog

**129. Which of the following correctly states the relationship between type I and type II errors?**

    a.  Type I error and type II error will both decrease if the significance level goes down
    b.  Type I error will increase and type II error will decrease if the significance level goes down
    c.  Type I error will decrease and type II error will increase if the significance level goes down
    d.  Type I error and type II error will both increase if the significance level goes down

**130. Which name is associated with mental health consultation?**

    a.  Caplan
    b.  Satir
    c.  Adler
    d.  Holland

**131. A counselor assigns his client reading to do outside of the therapy sessions. What type of therapy is likely being utilized?**

    a.  Busy work
    b.  Behavioral therapy
    c.  Bibliotherapy
    d.  Cognitive-emotive therapy

**132. Most mental health professionals believe:**

    a.  in one developmental theory.
    b.  that no one theory of development completely explains the process.
    c.  that all developmental theories are, for the most part, inaccurate.
    d.  only in the more modern, newly formulated theories of development.

**133. An African American client asks the counselor, who is Caucasian, how the counselor expects that the difference in race will affect their relationship. Which of the following is the most appropriate response?**

    a.  "Race won't have any effect on our relationship."
    b.  "There are likely cultural differences that will be important to explore."
    c.  "I consider the person and not the person's race."
    d.  "How do you think it will affect the relationship?"

**134. A counselor has decided to organize a group therapy session that will be open only to clients suffering from depression, and will not allow new clients to join once the sessions have started. What type of group therapy is being offered?**

    a.  Heterogeneous, closed group
    b.  Homogeneous, open group
    c.  Homogeneous, closed group
    d.  Heterogeneous, open group

**135. A client wants to understand why she continues to bite her nails. The counselor asks her questions to determine her thoughts before, after, and during her episodes of nail biting. What type of therapy is being utilized?**

a. Psychoanalytic
b. Behavioral
c. Cognitive
d. Transcendental

**136. The counselor is conducting a smoking cessation class for a group of clients, and two clients are adamant that they plan to resume smoking after discharge from the rehab facility. Which of the following is the best solution?**

a. Exclude the two clients from the group
b. Warn client that smoking could endanger their lives
c. Arrange for the two clients to meet a person with lung cancer from smoking
d. Provide information about symptoms of concern, such as increased cough

**137. Rational-emotive behavior therapy follows a five-step system using ABCDE, where D stands for:**

a. the disadvantages of the belief.
b. the direction of the motivation.
c. the demands on the client.
d. disputing the irrational belief.

**138. The counselor administers the Geriatric Depression Scale, which has 15 questions to which the client must answer "yes" or "no," with each "yes" answer scored as one point. Which of the following scores indicates depression?**

a. >3
b. >5
c. >8
d. >10

**139. Which of the following pairs does NOT accurately represent one of Ann Roe's eight occupational fields?**

a. Unskilled labor, service work
b. Managerial, general cultural
c. Arts and entertainment, technology
d. Outdoor work, scientific work

**140. According to Masters and Johnson, the human sexual response consists of how many phases?**

a. Two
b. Six
c. Three
d. Four

**141. When developing an education plan for a group of homeless clients with alcohol use disorder, the most important information to include is probably information about which of the following?**

    a.  Community resources
    b.  Inpatient facilities
    c.  Personal responsibility
    d.  Medications to control alcohol use disorder

**142. Who is considered the Father of Sociology?**

    a.  Sigmund Freud
    b.  Alfred Adler
    c.  Eric Berne
    d.  Emile Durkheim

**143. A client is taking a "tricyclic" medication. What type of drug is this?**

    a.  Antipsychotic
    b.  Antidepressant
    c.  Antianxiety
    d.  Sedative

**144. A career counselor who adheres to Holland's theory of career choice may have his clients take the _____ to help determine personality types.**

    a.  MMPI
    b.  KOIS
    c.  SDS
    d.  SCII

**145. The APA is a national organization for psychologists. The _____ is a national organization for counselors.**

    a.  APGA
    b.  NCE
    c.  ACA
    d.  NASP

**146. A counselor is sent a client who is "culturally different" from himself. Is it ethical for the counselor to counsel this client?**

    a.  Yes
    b.  No
    c.  It is only acceptable if the client agrees to avoid any culture-related discussion
    d.  It depends upon how culturally different the client is from the counselor

**147. Dr. Miller wants to investigate certain variables in his college class. He is going to test his statement that all of the students in his class with IQ scores above 120 will finish the term with higher grades than all of the students in his class with IQ scores below 120. This statement is an example of a:**

    a.  research question.
    b.  directional hypothesis.
    c.  nondirectional hypothesis.
    d.  null hypothesis.

148. People born between the years 1965 and 1980 in America are commonly referred to as
    a. Baby Boomers.
    b. Baby Busters.
    c. Generation X.
    d. Millennials.

149. A counselor has been working for months with victims of interpersonal violence and begins to feel exhausted, emotionally and physically, and feels increasingly unable to care about or care for the needs of clients. Which of the following may best account for this change?
    a. PTSD
    b. Compassion fatigue
    c. Burnout
    d. Depression

150. A teen client (who is usually quite slovenly), tells his counselor that he's willing to shower, comb his hair, and dress well on Friday nights because it gains him the attention of a girl he likes. What operant conditioning principle is at work here?
    a. Self-instructional principle
    b. Token economy principle
    c. Premack principle
    d. Self-efficacy principle

151. Psychoanalytic family therapy is to _____ as structural family therapy is to _____.
    a. Ackerman; Satir.
    b. Ackerman; Minuchin.
    c. Bowen; Satir.
    d. Minuchin; Bowen.

152. Ken belongs to a group whose aim is to prevent substance abuse among teens and young adults. In this group, the leader teaches members various coping skills and healthy behaviors. According to Caplan, this would be an example of:
    a. a primary group.
    b. a secondary group.
    c. a tertiary group.
    d. a preventative therapy group.

153. Most ethical issues are related to:
    a. an inappropriate relationship between counselor and client.
    b. duty to warn.
    c. confidentiality.
    d. supervision issues.

**154.** A client with agoraphobia has finally come to the counselor's office but begins to hyperventilate when the counselor shuts the office door. Which of the following is the most appropriate response?

    a. Touch the client's arm to help calm the client
    b. Advise the client that she is safe and the door is closed to ensure privacy
    c. Ask the client if she would be more comfortable with the door open
    d. Remind the client to breathe normally

**155.** A client who has developed a unilateral tremor of the left hand is referred to a counselor to determine if the cause is functional. The counselor notes that when the client is asked to move the right hand in circles, the tremor stops and the left hand also moves in a circle. Which of the following does this positive finding on the tremor entrainment test suggest?

    a. The cause of the tremor cannot be determined
    b. The cause of the tremor is neurological
    c. The client is faking the tremor
    d. The tremor is functional

**156.** If a client who was voluntarily committed to a psychiatric facility wants to leave and is restrained from doing so by a counselor, this may constitute which of the following?

    a. Assault and battery
    b. Intentional tort
    c. Negligence
    d. False imprisonment

**157.** What is NOT one of the differences between individual counseling and family counseling?

    a. The change in locus of pathology
    b. The different focus of treatment
    c. The redirected unit of treatment
    d. The longer duration of treatment

**158.** A researcher wants to conduct a study looking at the effects of systematic desensitization on agoraphobia. In this case, the independent variable is _____ and the dependent variable is _____.

    a. agoraphobia; systematic desensitization.
    b. systematic desensitization; agoraphobia.
    c. systematic desensitization; group effects.
    d. agoraphobia; group effects.

**159.** A client who has repeated complaints of various health problems (pain, nausea, headache, muscle ache, abdominal cramping) that prevents her from attending university classes or working in her place of employment has been diagnosed with probable factitious disorder. The counselor should assess the client for which of the following common co-diagnoses?

    a. Conduct disorder
    b. Anorexia nervosa
    c. Personality disorder
    d. Bipolar disorder

308

**160. A client may utilize the ego defense mechanism of *sublimation* in order to do which of the following?**
   a. Voluntarily block unpleasant emotions
   b. Negate an intolerable experience
   c. Retreat to an earlier stage of development
   d. Redirect socially unacceptable impulses

**161. A researcher who observes a strong negative correlation between income and mental illness would conclude that:**
   a. being poor causes mental illness.
   b. having wealth makes one resistant to mental illness.
   c. those with lower incomes tend to suffer from higher rates of mental illness and those with higher incomes tend to suffer from lower rates of mental illness.
   d. lower income levels lead to lower levels of mental illness.

**162. A 40-year-old client presents with complaints regarding not feeling comfortable socially. He states that after gaining weight he now finds social situations to be overwhelming. He has stopped attending church and recreational activities, and does not engage in new activities, although before he was known for being adventurous. A likely diagnosis would be:**
   a. borderline personality disorder.
   b. avoidant personality disorder.
   c. schizotypal personality disorder.
   d. depressive disorder.

**163. A client repeats the word "cake" over and over when asked if he'd like dessert. This is an example of which of the following?**
   a. Associative looseness
   b. Perseveration
   c. Tangentiality
   d. Echolalia

**164. If a counselor has a client whose managed care plan allows only 20 visits per year, at what point in the therapy should the counselor consider the implications of this limit?**
   a. At the initial visit
   b. At the half-point of therapy
   c. Five visits before termination
   d. At termination

**165. A group cognitive behavioral therapy (CBT) approach that focuses on relapse prevention for substance use disorders will likely do which of the following?**
   a. Stress the importance of attending Alcoholics or Narcotics Anonymous® (AA) meetings
   b. Stress mindfulness and accepting oneself
   c. Help clients identify situations that make them vulnerable to relapse
   d. Advise clients to serve as mentors for each other

309

166. A client diagnosed with depression and suicide ideation suddenly appears to feel better and think more clearly. His risk of suicide is now:

    a. increased.
    b. decreased.
    c. the same.
    d. no longer a risk at all.

167. Sallie attends two different therapy groups in an attempt to find one that suits her. In group A, the leader uses high levels of emotional stimulation, frequently uses caring functions, and uses low amounts of executive direction. In group B, the leader uses low amounts of emotional stimulation, low amounts of caring functions, high use of executive behavior, and low amounts of meaning attribution. According to Yalom, which group leader is more effective?

    a. Group A's leader is more effective
    b. Group B's leader is more effective
    c. It depends which Sallie likes better
    d. Neither leader is more effective

168. What are two contrasting elements of group dynamics?

    a. Content and context
    b. Process and product
    c. Context and product
    d. Content and process

169. When did group counseling start to be explored as an alternative or complement to individual counseling?

    a. In the mid-1800s
    b. After the 1940s
    c. In the 1990s
    d. In the early 1900s

170. The term "identity crisis" originated with which theorist?

    a. Jean Piaget
    b. Sigmund Freud
    c. Erik Erikson
    d. Albert Watson

171. A husband and wife present for help with her substance use. She had been recreationally using cocaine on some weekends, and indicates that she has a strong desire to stop, but has been unsuccessful in stopping before. The precipitating incident was an episode of driving under the influence on a weeknight that resulted in her arrest, impounding of the family car, and considerable fines, charges, and increases in automobile insurance. This is the second driving incident in the last two years. The most appropriate diagnosis for the wife, given the relevant details would be:

    a. stimulant intoxication.
    b. stimulant dependence.
    c. stimulant use disorder.
    d. stimulant use withdrawal.

**172. A counselor observes an ethics violation by another counselor. Which of the following is NOT a reason for the counselor who observed the activity to refrain from reporting it?**

a. A third counselor has been retained to review the counselor whose actions are in question.
b. A personal relationship exists between the two counselors.
c. Confidentiality rights would be violated.
d. The issue can be resolved informally.

**173. Becky is an elementary school student who displays a number of attention-seeking behaviors which are disruptive in the classroom. Her teacher was approached by a local university researcher to refer students for an experiment. The teacher and her parents ask Becky if she would like to participate in the study and she agrees. The research team has collected baseline behavioral data on Becky from the teacher. Early in the study, they find that her behavior is much improved compared to the baseline. Which of these is the most likely explanation for Becky's better behavior during the experiment?**

a. The Rosenthal effect
b. The Pygmalion effect
c. The Hawthorne effect
d. The Placebo effect

**174. Jennifer, a Brandon High School graduating senior, took the Geneva Advanced Placement test in mathematics and earned 177 points out of a total of 200 points. This score would most likely be used to determine that Jennifer did as well as or better than:**

a. 86% of the freshmen at Coolridge Community College.
b. 73% of the college students majoring in mathematics in the United States.
c. 89% of the graduating seniors at Glenbrook High School.
d. 77% of the mathematics team members from Highland High School.

**175. In a group therapy session, a client describes her experience related to telling her friends and family about her mental health condition, and the counselor points out that another group member had a similar experience. This is an example of which of the following?**

a. Diagnosing
b. Facilitating
c. Linking
d. Redirecting

**176. Which is NOT considered a weakness of Adlerian counseling?**

a. It is not firmly based in research
b. Its concepts and terms can be overly vague
c. It is a rigid and inflexible approach
d. Its approach is very narrow in nature

**177. What is NOT one of the strengths or benefits of Rogerian counseling?**

a. Acceptance
b. Concreteness
c. Openness
d. Versatility

**178. Robert Havighurst is identified with all BUT which of the following?**

    a. Stages of growth, each of which must be completed to reach the next one
    b. Stages of growth resulting in successively higher levels of cognitive function
    c. Developmental tasks arising from maturation and environmental influences
    d. Developmental tasks that are acquired via maturation, social learning, and effort

**179. How did Albert Ellis view "self-talk" in his theory?**

    a. As the source of our emotional disturbances
    b. As the symptom of neurosis or even psychosis
    c. As a therapeutic technique for solving problems
    d. As a kind of mental chatter that is to be ignored

**180. As a leader of a group, Barb is very structured. She sets and directs all of the group's goals and activities and hardly ever asks the participants for input. Most likely, Barb has a(n) _____ style of leadership.**

    a. laissez-faire
    b. democratic
    c. authoritative
    d. authoritarian

**181. In a support group, one client monopolizes the conversation, talking about the same problems over and over and preventing others from participating. The counselor has spoken with the client privately about the importance of allowing others to speak and not interrupting others, but the behavior persists. Which of the following is the most effective response?**

    a. "Remember what we discussed about your interrupting other group members."
    b. "Please stop interrupting other members when they are trying to speak."
    c. "When you interrupt others, I'm concerned that some group members are unable to participate."
    d. "You've already expressed your feelings about this topic many times."

**182. During the working stage of the group, the leader's role is to:**

    a. establish a trusting climate.
    b. provide a role model.
    c. deal with feelings.
    d. support risks.

**183. The contingency model of leadership states that leadership is determined by:**

    a. personality and situation.
    b. popularity and personality.
    c. situation and popularity.
    d. situation only.

**184. Which of the following is the most appropriate screening tool for a 16-year-old with suspected drug or alcohol abuse?**

    a. CRAFFT
    b. AUDIT
    c. CAGE
    d. DAST

**185. Which of these is correct regarding a release of information?**

a. This document is signed by the client before confidential information can be given to another professional or agency
b. This document is signed by the counselor and given to the client to disclose procedures before the counseling relationship starts
c. This document is signed by another professional or agency before a counselor can give confidential information to them
d. This document is signed by the client and given to the counselor before another professional or agency can give the counselor information

**186. All of the following are postulates of Hoppock's theory EXCEPT that:**

a. everyone has basic needs, and a person's reaction to these needs influences occupational choice.
b. people tend to move toward careers that serve their needs.
c. self-awareness and understanding are the bases upon which a person chooses an occupation.
d. people are most fulfilled by careers that are in the same field as their passions.

**187. Behavior changing as a result of just being part of an experiment is called the ________________ while believing that someone with an extensive vocabulary is better at communicating is called the __________________.**

a. halo effect; Rosenthal effect.
b. Hawthorne effect; Rosenthal effect.
c. Hawthorne effect; halo effect.
d. placebo effect; Rosenthal effect.

**188. If a client who is a pathological gambler insists to the counselor and to his spouse that he can control his gambling by limiting the time spent at the casino and the dollar amount he spends each week, which of the following approaches to treatment for process addiction is the client advocating?**

a. Cognitive behavioral therapy
b. Abstinence
c. Harm reduction
d. Desensitization

**189. When administering tests to a client, the counselor should always:**

a. educate the client as to how the tests were developed.
b. inform the client of the limitations of testing.
c. assure the client of the absolute accuracy of psychological testing.
d. keep as much information from the client as possible.

**190. Which of the following is the correct sequence of stages in Piaget's Theory of Cognitive Development?**

a. preoperational, sensorimotor, formal operational, concrete operational
b. preoperational, sensorimotor, concrete operational, formal operational
c. sensorimotor, preoperational, formal operational, concrete operational
d. sensorimotor, preoperational, concrete operational, formal operational

**191. If an aggressive, hostile client has managed to remove a towel rod and is brandishing it as a weapon, the counselor's first priority should be to do which of the following?**

    a. Disarm the client
    b. Subdue the client
    c. Protect self and others
    d. Leave the client's immediate environment

**192. How can tests aid a counselor with a new client?**

    a. They can help see if the client's needs are in the counselor's range of services
    b. They can help the counselor to obtain a greater understanding of the client
    c. They can help the client to obtain a greater degree of self-understanding
    d. They can help with any or all of these purposes in the counseling process

**193. Jim's new therapist believes in the uniqueness of each person. She talks about the importance of social influences on an individual. She tells Jim that everybody has a sense of inferiority, and as a result is always striving to attain superiority. Her counseling goals are to help Jim understand his lifestyle, or unified life plan, which gives meaning to his experiences, and to help him identify social and community interests most appropriate for him. She also wants to help explain Jim to himself. The techniques she uses in her therapy include life histories, homework assignments, and paradoxical intentions. The therapeutic modality that best describes this therapist's approach is:**

    a. client-centered therapy.
    b. Gestalt therapy.
    c. individual psychology.
    d. transactional analysis.

**194. Which of the following is NOT true of standard deviation?**

    a. Standard deviation describes the variability within a distribution of scores
    b. Standard deviation is basically the mean of all the deviations from the mean
    c. Standard deviation is a term of quantity, which is equal to the term variance
    d. Standard deviation is an excellent way to measure the dispersion of scores

**195. If a client with OCD is undergoing Exposure and Response Prevention therapy and the client has established a goal of being able to go into a store to shop for groceries, which of the following is the next step for the client?**

    a. Find a friend to accompany the client to the store
    b. Sign a contract committing to reaching the goal
    c. Create a fear ladder
    d. Establish a time frame for achieving the goal

**196. Harry Stack Sullivan theorized about "euphoria" and:**

    a. tension.
    b. stress.
    c. loss.
    d. abandonment.

**197. According to John Holland's six personality types, a client falls into the "realistic" personality type. Which of the following careers would he perhaps be well suited for?**

a. Carpenter
b. Doctor
c. Artist
d. Counselor

**198. Which of these is correct regarding ethical issues in family counseling?**

a. The counselor's attitude toward gender roles is irrelevant to family counseling
b. Due to confidentiality, the counselor should not report child abuse and incest
c. If the counselor diagnoses a family member, it could be used later on in a court of law
d. Family roles and family dynamics are the same, irrespective of a family's culture

**199. Which of the following feedback is specific and descriptive?**

a. "You were very sarcastic in the group meeting today."
b. "Marvin became upset when you made a joke about his failure to maintain sobriety."
c. "You tend to be thoughtless when you address other clients in the group."
d. "You should treat others with more respect in group meetings."

**200. When did the State of Virginia pass the first general practice counselor licensure law?**

a. 1954
b. 1962
c. 1976
d. 1981

# Answer Key and Explanations for Test #1

**1. A:** A cross-sectional study involves a research study using people who are similar in all areas except the variable that is being studied. For instance, one might wish to measure the intelligence level of a group of people of differing ages. However, measuring the intelligence level of differing ages during the same year does not account for lifestyle issues, differing resources that were available to the older subjects vs. the younger ones, etc. This is one of the criticisms of cross-sectional studies. Longitudinal studies are often preferred because they measure a variable over the lifespan (or a number of years) of each particular subject.

**2. C:** Tests administered using modified conditions may or may not yield results equivalent to those obtained using standardized conditions. There are no general agreements about how to modify tests for individuals with disabilities. Since testing individuals with disabilities is a fairly new concept, more research is needed to investigate equivalency of modified test administrations to standardized test administrations. Another topic of further consideration is how the test examiner will interpret results when a test has been modified.

**3. D:** If a client with antisocial behavior begins to stroke the counselor's arm and hand suggestively during a session, the most appropriate response is "Remove your hand. We are discussing your plan of care, and you don't need to touch me." It is imperative that the counselor maintain boundaries and respond to inappropriate behavior firmly and assertively but should avoid expressing judgment or anger. The counselor should also avoid making threats in response to the behavior.

**4. A:** The main purpose of norms is to provide meaning to test scores. A score of 100 means nothing if one doesn't know what receiving a score of 100 means. Norms provide a basis for comparison of scores against each other and against the standard. With knowledge of the standard, comparisons can be made. Answer B and C refer to concepts in reliability. Knowing whether a distribution is normal gives the test user information, but it does not provide information about the norms themselves.

**5. A:** The professional career counselor refers to leisure activities as those activities or hobbies with which a person is involved outside of work. These activities are referred to as avocations. A career counselor would discuss these activities with clients in order to better understand them.

**6. C:** Ipsative interpretation means comparing multiple subtest results for one individual with themselves only with no comparison to other people's results. Norm-referenced means comparing the individual's score(s) to others. Criterion-referenced means comparing the individual's score to a preset criterion. The WAIS-IV measures a number of different aptitudes. In this example, the tester is comparing one individual's various scores on different subtests with each other, which is an ipsative interpretation.

**7. B:** The Diagnostic and Statistical Manual of Mental Disorders classifies intellectual disabilities in relation to Wechsler IQ scores. A score of 50 to approximately 79 indicates mild intellectual disability. Moderate intellectual disability is 35-55, with severe intellectual disability falling between the scores of 20 and 40. Profound intellectual disability is below 20 or 25. One can see by the overlap of the ranges that the number itself is not enough to make a determination. A number of factors besides the subject's score must be taken into consideration in determining the subject's true level of impairment, such as communication skills, self-care, and self-direction, to name just a few.

**8. C:** Donald Super developed the archway model as a graphic depiction of the many factors that determine an individual's self-concept. One pillar of the arch corresponds to internal variables such as aptitudes, interests, needs, and accomplishments. The other pillar represents external factors such as family, community, and the work market. The arch between the pillars is the self. John Holland developed a typology identifying six modal personality orientations. He also created the Vocational Preference Inventory and the Self-Directed Search for determining a person's predominant Holland personality type. Linda Gottfredson created a developmental theory of careers in the 1980s called "circumscription and compromise" which emphasizes vocational self-concept. John Krumboltz was responsible for the learning theory of career counseling (LTCC) which is based on Albert Bandura's social learning theory.

**9. D:** If the treatment for a 26-year-old female client with bulimia nervosa sets limits regarding the client's eating habits, the limit that is counterproductive is assigning daily "grades" for compliance with eating limits as this may be viewed as punishment, especially if the client's grades are low. A better approach is to use positive reinforcement when the client does well. Other reasonable limits include requiring the client to eat in the dining room, keep a food diary, discuss reactions to different types of food, and stay out of the bathroom for 2 hours after eating.

**10. B:** Unconditional positive regard is central in client-centered counseling. Carl Rogers emphasized personal warmth, empathy, acceptance, and genuineness when he described his approach. He focused on giving support and providing total acceptance without limits. Conditions of worth are in direct opposition to what Rogers believed. Existentialism and self-actualization are not associated with Carl Rogers in any way.

**11. D:** Appraisal can be any means by which a counselor assesses the client. Sometimes the assessment may be in the form of an IQ test, mental status exam, psychodynamic evaluation, group test, or even just clinical interview and observation. Testing can be used to aid the client in choosing a career, point toward possible psychological disorders, or place a child in an appropriate class (given intelligence level or disabilities). Appraisal is simply a way to collect information about the client so that the counselor can be more effective in the therapeutic relationship. Interventions occur following the appraisal process.

**12. B:** A client who is devoutly religious and believes her disability is punishment for sins may benefit most from pastoral counseling because a pastor who is trained as a therapist may help the client balance religious and health beliefs in a more realistic manner. Pastoral counselors often carry out both psychological and spiritual counseling, providing the client with the support of the faith community. Pastoral counselors may represent many different faiths and branches of religions.

**13. D:** Alternate or parallel forms of reliability involve giving two different versions of the same test to the same group of people. If the test is reliable, there will be very little difference between the scores received on both tests. Split-half reliability involves dividing a test into two parts and comparing the scores on the first part with the scores on the second part. If the test is internally consistent, the scores on each half of the test will be nearly identical. Scorer reliability is used when two or more individuals score the same test. If the test has scorer reliability, each scorer scores nearly all the items on the test the same way. Test-retest reliability involves obtaining nearly identical scores on the same test even when the test is given at a later date.

**14. C:** Accreditation is what an institution receives when it meets certain established standards or qualifications. Colleges, universities, and specialized programs of study may receive accreditation via regional agencies of the US Department of Education; health care facilities are accredited via the

Joint Commission (formerly JCAHO). Accreditation is granted only to an institution or a program and not to individuals.

**15. A:** If a couple who each have children from previous marriages are planning to marry and during premarital counseling the male states, "I've already told my children that they have a new mother and they are to her 'Mom,'" this is the cause for most concern because he is attempting to force the children to replace their biological mother rather than allowing time for a relationship to form with the stepmother. Being realistic about custody agreements, feelings, and children's relationship with biological parents is important so that these issues can be discussed in order to prevent later conflicts.

**16. B:** When completing the client assessment and developing the plan of care with a client with an eating disorder, it is especially important to ask the client about self-injurious behavior. Clients with eating disorders often engage in superficial self-mutilating behaviors, such as cutting, burning, and hair pulling, and these actions may increase as an outlet for the client's emotional distress as the eating disorder is controlled. All clients with eating disorders should be screened for self-injurious behavior and should be monitored carefully during therapy.

**17. B:** A vocational assessment usually has a number of steps, beginning with the initial rehabilitation assessment and followed by a functional capacity evaluation. The next steps include a physical conditioning assessment and vocational assessment and then functional education and physical conditioning to prepare for work. Once a vocation is selected, then a workplace assessment, an ergonomic assessment and risk assessment are carried out. The last steps may include vocational counseling, labor market analysis, on-the-job training and job search and placement assistance.

**18. D:** Couples therapy focuses most specifically on conflicts and breaking out of destructive habits. Family therapy may touch on these issues but is more largely focused on the family as a system and the interrelationships within. Existential and psychodynamic therapies do not address breaking out of destructive habits, although psychodynamic therapy may address unresolved conflicts.

**19. B:** In Sigmund Freud's theory of psychosexual development, the Oedipus complex and Electra complex take place in the Phallic Stage. It is during this stage of development that the child faces the greatest sexual conflict. These two complexes refer to the child's unconscious desire to possess the opposite-gender parent and eliminate the same-sex one. The natural love of child for parent moves toward a sexual energy in the Phallic Stage, thus changing the dynamics of the relationship. This desire remains unconscious; it is repressed.

**20. A:** HIPAA, the Health Insurance Portability and Accountability Act, is a national law and does NOT vary from one state to another. It dictates standards for protecting the privacy of patient information in the health industry, including records of psychotherapy. It regulates the transmission of patients' or clients' records, and the exchange of information for insurance claims whether or not electronically transmitted.

**21. D:** Regression is a defense mechanism theorized by Sigmund Freud. Freud believed that some people, when confronted with high levels of stress, may regress to a prior time in their lives when they felt safe and protected. Many times, this regression may be to an earlier psychosexual stage in which the client is now fixated. For example, an individual who was fixated at the oral stage may regress to sucking his thumb when faced with the extreme stress of a terminal illness diagnosis. The defense mechanism works for the client because the thumb-sucking reduces the client's stressful feelings.

**22. C:** Jung coined these terms. He believed the collective unconscious is determined by the evolution of the human species, and that it contains universal brain response patterns he called archetypes. Adler was known for emphasizing birth order as a psychological influence, and he used the term "family constellation." Freud is famous for coining the terms id, ego, and superego as the basic personality structures. He also contributed many other terms, such as "ego defense mechanisms," "repression," "sublimation," "projection," "introjection," "reaction formation," etc. Aaron Beck coined the term "automatic thoughts" which are similar to Freud's "preconscious."

**23. C:** Albert Ellis developed rational emotive therapy (RET) in the mid-1950s. He believed that, in many cases, people are unhappy, and choose negative behaviors because of irrational thought processes. He felt there were three types of unrealistic views: people feel they must perform well to be approved of by others, must be treated fairly by others, and must have things go their way...or they will be unhappy. The RET therapist works to change irrational beliefs and promote rational self-talk. The therapist will challenge irrational thoughts and even assign homework to aid in combating irrational thinking and promote positive thoughts, feelings, and behaviors.

**24. A:** Arnold Gesell was a maturationist who believed that given a normal environment a child's growth and development were predetermined by genetic makeup. He felt that children developed in a predictable, orderly way with little influence from the environment including the parents. A belief that development is most influenced by the environment would be akin to the position of a behaviorist. There are many other theories that hold that development is the product of both nature and nurture, but Gesell's was not one of them. The position that development is primarily influenced by either one or the other would be unusual for most developmental theories, which tend to apply their beliefs about development more uniformly to the majority of human beings.

**25. A:** An independent variable is the experimental factor in an experiment. It is the element in the experiment that is changed or manipulated. By contrast, the dependent variable in an experiment is the one that is measured, and watched in relation to what is done with the independent variable. If the dependent variable is changed by the manipulation of the independent variable, one might conclude that the independent variable had an effect upon the dependent variable. Of course, one must still determine if one actually caused the other.

**26. B:** Empathy is a critical tool in counseling because it assists the counselor in understanding the internal workings of the client's mind. It's important to note that the term "empathy" (when used in relation to therapy), does not have the same meaning as it does in general use. Empathy does not refer to feeling the same feelings as the client, or having sympathy for the client. Rather, it's a way to experience the world as the client does, and thus gain a deeper understanding of the client's thoughts and feelings.

**27. B:** A therapeutic alliance is the bond of confidence and mutual understanding established between the counselor and client. The clubhouse model and window of opportunity have nothing to do with counseling. The therapeutic window normally describes a range of time or dose of medication at which positive effects of a specific intervention will be noticed.

**28. D:** The NCC certification is considered a generic counselor certification. NCSC, CCMHC, and MAC are all specialty counselor certifications that may be obtained from the NBCC following certification of the NCC credential.

**29. C:** Wrenn stressed developmental needs as the focus of the counseling profession. Developmental needs are normal and hence not necessarily neurotic. He did not emphasize needs of the group over those of the individual or vice versa.

**30. B:** Proxemics is the study of proximity. It refers to personal and interpersonal space and territoriality. Proxemics studies how an individual's proximity to others and things impacts that individual. The term was introduced by the anthropologist Edward Hall in 1966. He found there were measurable distances between people based upon specific circumstances and interactions. Proxemics defines certain types of space: fixed-feature, semi-fixed feature, and informal space. It also defines intimate, personal, social, and public distances, as well as specifying a variety of behavioral categories.

**31. B:** The Smith-Hughes Act (1917) granted federal funds for vocational education and guidance. The National Defense Education Act (1958) provided money for the training of school counselors. California passed a law in 1962 requiring that marriage, family and child counselors must be licensed. Counseling services to veterans in the Veterans Administration expanded following World War II.

**32. B:** The statement by a client in CBT for major depressive disorder suggesting that the client is applying principles learned in therapy is, "I can't fix this situation, so I'm going to think about taking a vacation." One of the goals of CBT is to help clients to think differently about situations and to use thought-stopping exercises when they begin to obsess over problems, such as a situation they can't fix. Clients use imagery, such as imagining taking a vacation, to help to have more positive thoughts.

**33. C:** Unlike individual therapy, family therapy believes that one family member's behavior influences all other members' behavior in a circular manner. What one person in the family does affects everyone else. Family members do not act independently of one another. Problems concern everyone, not just one person. The linear model of causality reflects individual therapy. An individual's behavior causes something to occur independent of other factors.

**34. D:** The basic idea behind operant conditioning is that the consequences of behaviors have an effect on the individual's choice to engage in those behaviors. There are four types of operant conditioning, two of which weaken behaviors, and two of which can strengthen it. Punishment is one type of operant conditioning that weakens the behavior. Put simply, it involves giving a negative consequence every time the behavior occurs. For example, a client who wishes to stop swearing may snap a rubber band on his wrist whenever he swears. The sharp, uncomfortable sensation of the snap, as well as the embarrassment of snapping the wrist in public, pairs a negative consequence with the behavior of swearing. The negative consequence may cause the unwanted behavior to eventually cease.

**35. C:** Donald Meichenbaum's stress inoculation training (SIT) was developed to help individuals cope with the aftermath of stressful events, and also to serve to "inoculate" people against future stressful reactions. There are three stages to SIT. In the initial "conceptualization" stage, the focus is on the relationship between client and counselor. "Skill acquisition" and "rehearsal" are the focus of the second stage of SIT, which teaches coping skills to the client. The third stage of "application" and "follow through" deals with, as stated, the application of the techniques learned. SIT can be conducted with individuals, couples, or groups.

**36. D:** Norm-referenced tests compare the individual to others who took the same test. How one compares with others is more important in norm-referenced testing than how much one knows. Criterion-referenced tests compare one's score to an established criterion, such as the cut-off score on the NCE; they do not rank a score within a group. They also do not compare one's score to others as norm-referenced tests do.

**37. A:** Wundt established the first psychological laboratory in 1879. Sigmund Freud first used psychoanalysis to treat mental illness in 1890. Jesse Davis first began work as a counselor in a Detroit high school in 1898. Clifford Beers exposed conditions in mental health institutions in his book A Mind That Found Itself, published in 1908.

**38. C:** Hoppock and Roe are classified as developmentalists when it comes to career choices. They believe that early development and early experiences have a large impact on career choice. Krumboltz is a behaviorist and does not ascribe to early development an influence on career choice. Holland believes that environment interacts with personality characteristics when one chooses a career. Krumboltz and Holland believe that the environment plays a role in career choice, but Krumboltz looks at learning, not personality.

**39. B:** Eric Berne is a psychologist who formulated a "life script" theory that addresses personality development and interpersonal relationships. The theory states that people form a life script early in their childhood years that sets the stage for how their future will develop. Individuals make decisions in their early life to live their life in a particular way as a means to ensure survival (based upon a number of considerations such as parental, social, and cultural). Transactional analysis (TA) is a psychotherapy used to make changes to an individual's life script in order for a happier, healthier life to develop.

**40. D:** The four essential components of informed consent before a client can make a decision about care are:

- **Voluntarism**: The client must be free to make the decision without coercion, manipulation, or threats although persuasion may be utilized.
- **Competence**: The client must be mentally competent enough to make decisions.
- **Disclosure**: The healthcare provider must provide full disclosure about treatment, including what comprises the treatment, any alternate options, and the purpose.
- **Comprehension**: The client must be able to understand the implications of treatment.

**41. B:** If, at a dinner party, the counselor encounters a client and, in the presence of four other guests at the party, the client tells the counselor that he feels guilty because he committed a serious crime, the communication is not privileged because the client made the confession in front of other guests so there was no expectation of confidentiality. Communication is privileged if the other person present has been granted the right, in writing, to be present, such as a family member or attorney.

**42. A:** A t-test is used to see if the mean scores of two groups differ significantly. Since the researcher did not have more than two groups, he would most likely use this test. A one-way analysis of variance is used when there are, for example, three groups and a t-test can no longer be used. A factorial ANOVA is used not only to see if mean scores testing two or more factors (variables) differ significantly, but also to see if they interact with one another significantly. A multivariate analysis of variance is used with more than one dependent variable, therefore precluding the use of a factorial ANOVA.

**43. A:** If a client who has been in recovery from cocaine addiction is laughing and telling the counselor about the good times he had when he was using cocaine and how much better his social life was, the counselor should suspect that the client may be having a relapse, especially since the client is focusing on positive aspects of addiction rather than negative. Other indications of relapse include sudden changes in behavior, complaints about treatment, excessive fatigue and/or irritability, depression and/or suicidal ideation, contact with previous associates, and stopping participation in therapy.

**44. C:** An appropriate statement for a counselor to make on a social networking site about working with clients is no statement whatsoever about specific clients or workload. The counselor should not describe clients even in general terms without naming them because people may be able to determine to whom the counselor refers by the description. Additionally, complaining about work ("I have to see way too many clients...) suggests that the counselor is not able to give adequate attention to clients.

**45. C:** Construct validity is described as the extent to which a test measures a specific theoretical construct, such as the construct of self-esteem. Content validity is described as the extent to which the items on a test are examples of the construct that the test measures. Criterion-related validity is described as the extent to which a test correlates with independent behaviors or events. In the case of this question, the independent behavior or event is the student's grade point average used as a measure of academic success. Concurrent validity is described as a form of criterion-related validity whereby the test administration and criterion measure happen at almost the same time. This method of criterion-related validity is not predictive.

**46. D:** The values clarification process has three steps: (1) choosing, (2) prizing, and (3) acting:

- Choosing: Considering options and freely choosing a value that feels appropriate for the individual rather than one imposed by others.
- Prizing: Feeling positive about the value and explaining or justifying the value to others.
- Acting: Applying the value to life experiences and interactions with others.

**47. C:** Reasoning is a means by which one processes information in order to reach a conclusion. There are several forms of reasoning, two of which are inductive reasoning and deductive reasoning. Inductive reasoning is reasoning that flows from the specific to the general, such as knowing something about one member of a group, and then generalizing that to the entire group the individual belongs to. Deductive reasoning is the opposite. In deductive reasoning, knowledge of a particular group is generalized to each of the individuals within that group. It is of course, not best to rely on only one type of reasoning to reach a conclusion.

**48. A:** The James-Lange Theory of Emotion was proposed in 1884. It is a combination of the ideas of William James and Carl Lange. The theory states that one's body reacts to a stimulus first and is then followed by the emotional reaction. For example, a spider lands on an individual's arm. The individual jumps and screams in reaction. The individual then interprets the body's reaction as fear, thus leading to actually feeling the emotion of fearfulness. This idea of the physiological response preceding the emotional one was new at the time, and one of the first theories used to explain the science of emotion.

**49. B:** The operational definition allows researchers to understand how something is being measured. Happiness, for example, cannot be simply measured. However, measuring the number of smiles in a day is one possible operational definition of how to measure happiness. An operational definition is very important in psychological research, because without it an experiment or study could not be replicated. It is important for replication to be done if a study is to be considered scientific. The operational definition tells the reader exactly how the study was done so that it can be carefully and methodically replicated in the future.

**50. D:** If, in a support group, the counselor observes that one member routinely takes over the discussions and sometimes bullies others, this might be described as a group pattern. A group pattern refers to processes, the ways in which a group may act. Patterns may vary widely, and some—such as one person taking over—may be detrimental to the group because other members may feel intimidated. The group leader needs to be alert to the patterns that are developing in a group.

**51. D:** Social Psychology deals primarily with groups and other social factors. This area of psychology studies issues such as how individuals behave in group settings, how social interaction affects the individual, and how the individual impacts upon society. Simply put, Social Psychology combines Psychology and Sociology. While Psychology studies the individual and internal processes, Social Psychology looks more at the individual's connections to others in society. This discipline believes that society plays a large role in how the individual views himself, his place in the world, and his behavior, as well as the choices he makes.

**52. D:** Stimulus generalization occurs when, after conditioning, the subject responds almost identically to a stimulus that is similar to the conditioned stimulus. Higher-order conditioning is a procedure by which a neutral stimulus becomes a conditioned stimulus through the association with an already established conditioned stimulus. A conditioned response is a response that is elicited by a conditioned stimulus. It occurs after the conditioned stimulus is associated with an unconditioned stimulus. Stimulus discrimination occurs when a stimulus that resembles a conditioned stimulus fails to evoke the conditioned response.

**53. B:** The p-value indicates the probability that the null hypothesis is correct (i.e., that there is no relationship between the variable being controlled and the variable being observed). A p-value that is <0.05 indicates a less than 5% probability that no relationship exists between the two variables. The p-value does not speak to the likelihood of error in the experiment, the relative size of the effect being studied, or the study design.

**54. D:** Managing a counseling program can require skill in some or all of these areas: strategic planning, program design and development, budgeting, personnel management, supervision, evaluation, and marketing and public relations.

**55. A:** The type of exercise that may best reduce symptoms of anxiety and depression is aerobic exercise, such as jogging, walking, gardening, and riding bicycles. Mental health clients often lead relatively sedentary lives because of their symptoms and adverse effects associated with their medications, increasing their risks for obesity, diabetes, and heart disease. An exercise regimen should be part of lifestyle changes and should include a minimum of 30 minutes of aerobic exercise at least 3 times weekly.

**56. D:** While ideally a counselor should examine preconceptions and set them aside prior to meeting with the client, once the counselor recognizes that his opinions may be colored by preconceptions, he should acknowledge them and set them aside so that he can establish a good working relationship with the client. Since the client is likely unaware of the counselor's preconceptions, apologizing is not necessary, nor is overcompensating by spending extra time with the client.

**57. B:** An ipsative scale gives information about a single individual. There are no comparisons made between the individual and others. A normative scale gives information about individuals but allows the examiner to make comparisons between the single individual and others. The key difference between ipsative scales and normative scales is whether comparisons can be made. No comparisons can be made when an ipsative scale is used.

**58. B:** Cause and effect is attainable only through an experiment. A correlational study looks only at the relationship between variables. A naturalistic observation involves simply observing subjects in their own environment. No cause and effect is even intended here. A survey involves distributing a questionnaire or survey to participants. Again, no cause and effect is intended.

**59. B:** While getting drunk at a party at age 18 is likely foolish, rape is a criminal action, and the client's getting drunk was in no way an invitation to rape. If the client states, "I'm so stupid. It was my fault! I shouldn't have gone to the party!" the best response is "You're not to blame for someone else's actions. It's not your fault" because the client is experiencing guilt and self-blame, common emotional responses to trauma.

**60. A:** The first intelligence test was developed in 1905 by Alfred Binet and Theophilus Simon. They began work on the test as a means to identify students with low intellectual abilities who could benefit from specialized education. Work continued on the test for some time following. The Stanford-Binet Intelligence Scale was developed out of that original test, and consists of four areas: verbal reasoning, quantitative reasoning, abstract/visual reasoning, and short-term memory. A larger, more diverse sample was used in its development, and it improved upon the original test by further correcting for racial and gender issues.

**61. C:** It was the social context that determined the behaviors of both the guards and the prisoners. In the Stanford prison study, the setting was so realistic that the participants became guards and prisoners. Their personal identities were masked by the context of being in a prison as either a guard or a prisoner. Even the researcher, Dr. Zimbardo, who took on the role of the prison warden, had to be reminded by one of his own graduate students that this was a research study and not a prison.

**62. B:** A t-test is performed when there is one independent variable (Nicorette gum), one experimental group (smokers attempting cessation who are instructed to use Nicorette gum), and one control group (smokers attempting cessation without any interventions). Pearson's r is used in correlational studies. An ANOVA is used when there is more than one independent variable or more than one experimental group. A chi-square is used to determine if obtained results differ at all from chance.

**63. C:** According to Gottfredson, younger children tend to choose occupations that fit their sex. Gottfredson's theory is developmental. She stated that since children of this age tend to identify certain occupations with either the male or the female gender, it follows that they will choose occupations based on gender roles or stereotypes. Orientation to sex roles is the name of her second developmental stage (ages 6-8). Preadolescents tend to choose occupations consistent with their social values since they are in Gottfredson's stage of orientation to social valuation (ages 9-13). Children of this age may also rule out occupations they feel are inappropriate to their intelligence or levels of ability. Adolescents, who are in Gottfredson's stage of orientation to internal unique self (age 14 and older), tend to choose occupations based on their awareness of their own personal characteristics.

**64. A:** Gottfredson stated that orientation to size and power occurs from age 3-5 when children have neither; when they still think concretely; and when they are just beginning to understand what being an adult means. Orientation to sex roles takes place from age 6-8 when children learn that adults have different roles and that many occupations are sex-typed. Orientation to social

324

valuation happens from age 9-13 when children gain greater awareness of peer, family, and community values and of the variation among the social valuations of different occupations. Finally, orientation to the internal unique self transpires from age 14 on when children's aspirations, interests, and values influence their occupational preferences and choices.

**65. B:** Electroconvulsive therapy (ECT), also known as "shock treatment," is often thought of as a controversial treatment. However, ECT has been found to be effective with some clients, and especially those with severe depression. ECT was developed in 1938, and because of the stigma associated with it in the 1960s, its practice declined. In ECT, two small electrodes are placed on the client's head and administer a small electrical current. The current causes a seizure that lasts less than one minute. Contrary to popular belief, ECT is not significantly painful and in some cases, clients can even sleep through it.

**66. B:** Enmeshment and disengagement are concepts in Minuchin's theory of family therapy. Adler looked at goals of behavior, social interest, and overcoming feelings of inferiority. Ackerman was a psychoanalytic family therapist who looked at unconscious motives and early relationships. Haley considered understanding levels of communication and organization and finding the myths that keep behavior going.

**67. B:** The counselor cannot acknowledge that the client is being seen by someone at the clinic in any manner. An appropriate response is to simply explain that you cannot discuss the presence or absence of any clients in the clinic, nor can you discuss details of clients. Be prepared with a uniform statement that all counselors at the clinic use in situations like this.

**68. B:** Rogerian counseling, of those listed, would be the most appropriate because it has an emic orientation—i.e., it emphasizes individual differences rather than similarities and would take into account the client's different cultural backgrounds and respect these. Traditional Freudian psychoanalysis has a more etic orientation—i.e., it uses the same techniques for everybody regardless of their individual backgrounds. As Atkinson (2004) suggested, traditional "time-bound, space-bound, cathartic psychotherapy" would probably not be as relevant to many cross-cultural clients. Maslow's theory of self-actualization is popular in American culture for its emphasis on individualism and realizing one's full potential. However, Juan's culture emphasizes familismo (familism), manifest in a strong identification with and attachment to one's family; and Mai's culture emphasizes collectivism, embodied in a strong identification with the good of the whole group over the needs of the individual. Thus, a Maslovian approach would likely be too individualistic and self-centered for these clients. Fritz Perls' Gestalt therapy also has a strongly self-centered orientation, and would also be less appropriate for multicultural counseling purposes.

**69. B:** Hypnosis may be best described as a deep state of relaxation. It is during this relaxed state that the mind is quieted and open to suggestion. Franz Mesmer (the "father of hypnosis") is credited with developing the technique, but it wasn't called hypnosis until the 1800s when James Braid experimented with trance-like states on patients. Jean-Martin Charcot used hypnosis successfully to treat hysterics, and Sigmund Freud used hypnosis in his work as well. Hypnosis is sometimes vilified as nothing more than a parlor trick, but, in reality, it can be highly effective in therapeutic settings when conducted by a trained hypnotherapist.

**70. D:** Self-efficacy is the belief that one can overcome obstacles. Self-efficacy is a factor in cognitive-behavior therapy, which seeks to change the client's thoughts in an effort to also change the client's behavior. Bandura believed that self-efficacy was very important if therapy was to be successful. By telling oneself messages such as "I can do this," self-confidence is enhanced and eventually the client puts increased effort forth to solve problems, which eliminates many long-term difficulties. Constructive self-talk is also often used in cognitive-behavior therapy, which aids in the development of self-efficacy.

**71. A:** John Watson is a well-known behaviorist who believed that any behavior can be learned. He claimed that if he were given any child and allowed to raise that child however he saw fit, he could make the child turn out however he dictated, regardless of the child's talents and abilities. His most famous experiment, the Little Albert experiment, involved conditioning a young boy to fear a white rat. He was also able to generalize that fear to other furry, white objects. Watson never deconditioned the child, so the experiment is often used as an example of unethical research. Behavioral modification and conditioning are still widely used today in therapy.

**72. C:** Transition is a stage within the "tentative" period, not a main period itself. The three main periods of Ginzberg, Ginsburg, Axelrad, and Herma's developmental theory are fantasy, tentative, and realistic.

**73. A:** The best way to reduce errors in research is to have a large sample size—the larger the better. Larger sample sizes are more likely to realistically reflect a population, decrease the margin of error, minimize the risk of samples being atypical, and enhance the ability to identify outliers.

**74. C:** The SBIRT (Screening, Brief Intervention, Referral to Treatment) program is specifically designed for substance users at risk but not yet dependent. The goal is early intervention as a preventive measure. The three primary functions of the program include: Screening (using various tools such as AUDIT or CRAFFT), brief intervention or therapy (ranging from discussion to 4-6 sessions), and referral to treatment for those at highest risk.

**75. C:** The existential perspective reflects on the human condition and what it means to be human; or in other words, what the meaning of life is. When it comes to rational-emotive therapy, the therapist helps individuals move from irrational to rational thoughts. Reality therapy focuses on helping individuals formulate realistic plans for improvement. Transactional analysis involves looking at individuals' "transactions" as they go through their life scripts (parent, adult, child).

**76. C:** Instrumental aggression occurs when a child wants a toy that another child has and he tries to get that toy by pushing or attacking the other child in some way. Hostile aggression occurs when a child intentionally hurts another child because he wants to hurt the other child. Physical aggression occurs more often in boys than in girls and is any form of harm or physical injury such as pushing, hitting, biting, or kicking. Relational aggression more often occurs in girls and involves the use of social exclusion, malicious gossip, or peer manipulation in order to damage another person's peer relationships.

**77. D:** In the past, work was viewed as a way to earn a wage in order to support a family. In recent years, however, choice of "work" has become more an issue of self-expression than simply a means to earn a living. Individuals now view the type of work they do as an extension of who they are. Social expectations often assume that an individual will choose work that they like, and that they are good at, rather than simply one that pays a good wage. Particular careers are also seen to exude a certain status, which also may be valued more the need to support oneself or a family.

**78. C:** Discussing members' problems is NOT an example of resistance. Discussing members' problems is a common activity in therapy groups. Seeming unable to set goals, talking too much or too little, and arriving late for group meetings are all examples of resistive behaviors that would impede group progress.

**79. C:** Caplan's model ranks groups according to their purpose. A tertiary group usually deals with more serious, longstanding individual difficulties.

**80. C:** Correlational studies that utilize two separate data points, in this case television viewing and academic performance, and are best represented in a scatterplot. The two main data points are divided onto the X and Y axis and then each data set is plotted using a dot. The dots combine to demonstrate correlation (the dots are all roughly following a trend that is either increasing or decreasing in slope) or a lack of correlation (the dots are completely and randomly scattered with no identifiable pattern).

**81. D:** If someone is thinking about suicide, asking that person about suicide will not plant the seed or push her into committing suicide. It is important that the counselor asks clients about suicide so that they can get the help they need. It is necessary to assess suicidality whenever it is suspected that someone is contemplating it or behaving in ways that may suggest that she is contemplating it. It is best practice to assess for suicidality at each session with clients. Suicide knows no age boundaries. Females attempt suicide at a rate three times higher than males, but males are successful more often, usually because they use more lethal methods than females.

**82. A:** Psychology seems often to be about what is abnormal or what has gone wrong in an individual's life. Positive Psychology, however, is about what goes right over the lifespan. It moves the focus from studying abnormal development and problems in everyday living to concentrating on the strengths of individuals and how they can get the most out of life. It is a relatively new area of psychology and still developing. It concentrates on three main areas: positive emotions, positive traits, and positive institutions. The focus is to enhance an individual's experiences in life.

**83. C:** Logotherapy, developed by Viktor Frankl, is an existential psychology that focuses on the search for meaning. The human spirit plays an integral role in Logotherapy, which is more about the human will or spirit, rather than related to religion or a relationship with God. Frankl taught that everything can be taken away from us in life, except for our will to find meaning in our lives. Logotherapy seeks to aid individuals in overcoming obstacles with the power of the human spirit. Frankl theorized that we can find meaning in our lives through deeds, by experiencing a value, or through suffering.

**84. A:** If the counselor is assessing an older adult who experienced an "accidental" overdose of drugs and alcohol for possible suicidal ideation, when assessing the client for depression, the most effective initial query is, "What has changed in your life or health over the last 6-8 months." This question does not challenge the client's assertion that the overdose was accidental, so the client may be more forthcoming about events that may have triggered or indicate depression.

**85. C:** A correlational research design looks at the relationship between two variables (the amount of TV viewing and academic performance). An AB or ABAB design is a two-part continuous measurement design in which the experimenter has established a baseline (A) and introduces an intervention (B). The ABAB design is intended to rule out confounding variables by seeing whether the second AB pattern yields the same results. A time-series or continuous measurement design looks at one person across time using a number of measurements throughout the study.

**86. D:** Aversive conditioning is a classical conditioning approach. Behavioral therapists use aversive conditioning to pair negative stimuli with the behavior that needs to be changed. The idea is for the reward value of the unwanted behavior to be eliminated, so that the client will no longer choose to engage in it. A common example for aversive conditioning is a client who has a drinking problem. The counselor may recommend medication that induces nausea when alcohol is consumed. The negative experience of nausea when drinking replaces the pleasurable experience of drinking, which eventually may result in the client choosing to stop drinking altogether.

**87. C:** An individual's profile of the six personality types may be differentiated (i.e., it has significant highs and lows among the types), or it may be undifferentiated (i.e., the profile tends to be more flattened among the various types). Pairs of types which are on adjacent sides of the hexagon are more psychologically alike, so answer A is incorrect. Pairs of types which are on non-adjacent sides of the hexagon are less psychologically alike, so answer B is incorrect. Congruence refers to similarity or sameness between the individual's personality type and the type of environment the individual is in not to pairs of personality types, so answer D is incorrect.

**88. A:** The primary purpose of administering the Digit Repetition Test to an older adult client is to assess attention. The counselor asks the client listen to numbers and then repeat them, beginning with two random single-digit numbers. If the client gets this sequence correct, the counselor then states 3 numbers and continues to add one number each time until the client is unable to repeat the numbers correctly. People with normal intelligence (without retardation or expressive aphasia) can usually repeat 5-7 numbers, so scores <5 indicate impaired attention.

**89. A:** If a client has frequent panic attacks that have become debilitating and that prevent him from socializing with others despite his taking antianxiety medication, the initial intervention should be to help the client recognize precipitating factors. If the client can understand triggers, such as a crowded room or excessive noise, the client will be better able to interrupt the escalation of anxiety to panic and to develop a plan to avoid panic attacks.

**90. B:** Frank Parsons, established Boston's Vocation Bureau in 1908. In his book, Choosing a Vocation (published in 1909), he established the trait-factor guidance approach. Jesse Davis was the first identified school counselor who he began working in a high school in Detroit in 1898. E. G. Williamson modified Frank Parsons' trait-factor approach in his book How to Counsel Students published in 1939. Clifford Beers published his book A Mind That Found Itself in 1908 exposing unethical and unhealthy conditions in mental health institutions of the time.

**91. A:** The independent variable is the one that the researcher manipulates or changes. The dependent variable is "dependent" upon the changes that the researcher is making. Therefore, the dependent variable is the one that shows whether or not the manipulation of the independent variable is effective. The dependent variable is related to outcomes. Leaving variables unattended is not appropriate in most experimental research.

**92. D:** Just like with any new client, the counselor would have the parent or guardian provide some background information and get insurance information. Each state has guidelines about when adolescents must sign their own consent-for-treatment forms, but usually the age is 14 or 15.

**93. C:** Stratified sampling refers to selecting individuals who represent major subgroups in the population. The subgroups represented could be ethnic groups, age groups, gender, teenagers, married people, etc. Selecting naturally occurring groups is known as cluster sampling. The naturally occurring groups could be classrooms, apartment complexes, city blocks, neighborhoods, etc. Selecting samples of convenience or of volunteers refers to non-random or non-probability samples or "other" samples. These will not necessarily yield a normal score distribution, but may offer very valuable data. Selecting individuals so that each has equal chances of being selected is known as random sampling.

**94. C:** The Wechsler Adult Intelligence Scale consists of several subtests divided between "verbal" and "performance" categories. The results of the test include three scaled scores, which are a verbal

IQ score, a performance IQ score, and a full-scale IQ score. A full-scale score of 130 and above indicates a subject performing in the "very superior" range. 120-129 is the "superior" range, 110-119 is "high average," and 90-109 is "average." The "borderline" range is a score of 70-79, with 69 and below being in the "extremely low" range.

**95. C: Conversion disorder**: Sudden onset of sensory (seeing, hearing) or motor (paralysis, weakness) deficits without identifiable physical cause. *La belle indifference* (unconcern) is common. **Somatization disorder**: Combinations of multiple physical symptoms, usually involving pain and sexual, gastrointestinal, and/or pseudoneurological symptoms. **Pain disorder**: Pain that is unrelieved by analgesia and is affected by psychological status. **Body dysmorphic disorder**: Preoccupation with imagined physical defect or exaggeration of a physical defect, such as belief that one's nose is hideous, and often seeking surgical correction.

**96. A:** Psychosurgery refers to surgery that removes or destroys brain tissue in order to improve a mental health condition. Egas Moniz developed the "prefrontal lobotomy" to surgically sever the frontal lobe. He believed that severe mental illnesses could be alleviated by this surgery. Moniz was awarded the Nobel Prize in 1949 for his work, but since prefrontal lobotomies often leave patients in a vegetative state, this treatment is no longer used. Today, psychosurgery is considered a last resort and is performed in a far more precise manner.

**97. A:** Historical analysis is analytical research done mainly via analysis of documents, and as such is not interactive in nature. Ethnographies, dramaturgy, and case studies are examples of interactive research, conducted via interviews and observation. Both interactive and non-interactive research designs are qualitative research designs.

**98. B:** Lev Vygotsky was a Russian psychologist with an interest in development, education, and sociocultural issues. He looked at development in terms of the entire lifespan rather than in stages. Vygotsky believed that the cultural context within which development occurs is critical, and that language plays a large role in that development. In Vygotsky's theory, the social environment an individual resides in has a significant impact upon cognition, with culture playing a major role in the thought patterns of the individual. Vygotsky's ideas are often compared with Jean Piaget's work. However, Piaget believed that children act independently, while Vygotsky saw social learning as a guiding force.

**99. C:** A counselor who wants to consult or contact another professional, a client's family member, or someone else who works with a particular client must have the client give written permission to contact and share information. If the counselor gets contacted by someone who has contact with the client, the counselor cannot acknowledge that the client is being seen unless the client has signed a release-of-information.

**100. B:** Biofeedback is a means to measure involuntary physiological behaviors and report them to the client. It grew out of an interest in the mind-body connection and has been shown to be quite useful in some cases. By using cognitive-control methods, clients can learn to control physiological responses, and therefore manage such things as chronic pain, irritable bowel syndrome (IBS), high blood pressure, and headaches. It is also often used with stress-related issues such as depression, anxiety, and sleep disorders, and is being used with some psychiatric disorders as well. Because biofeedback can sometimes be used to voluntarily control involuntary (automatic physical) responses, its potential is significant.

**101. D:** While all of Sigmund Freud's theories have been criticized over the years, his view of female sexuality would be the most controversial. Freud worked in therapy with many female clients, and came to believe that females are weaker than males and certainly inferior in many other ways as well. For example, he believed that female sexual organs were inferior and that clitoral orgasm was an immature response. Superego development in females was also viewed as weak, and he considered females for more susceptible to neurotic behavior.

**102. B:** When engaging in psychoeducation with a client who has schizophrenia and the client's family, the counselor should include impaired cause and effect reasoning as an early sign of relapse. Other indications included increasing lethargy and inability to sleep, social isolation, mood swings, disinhibition, neglect in appearance, increasing forgetfulness, and increased negativity. It's essential that the client and family understand the importance of managing medications and looking for signs of relapse so it can be prevented or interventions taken to minimize the severity of the relapse.

**103. A:** An action or activity, defined as an external event, is the first step in therapy. This induces a belief, evident in the form of a self-verbalization. Third, there is a consequent affect (i.e., a feeling derived from the belief). This affect may be rational or irrational. (D and E stand for disputing and effect.)

**104. A:** The most noticeable finding in the Stanford Prison Study was that the individuals who played one role or another really took on their role. As prisoners, these individuals in a very short time began to display behaviors such as distress and panic, which emulated the behaviors a "real" prisoner displays. It did not matter how the guards treated them or acted toward them, the fact that they became like "real" prisoners was the key finding. Individuals who played guards took on behaviors of "real" guards; and individuals who played prisoners took on behaviors of "real" prisoners.

**105. D:** William Glasser's choice theory states that all behavior consists of either "what we do," "what we think," or "what we feel." He theorized that one can only control one's own behavior, and that every behavior chosen is an attempt to meet one's internal needs at the time. Unlike the stimulus-response theories that are popular for controlling behavior and encouraging change, Glasser believed that only the individual can control himself, and it's not possible to do so with reinforcements or other such inducements. He further theorized that for people to be happy with their lives, they need to find ways to meet their inner needs.

**106. B:** Techniques involving setting goals or keeping a diary are extensions of behavioral therapy. Most other therapies do not involve keeping track of behaviors or setting specific goals. A psychodynamic approach would use techniques like free association; gestalt approach would use techniques like psychodrama or exaggeration; and the existential approach would use imagery or awareness activities.

**107. B:** Millions of men suffer from depression each year, yet relatively few are likely to seek help for it. Instead of enlisting the aid of a medical professional, men often self-medicate with drugs or alcohol, which merely masks the symptoms rather than addressing them. Furthermore, depression in men is often overlooked because their symptoms are sometimes not what is expected of a depressed individual. Instead of the typical sadness, male depressive symptoms are often such things as irritability, anger, and aggressive acting-out. Attention to older men is also needed because illness and medications can mask depressive symptoms and cause elderly men to be less likely to receive help.

**108. D:** The symptoms of schizophrenia create a significant change in the client's personality and are characterized in three ways. "Positive" symptoms are things that should not be present (such as delusions and hallucinations). Symptoms characterized as "negative" are missing aspects that should be present (such as "normal" emotional reactions or speech patterns). "Disorganized" symptoms would be issues such as inability to communicate with others appropriately or difficulty interpreting others.

**109. A:** Empathic understanding refers to the ability to perceive and appreciate a client's subjective feelings and thoughts. The term congruence is often used to refer to counselor openness and genuineness, meaning the therapist is authentic and integrated during the session. (Congruence can also mean agreement between a client's beliefs and behaviors.) Unconditional positive regard refers to acceptance, meaning the counselor is not judgmental of the client. Reflection refers to repeating what the client has said, emphasizing the emotional content of each statement.

**110. C:** If a Puerto Rican client almost always comes late to his therapy appointments, this is probably because of cultural ideas of time, which are more relaxed than common in the continental United States, where people are expected to be on time. When assigned a time for a meeting, the client may believe that coming at "about" that time is acceptable and does not intend to be disrespectful or to display passive-aggressive behavior, and this behavior is usually not related to poor time management but rather a perception that other things, such as family concerns, are more important.

**111. C:** An appropriate response when caring for a client who admits to being a victim of intimate partner violence is, "I'm worried about your safety." The counselor should avoid making disparaging remarks about the partner, such as "Your partner is a thug" because this may make the client defensive. The counselor should also refrain from giving advice, such as "You should call the police" as this may seem coercive. The counselor must allow the client to retain control and resist the urge to solve all the problems: "Don't worry. I'll take care of everything for you."

**112. C:** If a client is in a manic phase of bipolar disorder and is speaking very rapidly and incoherently, the most appropriate response is "I'm having trouble understanding. Could you speak more slowly." This puts the focus on the problem that the counselor is having rather than on the client. Phrasing should avoid suggesting that the client has a problem because the client is likely to resist any such idea during the manic phase. The counselor may need to repeat this phrase a number of times in order to continue communication.

**113. A:** Most ethical guidelines suggest that the best course of action is to confront the impaired professional first and then report him to the licensing board if he continues to come to work impaired.

**114. C:** It is possible for a counselor to be licensed in several different states of the country at the same time. Licensing requirements are established by the passage of law at the state level. There is no licensure at the national level. Licensure requirements are not the same from one state to another; there are variations in requirements depending upon the state. Counselors cannot move their licenses from one state to another if they relocate. However, a counselor can obtain licensure in more than one state.

**115. C:** A Type I or alpha error is rejecting the null hypothesis, which states that there is no difference in the results, when it is true. A type II or beta error is accepting the null hypothesis when it is wrong and there actually is a difference.

**116. C:** Considering anticipatory guidance, it is generally recommended that the parent and/or counselor begin discussions about methods to avoid gangs, drugs, alcohol, and abusive relationships when the child is between 11 and 14, depending on the maturity of the child and the environmental influences. Early adolescence is a time of physical changes (secondary sexual characteristics develop), cognitive changes (difference in thought patterns and awareness), and socio-behavioral changes (peer pressure).

**117. A:** A useful exercise for a client who has perfectionist tendencies and unrealistic expectation of himself and others is to make a list of those things in his life that are in his control (diet, exercise, tasks) and those things that are outside his control (weather, workload, other people). The lists then can serve as a starting point for a discussion because they likely include those things that have been causes for concern to the client.

**118. D:** Group therapy, group counseling or group work refer to interventions done with more than three people at once. Group cohesion refers to the bond formed by group members. Group practice refers to a number of providers practicing in a single business entity. Group dynamics refers to the interactions between group members.

**119. B:** A basic idea of cognitive-behavioral therapy is that we can't change the world around us or many of the events that occur in our lives, but we can change how we think and feel about everything. In cognitive-behavioral theory, our thoughts cause our feelings and behaviors. Since thoughts can be faulty, they can cause us to feel, and choose behaviors, that are problematic. By changing inappropriate thoughts, we can change how we think and feel about situations, and also how we choose to behave in response to those situations, even when we can't change the situations themselves.

**120. D:** If a client with a history of substance abuse receives a coupon for a free meal at a local fast-food restaurant each time a urine test for drug use is negative, the type of therapy that the client is likely undergoing is motivational enhancement therapy. This type of therapy utilizes a reward system for positive behavior, such as a negative drug test. Rewards help to build self-esteem and are tangible recognition of progress.

**121. D:** Conducting scientific studies is important for the advancement of knowledge in psychology. However, how does one know if those studies, and the results of those studies, are trustworthy? A statistical significance means that the differences between two variables are great enough that it's not likely that those differences are due to chance. A minimum level of statistical significance of 0.05 is often necessary for concluding that the differences seen aren't simply a fluke. In fact, when a test is said to be statistically significant, they're saying that there is a 95% chance that the experiment's results are not due to chance.

**122. D:** If an adolescent client with muscular dystrophy has become wheelchair bound but appears to be adjusting well and denies distress over the change in his mobility status although the counselor is concerned that the client is in denial, the counselor should focus therapy on assisting the client to develop strategies for managing wheelchair use. It's important that the counselor not impose the expectation that the client is in denial on the client, who may, in fact, have a more positive outlook or even feel relief at having less struggle to remain mobile.

**123. C:** A client who has been diagnosed with bipolar disorder but has consistently refused to take medications or attend therapy, insisting that he has been misdiagnosed and has only "mild stress" is probably experiencing denial, an ego defense mechanism. Denial occurs when a client refuses to acknowledge a painful truth, such as a diagnosis of bipolar disorder. Denial may also include the failure to recognize the behavior or attitudes that allow problems to continue.

**124. B:** Adolescents may resist treatment because of concern about body image and loss of control or because of unrealistic ideas about their own invincibility. They often can't articulate or even understand their motives in doing something, so asking for a reason may be pointless. Using words such as "must" or "should" may result in resentment, so engaging the adolescent in the treatment plan, "What do you think you can do to make these treatments easier for you?", shows respect for the adolescent's autonomy and opens a discussion with the focus on what the adolescent is thinking.

**125. B:** In Rogerian counseling, Rogers reacted against the directive psychoanalytic approach, which put the counselor in charge of advising, teaching, and interpreting, as described in Answer A. Rogers' focus was on the phenomenological reality of the individual client and the client's feelings. Answer C, which describes the therapeutic process as holistic, focused in the present, and based on existential concepts, reflects the bases of Fritz Perls' Gestalt therapy. Answer D, which describes the therapy process as helping clients to gain insights into themselves, describes a goal of Individual Psychology, pioneered by Alfred Adler and Rudolph Dreikurs.

**126. C:** This is blatantly unethical due to the potential for harm to the client that exists. This is considered sexual misconduct and is therefore unethical and a punishable offense. While the professional treatment was terminated, the counselor is still the counselor to the client, should she ever need to return for treatment.

**127. A:** If a caregiver for her mother, who has moderately-severe Alzheimer's disease, reports that her mother has been wandering at night and has gotten lost and been brought back home by the police, the best advice is likely to place a latch at the top or bottom of the door as most people with Alzheimer's disease are unable locate the latches. Alarms on door can be very frightening and may just result in the individual running away from the house. Movement sensors tend to be ignored after people get used to the sound, and people should never be locked in their rooms for safety reasons.

**128. C:** The **Dementia Severity Rating Scale** is the tool that is most appropriate to assess a client with cognitive impairment to determine the client's ability to function in the home environment because it includes questions about community affairs, home activities, and personal care. The **Memory Impairment Screen** is recommended for ethnic minorities because it lacks the language and educational bias found in some tools. **MMSE** assesses orientation, attention, language recall, perception, and the ability to follow directions and do calculations. **Mini-Cog** is a short 3-item tool that includes the clock drawing test.

**129. C:** If the significance level of an experiment goes down, the type I error will also go down and the type II error will go up. Answers A and D are wrong because type I and type II errors will not both go in the same direction relative to the significance level. Type I and type II errors have an inverse relationship (i.e., as one goes up the other will go down). Type I error is wrongly rejecting the null hypothesis and type II error is wrongly accepting the null hypothesis. Answer B is the reverse of the correct answer.

**130. A:** Gerald Caplan conceptualized mental health consultation by describing numerous types such as client-centered consultation and consultee-centered consultation. Satir is a well-known family therapist. Adler is a Neo-Freudian theorist. And Holland is associated with career counseling.

**131. C:** Bibliotherapy is just as it sounds, a type of therapy that uses reading material to enhance the therapeutic experience. Bibliotherapy often involves the simple assignment of reading material that would be meaningful to the client and the direction the therapy is taking. However, it can also include activities and exercises related to the reading assignment. The use of bibliotherapy has various applications, depending upon the client, symptoms, and treatment being used. It can be a time-saving method used to significantly advance the course of therapy. Some people also view bibliotherapy as a self-help technique when not used in the traditional therapeutic setting.

**132. B:** Each theorist lends a particular emphasis to their theory of development. For instance, Sigmund Freud has a psychosexual bent to it, while Erik Erikson was psychosocial. Lawrence Kohlberg was interested in moral development, and Jean Piaget focused on cognitive issues. Of the various development theorists, each placed their own unique slant on the material, based upon their own experiences and research. Most mental health professionals today see value in all of the theories, discarding some parts and adopting other components in their own practice. Few practitioners, however, would adhere completely to only one developmental theory.

**133. B:** If an African American client asks the counselor, who is Caucasian, how the counselor expects that the difference in race will affect their relationship, the most appropriate response is, "There are likely cultural differences that will be important to explore." Suggesting that race will have no effect or that race is not a factor may give the client the impression that race and culture are not important and have no role in people's lives. Answering the question with a question is technique of avoidance.

**134. C:** A homogeneous group is one in which the members share a similarity. By contrast, the heterogeneous group is one made up of individuals who may not share a commonality. An open group allows new members to join throughout the therapy sessions, but a closed group does not admit new members to the group once the group therapy sessions have begun. The length of the group therapy sessions, the number of sessions, and any other factors are not dictated by these distinctions. Some types of groups, with particular populations, are more effective with one type of group or another, and the decision of which to offer should be made on a case-by-case basis.

**135. C:** Behavior therapies focus on eliminating or changing the client's undesirable behavior, unlike psychoanalysts who focus on unconscious thoughts and the origins of the reasons behind behaviors. In order to investigate abnormal behaviors, cognitive therapists emphasize the client's thoughts. They believe that if the client's thoughts and feelings change, then so will the unwanted behavior. Cognitive therapists are more conversational in their approach than cognitive-behavioral therapists, who use a lot of exercises and training sessions. The cognitive approach seems more traditional than the cognitive-behavioral approach.

**136. D:** Most people with reasonable cognitive ability understand that smoking is bad for their health, so threatening them or scaring them is not likely to motivate them to quit. Realistically, success rates for smoking cessation are often low, so the counselor should consider that not everyone will be successful at quitting and should provide information as a preventive measure about symptoms of concern, such as increasing cough, purulent or bloody sputum, and increased shortness of breath.

**137. D:** The ABCDE system is as follows: A is the external event; B is the belief about the event; C is the accompanying feeling; D is the disputing of the irrational belief that is causing the accompanying feeling; and E is the change that is made in the self-talk as a result of the therapy process.

**138. B:** On the Geriatric Depression Scale, a total score of >5 indicates depression. The GDS comprises 15 questions about satisfaction with life ("Are you basically satisfied with your life?", feelings about life ("Does your life feel empty?", "Do you feel your situation is hopeless?"), and feelings in general ("Are you in good spirits?", Do you feel happy most of the time?", "Do you feel worthless?") Each yes answer is scored with one point.

**139. A:** Unskilled labor represents one of Roe's six levels of occupations (not one of her eight fields). The eight fields she identified were: service (only this half of answer A is correct), business contact, managerial, general cultural, arts and entertainment, technology, outdoor, and science. The six levels she identified were: professional and managerial (highest level); professional and managerial (regular); semi-professional and managerial; skilled; semiskilled; and unskilled.

**140. D:** William Masters and Virginia Johnson studied the physiological responses of hundreds of subjects to determine that there are four phases of sexual response. The first phase is "excitement" and lasts from minutes to hours. During this phase there is increased genital blood flow and muscle tension. "Plateau" is the next phase and consists of such responses as increased pulse rate, rapid breathing, and raised blood pressure. The third phase of "orgasm" brings intense pleasure and extreme completion of neuromuscular tension. The human sexual response concludes with the fourth stage of "resolution" with the arousal dropping off, and the return to a normal resting state.

**141. A:** When developing an education plan for a group of homeless clients with alcohol use disorder, the most important information to include is probably information about community resources, including shelters, food banks, free meals, free clinics, and self-help groups, such as Alcoholics Anonymous®. Inpatient care is often an unrealistic goal for homeless people with few or no financial resources unless care is mandated by the courts and covered by government programs. Clients who are homeless and addicted often have multiple problems, including dual diagnoses, which make personal responsibility difficult to achieve.

**142. D:** Emile Durkheim is considered by many to be the father of sociology. He is often credited with making sociology a science, and he conducted a great deal of research and educational endeavors on the subject, as well as wrote books and gave many lectures. He was one of the first sociologists to make use of statistical and scientific techniques. Durkheim believed that all parts of the society work together as a machine, which came to be known as "sociological functionalism." He is also known for his studies of religion, labor, crime, and suicide.

**143. B:** Tricyclic drugs are called antidepressant drugs because they regulate mood. They are called "tricyclic" because of their three-ringed molecular structure. They can correct chemical imbalances in the brain and raise the levels of serotonin and norepinephrine. Tricyclic drugs are available in several forms, including, pills, liquid, and injection. Some commonly used antidepressants are amitriptyline, nortriptyline, and protriptyline. Depending upon the particular drug used, side effects can include dizziness, bladder problems, dry mouth, and an increased heart rate, among other issues. It takes some time for the medication to work, so several weeks should be allowed before deciding if the medication is having its desired effect.

**144. C:** The MMPI (Minnesota Multiphasic Personality Inventory) is usually used by clinical psychologists to clarify diagnoses of mental disorders. The KOIS is the Kuder Occupational Interest Survey, which looks at matching career choices with interests, not personality characteristics. The SDS (Self-Directed Search) is the instrument developed by John Holland that looks specifically at six different categories of personality characteristics that may relate to certain career choices. The SCII (Strong Interest Inventory) is similar to the KOIS, as it looks at matching personal interests with possible career choices.

**145. C:** The APA is the American Psychological Association and is the national organization for psychologists. The ACA is the American Counselors Association and is the national organization for counselors. The NCE is the National Counselor's Exam. NASP is the National Association for School Psychologists.

**146. A:** A counselor can enter into a therapeutic relationship with a client, even if that client is culturally different. In such a situation, the term "cultural relativity" comes into play. Cultural relativity basically refers to the belief that a situation is relative to the culture in which it occurs. In the counseling setting, the therapist would address the issues presented by the client in terms of the client's culture. It would not be appropriate to do otherwise. For example, something that would be acceptable in the counselor's culture may not be acceptable from the client's perspective. Therefore, applying the client's issues to the counselor's culture would not be relevant (or helpful).

**147. B:** A hypothesis is a statement formulated by a researcher who then tests it to see if it is true or not. A directional hypothesis states that one group will have a significantly different score than another. (This is a hypothesis that would use a one-tailed test.) A research question is in the form of a question rather than a statement. A nondirectional hypothesis would state that there will be differences in the two groups, but will not state which group will have a higher or lower score. (This type of hypothesis would require a two-tailed test.) A null hypothesis would state that there is no difference between the two groups.

**148. C:** Individuals born after between 1965 and 1980 are what is commonly referred to as Generation X. The Baby Boomer generation included those born between 1946 and 1964. Those born between 1980 and 1996 are known as Millennials; they are also variously known as the Internet Generation. Generation Z is defined as those who were born after 1997. Note that the definitions of generations are not absolute, but are prone to overlap.

**149. B:** If a counselor has been working for months with victims of interpersonal violence and begins to feel exhausted, emotionally and physically, and feels increasingly unable to care about or care for the needs of clients, compassion fatigues best accounts for this change. Compassion fatigue includes a feeling of numbness toward others' suffering and problems and usually occurs after seeing or hearing the same type of suffering repeatedly. The individual may begin to feel overwhelmed by others' problems and to blame them rather than feel empathy.

**150. C:** Premack's Principle of reinforcement was developed by David Premack in 1965 out of a study completed with monkeys. It states that high-probability behaviors (HPB) will reinforce low-probability behaviors (LPB). In the case of this question, the client doesn't like to shower and dress well. However, he is willing to do so because of the attention it gives him from a girl he likes. In other words, he is willing to engage in behavior he doesn't like in order to get something that he does. The Premack Principle has a variety of uses, included its use in animal training.

**151. B:** Ackerman is best known for his work in psychoanalytic family theory, while Minuchin is best known for his work in structural family theory. Bowen was one of the pioneers of family systems theory. Satir's work focused on conjoint family therapy and was involved in communication patterns and meta-communication.

**152. A:** In Caplan's model, a primary group emphasizes a healthy lifestyle and/or coping strategies aimed at reducing the incidence of a certain problem. In this case, it is substance abuse. This kind of group could also be aimed at preventing teen pregnancy, preventing divorce, etc.

**153. C:** Confidentiality is a major ethical consideration for the mental health professional, and it is also tested the most often. Confidentiality not only affects what is said during counseling sessions, but also involves the storage of records, testimony in court, communication between professionals, and many other areas of practice. The scope of "confidentiality" is so far reaching that it even protects the client after death. When in doubt about any issue related to confidentiality, a counselor should consult the ACA Code of Ethics and other practitioners for assistance. The rules are clear, but situations can sometimes arise that make them difficult to interpret.

**154. C:** If a client with agoraphobia has finally come to the counselor's office but begins to hyperventilate when the counselor shuts the office door, the most appropriate response is to ask the client if she would be more comfortable with the door open. Hyperventilation is often the first indication of panic. While there may be privacy concerns, the immediate response should be to prevent escalation of the panic response. A client experiencing a panic attack may construe any touch as threatening.

**155. D:** If a client who has developed a unilateral tremor of the left hand has a positive finding on the tremor entrainment test (tremor stops when ask to move the right hand in a circle and left hand entrains/copies the right), this suggests that the cause is functional and that the diagnosis is conversion (functional neurological symptom) disorder. However, the diagnosis should not be based on a single finding but rather on the client's overall clinical picture.

**156. D:** If a client who was voluntarily committed to a psychiatric facility wants to leave and is restrained from doing so by a counselor, this may constitute **false imprisonment** as the client has the legal right to leave, even against medical advice. **Assault and battery** may occur if a client was treated without consent or threatened. **Intentional torts** are voluntary purposeful actions intended to bring about a physical or mental consequence. **Negligence** is providing substandard care.

**157. D:** The duration of treatment in family therapy is usually shorter than in individual therapy. Family therapy generally tries to resolve current problems within a family via brief counseling. The locus of pathology in family counseling is viewed as being within the social context, typically the family, rather than as being within the individual. The focus of the interventions in family therapy is on the family rather than on the individual even though one individual in the family may be the identified patient. The unit of treatment intervention is the family rather than an individual in family counseling.

**158. B:** The independent variable is the one that the researcher is going to manipulate, in this case the intervention of systematic desensitization. The dependent variable is the variable impacted (or not) by the independent variable, in this case, agoraphobia.

**159. C:** If a client has repeated complaints of various health problems (pain, nausea, headache, muscle ache, abdominal cramping) that prevents her from attending university classes or working in her place of employment has been diagnosed with probable factitious disorder, the counselor should assess the client for the common co-diagnosis of personality disorder. Clients often have dysfunctional relationships with partners or other family members and have difficulty developing attachments.

**160. D: Sublimation**: The client redirects socially unacceptable impulses to acceptable actions, such as when the victim of a crime redirects anger toward becoming an advocate for other victims. **Regression**: The client retreats to an earlier stage of development, such as by being more dependent. **Suppression**: The client voluntarily blocks unpleasant emotions, such as by refusing to think about an event. **Repression**: The client involuntarily blocks unpleasant emotions, such as being unable to remember being raped.

**161. C:** A strong negative correlation between income and mental illness would indicate that those with lower incomes tend to suffer from higher rates of mental illness and those with higher incomes tend to suffer from lower rates of mental illness. A correlation does not necessarily indicate causation, which is inferred in the other three options.

**162. B:** The client is describing the features of avoidant personality disorder. Criteria include being worried about social situations, unwillingness to try new activities, avoiding activities once found enjoyable if they are social.

**163. B: Perseveration**: Client repeats the same word phrase over and over, such as "cake," in response to a question. **Associative looseness**: Client shifts comments from one topic to another but is unaware the ideas may be incoherent. **Tangentiality**: Client introduces unrelated topics and never returns to the point of the communication. **Echolalia**: Client repeats words or phrases that the client hears. For example, if a counselor states, "It's time to go home," the client might repeat, "it's time to go home," over and over or may shorten it to "home, home, home, home."

**164. A:** If a counselor has a client whose managed care plan allows only 20 visits per year, the counselor should consider the implications of this limit at the initial visit. Ethically, a counselor cannot abandon a client who needs more than 20 visits, so the counselor should consider options: full private pay, payment on a sliding scale according to income, referral to another type of covered service (such as a psychiatrist), or referral to a free clinic. In some areas, resources are very limited for clients with limited ability to pay although some may qualify for assistance through Medicaid.

**165. C:** A cognitive behavioral therapy (CBT) approach that focuses on relapse prevention for drug use disorders will likely help clients identify situations that make them vulnerable to relapse. Therapy may include training in behavioral skills and the use of cognitive interventions to assist them to identify triggers or situations that result in relapse as well as to provide tools they can use if faced with a situation that is placing the client at risk, such as when associates are engaging in addictive behavior.

**166. A:** Suicide ideation is often a result of depression. When depressed, the client will show significant changes to his usual behavior, which could include changes in eating, sleeping habits, work behavior, relationship problems, and many other possible factors. When a client has been in the midst of a depression for some time, and suicide has been a significant factor, one of the times the risk is highest is when the client appears to suddenly feel better. Friends and relatives will often drop their guard at that time, but it is then that the client is more likely to attempt suicide because he or she made the final decision, feels the relief of being out of conflict, and is ready to act.

**167. D:** According to Yalom, a poor style of group leadership includes low or high emotional stimulation, low or high executive behavior, low use of caring function, and low use of meaning attribution. Yalom found that effective leaders used moderate amounts of emotional stimulation and executive direction, frequent use of caring functions, and consistent use of meaning attribution. Thus, both group A's and group B's leaders have styles that fit Yalom's definition of poor group leadership. According to Yalom, it does not depend on which of these two leaders Sallie likes better since neither one uses the techniques of an effective group leader.

**168. D:** Content is the subject under group discussion, and process is how the discussion or interaction is taking place. Context contrasts with content and means the setting in which the content exists. Product contrasts with process in that it is the result of a process.

**169. B:** Prior to the 1940s, psychological problems were seen as best dealt with through individual therapy. Kurt Lewin, known for his early research and theory on groups, started exploring the concepts of group dynamics and group therapy in the 1940's. The concept of group therapy also naturally evolved out of other group dynamics that have been present throughout history. Religious groups, fraternal organizations, schools, and even the basic family unit have all reflected both the positive and negative attributes of group dynamics. It was to be expected that psychology would also embrace the group setting as a means by which to deal with personal and interpersonal issues, and a great deal of progress has been made in the professional treatment of individuals within the group therapy setting.

**170. C:** Erik Erikson theorized that adolescents experiment with a variety of roles in an attempt to "find themselves," or determine who they really are. In Erikson's stages of psychosocial development, it is during the teenage years that the individual seeks a clear sense of identity in occupation, politics, religion, and sex roles. The age range for this is considered to be from age twelve to eighteen. The term "identity crisis" has come to be loosely used in society, referring to something that can occur later in the lifespan, but the term originated with Erikson as a feeling during teenage development.

**171. C:** The DSM-5 no longer separates substances abuse and dependence but now places all disorders under substance use disorder, substance intoxication, and substance withdrawal. Stimulant use disorder involves the need for escalating amounts of a substance to achieve intoxication, withdrawal symptoms, compulsive use in spite of a desire to stop, compromised social, occupational/educational, familial, and/or other important role compromise due to the use of an intoxicating substance, and includes severe physiological or compulsive use features. Severity is decided by the number of symptoms, and can be classified as mild, moderate, or severe.

**172. B:** All counselors have an ethical responsibility to not only hold themselves to a strict code of ethics, but also to expect it of other counselors. When an ethics violation has taken place, all efforts should be made to resolve the issue informally. Failing an informal resolution, the violation should be reported to the appropriate agency, licensing board, or other authority. However, if reporting the violation will also violate confidentiality rights, or if the counselor's work in question is currently being evaluated for possible infringement, then the ethics violation need not be reported.

**173. C:** The Hawthorne effect refers to the way experimental subjects' behavior can change when they receive attention and/or know that they are participating in research. Since Becky's disruptive behaviors were identified as attention-seeking, the extra attention she gets in the experiment likely satisfies her need for more individual attention. Knowing she is participating in research also may make her feel special, and thus motivate her to be on her best behavior for the scientists. The Rosenthal effect refers to changes in the subject's behavior caused by the researcher's expectations, attitudes, or behaviors. The Pygmalion effect is another name for the Rosenthal effect. There is no information in the question pertaining to any possible influence by the researchers' expectations. The placebo effect refers to the phenomenon of control subjects' behavior changing even though they have not been given any experimental treatment. The question does not state that Becky was a control subject.

**174. C:** Although Jennifer's score (177 out of 200) remains the same, the interpretation of her score will be different based on the norm group to which her score is being compared. It is inappropriate to compare Jennifer (a graduating high school senior) to freshmen at a community college, to a group of college mathematics majors, or even to a group of high school mathematics team members, because Jennifer is not a member of any of these groups. She is a graduating senior high school student. Therefore, it is most appropriate to compare Jennifer's score to those of a similar group of graduating seniors. It is important to compare one's score to a norm group closest to the group to which the individual belongs.

**175. C:** If, in a group therapy session, a client describes her experience related to telling her friends and family about her mental health condition, and the counselor points out that another group member had a similar experience, this is an example of linking. Linking is showing a connection between one statement or action and another. The group leader may help the members to see the connection through directly pointing it out or leading the group to the discovery.

**176. C:** Actually, Adler's therapy is considered to be versatile. It is also useful for treating specific disorders. Criticisms of Adlerian counseling include the lack of a firm research base; the vagueness of many of his terms and concepts and lack of "how-to" counseling instructions; and the inherent narrowness of his approach.

**177. B:** Concreteness is NOT one of the strengths of Rogerian counseling. One of its criticisms is its lack of concreteness. One of Rogers' techniques is the therapist's acceptance of the client, which benefits the client. Other strengths of Rogers' client-centered counseling include the openness of the theory, its evolution, and its applicability to a wide range of problems.

**178. B:** Havighurst's stages of growth were not specifically focused on cognitive development alone. Developmental stages resulting in progressively higher levels of cognitive function would be a more accurate description of Jean Piaget's cognitive developmental theory. Havighurst did identify stages of growth; each one requiring completion to reach the next. Havighurst also believed that developmental tasks arise from a combination of physical maturation, cultural, and social influences, combined with the individual's values and desires. These tasks consist of knowledge, skills, attitudes, and behaviors, which are attained via a combination of maturation, social learning, and personal effort.

**179. A:** In his rational emotive behavior therapy (REBT) theory, Ellis stated that irrational belief systems, self-talk, and crooked thinking cause emotional disturbance and inappropriate affects and behaviors. While Ellis believed that self-talk is the source of emotional disturbance, it is not necessarily a symptom of neurosis or psychosis; Ellis was a cognitive-behavioral psychologist who had earlier subscribed to Freudian psychoanalysis but came to reject it by the early 1950s. In Ellis' paradigm, self-talk is not a problem-solving technique but a problem itself. While self-talk might be considered a kind of mental chatter, Ellis did not teach that it should be ignored, but rather that one should actively work to change irrational beliefs and behaviors through rational analysis and cognitive reconstruction.

**180. D:** A laissez-faire leadership style could be considered a "hands-off" style in that there is no participation from the leader. The group participants make all the decisions and set their own goals and activities. A democratic leader encourages members to make their own decisions, and all members discuss the goals and activities. There is no authoritative leadership style as it applies to group counseling.

**181. C:** If one client monopolizes the conversation in a support group, talking about the same problems over and over and preventing others from participating, and speaking privately about the matter to the client did not change the client's behavior, the most effective response focuses on the results of the action rather than blame: "When you interrupt others, I'm concerned that some group members are unable to participate." Many groups include members who tend to monopolize the communication until other members become angry and/or exasperated.

**182. D:** The leader serves as a role model during the transition stage of the group, as well as establishing a trusting climate for the group, providing support, and addressing resistances and anxiety. During the termination stage, the leader's role is to deal with feelings, reinforce changes, and help members make plans. During the orientation stage, the leader's role is to help identify goals and structures and begin the modeling process. The leader in the working stage provides reinforcement, links themes, supports risks, and encourages translating insight into action.

**183. A:** According to the contingency model of leadership, an individual becomes a leader because of both personality issues and situational factors. It further states that both leaders and followers influence each other. In this model, leaders either focus their leadership duties on completing particular tasks or direct their attention toward the relationship between the members of the group. According to this model, the ideal style of leadership varies depending upon the situation. A task-oriented leadership style is better if the situation is harsh, with the relationship style better in easier times.

**184. A:** CRAFFT is the most appropriate tool for screening children and adolescents under age 21 for drug and alcohol use.

| C | Have you ever ridden in a CAR driven by someone (including self) who was "high" or had been using alcohol or drugs? |
|---|---|
| R | Do you ever use alcohol or drugs to RELAX, feel better about yourself, or fit in? |
| A | Do you ever use alcohol or drugs while you are by yourself or ALONE? |
| F | Do you every FORGET things you did while using alcohol or drugs? |
| F | Do your family or FRIENDS every tell you that you should cut down on your drinking or drug use? |
| T | Have you ever gotten into TROUBLE while you were using alcohol or drugs? |

**185. A:** A release of information form is to be signed by the client before confidential information can be released by their counselor to another professional or agency. It should specify what information can be released, to whom, and for what period of time. This is similar to the information release that clients sign for medical doctors to release their information to other doctors. A release of information is not a document given to a client by a counselor to disclose what procedures may be used before the counseling relationship begins, as this would be a statement of disclosure. The information release is not signed by the other professional or agency to receive the confidential information, but by the client who is giving permission. The information release is not for another professional or agency to give the client's information to the counselor. This would only happen if the other professional or agency were one that had also worked with the client in some capacity. In this case, the client would sign the release for the other professional or agency and give it to them not to the client's counselor.

**186. D:** Hoppock's theory of career choice suggests that people choose careers that meet some personal needs. As part of this theory, Hoppock postulates that everyone has personal needs and that an individual reacts to these needs when making career choices. Making career choices involves self-awareness and understanding. Those career choices may not necessarily be in the same field as their passion if, for instance, their needs are based on finances or meeting external expectations.

**187. C:** The halo effect is the tendency to generalize about a person based on one trait. In this case, assuming an individual is a better communicator simply because they have an extensive vocabulary is an example of the halo effect. The placebo effect is when an ineffective or inert substance is given to participants and participants report positive changes due to the simple belief that they were given something that would cause improvement. The Rosenthal effect or Pygmalion effect suggests that the researcher's beliefs impact the outcome of an experiment. The Hawthorne effect is the tendency for participants to change their behavior just because they are participants in a research study.

**188. C:** If a client who is a pathological gambler insists to the counselor and to his spouse that he can control his gambling by limiting the time spent at the casino and the dollar amount he spends each week, this approach to treatment for this process addiction is part of harm reduction therapy. Unfortunately, because of the addictive quality of pathological gambling, most people cannot successfully control their habit in this manner and may benefit more from other types of therapy, such as cognitive behavioral therapy and participation in Gambler's Anonymous.

**189. B:** Testing results can be affected by many factors. They also provide information collected at a particular point in time and in a particular situation, where many factors can affect the results. For ethical reasons, the client should be informed of the limitations of testing and made as comfortable as possible with the testing situation and results. The counselor should also keep in mind the limitations of the testing results, and not rely too heavily on any one test or test results.

**190. D:** Piaget's stages of cognitive development are 1) sensorimotor (birth to 2 years) during which the child learns about himself and his environment through sensory perceptions and motor activities; 2) preoperational (2-7 years) in which language develops and the child is egocentric; 3) concrete operational (7-11 years) during which the child begins to think logically but still has trouble with abstract concepts; and 4) formal operational (11 years to adulthood) during which the child develops the capability of logical thought, deductive reasoning, and systematic planning.

**191. C:** If an aggressive, hostile client has managed to remove a towel rod and is brandishing it as a weapon, the counselor's first priority should be to protect self and others. Unless the counselor has had special training in dealing with clients with weapons, the counselor should not attempt to disarm or subdue the client and should keep something between the counselor and the client, such as a pillow or chair, and maintain a distance beyond 4 feet. The counselor should summon help and try to clear the room if other clients are present.

**192. D:** To help a counselor decide if a client's needs are within the counselor's range of services, to help a counselor gain understanding of the client, and to help a client gain self-understanding are only a few of the ways that test can inform the counseling process.

**193. C:** Alfred Adler and Rudolph Dreikurs were proponents of individual psychology. All of the terms used in the question come from this approach. Client-centered or person-centered therapy was developed by Carl Rogers and includes concepts such as the process of becoming, the client-therapist relationship, unconditional positive regard, congruence or genuineness, and empathic understanding. Gestalt therapy, proposed by Fritz and Laura Perls, is based on existential principles. It has a viewpoint derived from holistic systems theory, and its focus is on the here-and-now of perceptions and feelings. Its name refers to a "unified whole," and it uses concepts of perception to understand and integrate the self. It makes use of the figure-ground concept (proposed by Edgar Rubin) in differentiating between focused figures (main issues) versus their ground (or background)) relationships. The analogy is that a foremost need is a figure and other needs are the ground, and as the main need is met, this completes the gestalt or whole. Transactional analysis was pioneered by Eric Berne, who posited that the personality has three ego states: parent, adult, and child. Berne states that a life script develops during childhood and influences one's behavior. He regarded many transactions between people as games played to avoid intimacy.

**194. C:** Standard deviation is NOT the same as variance. Variance is the square of the standard deviation, or SD2. SD is a description of the variability within a distribution of scores. It is also the mean of all the deviations from the mean. SD is an excellent measure of the dispersion of scores; it describes the dispersion of scores better than the variance does.

**195. C:** If a client with OCD is undergoing Exposure and Response Prevention therapy and the client has established a goal of being able to go into a store to shop for groceries, the next step for the client is to establish a fear ladder, usually a number of incremental steps the client will take in order to reach the goal (the last step in the ladder). For example, the first step may be to drive by the store and watch people entering and leaving the store every day for a week. The client performs each step until the client's anxiety begins to decrease before moving on to the next step.

**196. A:** Harry Stack Sullivan theorized that "euphoria" occurs in the absence of internal "tension," and tension manifests itself as the opposite extreme. There are four types of tension, with biological needs (such as the need for food and water) causing the first type of tension. Sleep is not included in Sullivan's first type of tension, because he considers it a separate type of need, deserving of its own "type." Perhaps the most critical of the types of tension is the third, "anxiety." Anxiety can be caused in various ways and exist on a variety of levels, depending upon the individual situation. The final type of tension is related to "fear."

**197. A:** John Holland believed that everyone's personality falls into a particular category. He created the Vocational Preference Inventory (VPI), which is a test that measures an individual's particular type and matches it to a career choice that would fit that type. He used a hexagon shape to depict six types of career: realistic, investigative, artistic, social, enterprising, and conventional. Within each type on the hexagon is the variety of actual jobs that would fall into those categories. For example, the "realistic" personality type would include jobs such as a carpenter because it includes people who like to work with tools.

**198. C:** If a counselor applies some diagnostic label to a member of a family, this could be used later in court. For example, a counselor's information might be used in child custody hearings or divorce proceedings. This is an ethical issue that family counselors must consider. The counselor's attitude toward gender roles is NOT irrelevant. The counselor's idea of the role of women in families, for example, will make a meaningful difference in family counseling. Whether the counselor believes in traditional gender roles or not will also affect the course of counseling. Despite confidentiality, a counselor should NOT keep child abuse or incest a secret as the law requires such abuse to be reported. When a family is culturally different, the counselor needs to be aware that the family roles and family dynamics will also be different according to that family's culture of origin.

**199. B:** The feedback that is specific and descriptive is "Marvin became upset when you made a joke about his failure to maintain sobriety" because it gives the essential facts. "You were very sarcastic in the group meeting today" is evaluative ("very sarcastic") without outlining the specific problem. "You tend to be thoughtless when you address other client in the group" is too general. "You should treat others with more respect in group meetings" is giving advice ("you should") as opposed to feedback.

**200. C:** 1976 was the year that the State of Virginia passed the first general practice counselor licensure law. In 1954, the Office of Vocational Rehabilitation was created. In 1981, the Council for the Accreditation of Counseling and Related Educational Programs (CACREP) was established. In 1962, the State of California passed a law for the licensure of marriage, family, and child counselors.

# NCE Practice Test #2

**1. The Wisconsin card sorting test is used with clients with traumatic brain injury to assess which of the following?**
- a. Fine motor skills
- b. Language skills
- c. Memory
- d. Cognitive reasoning

**2. What is the fourth stage of Jean Piaget's four stages of cognitive development?**
- a. Sensory Motor Stage
- b. Preoperational
- c. Concrete Operations
- d. Formal Operations

**3. The mother of a young adult with autism spectrum disorder and severe impairments states she is often so tired at the end of the evening that she breaks down and cries. Which of the following is the care support that is probably the most essential at this time?**
- a. Respite care
- b. Support group
- c. Volunteer visitor
- d. Spiritual support

**4. A bipolar client who is very nervous about transitioning into the community from a sheltered environment may benefit from which of the following?**
- a. A support group
- b. A 12-step program
- c. Antidepressants
- d. Peer counseling

**5. Super describes four stages of career development, beginning in adolescence with the _____ stage, in which a person fantasizes and role-plays in order to clarify the emerging self-concept. In the _____ stage the self-concept adjusts to fit the stabilized career choice and the person tries out various options.**
- a. maintenance; establishment
- b. establishment; maintenance
- c. establishment; exploratory
- d. exploratory; establishment

**6. A 16-year-old male admitted to the mental health unit for alcohol use disorder has repeatedly failed to maintain sobriety and consistently missed support meetings while partying with his friends. Which of the following is the most likely reason that the client is not compliant with treatment?**
- a. Disturbance of body image
- b. Embarrassment
- c. Fear of being different from peers
- d. Guilt about illness

**7. Which of the following is NOT true about standardized scores?**

    a. Standardized score scales allow comparison of different test scores for the same individual

    b. Standardized scores enable comparisons of scores between or among different individuals

    c. Standardized scores indicate the individual's distance from the mean in standard deviations

    d. Standardized scores may be discontinuous and may employ units which are not equivalent

**8. Which is true of open vs. closed therapy groups?**

    a. In an open group, anyone is allowed to join the group

    b. In an open group, members who leave are replaced

    c. In a closed group, only certain members may join

    d. In a closed group, members who leave are replaced

**9. For a therapy group composed of adults with a single group leader, what is generally considered to be the optimum group size?**

    a. 3

    b. 8

    c. 5

    d. 10

**10. What is the cause of cyclothymia?**

    a. Prenatal drug use

    b. The cause is unknown

    c. Child abuse

    d. Chromosomal deficiencies

**11. Which of these is true of quantitative research?**

    a. This kind of research tends to use naturalistic observation of individual behaviors

    b. This kind of research tends to use impressions, feelings or judgments of researchers

    c. This kind of research has as its primary goal the description of the nature of reality

    d. This kind of research tends to investigate with a goal of finding causal relationships

*) qualitative* (handwritten annotation)

**12. The social-learning perspective is to the psychodynamic perspective as _____ are to _____.**

    a. bodily events; social and cultural forces

    b. social and cultural forces; bodily events

    c. environmental conditions; unconscious dynamics

    d. unconscious dynamics; environmental conditions

**13. Which of the following behaviors would differentiate aggression from anger?**

    a. Passive-aggressive behavior

    b. Holding clenched fists

    c. Yelling and shouting

    d. Verbal threats

**14.** A single mother and a teenage son present for relationship problems. The son is actively defiant of instructions, argues regularly over minor requests, and can be spiteful and resentful over normal parenting efforts. School performance is marginal, but only one unexcused absence has occurred during the current school year, which is nearing its end. The most appropriate diagnosis would be:

    a. oppositional defiant disorder.
    b. conduct disorder.
    c. intermittent explosive disorder.
    d. parent-child relational problem.

**15.** A client who is an ethnic minority states that she has been passed over for promotion three times even though she is better qualified and received better reviews than those that were promoted. This is most likely an example of which of the following?

    a. Discrimination
    b. Suppression
    c. Oppression
    d. Racism

**16.** What did the Milgram experiment teach us about authority?

    a. People usually will not obey authority
    b. People usually will obey authority
    c. Sometimes people will obey authority
    d. People generally disregard authority

**17.** Mike Brown has completed gender reassignment surgery (male-to-female) and is now legally Mikaela Brown. Mikaela states that she is still attracted to females and not males. Her sexual orientation should be most appropriately classified as which of the following?

    a. Lesbian
    b. Heterosexual
    c. Homosexual
    d. Bisexual

**18.** People are said to be products of five different cultures. Two are inevitable culture sources (a culture of human biology and a culture of ecology, which refers to the climates in which people live). Which is NOT one of the other three?

    a. Racio-ethnic
    b. Linguistic
    c. Regional
    d. National

**19.** Which is NOT an aspect of a "closed group" therapy session?

    a. Stronger cohesiveness within the group
    b. Less cost-effective for the counselor
    c. Greater diversity among members
    d. Members that leave are not replaced

**20. Screening for intimate partner abuse should be done for which female clients?**

a. Age 12 or older
b. Age 14 or older
c. Age 16 or older
d. Age 18 or older

**21. All of the following are physical characteristics of Down Syndrome EXCEPT:**

a. short, stocky build.
b. almond-shaped eyes.
c. large hands and feet.
d. flattened face.

**22. The counselor is seeing a client who has just started electroconvulsive therapy for severe depression. How many minimum ECT treatments are generally required before a client shows sustained improvement?**

a. 3
b. 6
c. 12
d. 15

**23. Which of the following terms is associated with transactional analysis?**

a. Free association
b. Unconditional positive regard
c. Irrational beliefs
d. Complementary transactions

**24. A counselor has written an article that he wants to submit to a professional journal. This article needs to be in:**

a. MLA format.
b. APA format.
c. either MLA or APA format.
d. none of the above.

**25. Which of the following is not a behavioral therapy?**

a. Flooding
b. Skills training
c. Exposure
d. Unconditional positive regard

**26. During a staff meeting, one counselor folds his arms across his chest and rolls his eyes while another counselor speaks about a problem she has encountered with a client. This is an example of which of the following?**

a. Sexual harassment
b. Normal response to disagreement
c. Horizontal violence
d. Workplace discrimination

27. A counselor has been involved in a counseling relationship with a client for six months, when he is presented with a small gift from the client. What should the counselor do?
   a. Accept the gift and thank the client
   b. Decline the gift with an explanation of why it's inappropriate to accept it
   c. Request that the gift be given only once therapy is complete
   d. Accept or decline depending upon the circumstances

28. A 16-year-old girl is being treated with fluoxetine and cognitive behavioral therapy for severe anxiety and depression 6 months after the death of her mother. For which of the following must the girl be regularly monitored and assessed?
   a. Substance abuse
   b. Polypharmacy
   c. Suicidal ideation
   d. Noncompliance

29. If utilizing exposure therapy with a client with severe phobias, which of the following approaches is likely to have the most long-lasting effect?
   a. In vivo spaced exposure
   b. In vivo massed exposure ("flooding")
   c. Spaced imagery exposure
   d. Massed virtual exposure

30. Everyone says that Jack and Samantha are alike in every way, and it isn't long before they marry. What might explain their relationship?
   a. Biological processes
   b. Attribution theory
   c. Consensual validation
   d. Conformity

31. A client with schizophrenia has both delusions and hallucinations. Which of the following types of hallucinations pose the greatest threat to the client or others?
   a. Auditory command hallucinations
   b. Visual hallucinations
   c. Formication tactile hallucinations
   d. Gustatory hallucinations

32. Clients typically go through four phases in response to a stressor, culminating in an acute crisis. If a client has tried problem-solving techniques and found them to be unsuccessful in alleviating stress, which of the following phases is the client experiencing?
   a. Phase 1
   b. Phase 2
   c. Phase 3
   d. Phase 4

33. Which of the following is true regarding payment for counseling?
   a. Payment to master's degree-level counselors is only automatic if they are licensed
   b. Master's degree-level counselors do not receive payment even if they are licensed
   c. Some counselors are reimbursed by insurance through a supervising psychologist
   d. Counselors in private practice may not require direct payments from their clients

**34.** The counselor says a word to his client and he answers back with the first thing that comes to mind. What theorist developed the method the counselor is using?

    a. Jean Piaget
    b. Alfred Adler
    c. Carl Jung
    d. Sigmund Freud

**35.** Binge eating coupled with inappropriate methods of controlling one's weight may be a symptom of what disorder?

    a. Pica
    b. Anorexia nervosa
    c. Rumination disorder
    d. Bulimia nervosa

**36.** A behaviorist family counselor instructs the parents of a 12-year-old boy to tell their son that, when he gets his homework done, he can play his Xbox. This is an example of:

    a. positive reinforcement.
    b. the Premack principle.
    c. quid pro quo.
    d. negative reinforcement.

**37.** In the Milgram studies, Milgram and his colleagues found that volunteers were more likely to disobey orders to continue administering electric shocks to the subject under all of the following circumstances EXCEPT when:

    a. the experimenter wearing a lab coat was replaced by a man dressed in street clothes.
    b. the order to give an electric shock was delivered by telephone.
    c. the volunteer's role was to instruct someone else to administer the electric shock.
    d. the location of the experiment was moved from Yale's campus to an office building.

**38.** Giving a positive consequence every time a desired behavior is engaged in could be considered:

    a. negative reinforcement.
    b. positive reinforcement.
    c. aversive conditioning.
    d. extinction.

**39.** When conducting research, two counselors administer the same evaluation instrument to one group of clients participating in a support group, but the counselors get markedly different results. What type of problem does this suggest?

    a. Reliability
    b. Measurement
    c. Validity
    d. Comprehension

**40.** Which of the following is true about the correlation coefficient?

    a. A perfect correlation coefficient can be a positive one but cannot be negative
    b. A correlation coefficient shows the relationship between two sets of numbers
    c. A correlation coefficient shows a cause and effect relationship between variables
    d. With a strong correlation, knowing one score will not help to predict another score

**41. A client with symptoms consistent with narcolepsy-cataplexy should be referred to a physician for which of the following types of testing?**

a. Thyroid function
b. Liver function
c. Blood glucose
d. Hypocretin

**42. *Tarasoff vs. Board of Regents* of the University of California was a landmark case which brought to light the:**

a. duty of the counselor to warn individuals or groups about the potential of imminent danger.
b. standard of practice of obtaining releases of information in order to share information with individuals or agencies.
c. rights a client has as an individual with disabilities.
d. potential harm an impaired professional may inflict on his clients.

**43. What are the four levels of data measurement used to determine the statistics used?**

a. Nominal, random, stratified, cluster
b. Ordinal, purposeful, cluster, nominal
c. Ratio, random, cluster, interval
d. Nominal, ordinal, interval, ratio

**44. The counselor is carrying out a spiritual assessment using the FICA tool (Faith, Importance, Community, Address). Which of the following is the first question that the counselor should ask?**

a. "What importance does your faith have in your daily life?"
b. "Do you have a faith or belief system that gives your life meaning?"
c. "What faith issues would you like me to address in your care?"
d. "Do you participate and gain support from your faith community?"

**45. A male client has been following a female client and claims that the female is "flirting" with him and using "sexual innuendos"; however, the female client complains that the male client is harassing and scaring her, and staff observations concur with the female client's complaints. The male client is most likely exhibiting which of the following?**

a. Introjection
b. Projection
c. Compensation
d. Identification

**46. What does "reliability" in testing refer to?**

a. How sure the researcher can be, before the test is taken, of what the outcome will be
b. How accurate the test is
c. How consistent the test results are
d. How many samples were used in evaluation of the test

**47. When developing an individualized Goal Attainment Scale (GAS) with a client, how would the counselor score an expected outcome?**

    a.  -1
    b.  0
    c.  +1
    d.  =+2

**48. In order to facilitate growth in a client, the counselor uses all of the following strategies EXCEPT:**

    a.  confrontation.
    b.  reflection.
    c.  abandonment.
    d.  interpretation.

**49. Which of the following Neo-Freudian theorists most strongly believed that behavior can be understood best in terms of social interactions and interpersonal relationships?**

    a.  Erich Fromm
    b.  Harry Stack Sullivan
    c.  Wilhelm Reich
    d.  Karen Horney

**50. A correlation coefficient shows:**

    a.  how strong the relationship between two variables is.
    b.  the direction of two variables' relationship.
    c.  the degree of relationship between two variables.
    d.  all of the above.

**51. In _____ therapy, the therapist uses logical arguments to challenge a client's unrealistic beliefs or expectations.**

    a.  client-centered
    b.  rational-emotive behavior
    c.  existential
    d.  aversive conditioning

**52. How does consultation differ from counseling?**

    a.  It uses different skills than counseling does
    b.  It is for resolving, not preventing, problems
    c.  It is a voluntary, work-related process
    d.  It is process-oriented, not content-oriented

**53. Who of the following is known for person-centered counseling?**

    a.  Rollo May
    b.  Carl Rogers
    c.  Fritz Perls
    d.  Aaron Beck

**54. What do "title and practice-control" laws mean?**

   a.  These are laws stating that one cannot practice counseling without using the title of LPC

   b.  These are laws stating that one can practice counseling without a license, but cannot use the title

   c.  These are laws stating that one cannot practice counseling without a professional counselor license

   d.  These are laws stating one may not get a professional counseling license without using the title

**55. All of the following are characteristics of an open group EXCEPT that:**

   a.  members can join and leave at any time.

   b.  the number of sessions is undetermined.

   c.  there is good cohesion.

   d.  group meetings are usually held in a hospital setting.

**56. What is e-therapy?**

   a.  Therapy that focuses on regularly spaced client evaluations

   b.  Online psychological treatment

   c.  A new version of cognitive-emotive therapy

   d.  A psychoanalytic treatment modality

**57. The Theory of Work Adjustment (TWA) focuses on work in relation to the individual's:**

   a.  environment.

   b.  psyche.

   c.  emotional development.

   d.  phobias.

**58. Popular techniques of what approach are role playing, "empty chair," and "making the rounds"?**

   a.  Client-centered

   b.  Psychoanalysis

   c.  Gestalt

   d.  Adlerian

**59. Research on gay and lesbian parents indicates:**

   a.  their children are maladjusted.

   b.  they are as dedicated to and effective at child rearing as are heterosexual parents.

   c.  they are less dedicated to child rearing than heterosexual parents.

   d.  their children are parented harshly and inconsistently.

**60. In the landmark 1976 Tarasoff case, the California court ruled that failure to warn an intended victim is professionally irresponsible. Out of what event did this ruling come?**

   a.  A university psychologist by the name of Tarasoff was murdered by one of his clients

   b.  A client named Tarasoff, under the care of a university psychologist, was murdered

   c.  A university psychologist murdered his client, Tatiana Tarasoff, and her family sued

   d.  A client of a university psychologist murdered Tatiana Tarasoff and her family sued

**61. If college graduates typically earn more money than high school graduates, this would indicate that level of education and income are:**

    a. causally related.
    b. positively correlated.
    c. negatively correlated.
    d. unrelated.

**62. What kind of tests are the Rotter Incomplete Sentences Blank and the Draw-A-Person Test?**

    a. Specialized personality tests
    b. Specialized achievement tests
    c. Projective personality tests
    d. Inventory personality tests

**63. Presenting stimuli in different sequences to reduce "order of presentation" influences in an experiment is called:**

    a. countertransference.
    b. counterculture.
    c. counterbalancing.
    d. countercounseling.

**64. Which is most accurate statement regarding the duration of a therapy group?**

    a. When a therapy group is first formed, nobody knows exactly how long the group will exist or run
    b. When a therapy group is first formed, it is generally accepted that it will run for about six months
    c. When a therapy group is first formed, the group members decide on how long they want it to run
    d. When a therapy group is first formed, the leader should set its duration and advise the members

**65. Elisabeth Kübler-Ross identified five stages that grieving people experience. Which of these accurately identifies these five stages?**

    a. Shock, Panic, Sorrow, Depression, Acceptance
    b. Denial, Anger, Bargaining, Depression, Acceptance
    c. Depression, Fear, Bargaining, Stoicism, Acceptance
    d. Fear, Withdrawal, Bargaining, Resignation, Peace

**66. During the initial interview, the client states repeatedly that his boss is to blame for all of the client's problems and that the boss "is going to pay." The counselor should respond by asking which of the following questions?**

    a. "Why do you feel that way?"
    b. "What thoughts have you had about hurting your boss?"
    c. "Can you think of other reasons for your problems?"
    d. "Do you think that this anger toward your boss is productive?"

67. **What is the MOST concerning sign to look for in assessing the risk of suicide in a client?**

    a. A lifting of depression due to the relief of having made a decision
    b. An unnatural sense of gaiety as all responsibilities are discarded
    c. Frequent explosions of hostility or rage directed at other people
    d. Establishment of a definite plan and having the means available

68. **Jenny recently lost her job and fell behind in her mortgage payments, so now she is facing foreclosure. She is seeing a counselor to help her cope with the stress in her life. She feels like a failure and wants her self-esteem to be higher, and she feels that she is not living up to her potential. Her counselor tells her that her first priorities are to fulfill her more basic needs, such as applying for food stamps so she will not go hungry and getting help with her housing situation so that she meets her needs for safety and physical security. The counselor tells her that once she has addressed these basic needs, she can then address her higher-order needs for self-esteem and fulfilling her potential as a person. Which theorist has most influenced Jenny's counselor?**

    a. Abraham Maslow
    b. Edward Thorndike
    c. Erik Erikson
    d. Harry Stack Sullivan

69. **Which of these is true of qualitative research?**

    a. This kind of research assumes social elements have a single objective reality
    b. This kind of research tends to study groups, such as samples or populations
    c. This kind of research assumes that different realities are socially constructed
    d. This kind of research tries to avoid influencing its data collection instruments

70. **In career development and counseling, what is meant by the compensatory vs. spillover theory of leisure?**

    a. Individuals who are dissatisfied with their jobs compensate by engaging in excessive leisure activities
    b. Individuals whose leisure interests tend to spill over into the workplace are not as productive
    c. Individuals may compensate for work with different leisure activities or their work may spill over into their leisure activities
    d. Individuals may compensate for leisure by working harder or leisure activities may spill over to work

71. **What does the Likert scale measure?**

    a. Attitudes and feelings
    b. Statistics
    c. Physical health
    d. Mental health

72. **Which of the following is NOT a central concept in existential therapy?**

    a. Guilt
    b. Anxiety
    c. Free association
    d. Search for meaning

**73. Which of these is a limitation to confidentiality in the ethical practice of counseling?**

    a.  Clerical staff in the counseling office will see client information

    b.  A health insurance company or HMO will see client information

    c.  A counselor gets helpful advice about a client from a colleague

    d.  All of these situations represent valid confidentiality limitations

**74. Clients with bipolar disorder are often treated with interpersonal and social rhythm therapy. This therapy helps clients do which of the following?**

    a.  Recognize triggers to mood changes

    b.  Manage stress

    c.  Establish consistent sleep and physical activity schedules

    d.  Cope with bipolar disorder

**75. The counselor is working with an 8-year-old child who has been suspended from school because of anger issues. The counselor notes that the child has many bruises in various stages of healing, including on the left side of the face, and the child seems anxious when the parent is in the room. However, the child denies any abuse. Which of the following should the counselor do?**

    a.  Ask the child's parents about abuse

    b.  Monitor the child carefully in the future

    c.  Report possible child abuse to the appropriate authorities

    d.  Advise the parents to take the child to a pediatrician to determine the cause of bruising

**76. Which of the following is the most effective method of confronting a client who routinely misses group support meetings, making various excuses, but claims that the support group is very helpful?**

    a.  "You keep making excuses as to why you don't attend."

    b.  "Your behavior suggests that you don't really want to attend the group."

    c.  "You don't come to group but you say it's helpful. How do you feel about this contradiction?"

    d.  "Why do you keep missing the group if it's helpful?"

**77. A counselor who works for a county agency also has a small private practice. She screens all clients at the county agency and refers those clients with the best insurance benefits to her private practice. This counselor is:**

    a.  following standard procedure for many public agencies.

    b.  acting unethically.

    c.  engaging in a dual relationship.

    d.  practicing beyond her scope of practice.

**78. A client in the depressive stage of bipolar disease experiences "all or nothing" negative automatic thoughts and states, "I'm a complete failure at everything I try to do." The counselor is using cognitive behavioral therapy to alter dysfunctional thinking. Which of the following is the most appropriate intervention?**

    a.  Assist the client to develop a list of positive achievements

    b.  Reassure the client that the feelings are the result of the depression and not real

    c.  Remind the client how the client felt during the manic stage of the disorder

    d.  Ask the client to describe supporting and disputing evidence for this statement

79. **Which theorist is well known for his work with prejudice?**
    a. Allport
    b. Skinner
    c. Jung
    d. Freud

80. **According to Freudian theory, where does the conscience reside?**
    a. Superego
    b. Ego
    c. Id
    d. Preconscious

81. **A client reports only occasional social drinking and denies the use of illicit drugs but within 2 days of hospitalization for depression, the client becomes increasingly agitated with noticeable hand tremors and complains that she feels as though bugs are crawling under her skin. Which of the following should the counselor suspect?**
    a. The client is exhibiting signs of bipolar disorder
    b. The client is undergoing alcohol withdrawal
    c. The client is exhibiting signs of heroin withdrawal
    d. The client is experiencing signs of panic disorder

82. **Which is correct regarding the notion of world views?**
    a. An emic worldview is the belief in a global view of all of humanity
    b. An etic worldview is the belief in taking each group's perspective
    c. An etic worldview is the belief we are more similar than different
    d. An emic worldview is the belief in transcending all our differences

83. **The difference between confidentiality and privileged communication is:**
    a. "privileged communication" is a legal term and confidentiality is an ethical concept.
    b. "confidentiality" is a legal term and privileged communication is an ethical concept.
    c. privileged communication is enforced only when a client asks something to be privileged.
    d. confidentiality is enforced only when a client asks that something be kept confidential.

84. **Tiedeman's decision-making model saw career decisions as being made up of two phases. What were these?**
    a. Anticipation or examination and execution or fulfillment
    b. Anticipation or preoccupation and implementation or adjustment
    c. Preoccupation or examination and correction or adjustment
    d. Examination or definition and realization or completion

85. **An experienced counselor is the supervisor for a new counselor and is asked to attend her wedding. Would it be ethical to do so?**
    a. It would not be ethical to attend her wedding
    b. It would depend on the counselor's role in the festivities
    c. Yes, but only if the counselor doesn't bring a gift
    d. Yes, the counselor should be able to attend her wedding without a breach of ethics

356

86. The emphasis for which type of group is on prevention and development of healthy behaviors?
    a. Secondary
    b. Tertiary
    c. Primary
    d. Homogeneous

87. What does Title IX of the educational amendments provide?
    a. Remedial reading instruction
    b. A ban on sex discrimination
    c. Equal sports for both sexes
    d. Equal class sizes in schools

88. The Education Act for All Handicapped Children (PL 94-142) requires that:
    a. all children who are handicapped be seen by a counselor who specializes in disabilities.
    b. a free and appropriate education be provided for all children with disabilities.
    c. children with handicaps be placed in the most restrictive environment in the schools.
    d. children with handicaps be sent to special schools or institutions.

89. What are Lawrence Kohlberg's three levels of morality?
    a. Instinctual, Intellectual, and Physical
    b. Oral, Latency, and Genital
    c. Pre-conventional, Conventional, and Post-conventional
    d. Optional, Formulaic, and Oppositional

90. The process of saying freely whatever comes to mind in connection with dreams, memories, fantasies, or conflicts, in the course of a psychodynamic therapy session, is referred to as:
    a. systematic desensitization.
    b. flooding.
    c. free association.
    d. exposure treatment.

91. An apparent treatment success that is due to the client's expectation or hopes rather than the treatment itself is called:
    a. the placebo effect.
    b. the nocebo effect.
    c. the therapeutic window.
    d. an empirically validated treatment.

92. A 28-year-old client has a dual diagnosis of bipolar disorder and substance abuse (cocaine, alcohol). Which of the following is the first outcome goal for the client?
    a. Interact appropriately with others
    b. Become active in drug and alcohol-free activities
    c. Develop a plan for activities during free time
    d. Take only medications that have been prescribed

**93.** A client feels his coworker's recent promotion was not because of the coworker's own merit, but simply because of company restructuring. He feels his own promotion, however, is a reflection of his own professional abilities. In social psychology/cognition, this might be called:

   a. sour grapes.
   b. transference.
   c. attribution.
   d. latent hostility.

**94.** A married couple presents for counseling. Evaluation reveals that the wife comes from a dysfunctional, neglectful, alcoholic home and has little trust or tolerance for relationships. Consequently, their marriage is marred by constant arguing and distrust, frequent demands that he leave, episodes of impulsive violence, alternating with brief periods of excessive over-valuation (stating that he is the "best thing that ever happened" to her, "too good" for her, etc.). Which is the most likely diagnosis for the wife?

   a. Anti-social personality disorder
   b. Histrionic personality disorder
   c. Borderline personality disorder
   d. Narcissistic personality disorder

**95.** In order for a client with a psychiatric diagnosis to qualify for disability benefits under the Social Security Administration, the client must be unable to engage in substantial gainful activity because of the disability for what minimum period of time?

   a. 6 months
   b. 12 months
   c. 18 months
   d. 24 months

**96.** When working with individuals from different cultures, the effective counselor may not:

   a. use language similar to the client's.
   b. maintain good eye contact at all times.
   c. be cognizant of the context.
   d. honor religious beliefs.

**97.** Which describes a violation of the "scope of practice" ethical standard?

   a. A counselor suggests a set of positive affirmations to her client after the counselor has discussed positive affirmations at length in session
   b. A counselor uses EMDR with a client who insisted on this method of treatment
   c. A counselor confronts her client about the negative thought patterns in which the client is engaging on a regular basis
   d. A counselor seeks consultation from a colleague on a difficult case

**98.** From which perspective are the group goals to enable members to pay close attention to their here-and-now experiences so they can recognize and integrate disowned aspects of themselves?

   a. Gestalt
   b. Psychodynamic
   c. Reality
   d. Existential

**99. When publishing research, it is LEAST appropriate to:**

a. give credit to other contributors or sources.
b. not plagiarize.
c. submit material to only one journal at a time.
d. submit material to several journals at a time.

**100. Which of the following adult attachment styles best describes clients who feel uncomfortable with close attachments because of fear of getting hurt and who have difficulty expressing feelings and few close relationships?**

a. Anxious-preoccupied
b. Dismissive-avoidant
c. Fearful-avoidant
d. Secure

**101. The counselor is assessing a victim of violent trauma. Which of the following is an essential initial step?**

a. Ask questions about the trauma, rapidly increasing the specificity
b. Explain the procedure for screening and assessment
c. Stress the importance of focusing on the future
d. Stress that it's important for the client to answer every question

**102. A client has met the criteria for binge-eating disorder and averages 8 or 9 binge-eating episodes per week. How would the severity of the disorder be classified?**

a. Mild
b. Moderate
c. Severe
d. Extreme

**103. B.F. Skinner found that deprivation will ___ the probability of an operant.**

a. decrease
b. increase
c. not affect
d. sporadically alter

**104. The client is having difficulty deciding what career she would like to pursue. The counselor gives her a test that will help her make an informed choice. What type of test did the counselor give her?**

a. An achievement test
b. A psychoanalytic test
c. An aptitude test
d. A personality test

359

**105.** A counselor gives a questionnaire to a group of respondents to measure their opinions on certain topics. Each question has seven possible choices: Strongly Agree, Agree Somewhat, Agree, Neutral, Disagree, Disagree Somewhat, and Strongly Disagree. This measurement technique is known as:

    a.  a Likert scale.
    b.  a scatterplot.
    c.  a Kruskal-Wallis test.
    d.  a Wilcoxon signed-rank test.

**106.** A client who was the victim of sexual assault tells the counselor that she will never feel safe again. In response, the counselor asks the client if she feels safe at the moment and what she will need to do to feel safe when she goes home. This is an example of which of the following techniques?

    a.  Thought stopping
    b.  Cognitive restructuring
    c.  Reframing
    d.  Labeling distortions

**107.** All of these are characteristics of test reliability EXCEPT:

    a.  stability.
    b.  equivalence.
    c.  internal consistency.
    d.  predictive.

**108.** If a family member of a client asks the counselor what constitutes probable cause for involuntary commitment, which of the following is the best response?

    a.  "You should ask an attorney about that."
    b.  "The person is a threat to herself or others."
    c.  "The person is uncooperative with the family."
    d.  "The person is no longer able to work and is homeless."

**109.** The sensorimotor period is part of whose developmental stage theory?

    a.  Freud
    b.  Piaget
    c.  Erikson
    d.  Kohlberg

**110.** In which is the focus on the meaning of life and the relevance of the individual experience?

    a.  Existential counseling
    b.  Adlerian counseling
    c.  Gestalt therapy
    d.  Reality therapy

**111.** Which of these psychologists' theories completely ignore the unconscious?

    a.  Glasser's reality therapy, Rogerian counseling, and behaviorism
    b.  Freudian psychoanalysis, Jungian, and Adlerian counseling
    c.  Karen Horney, Erich Fromm, and object relations theory
    d.  Rollo May, Victor Frankl, Abraham Maslow's existentialism

**112. Many counselors and clients, in the therapeutic setting, would say that ___ is very difficult to deal with.**
   a.  silence
   b.  catharsis
   c.  role reversal
   d.  ambivalence

**113. A client has experienced complicated grief after the death of her father, with whom she had a "love-hate" relationship as he tended to be overbearing and judgmental. However, the client's level of enmeshment was high because the father discussed his marital problems with his ex-wife (the client's mother) with the client and used her to carry messages. Which of the following is likely the cause of the client's complicated grief?**
   a.  Chronic depression
   b.  Anger
   c.  Introjection
   d.  Unresolved conflicts

**114. The Id, Ego, and Superego are attributed to which psychoanalyst?**
   a.  Erik Erikson
   b.  William Perry
   c.  Sigmund Freud
   d.  Alfred Binet

**115. During the past several sessions, a heated discussion has occurred between the father and the mother. The gist of the argument stems from the mother's constant attention being focused on the daughter. This is an example of:**
   a.  negative attention seeking.
   b.  disequilibrium.
   c.  enmeshment.
   d.  triangulation.

**116. What should the counselor do if a client requests to see his confidential file?**
   a.  Immediately give the client access to the file
   b.  Explain to the client that such information is confidential and for the counselor's eyes only
   c.  Accept or decline depending upon the circumstances
   d.  Ignore the request

**117. A client repeatedly justifies destructive behaviors with excuses that attempt to depict them as beneficial. What Freudian defense mechanism is he making use of?**
   a.  Rationalization
   b.  Depression
   c.  Reaction formation
   d.  Sublimation

**118. When working with a client with conduct disorder who has exhibited sociopathic behavior, which of the following comments by the client is the most cause for concern?**

    a.  "That pretty little daughter of yours goes to Farmin School, doesn't she?"
    b.  "I'll bet you have no friends outside of work."
    c.  "I know more about you than you know about me."
    d.  "This therapy is a complete waste of time."

**119. The counselor is seeing a client with a history of trichotillomania and plans to begin habit reversal training. Which of the following is the first step in HRT?**

    a.  Contingency management
    b.  Awareness training
    c.  Competing response training
    d.  Relaxation training

**120. Which of these is NOT commonly cited as a reason for counseling program evaluation?**

    a.  The emphasis on accountability in the human services field
    b.  A strong need to show the efficacy of counseling in general
    c.  A need to show efficacy of specific theories and techniques
    d.  A need to show the effectiveness of a particular counselor

**121. Compared with high school students who enter the workforce right after graduation, students who go to college can expect to:**

    a.  be hired at lower wages.
    b.  earn about $10,000 more per year.
    c.  work longer hours.
    d.  be hired to fill more unskilled positions.

**122. The severity of anorexia nervosa in adults is based on the client's BMI. If a female client has a BMI of 16.2 kg/m², how would the severity be classified?**

    a.  Mild
    b.  Moderate
    c.  Severe
    d.  Extreme

**123. A client with schizophrenia and a history of violent behavior in response to "voices" has been pacing about his room and suddenly begins shouting at the counselor "Get away from me! Let me out of here!" Considering the 5-phase aggression cycle, the client is most likely in which of the following phases?**

    a.  Crisis
    b.  Recovery
    c.  Triggering
    d.  Escalation

**124. Which of these is NOT included in the study of kinesics and proxemics?**

    a.  Facial expressions
    b.  Verbal expressions
    c.  Physical body gestures
    d.  Seating arrangements

125. If a client who has been hospitalized for treatment is resistant to discharge because of fear that she will be unable to function independently, which of the following is the most appropriate response?

    a. Remind the client that she has family waiting for her at home
    b. Review the progress the client has made
    c. Reinforce to the client that she no longer needs hospitalization
    d. Remind the client that she was also resistant to hospitalization

126. Which of these is NOT correct regarding standard scores?

    a. A standard score is obtained by converting raw score distributions
    b. A z-score is a type of standardized score which is commonly used
    c. An n-score is a type of standardized score that is commonly used
    d. A t-score is a type of standardized score which is commonly used

127. A couple comes in to see a counselor who specializes in sex counseling. Before the counselor agrees to treat the couple for sex counseling, she refers the couple for:

    a. a physical examination and medical history consultation by a medical practitioner.
    b. a clinical assessment and interview.
    c. sensate focus exercises.
    d. an exploration of the marital relationship.

128. In the steps of developing a counseling program, which of the following should come FIRST?

    a. Operating the program
    b. Conducting a pilot study
    c. Evaluating the program
    d. Development of a plan

129. With which type of therapist would rapport be established the quickest?

    a. Rogerian therapist
    b. Gestalt therapist
    c. Freudian therapist
    d. Rational-emotive therapist

130. An adoptive parent complains to the counselor that the adoptive daughter never says, "Thank you." In which of the following situations does the complaint suggest that the problem may lie with the parent rather than the child?

    a. The child does not say "thank you" when the parent treats her and her friends to a movie
    b. The child does not say "thank you" for room and board (bedroom, food)
    c. The child does not say "thank you" when the parent buys her something special
    d. The child does not say "thank you" when the parent agrees to pay for horseback riding lessons

131. In contrast to feeling sorry for the client, the counselor needs to demonstrate _____ toward the client.

    a. empathy
    b. sympathy
    c. emotionality
    d. stability

**132. In what therapeutic approach is the counselor's emphasis on being authentic while concentrating on verbal and nonverbal messages?**

    a. Existential counseling
    b. Behavioral counseling
    c. Gestalt therapy
    d. Rational-emotive therapy

**133. One of the goals of family therapy is to help facilitate adaptability. Adaptability from a family therapy perspective means:**

    a. obtaining a balance between stability and change.
    b. reaching consensus.
    c. obtaining a state of enmeshment.
    d. reaching the status quo.

**134. The counselor should be aware that which of the following common drugs may be associated with depression?**

    a. Isotretinoin (Accutane®)
    b. Beta blockers
    c. Calcium channel blockers
    d. Digoxin (Lanoxin®)

**135. One method of assessing a client's ability to concentrate is to ask the client to do which of the following?**

    a. Give the name of the previous president
    b. State the client's social security number
    c. State the client's current location
    d. Count backward from 100 in serial 7s

**136. In career self-efficacy theory, which of these is NOT one of the three elements that will be influenced by an individual's expectations?**

    a. Choice
    b. Competence
    c. Performance
    d. Persistence

**137. In dual-career families, the woman typically:**

    a. starts her family before entering the workforce.
    b. decides not to have children.
    c. has an established career before having children.
    d. work a part-time or flexible job.

**138. If a 30-year-old client with paranoia and schizophrenia states he does not want his parents (who are paying for his care) to visit because he believes they are "possessed by devils," the counselor should do which of the following?**

    a. Ask the physician to intervene
    b. Allow the parents to visit
    c. Respect the client's request
    d. Suggest the parents get a court order to allow visits

**139. Which of the following is the best synonym for the term appraisal?**

   a. Assessment
   b. Evaluation
   c. Measurement
   d. Testing

**140. Cases of _____ lead to the most malpractice lawsuits for any mental health provider, including counselors and psychologists.**

   a. dual relationships
   b. failure of duty to warn
   c. sexual misconduct
   d. breach of confidentiality

**141. An 18-year-old client is away from home at a university and has always had a very close relationship with her mother, whom she calls every day to ask for guidance and support. The client has made four visits to the infirmary with vague complaints of headache and stomach ache and is increasingly anxious and having difficulty making decisions. Which of the following types of crises is the client likely experiencing?**

   a. Maturational/Developmental
   b. Dispositional
   c. Life transitions
   d. Traumatic

**142. The standard error of measurement is NOT:**

   a. a measure of reliability.
   b. a measure of validity.
   c. the confidence band.
   d. confidence limits.

**143. Which of the following is an example of hypomentalism?**

   a. A client on the autism spectrum cannot pick up clues from another person's tone of voice or eye contact
   b. A client with schizophrenia believes he is under surveillance by the government
   c. A client with psychosis believes that he is receiving messages through the television
   d. A client with a psychotic spectrum disorder believes the counselor is in love with her

**144. Which of the following is NOT true of the FERPA?**

   a. The acronym stands for the Family Educational Rights and Privacy Act of 1974
   b. This law is also referred to as the Buckley Amendment
   c. The intention of this act was to protect individuals' privacy
   d. It gives students' parents access to their counseling records

**145. A 62-year-old homeless man hospitalized for schizophrenia is to be discharged but has no place to go and no income. Which of the following is of primary importance in preparing for discharge?**

   a. Specific directions for medication or treatments, including side effects
   b. Information sheets outlining signs for all risk factors
   c. List of safe shelters and assistance in applying for welfare assistance or Social Security
   d. Follow-up appointment dates, with physicians, labs, or other healthcare providers

**146. Gender bias would be LEAST aroused by which of the following?**
  a. A woman who works in human resources
  b. A man who is a nurse
  c. A woman who drives a semi-truck
  d. A man who designs footwear

**147. The Yerkes-Dodson law states that people perform better:**
  a. under high levels of arousal.
  b. under low levels of arousal.
  c. under moderate levels of arousal.
  d. without notable arousal.

**148. B.F. Skinner would say that religion is:**
  a. an example of behavioral control through conditioning.
  b. an exception to the behavioral rule.
  c. a means of mind control.
  d. central to human existence.

**149. When conducting a cultural formulation interview, which of the following topics is explored first?**
  a. Cultural definition of the problem
  b. Cultural factors affecting current help seeking
  c. Cultural perception of cause, context, and support
  d. Cultural factors affecting self-coping and past help seeking

**150. As founder of many child development centers, _____ could be attributed with being one of the first family counselors.**
  a. Satir
  b. Ackerman
  c. Adler
  d. Rogers

**151. Disadvantages of closed-ended questions include all of the following EXCEPT:**
  a. the client fails to disclose personal information.
  b. the client fails to come up with an answer to the questions.
  c. the client fails to continue to dialogue with the counselor.
  d. the client fails to provide important information.

**152. The DSM system of diagnosis is based on:**
  a. a model set up by insurance companies.
  b. an educational model.
  c. the medical model.
  d. an integrated model of doctors and lawyers.

**153. What is Abraham Maslow's "Hierarchy of Needs"?**
  a. A theory of personality
  b. A theory of human motivation
  c. A psychoanalytic theory
  d. A needs-based counseling concept

**154. Which of the following types of psychotherapists would be most likely to use free association and transference?**

  a. Rational-emotive behavior therapists
  b. Behavior therapists
  c. Psychodynamic therapists
  d. Client-centered therapists

**155. What is the Rorschach also called?**

  a. The random sample test
  b. The personality evaluation
  c. The inkblot test
  d. All of the above

**156. Many mental health professionals apply to HMOs and PPOs to be on their provider lists. What is the reason for their doing this?**

  a. To enhance their professional reputations
  b. To allow clients to be referred to them
  c. To comply with national and state laws
  d. To gain membership in the organizations

**157. In a group therapy setting, what is a "blocker"?**

  a. Someone who blocks the others from taking up previous discussions
  b. A counselor who severely restricts group discussion
  c. A member who blocks others from veering off topic
  d. A group member who blocks new ideas

**158. In Salvador Minuchin's structural family therapy, there are _____ between family subsystems; if these are too rigid, they lead to _____, and if they are too diffuse, they can lead to _____.**

  a. transactional patterns; opposition; fragmentation
  b. boundaries; disengagement; enmeshment
  c. alignments; coalitions; conflicts
  d. structural maps; withdrawal; disorganization

**159. One of the more common techniques used by marriage and family therapists is reframing. Which of the following is an example of reframing?**

  a. A counselor listens intently to the family's discussion of an event and points out what happened at point A, point B, and point C
  b. A counselor has the members of a family each take turns talking about how they felt about a specific incident
  c. A counselor suggests that a mother's constant questioning of the daughter regarding a recent party the daughter attended could be interpreted by the daughter as mistrust rather than love and concern
  d. A counselor outlines exactly how individuals in the family are to argue by setting up fair-fighting rules

**160. Which of the following does NOT correctly pair a model of consultation with the person who developed it?**

    a.  Caplan – mental health consultation model
    b.  Bandura – social learning consultation model
    c.  Bergan – process consultation model
    d.  Schein – purchase consultation model

**161. A test is considered "standardized" if it includes all of the following EXCEPT:**

    a.  clearly specified procedures for administration.
    b.  clearly specified procedures for scoring.
    c.  questions have multiple correct answers.
    d.  normative data.

**162. Roger Gould believed that there were different "protective devices" people have. Which of these is the most accurate definition of protective devices according to Gould?**

    a.  Coping strategies
    b.  Defense mechanisms
    c.  False assumptions
    d.  Absolute truths

**163. Career counseling based on Bandura's social cognitive theory emphasizes all of these concepts EXCEPT:**

    a.  personal agency.
    b.  positive uncertainty.
    c.  self-efficacy.
    d.  vicarious learning.

**164. Which of these is true about professional liability insurance for counselors?**

    a.  This insurance is always required by law in every state of the U. S.
    b.  This insurance is required by law in some states, but not in others
    c.  This insurance is not required by law and is an unnecessary expense
    d.  This insurance is not recommended since it invites litigation

**165. A client who lost his job because of his inability to complete his work tasks yells at the counselor that she is "mean and stupid" and ruining his life. Which of the following ego defense mechanisms is the client using?**

    a.  Identification
    b.  Displacement
    c.  Sublimation
    d.  Projection

**166. The purpose of free association in psychoanalysis is:**

    a.  to bring conscious material into the unconscious.
    b.  to bring unconscious material into the conscious.
    c.  to allow for a break from the stress of analysis.
    d.  to decipher meaning from dreams.

**167. The best kind of random sampling technique that would include 10% Asian, 10% Hispanic, and 15% African American, as well as individuals from the majority ethnic group, would be a:**

    a. mixed randomized sampling technique.
    b. stratified sampling technique.
    c. cluster sampling technique.
    d. random chance sampling technique.

**168. A client who is post-amputation of a lower limb and insists he needs no physical therapy or rehabilitation is probably experiencing which of the following?**

    a. Self-confidence
    b. Denial
    c. Delusions
    d. Fear

**169. Which theorist conducted experiments regarding imprinting?**

    a. Jean Piaget
    b. Albert Bandura
    c. Konrad Lorenz
    d. Sigmund Freud

**170. A child who throws food at the dinner table is removed from the dining area and told to sit on the stairs for five minutes. This discipline technique is known as:**

    a. coercion.
    b. the Premack principle.
    c. shaping.
    d. time-out.

**171. A formal mental status examination covers all BUT which of the following areas?**

    a. Appearance and behavior
    b. Thought processes, mood and affect
    c. Intellectual functioning, sensorium
    d. Personality, brain dysfunctions

**172. Which is most accurate regarding homogeneous vs. heterogeneous therapy groups?**

    a. Homogeneous groups are too much alike to experience effective group dynamics
    b. Heterogeneous groups may have more difficulty being able to relate to each other
    c. Heterogeneous groups are not as similar to the real world as homogeneous groups
    d. Homogeneous groups are more likely to simulate interactions among the members

**173. What is "group content"?**

    a. The manner in which the group processes information
    b. Analysis of the group's interactions
    c. The material that is being discussed within the group
    d. The details of individuals forming the group

**174. A focus on confronting clients and pushing them to choose the present instead of allowing the past to affect them is:**
- a. person-centered therapy.
- b. classical conditioning.
- c. self-efficacy.
- d. Gestalt therapy.

**175. Dual-career families engage in leisure time:**
- a. more often than families with one wage earner.
- b. that is costlier than that of families with one wage earner.
- c. less often than families with one wage earner.
- d. as often as families with one wage earner.

**176. Most counselors incorporate several therapeutic theories in their work. This would be what type of approach to counseling?**
- a. Psychoanalytic
- b. Eclectic
- c. Integrative
- d. Cognitive

**177. Which of the following statements most likely indicates suicidal ideation and risk for suicide?**
- a. "My children would be better off without me."
- b. "I can't stop crying when I think about my mother's death."
- c. "My brother thinks he is so much better than I am."
- d. "Sometimes, I think this therapy is totally pointless."

**178. There are long silences, several members of the group are acting out, and it seems like all the group members are expressing frustrations with both the structure of the group and the way the group leader is functioning. Most likely this group is in the _____ state of the group process.**
- a. working
- b. initial
- c. transition
- d. closing

**179. Which demographic is projected about the U.S. population by the year 2050?**
- a. The numbers of Hispanic Americans will exceed the numbers of White Americans
- b. The largest numbers of Americans in the U.S. population will be Non-Hispanic Whites
- c. All of the minority groups combined will outnumber the Non-Hispanic White population
- d. Non-Hispanic Whites will outnumber all the minority groups combined in the population

**180. A person received a t-score of 40. This means that:**
- a. her score fell one standard deviation below the mean.
- b. her score is very low.
- c. there is an error.
- d. her score is higher than average.

**181.** Active symptoms of schizophrenia involve an _____ of normal thinking processes; passive symptoms involve the _____ of normal traits and abilities.

    a.  exaggeration; exaggeration
    b.  exaggeration; absence
    c.  absence; exaggeration
    d.  absence; absence

**182.** While involved with a research study, a counselor learns that several of her students are using confidential material in an unethical manner. She had no prior knowledge of this, and all of her safeguards for professional practice were appropriate. Is she, as the principal researcher, responsible for the student's behavior?

    a.  No, if professional safeguards were in place, the counselor is not responsible
    b.  Yes, the counselor is ultimately responsible
    c.  Only the students who acted unethically are to be held responsible
    d.  The counselor would only be responsible if she had knowledge of what was occurring and did nothing to stop it

**183.** There is a distinction between group content and group process. An example of group process would be:

    a.  Sarah monopolizes the group by continuously talking and doesn't allow other participants to contribute to the discussion.
    b.  Joe says, "I think today's topic should be what to do on a first date."
    c.  Randy rolls his eyes every time Karen says something.
    d.  both A and C.

**184.** Haley's strategic family therapy assumes that:

    a.  the client's symptoms are serving a protective function.
    b.  the power hierarchy of the family is confused.
    c.  the real problem is the family communication pattern.
    d.  All of the above.

**185.** Of the following, which is the loosest acceptable p-value bound if a researcher needs to demonstrate that something is 98% statistically significant?

    a.  $p < 0.05$
    b.  $p < 0.01$
    c.  $p < 0.001$
    d.  $p < 0.10$

**186.** _____ is a humanist approach that emphasizes the tragic aspects of life, the burden of responsibility, and the need to face the inevitability of death.

    a.  Social interest
    b.  Psychoanalysis
    c.  Existentialism
    d.  Self-actualization

**187. What is meant by the term "regression toward the mean?"**

   a. It means that most individuals are more likely to score near the mean on most standardized tests

   b. It means that most individuals' standardized test scores will go down from a pretest to a posttest

   c. It means that those individuals scoring near the mean on a pretest will score lower on a posttest

   d. It means that most scoring very high or low on a pretest will score nearer the mean on a posttest

**188. Which early theorist engaged in group therapy?**

   a. Alfred Adler

   b. Carl Jung

   c. Sigmund Freud

   d. Carl Rogers

**189. A client comes to a counselor because her house recently burned down and her husband has left her. She is depressed, and expresses suicidal ideation. Which of the following would the counselor consider?**

   a. Referral to an inpatient program

   b. Individual psychotherapy

   c. Group therapy

   d. Vocational counseling

**190. A group has co-leaders. That is, there are two trained counselors who are facilitating the group together. All of the following are advantages of co-leadership groups EXCEPT that:**

   a. more support and attention are provided to group participants.

   b. there is less time spent observing participants.

   c. effective modeling of appropriate behavior is provided to the participants.

   d. participants often view co-leaders as parents.

**191. A 27-year-old male with a history of drug and alcohol abuse, stealing, and bullying behavior has been working with the counselor on educational issues related to substance abuse, self-esteem, and anger. Which of the following are the primary determinants of effectiveness of education?**

   a. Observed behavior modification and compliance

   b. Self-reported behavior modification and compliance

   c. Positive reports from probation officer

   d. Drug and alcohol abstinence verified by testing

**192. Which of these tests has multiple forms for administration to differently aged subjects?**

   a. Wechsler Intelligence Scales

   b. Stanford-Binet Intelligence Scales

   c. Miller Analogies Test (MAT)

   d. Scholastic Assessment Test (SAT)

**193. Donald Super identified four theaters of life in which we play roles. The home is one of them. Which of these is NOT one of the other three?**

a. Community
b. School
c. Workplace
d. Church

**194. A client arrives complaining of feeling restless. She describes mood swings and times of hopelessness followed by periods of high energy and creativity in which she can go for days without sleep. What is her likely diagnosis?**

a. Depressive disorder
b. Bipolar disorder
c. ADHD
d. OCD

**195. Pat's therapist tells her that "self-talk" and "crooked thinking" cause emotional disturbances. He believes we all have the potential to think rationally. He uses techniques like role-playing and imagery to help Pat work through some of her issues. He also follows an A-B-C-D-E system. Pat's therapist believes that we are not influenced by the events we experience, but by our interpretation of them. Pat's therapist subscribes to which of these therapeutic approaches?**

a. Existential therapy (May, Frankl, Yalom)
b. Rational Emotive Behavior Therapy (Ellis)
c. Reality Therapy (Glasser)
d. Multimodal Therapy (Lazarus)

**196. Which of these is NOT an issue for adults in career transition that counselors should address during career counseling?**

a. Not wanting to undergo job transition
b. Obsolete job skills/a need for retraining
c. Lack of information/job-seeking skills
d. Changes in physical abilities or values

**197. When instituting suicide precautions, which client is likely at highest risk?**

a. A 15-year-old girl who overdosed on aspirin and then told her best friend
b. A 50-year-old woman who overdosed on pills and alcohol while her family was present
c. A 26-year-old man who threatened to jump out of a second story window
d. A 38-year-old man who shot himself in the chest while alone at home

**198. An infant first sucks on a nipple to nurse. Then the infant sucks on other things—a toy, Daddy's finger, etc. Later, this infant discovers other things to do with objects beyond sucking on them such as grasping them, shaking them, and otherwise manipulating them. These two behaviors were labeled by Jean Piaget with what terms, in order of their occurrence?**

a. Adaptation and assimilation
b. Adaptation and organization
c. Assimilation and accommodation
d. Accommodation and assimilation

199. Irvin Yalom specified that the functions of a therapy group leader should include: emotional stimulation, caring, meaning attribution, and executive leadership. Zander Ponzo found support for these same factors, and he also identified other factors found in successful groups. The factors Ponzo identified include all EXCEPT:

   a. participation.
   b. risk-taking.
   c. neutrality.
   d. conflict-confrontation.

200. Dr. Stanwyck has found a significant difference in the mean test scores of his two student groups. He has also found a significant interaction between their scores. He subsequently tested for significance on a second dependent variable as well. Now he wants to make one more analysis based on the information he has obtained related to the first dependent variable he tested—that of self-efficacy. In pretesting, he noticed that the college seniors in each group had higher average scores in self-efficacy than the college juniors in each group. Therefore, he now adjusts the groups' scores statistically to control for these initial differences before he compares his two test groups. What kind of test is he using?

   a. Factorial ANOVA
   b. MANOVA
   c. One-way ANOVA
   d. ANCOVA

# Answer Key and Explanations for Test #2

**1. D:** The Wisconsin card sorting test is used with clients with traumatic brain injury to assess cognitive reasoning. This test requires the client to classify cards by color, shape, or number, and the rules keep changing, so the client must pay close attention to feedback. The test is generally done on the computer, which automatically calculates the number of errors, including perseveration errors (where the client continues to classify to the same category after a rule change) and non-perseveration errors.

**2. D:** Jean Piaget's last stage of development, formal operations, is when the individual's thinking becomes less tied to reality, and they are more able to use abstract reasoning and formal logic. When faced with a problem during this stage, the child is able to systematically solve problems in a more methodical manner. Jean Piaget theorized that cognitive development is tied to one's ability to process new information. Piaget's stages, in order, are sensory motor (involving motor skill and sensory input), preoperational (increased verbalizations and crudely formed concepts), concrete operations (organized thought and logic), and formal operations.

**3. A:** Caregiving can be exhausting, so if the mother of a young adult with autism spectrum disorder and severe impairment is so tired that she begins crying, then she is overwhelmed and is most in need of respite care. The caregiver needs a break of even a few days in order to rest and have time for herself. If this is not possible, then part-time respite care in the home to allow the caregiver to relinquish caregiving for a few hours may help to reduce stress.

**4. A:** A bipolar client who is very nervous about transitioning into the community from a sheltered environment may benefit from a support group comprised of people dealing with similar issues. Support groups may have a mental health professional as a leader. Support groups are usually open groups that allow clients to choose whether or not to attend, but the groups provide a safe and supportive atmosphere where people can discuss shared concerns and methods of coping.

**5. D:** According to Super, adolescents explore career options, fantasize about various careers, and role-play as a means to narrow down their choices. Thus, they explore. In the establishment stage, individuals try out options and establish their careers. The maintenance stage is where the career path has already been established and now is being maintained.

**6. C:** A 16-year-old client who has repeatedly failed to maintain sobriety and consistently missed support meetings while partying with his friends has most likely done so out of fear of being different from his peers. Peer relationships are especially important to adolescents who are still developing a sense of self, so if an adolescent is involved in drinking with his friends, he may be reluctant to change the dynamic by remaining sober and may feel he will be abandoned or ridiculed if his behavior changes.

**7. D:** Standardized scores are continuous and the units they use are equal. Standardized scores do enable us to compare several different test scores for the same person. They allow normative or relative meaning, which enables comparisons between or among individuals. They do express the distance of an individual's score from the mean in terms of the particular standard score distribution's standard deviation.

**8. B:** In an open group, if a member leaves, a new member is admitted to replace the one who left. New members can provide stimulation, new ideas, and new resources. An open group does not mean that anybody can join it; the member's needs and personality should be appropriate for the group, as determined by the leader with input from group members. A closed group does not mean that only certain people may join it; it means that new members are not admitted. This can facilitate group cohesion and maintain trust within the group. Since new members are not admitted to closed groups, it follows that members who leave are not replaced, as they are in open groups.

**9. B:** The optimum group size for an adult group with no co-leader is generally considered to be 8 people. With young children who are 5 or 6 years old, an optimum group size would be 3 or 4. Groups may be larger with older children. For adults, 5 may be too small and 10 too large.

**10. B:** Cyclothymia is a mild form of bipolar disorder with a cause that is unknown. In this disorder, the mood swings from hypomanic behavior to depression symptoms. A client may be resistant to treatment because the hypomanic periods can also result in a significant increase in productivity and positive mood. However, friends and family will likely feel differently. Long-term treatment is necessary with this disorder because, like bipolar disorder, this has a recurring set of symptoms. Medication is often the primary treatment for cyclothymic disorder, but psychotherapy is also useful for support, education, and long-term management of the illness.

**11. D:** Quantitative research is more focused on finding relationships, often cause and effect relationships if they can be statistically proven. Answers A, B, and C all describe characteristics of qualitative research.

**12. C:** A hallmark of the psychodynamic perspective is the unconscious process, while the social-learning perspective deals with social aspects, specifically within environmental conditions. Bodily events or bodily functions would be more aligned with a biological approach of some sort.

**13. D:** The behavior that would differentiate aggression from anger is making verbal threats, as this often means that the client's anger is escalating, and the person's response may be disproportionate to the situation. Other indications of aggression include restless behavior and pacing back and forth, shouting in a loud voice, and using obscenities. The person may be very suspicious and exhibit disturbed thought processes and increased agitation and overreaction to stimuli. Aggressive individuals almost always have intent to hurt someone or something.

**14. A:** The degree of discord is substantial, and the level of verbal conflict is high, thus oppositional defiant disorder would be the most appropriate diagnosis. A parent-child relational problem tends to be less severe in nature, while conduct disorder is much more severe (i.e., involves violations of the rights of others, physical aggression, or property damage, persistent truancy, etc.). Intermittent explosive disorder addresses impulsive acts of aggression or violence (as opposed to premeditated or planned behaviors). Persistent conduct disorder carried into adulthood may meet criteria for antisocial personality disorder.

**15. A:** If a client who is an ethnic minority states that she has been passed over for promotion three times even though she is better qualified and had received better reviews that those who were promoted, this is most likely an example of discrimination, which is acting on racism (prejudice against others because of their ethnic identity) to deny opportunities to those who are different. Being a victim of discrimination can result in loss of self-esteem and depression as well as feelings of guilt and anxiety.

**16. B:** Following WWII, a common excuse used to explain some of the terrible acts committed was that the individual was just following orders. Inspired by this supposition, Stanley Milgram (in the 1960s) set out to explore the issue of authority and obedience. In his famous experiment, Milgram found that the majority of people, when faced with someone of authority, will do as they are told—even to the detriment of someone else. His experiment raised ethical issues about the treatment of subjects in psychological experiments, but the study itself is still heralded today as a significant contribution to the field of social psychology.

**17. A:** Once a person completes gender reassignment surgery and legally changes genders, that person is then considered the reassigned gender; thus, Mikaela is considered female, so her attraction to other females would result in her sexual orientation as lesbian. If she were attracted to males, she would be heterosexual. While she could also be classified as homosexual, this term is more commonly used for gay males, and she is no longer considered a male. She does not report a bisexual attraction to both genders.

**18. B:** Linguistic is NOT one of the five different cultures. Language is often a common feature in a national culture, and language may be an aspect of our ecological culture. Language is also often one part of an ethnic culture, along with practices, learning, and style of living. A specific language does not constitute one of the five distinct culture types.

**19. C:** The closed group promotes greater cohesiveness within the group because of the stability of the membership. With the same members interacting with each other during each session, the group members can form closer relationships, and will have fewer inhibitions as time goes by. There is a lack of diversity/change, but that can be a good thing depending upon the dynamics and goals of the group setting. The closed group is less cost-effective because as members may drop out or miss sessions, the counselor will not be able to replace them with new paying members.

**20. B:** While most screening for intimate partner abuse focuses on females age 18 or older, all female clients ages 14 and older should be screened as many very young females engage in sexual relationships, and this makes them vulnerable to intimate partner abuse. Additionally, some screening may also be appropriate for males, who are sometimes also the victims of abuse. Intimate partner abuse also occurs in same sex relationships, both male and female, so healthcare providers should be alert to those possibilities.

**21. C:** The chromosomal abnormality, Down syndrome, is the most common chromosomal disorder, occurring in 1 out of every 800 births. Individuals with Down syndrome suffer from intellectual disabilities, memory and speech problems, and slow motor development. They usually have some heart deformities, as well as being of short and stocky build. They have almond-shaped eyes, a flattened face, a protruding tongue, and an unusual crease running across the palm of the hand. Large hands and feet are not common characteristics of Down Syndrome.

**22. B:** If a counselor is seeing a client who has just started electroconvulsive therapy for severe depression, the counselor should be aware that a minimum of at least 6 treatments are generally required before a client shows sustained improvement. ECT is usually administered under an anesthetic three times weekly for 6-15 treatments. Most clients achieve the maximum benefit within 12-15 treatments so more are not warranted. Post-treatment effects include short-term memory impairment and mild confusion and disorientation.

**23. D:** Transactional analysis examines the interactions or complementary transactions that occur within an individual (parent, adult, child). Free association is paired with the psychoanalytic or psychodynamic approach. Unconditional positive regard is affiliated with the client-centered counseling of Carl Rogers. Irrational beliefs are associated with rational-emotive behavior therapy.

**24. B:** The standards for submission to most professional journals include using APA format. Most scholarly material is written in this form, at least in the mental health field. MLA format is often used in literary journals and comes from the journalism and communications fields.

**25. D:** The only technique that is not behavioral is unconditional positive regard, which is client centered, or Rogerian. A Rogerian-oriented therapist reflects back whatever a client says as a way to show empathy or unconditional regard. Behaviorists do not address feelings at all, so unconditional positive regard would not be something a behaviorist would consider offering to a client directly.

**26. C:** Horizontal violence can include physical contact (such as hitting and shoving) but most often it involves verbal or nonverbal expressions of hostility and conflict, including defensive postures (folded arms) and gestures meant to show contempt (rolling the eyes). Horizontal violence is a form of workplace bullying and may include name-calling, sarcastic statement, blaming, ignoring other's concerns, making inappropriate jokes, and interfering with others rights as well as punishing others inappropriately. Horizontal violence may cause the victim to lose self-esteem, emotional control, and motivation.

**27. D:** Giving a gift is sometimes, and in some cultures, a means of showing respect and gratitude in a way that monetarily compensating the counselor does not. In certain circumstances, accepting a gift may be an acceptable thing for a counselor to do. However, in deciding whether or not to accept a gift, a counselor must consider the client's motivation, the counselor's motivation (in wanting to accept or decline), the monetary value of the item, and of course the point at which the therapeutic relationship has reached. For instance, in some cases declining a gift may be detrimental to therapy. However, for the most part, it is generally best if the counselor does not encourage or accept gifts from those with whom they are in a therapeutic relationship.

**28. C:** Adolescents respond well to a combination of SSRI and CBT for the treatment of depression, but SSRI use in adolescents has been associated with increased suicidal ideation, so the patient must be carefully monitored and assessed for suicidal ideation. She and her family should be educated about this possible effect and warning signs. In some cases, adolescents may be asked to sign a no-suicide contract that clearly outlines the steps to take in the event they feel suicidal.

**29. A:** If utilizing exposure therapy with a client with severe phobias, the approach that is likely to have the most long-lasting effect is in vivo (actual) spaced exposure. Massed exposure (AKA "flooding") tend to be effective in the short-term, but the effect erodes more quickly than when exposure is spaced and progressive, allowing the client to adjust slowly to the exposure. Exposure therapy is part of a behavioral approach to treatment, and numerous different techniques are utilized.

**30. C:** When the thoughts and behaviors of two people are similar, they validate each other. In other words, each feels good in the presence of the other because of their similarities. Consensual validity is the term for this interpersonal dynamic, which helps to explain why people are attracted to those who are like them. Being similar also has the advantage of allowing for the enjoyment of common activities, and the increased ability to control the relationship (because of the increased understanding of how the other person thinks and feels), which also lends to the attraction.

**31. A:** If a client with schizophrenia has both delusions and hallucinations, the hallucinations that pose the greatest threat to the client and others are auditory command hallucinations during which a "voice" tells the client to carry out actions, which may involve self-injury or injury to others. Auditory hallucinations are the most common type although not all involve commands. Some clients hear clicks, music, or other noises rather than voices.

**32. B:** Of clients typically go through four phases in response to a stressor, culminating in an acute crisis, and a client has tried problem-solving techniques and found them to be unsuccessful in alleviating stress, the client is experiencing phase 2. Phases in crisis development:

- Phase 1: Exposure to a precipitating stressor and increased anxiety.
- Phase 2: Usual coping strategies fail to relieve stress.
- Phase 3: Stress increases. New strategies may be attempted and resolution or progression to phase 4 may occur.
- Phase 4. Acute stress

**33. C:** Some counselors work under the supervision of a psychologist or psychiatrist (particularly those with Master's degrees rather than Ph.D. or M.D. degrees), and insurance companies reimburse the supervising psychologist or psychiatrist who then remits payment to the supervising counselor. Payment to master's degree-level counselors is NOT automatic even if they are licensed. However, it is also NOT true that counselors with Master's degrees must remain unpaid unless they are licensed. Their payment would depend on whether they have a supervising psychologist or psychiatrist and upon applicable state laws. Some counselors can practice without a license in certain states as long as they do not use the title of a licensed professional counselor and do not advertise that they are licensed. Some counselors in private practice will not see clients unless they pay them directly.

**34. C:** Carl Jung, a student of Sigmund Freud, developed the Word Association Test (WAT). In the WAT, a single word is read to the client, who then responds as quickly as possible with whatever word comes to mind. The word the client responds with is recorded, but other factors are also noted such as speed of response and client behavior. The test was used to clarify issues of psychopathology, but also as a means of generally gleaning information about the client's personality. The WAT has also been used in the study of memory. The test was based on earlier ideas of mental associations.

**35. D:** Bulimia is an eating disorder, characterized by periods of binge eating followed by inappropriate methods of avoiding weight gain. The individual with bulimia will often lose control of efforts to avoid eating, only to binge uncontrollably. Following the bingeing behavior, the client will induce diarrhea, vomit, exercise excessively, or any other number of extreme methods. There are many possible causes of bulimia, including body image issues, biological factors, and control issues. Major life changes and stress can also be a factor in bulimic behavior. Cognitive-behavioral therapy is often chosen as a method of treatment, but psychotherapy is also often used.

**36. B:** This is an example of the Premack principle, which states that using a behavior of higher probability (playing Xbox) can motivate an individual to carry out a behavior of lower probability (finishing homework). Positive reinforcement would occur when a child produces a desired behavior and is provided with positive feedback and reinforcement to increase the chances that the child will produce the same behavior again. Negative reinforcement is the taking away of an undesirable consequence to increase the likelihood that the child will engage in the behavior again (Mom stops nagging if she cleans her room). Quid pro quo is another behavioral technique that essentially means one gets something for something: "I will do something for you if you do something for me."

**37. C:** In the baseline study, in which an experimenter wearing a lab coat instructed the volunteer to administer progressively more powerful electric shocks to a subject, Milgram's team found that the obedience rate (i.e., the percentage of participants who administered all planned shocks) was around 65%. Replacing the authority figure by someone who appeared to be an ordinary member of the public reduced the obedience rate to around 20%. When the orders were delivered by telephone, obedience rate also dropped to around 20%, though in this case, many volunteers pretended to obey the orders while not following through. When the experiment venue was moved off of Yale's campus, the obedience rate dropped below 50%. However, when the volunteers were not the ones directly initiating the electric shocks (i.e., they were instructing someone else to do so), the obedience rate climbed to well over 90%.

**38. B:** Positive reinforcement is a type of operant conditioning used in behavioral therapy. It's a way in which to strengthen a desirable behavior. An example of positive reinforcement would be if someone wanted a dog to sit upon command. Every time the dog successfully sits when given the command to do so, the dog would be rewarded with a positive consequence (such as a dog treat or pat on the head). Eventually the dog would come to identify the positive reinforcement with the behavior of sitting upon command, and therefore continue the wanted behavior on a consistent basis.

**39. A:** When the same evaluation instrument yields completely different results with different evaluators or different groups of individuals, then the problem is likely with the reliability of the instrument. Types of reliability include stability reliability (reliability over time), equivalence reliability (two different forms of the instrument should obtain the same results), and internal consistency reliability (used only if the instrument is measuring only one concept). Results should be precise and predictable to some degree. Validity refers to the degree to which the instrument actually measures that which it is intended to measure.

**40. B:** A correlation coefficient does show the relationship between two sets of numbers. A correlation coefficient ranges from -1.00, or a perfect negative correlation, to 1.00, or a perfect positive correlation. A perfect correlation can be either positive or negative. Correlation coefficients indicate the degree of relationship, but do not indicate any causal relationship between variables. When a very strong correlation exists between variables, knowing one score an individual got will enable fairly accurate prediction of another score that individual got.

**41. D:** A client with symptoms consistent with narcolepsy-cataplexy should be referred to a physician for testing for hypocretin, which is measured in the cerebrospinal fluid. Narcolepsy is an irrepressible and recurrent need to sleep, and cataplexy is a sudden loss of muscle tone triggered by laughing/joking. The narcolepsy-cataplexy condition typically is a sign of loss of cells in the hypothalamus that produce hypocretin. This loss is associated with an autoimmune reaction. In young people with narcolepsy without cataplexy but with a low level of hypocretin, cataplexy usually develops at a later time.

**42. A:** *Tarasoff* is a landmark case that led to improving services for mental health by requiring mental health practitioners to warn potential victims of imminent harm. Counselors are mandatory reporters that must take reasonable steps to protect possible victims from harm. Reasonable steps are those that any person who cares about another person would take to secure that person's safety. Usually that involves informing potential victims and law enforcement agencies.

**43. D:** In nominal measurement, the numbers represent categories such as male and female. In ordinal measurement, the numbers show differences in magnitude such as from high to low or vice versa. In interval measurement, the numbers have equal quantities throughout so that the interval between them is always the same; the interval between 10 and 11 being the same as the interval between 2 and 3. In ratio measurement the numbers are on a scale with a true zero and can be compared by ratios such as 400 being twice as much as 200. Random, stratified, cluster, and purposeful are types of sampling not types of measurement.

**44. B:** If the counselor is carrying out a spiritual assessment using the FICA (Faith, Importance, Community, Address) tool, the first question that the counselor should ask is, "Do you have a faith or belief system that gives your life meaning?" The questions go from the general to the specific. **FICA** is an abbreviated spiritual assessment:

| F | Faith | Do you have a faith or belief system that gives your life meaning? |
|---|---|---|
| I | Importance | What importance does your faith have in your daily life? |
| C | Community | Do you participate and gain support from a faith community? |
| A | Address | What faith issues would you like me to address in your care? |

**45. B:** If a male client has been following a female client and claims the female is "flirting" with him and using "sexual innuendoes" but the female client complains that the male client is harassing and scaring her, and staff observations concur with the female client's complaints, then the male client is most likely exhibiting projection, an ego defense mechanism in which the male client is projecting his own feelings of attraction onto the female client.

**46. C:** Reliability tells one if the test is able to give consistent results each time it is administered. A problem with determining this comes into play with the "memory factor" (as the same group may remember some of the answers during subsequent administrations), which can affect the validity of the test. There are also other types of reliability. For instance, "test-retest reliability" refers to the administration of the test, and "internal-consistency reliability" is about how the items of the test relate to each other.

**47. B.** When developing an individualized Goal Attainment Scale (GAS) with a client, the counselor would score an expected outcome as 0. The counselor and client develop a list of goals together and weigh the outcomes on a scale that includes both scoring and a precise description of achievement at that score so that client's progress can be quantified:

- -2: This is the least favorable outcome.
- -1: Outcomes is less than expected.
- 0: Outcome is that which was expected.
- +1: Outcome is greater than expected.
- +2: Outcome is the most favorable.

**48. C:** Confrontation is often used by counselors to point out discrepancies between a client's thoughts/beliefs and the behavior. Making the client aware of these discrepancies is a necessary skill for a counselor. When a counselor uses interpretation, she is pointing out the real meaning of a client's behavior. Reflection is another skill that a counselor uses to help clients. When a counselor reflects something back to a client, he is paraphrasing what the client said in order to emphasize the importance of the feelings associated with the statement and to project empathy. It is considered unethical to abandon a client.

**49. B:** Harry Stack Sullivan favored a social systems approach to understanding human behavior. He felt that human behavior is best understood in terms of social interactions and interpersonal relationships. Erich Fromm believed that individuals could develop self-fulfillment, or social character, through joining with other people and could become lonely and unproductive if they did not. He felt that society offers opportunities to experience mutual love and respect. Wilhelm Reich contributed to the body therapy manipulation movement, and he believed that repeated successful orgasms were necessary for mental health. Karen Horney believed that security motivates every individual and a lack of security causes anxiety. She felt that irrational attempts to repair disrupted relationships could turn into neurotic needs.

**50. D:** A correlation coefficient is a number that shows the degree of relationship between the two variables studied in an experiment. The numeric value of the correlation coefficient falls between +1.00 and -1.00, and there are two parts to each. The number of the correlation coefficient reveals how strong the relationship between two factors is—the closer the number is to 1.00, the stronger the correlation is (regardless of the sign). The closer the number of the correlation coefficient is to 0.00, the weaker the relationship. The sign (plus or minus) shows the direction of the two variables' relationship. A negative correlation's variables vary in opposite directions. A positive correlation's variables vary in the same direction.

**51. B:** In rational-emotive therapy, a client's irrational beliefs are challenged. In existential therapy, the focus is on the choices a client makes in order to find what is meaningful. Personal freedom and awareness are emphasized. In aversive conditioning, a person is conditioned using something aversive to stay away from or refrain from engaging in some inappropriate behavior. And client-centered therapy focuses on self-acceptance and self-exploration.

**52. C:** Consultation is a voluntary problem-solving process, and it is also work-related. It uses the same skills as counseling does, but in a different context, role, and function than in counseling. It is for resolving existing problems and also for preventing future problems. It may be content-oriented or process-oriented, or both.

**53. B:** Carl Rogers is known for person-centered or client-centered counseling. Rollo May is known for existential counseling. Fritz Perls is known for Gestalt therapy. Aaron Beck is known for behavioral/cognitive-behavioral counseling.

**54. C:** Title and practice-control laws state that one cannot practice counseling without a professional counselor license. Some states have laws saying that one may practice counseling without a license, but if doing so one may not legally use the licensed professional counselor (LPC) title. These are called "title-control" laws rather than "title and practice-control" laws. There is no law specifying that one cannot practice counseling without using the LPC title. Using the LPC title is not a requirement for obtaining a license.

**55. C:** Because group members can come and go at will, there is a chance that at each session there are different people. This characteristic of an open group lessens the cohesion of a group. At every session, someone new may join, and group participants have to get to know someone new. In order for a group to be cohesive, a greater amount of familiarity among group members is needed, as then they are more willing to open up and share with others. In an open group, it is also harder to nurture members and to sustain continuity compared with a closed group. A closed group has greater cohesiveness, stability, and predictability.

**56. B:** E-therapy is also sometimes called cyber-therapy, e-counseling, tele-therapy, or just online therapy or counseling. It can involve either individual or group therapy and is accomplished in a number of ways. Videoconferencing, chat rooms, e-mail, and instant messaging are some of the more common methods of providing counseling services. As e-therapy is still a new manner of conducting therapy, it is met with skepticism by some professionals and clients. However, e-therapy is a dramatically growing field and makes therapy possible for many clients who are otherwise unwilling, or unable to, attend the traditional therapy session.

**57. A:** The Theory of Work Adjustment (TWA) states that career outcome depends upon satisfaction and satisfactoriness. The former refers to the worker's needs and values in relation to the job, and the latter addresses the worker's skills for the position. How well those two elements fit together impacts the ultimate outcome. Simply stated, both the work environment and the individual must meet each other's needs for the interaction to be maintained, and work adjustment is dependent upon that interaction. How well the requirements of the two factors are met is called correspondence.

**58. C:** Gestalt therapy utilizes the empty-chair technique and making rounds, as well as psychodrama. Free association and dream analysis are popular techniques used by psychoanalysis. Adlerian counseling utilizes examination of clients' memories, catching oneself, and spitting in the client's soup. Client-centered counselors utilize active/passive listening, open-ended questions, positive regard, and reflection of feelings.

**59. B:** There is very little evidence to support that homosexual couples are poor parents. When gay and lesbian couples become parents, they generally are just as effective and caring as are heterosexual couples who become parents. The proportion of children who are maladjusted is just about equal for homosexual and heterosexual parents. The research shows that being gay or lesbian does not make a person a bad parent.

**60. D:** Tatiana Tarasoff was murdered by Prosenjit Poddar, who was a client of a university psychologist, and her family subsequently sued the Board of Regents of the University of California. The court ruled that if a therapist has reason to believe that a client may pose a serious danger of violence to one or more third parties, that therapist must either confine the client under state laws of psychiatric involuntary hospitalization, or else break confidentiality to notify the police and warn the intended victim(s). This is known as the Duty to Warn. Since this case, decisions in other court cases in other states have reaffirmed this legal precedent.

**61. B:** In the case presented, the more education a person has, the higher the person's salary will be. This describes a positive correlation in that as one variable increases, the other variable also increases. An example of a negative correlation would be: The hotter the temperature outside, the less hot soup people consume. In a negative correlation, one variable increases while the other variable decreases.

**62. C:** These tests are projective in nature. The Rotter's Incomplete Sentences Blank prompts the subject to complete partial sentences in the testing process. The Draw-A-Person Test prompts the subject to make a drawing of a person. The results are evaluated and interpreted by the counselor. Both tasks are unstructured or open-ended allowing the subject to project individual feelings, ideas, states, needs, etc., onto it. From this, the tester may gain insights to the subject's internal consciousness. Specialized personality tests include the Tennessee Self-Concept Scale, the Bender® Visual-Motor Gestalt Test, and the Luria-Nebraska Neuropsychological Battery. Specialized achievement tests include the GED test, the College Board's AP Program test, and the College-Level Examination Program (CLEP) test. Inventory personality tests include the MMPI, the California Psychological Inventory (CPI), the NEO Personality Inventory (revised), the Beck Depression Inventory, and the Myers-Briggs Type Indicator.

**63. C:** Counterbalancing is presenting stimuli in differing sequences to avoid influencing an experiment by the order of presentation. Countertransference is a process that can occur during therapy when an unresolved personal issue prevents a therapist from being objective. Counterculture is an alternative culture arising in opposition to the dominant values and behaviors of a society. "Countercounseling" is a made-up term.

**64. D:** When a therapy group is formed, the leader(s) should decide in advance how long it will run and should advise the members of this. The group's duration should not be unknown or indefinite.

There is no generalization that therapy groups should run for six months. The group members should not decide on its length, as they do not have the leader's knowledge or expertise.

**65. B:** Kübler-Ross identified the five stages of the grieving experience as: denial (refusal to believe one is dying); anger (resentment, feeling it is unfair to be dying/objecting to dying); bargaining (trying to make deals with God or others—e.g., "I'll give everything to charity if I can just live/I'll treat my family members better if I just don't have to die now/I'll be a better person if I can just have some more time," etc.); depression (a feeling of hopelessness and/or helplessness in the face of one's mortality; sadness over leaving bodily life and loved ones behind); and, finally, acceptance (a feeling of peace at having to come to terms with the fact of one's imminent demise). Shock, panic, sorrow, stoicism, fear, withdrawal, resignation, and peace are all emotions that a dying person could certainly experience, but they are not named as stages in Kübler-Ross' theory.

**66. B:** If, during an interview the client blames his boss for his problems and states that the boss is "going to pay," this is an implied threat. Because of the duty to warn those who might be in danger from a client with mental health issues, the counselor should ask directly, "What thoughts have you had about hurting your boss?" in order to assess whether there is a risk of violence.

**67. D:** If a suicidal person has made a definite plan to commit suicide and also has means such as sleeping pills or a gun available, this is a sign of serious risk that the individual will attempt suicide. Another sign of suicide risk is depression and a sense of hopelessness, so a lifting or relief of depression is not necessarily correct, although it has been seen that some clients demonstrate a lift of depression before suicide because they are at peace with the decision. An unnatural sense of gaiety at giving up responsibilities is not a common sign of serious suicide risk, but the giving away of valuables is another sign to be wary of. Frequent explosions of hostility or rage directed at others is a sign of disturbance, but this is more likely a sign of risk for murder or otherwise harming others than for suicide. Depression is anger turned inward at the self, and suicide is aggression against the self. A person who lashes out at others is less likely to commit suicide.

**68. A:** Abraham Maslow's humanistic theory posits a hierarchy of needs. The more basic needs such as food/water, shelter and safety must be met before higher-order needs, such as love, belonging, and self-esteem can be addressed, according to Maslow. Edward Thorndike is known for formulating the Law of Effect, which says that a reward reinforces the connection between a stimulus and a response; this law is fundamental to behaviorism. Erik Erikson is known for his psychosocial stage theory, identifying eight (later nine) stages, each of which contains a central crisis/conflict/task, which must be resolved in order to progress. Harry Stack Sullivan was a neo-Freudian theorist who stressed the importance of social/interpersonal relationships.

**69. C:** In contrast to quantitative research, which assumes that social factors belong to a single objective reality, qualitative research assumes that individuals and groups construct a multiplicity of realities. Answers A, B, and D all describe characteristics of quantitative research.

**70. C:** This theory states that some people compensate for things they cannot do in their jobs by engaging in leisure activities which are markedly different from what they do at work, while other people use the same skills and do similar activities in their leisure time as they have at work, so that their jobs are said to "spillover" into their leisure activity. This theory does not state that unhappy workers compensate with excessive leisure pursuits, nor does it state that people's preferences in leisure time reduce their job productivity. It also does not state that people try to make up for having leisure activities by working harder, nor that leisure interests spill over into their work lives.

**71. A:** The Likert Scale was developed in 1932 by Renis Likert, and is a psychometric, multi-item scale used for questionnaires. Likert wanted to develop a scientific way in which to measure psychological attitudes, and the factors that influence those attitudes and feelings. The scale is commonly used in surveys and other studies in which closed-ended questions are desired (ones that don't allow the respondent to answer in their own words). A Likert Scale survey asks the respondent to choose where on a scale (ranging from "strongly disagree" to "completely agree") their attitudes lay.

**72. C:** Free association is a technique commonly used in Freudian psychoanalysis. Guilt is a central concept of existential therapy; it occurs when we fail to reach our potential. Anxiety is also a central concept in existential therapy, and is considered to be the threat of non-being. Existentialists also believe that we search for meaning in life. They feel that we have freedom of choice and are responsible for our own fates. Thus, we struggle with being alone/not connected to others, and we search for the meaning of our existence.

**73. D:** All of the situations listed are limitations to confidentiality. These limitations include: 1) danger to the client or to others (requiring certain reporting); 2) discussing a case with other professionals who can help; 3) discussing a case with superiors or teachers if the counselor is still a student; 4) client requests for release of records; 5) a lawsuit is filed against a counselor; 6) court orders for release of information; 7) clerical office staff working with client records; 8) managed care providers and health insurance companies' requests for client information.

**74. C:** Interpersonal and social rhythm therapy helps clients with bipolar disorder establish consistent sleep and physical activity schedules. The clients utilize a self-monitoring instrument to monitor their daily activities, including their sleep patterns. Maintaining consistent patterns of activities and sleeping at the same time and for the same duration each night help to reduce manic and depressive episodes. Clients may also engage in cognitive behavioral therapy, family therapy, and group therapy. If symptoms are severe and the client does not respond to other treatments, electroconvulsive therapy (ECT) may be considered.

**75. C:** If a counselor working with an 8-year-old child who has been suspended from school because of anger issues notes that the child has many bruises in various stages of healing, including on the left side of the face, and the child seems anxious when the parent is in the room, but the child denies any abuse, the counselor should report possible child abuse to the appropriate authorities. Most children deny being abused even when the abuse is egregious, but there are numerous red flags (anger issues, bruising, anxiety) that point to abuse, and the counselor is a mandatory reporter.

**76. C:** If a client routinely misses group support meetings, making various excuses, but claims that the support group is very helpful, the most effective method of confronting the client is: "You don't come to group but you say it's helpful. How do you feel about this contradiction?" This approach keeps the focus on the client and the client's conflict but avoids judgmental statements that may cause the client to feel it necessary to defend the failure to attend group.

**77. B:** This is unethical. This scenario describes a situation in which the counselor profits from the referrals. If the counselor is working for a community agency, most likely she receives a salary for her work. Referring clients to her own private practice has the potential to harm the client and provides her with additional money. An ethical violation of scope of practice would be a scenario in which a counselor lacks appropriate training and supervision to perform or engage in some treatment. In a dual relationship violation, the counselor basically wears multiple hats in the relationship with the client—the therapist and a neighbor or friend.

**78. D:** If a client in the depressive stage of bipolar disease experiences "all or nothing" negative automatic thoughts and states, "I'm a complete failure at everything I try to do," and the counselor is using CBT to alter dysfunctional thinking, the most appropriate intervention is to ask the client to describe supporting and disputing evidence for this statement. Then, the counselor and the client discuss the underlying logic for the evidence that the client presents.

**79. A:** An irrational hostility toward another that is merely due to that individual's membership in a particular group is how Gordon Allport would define "prejudice." Allport believed that prejudice was a complex issue and caused by a variety of factors. He points out that the nature of prejudice is such that it can't be affected by the addition of rational facts. Situational issues such as economic factors, cultural factors, advertising, historical issues, and stereotyping are just a few of the possible influences upon the development of prejudice. Allport believed that prejudice should be regarded as a type of psychopathology, as it leads to such things as the increased use of defense mechanisms, passivity, and withdrawal.

**80. A:** According to Freudian psychoanalytic theory, the conscience resides in the Superego. The Id knows only what the individual wants; the Ego knows it can't always get what it wants and negotiates between the Id and the Superego. The Superego is the moral part of the mind, imposing rules and punishing inappropriate thoughts and actions. For this reason, the Superego (where the conscience is) causes the Ego to feel anxiety/guilt when the individual's behavior diverts from what is deemed morally acceptable. The Superego is an important part of the personality for obvious reasons. If the Superego is underdeveloped, the individual may not experience the necessary tension between the Ego and Superego, and thus act inappropriately in interpersonal relationships or in society in general.

**81. B:** If a client reports only occasional social drinking and denies the use of illicit drugs but within 2 days of hospitalization for depression, the client becomes increasingly agitated with noticeable hand tremors and complains that she feels as though bugs are crawling under her skin, the counselor should suspect the client is undergoing alcohol withdrawal. Onset of withdrawal symptoms from heroin is usually within 6-12 hours. These symptoms are not consistent with bipolar disorder or panic disorder.

**82. C:** An etic worldview puts more emphasis on our similarities than on our differences. An emic worldview puts more emphasis on differences that we must understand in order to help different cultural groups from their specific perspectives. Thus, it is a specific rather than a global view. Therefore, the belief in taking each group's perspective is emic, not etic. The emic worldview does not state that we need to transcend our differences, but rather to focus on them by taking each group's perspective in order to understand and help them.

**83. A:** Although the two terms may seem to come up within similar contexts, "privileged communication" is a legal term and "confidentiality" is an ethical concept. Things said during sessions are kept confidential within limits. Legally, when a counselor invokes privileged communication, this means that things revealed in confidential therapy sessions cannot be disclosed in court without the client's permission. The only exceptions would be when a mental health professional who has been hired by the court conducts an evaluation or other service that relates to some legal action. In these cases, the counselor or other mental health practitioner has to inform the client of the limits of privileged communication.

**84. B:** Tiedeman said that the continuous process of career decision-making is made up of the first phase of anticipation or preoccupation, which includes the following sub-phases: exploration, crystallization, choice, and clarification. The second phase is implementation or adjustment, which includes these sub-phases: induction, reformation, and integration.

**85. D:** There is a significant power differential between supervisors and supervisees. As a supervisor, the counselor must be diligently aware of any and all possible circumstances that might negatively affect his ability to competently conduct his role as a supervisor. Some activities can be beneficial to the professional relationship. Activities such as visits to the hospital or attendance at weddings and other significant events may enhance the relationship. However, other activities such as romantic involvements or business investments could prove detrimental and could be considered unethical.

**86. C:** There are three levels of groups—primary, secondary, and tertiary. Each level has a different focus or emphasis. The emphasis of a primary group is on preventing problems from occurring and developing healthy behaviors. The emphasis of a secondary group is preventative and remedial—its focus may be on the reduction of symptoms, lessening the severity of problems, and/or helping with overall adjustment to life stressors. The tertiary group can be thought of more as a "therapy" group in that its focus is on getting members of the group back to a more functional level of living. Tertiary groups may involve aspects of personality change and/or rehabilitation. One way to think about the three levels is in terms of severity—primary usually is very mild; secondary is mild to moderate; and tertiary is moderate to severe.

**87. B:** Title IX bans sex discrimination in academics and athletics in K-12 schools and colleges. Title IX has nothing to do with remedial reading. This law does not require that the same sports be available to both males and females, only that males and females be provided the same proportion of opportunities to participate in sports. This law has nothing to do with the sizes of classes in schools.

**88. B:** PL 94-142 guarantees free and appropriate education for all handicapped children. Another part of this law is that handicapped children are to be placed in the least restrictive educational environment that is most appropriate for a particular child. All handicapped children are to have an individualized educational plan as well. The least restrictive environment is most often in a public-school setting.

**89. C:** Lawrence Kohlberg was interested in moral development, and theorized stages by which this development occurs in the individual. There are several stages that fall under three "levels." Children begin the Pre-conventional level by doing whatever they can get away with, and end by beginning to see the needs of others (although still judging everything in terms of their own needs). In the Conventional level, the child acknowledges both others and the rules of society, feeling a duty to obey the rules. In the final level, Post-conventional, the individual understands society's role in making decisions, and answers to an inner conscience.

**90. C:** Free association is the technique of allowing the client to speak freely about whatever comes to mind. Free association is a technique used by psychoanalysts and psychodynamic therapists to summon unconscious thoughts and motivations. The other techniques are all used exclusively by behaviorists.

**91. A:** The placebo effect describes when improvement occurs just by the fact that someone is expecting improvement. The opposite, the nocebo effect, occurs when an innocuous substance (a sugar pill) causes a person to get sick or to feel worse. The therapeutic window describes a range of time or dose of medication at which positive effects will be noticed. An empirically validated treatment is one in which the treatment has been systematically tested and validated through some research and found to be successful.

**92. D:** The most immediate goal is to manage the client's symptoms with appropriate medications and for the client to take only prescribed medications rather than self-medicating with cocaine and alcohol. Clients with dual diagnoses can present challenges because they cannot abstain from all medications if their symptoms are to be controlled. Once they are properly medicated, they can begin to interact with others, express feeling, and develop plans for activities. When stabilized, they can begin to work on social skills and participate in alcohol/drug-free activities.

**93. C:** An area of study in social cognition is attribution. Attribution refers to the explanations people make for the behaviors that people engage in. Internal attributions deal with factors within the individual. External attributions assign the cause of behavior to outside factors. Generally, people tend to assign external causes for their failures in life, and internal causes to the failures of others. The success of others is often also seen as the result of external elements, while one's own success may more likely be attributed to internal causes.

**94. C:** The key features of borderline personality disorder (BPD) involve instability in relationships and affect, poor self-image, and high impulsivity. Violations of personal rights and apathy common to antisocial personality disorder are insufficiently pronounced. While evidence of histrionic behavior exists, the devaluation/over-valuation pattern common to BPD is not accounted for via histrionic personality disorder. Nor is the need for admiration, pervasive with narcissism, not otherwise addressed.

**95. B:** In order for a client with a psychiatric diagnosis to quality for disability benefits under the Social Security Administration, the client must be unable to engage in substantial gainful activity because of the disability for at least 12 months. The Office of Disability Adjudication and Review (ODAR) will review the client's medical records to determine the diagnosis, any co-occurring disabilities and their effects, treatment, and functional ability. Clients are evaluated for Social Security Disability Insurance (SSDI) and the Supplemental Security Income (SSI).

**96. B:** It is expected in our Western culture that we maintain good eye contact at all times. In the Eastern traditions, however, eye contact is averted in some situations. It is the counselor's job to know those subtle differences and respect them. An effective counselor may not use the same language as the client, but can utilize an interpreter to assist in translation. The effective counselor must also be cognizant of context and honor religious beliefs regardless of whether they different from their own.

**97. B:** EMDR (eye movement desensitization and reprocessing) is a specialization that requires additional training. Unless the counselor took the specialized training and had supervision, she cannot use EMDR in her practice. In this case, the counselor is functioning out of her scope of practice. Remember, the client insisted that this treatment methodology be used. The question did not say that the counselor was a trained EMDR practitioner.

**98. A:** The goal of Gestalt therapy is to enable members to pay attention to their here-and-now experiences so they can recognize and integrate disowned aspects of themselves. The goal of a psychodynamic-oriented group is to provide a climate to help members re-experience early family relationships. The goals of a reality-oriented group are to guide members toward learning realistic and responsible behavior and to develop identities that focus on success. The goals of an existential-oriented group are to provide conditions that maximize self-awareness and to remove obstacles to personal growth.

**99. D:** When reporting research, it is important to always give credit to any other source or individual who has contributed to the work, or from whom the researcher has drawn significant information. Work must also be original (unless indicated otherwise), and one should never plagiarize. Editorial must also be made aware of previous publication of the material, and only one journal should be submitted to at a time. If material is substantially based on the work of students, they should certainly be listed as principal authors.

**100. C:** Fearful-avoidant. Adult attachment styles:

- **Anxious-preoccupied**: Seek intimacy but may become overly dependent on others, sometimes causing others to back away, resulting in loneliness and questioning of self-worth
- **Dismissive-avoidant**: Feel a strong need for independence and may avoid intimacy with others, stating they have no need of attachments and suppressing feelings, resulting in few close friends.
- **Fearful-avoidant**: Feel uncomfortable with close attachments because of fear of getting hurt and who have difficulty expressing feelings and few close relationships.
- **Secure:** Feel positively about themselves and others and able to establish close relationships with others while maintaining a sense of independence.

**101. B:** If the counselor is assessing a victim of violent trauma, and essential initial step is to explain the procedure for screening and assessment. This allows the client to have some feeling of control. Additionally, the client should be assured that he or she can choose whether or not to answer, to answer later, to avoid answering. Questions about the trauma should be asked slowly, gradually increasing the specificity. The counselor should stress the importance of focusing on the client's current recovery.

**102. C:** If a client has met the criteria for binge-eating disorder and averages 8 or 9 binge-eating episodes per week, the severity of the disorder would be classified as severe. Severity classification:

- Mild: 1-3 binge-eating episodes per week.
- Moderate: 4-7 binge-eating episodes per week.
- Severe: 8-13 binge-eating episodes per week.
- Extreme: 14 or more binge-eating episodes per week.

**103. B:** B.F. Skinner found that deprivation will increase the probability of an operant. For example, a rat deprived of food for some time is far more likely to press a bar to receive food than a rat that has not been deprived of food. B.F. Skinner would view the rat's hunger, not as an internal process, but rather as an external, measurable one (i.e., the amount of time without food). Just as deprivation will increase an operant, satiation will decrease it. For instance, a rat that has been given his fill of food and water is much less likely to manipulate a bar in order to receive food.

**104. C:** The terms "aptitude test" and "achievement test" are often used interchangeably, but they are quite different from each other. Achievement is what one can do, while aptitude is what one has the ability to do. In the achievement test, the test measures what the subject currently knows. It is the type of test commonly used in the school setting. In the norm-referenced achievement test, the subject is measured against others who also took the test. In a criterion-referenced achievement test, the subject is measured against a previously set criterion. Aptitude tests differ from achievement tests in that they measure the subject's ability or interests in particular areas. Career testing would be a common example of an aptitude test that helps subjects choose a career based upon their interests.

**105. A:** The Likert scale is the type of question where the answer choices are graduated in order of degree according to the strength of the respondent's opinion. A scatterplot is a graphic depiction of the relationship between two variables for a group of test respondents. It plots the respondent's scores on a graph. The Kruskal-Wallis test is a nonparametric test used when there are more than two mean scores on a single variable. It is a nonparametric version of an ANOVA. The Wilcoxon signed-rank test is a nonparametric measure used when there are scores for two samples that are correlated.

**106. C:** If a client who was the victim of sexual assault tells the counselor that she will never feel safe again and the counselor asks the client if she feels safe at the moment and what she will need to do to feel safe when she goes home, this is an example of reframing. Reframing aims to stop the negative thoughts and to change the way of looking at something. Instead of focusing on a lack of safety, the counselor is reframing the issue to focus on proactive steps to feeling safe.

**107. D:** Predictive is a type of validity, not of reliability. It means that predictions made by a test are confirmed by later behavior. Stability refers to test-retest reliability using the same testing instrument with the same group at different times. Equivalence is a type of reliability using alternate forms of the same test with the same group and correlating the results. Internal consistency refers to the degree of correlation between different aspects of a test intended to address the same characteristic. This measure of reliability is often measured via a split-half method – where items addressing a shared characteristic are divided into two test "halves" and then administered to involved subjects. The degree of correlation between the two halves measures the instrument's internal consistency.

**108. B:** While laws may vary slightly from one state to another in relation to involuntary commitment, generally probable cause is present if a person is a threat to herself or others (and usually the threat must be imminent). A second criterion is usually that the person is too disabled to provide self-care; however, this last criterion can be interpreted in a wide variety of ways (the reason so many mentally ill individuals are homeless and living on the streets) and is rarely utilized.

**109. B:** Piaget's theory has the following stages: sensorimotor, preoperational, concrete operational, and formal operational (and later post-formal operations). Freud, Erikson and Kohlberg also have staged theories regarding human development, but none of them includes a stage named Sensorimotor.

**110. A:** Existentialism examines philosophical questions such as, "What is the meaning of life?" and "Is there life in the hereafter?" The focus of Adlerian counseling is on developing and maintaining social interests. The focus of Gestalt therapy is congruence and the here and now. Reality therapy is focused on becoming psychologically well by taking responsibility for oneself and formulating realistic plans.

**111. A:** Glasser's reality therapy ignores the unconscious in favor of focusing on the here and now and the concrete. Rogerian or person-centered counseling emphasizes acceptance, empathy and the therapeutic relationship, and deals more with surface issues disregarding innate drives and the unconscious. Behaviorism is famous for not caring about internal states, because what is learned can be unlearned, and only observable behaviors can be changed in this theory. Freud, Adler, and Jung all did a great deal of work regarding the unconscious. Karen Horney and Erich Fromm were neo-Freudians, and object relations theory (pioneered by Ronald Fairbairn, Melanie Klein, D.W. Winnicott, and others) is based on Freudian concepts. Existential theorists focus on internal motivations such as anxiety and guilt.

**112. A:** Silence is often difficult for anyone in a social setting, but it can be particularly troublesome for a counselor and client in the therapeutic setting when not properly understood. Society in general often views silence as a sign of disinterest, rudeness, or awkwardness. In therapy, however, silence can take on another meaning. Silence is not always best used with very disturbed clients. However, it can be a valuable tool for general use. Silence not only is a means to convey empathy and understanding at particular moments, but is also a means by which to encourage deeper thought and retrospection. It can also apply subtle pressure upon the client who is resistant or otherwise holding back.

**113. D:** If a client has experienced complicated grief after the death of her father with whom she was highly enmeshed because of her inappropriate role as go-between for her parents but had a "love-hate" relationship because he was overbearing and judgmental, the likely cause of the client's complicated grief is unresolved conflicts. The client may suppress grief for a time after the death but over time the conflicted feelings that the client has may intrude more and more, affecting functioning.

**114. C:** Sigmund Freud's theory of how the human personality is formed consists of five parts, one of which includes the Id, Ego, and Superego. The Id is all about the "pleasure principle" and animalistic instincts. It's the part of the personality that wants what it wants regardless of the circumstances. The Ego is referred to as the "reality principle" and needs to balance the needs of the Id with the reality of the situation. The Superego is the moral part of the personality and is concerned with issues of right and wrong.

**115. C:** This is an example of enmeshment, the diffusion of boundaries. Here the mother is trying to dominate or live her life through her daughter. An example of negative attention seeking would be if the daughter constantly misbehaved to get her mother or father to pay attention to her. Disequilibrium refers more to family structure than behaviors. Triangulation is described above.

**116. C:** A client's file should always be viewed as confidential and kept in a secure manner and location. There are few exceptions to this requirement that the client's file be kept private, but one would be the request of the client to see his or her own file. In some cases, however, it may be deemed counter to a positive counseling relationship for the client to see the file. In such cases, it is permissible to omit the parts of the file that would prove detrimental. Also, in cases where the client is considered to be incompetent, it would often be best to limit or deny access.

**117. A:** Rationalization is a Freudian psychoanalytic defense mechanism. It occurs when the ego rejects the real motive for the individual's behavior and substitutes it with a motive that will make the behavior seem more acceptable. A client is likely to feel anxiety when acting in a manner that, for whatever reason, runs counter to what he believes is right. In order to make himself feel better for his behavior, the client will come up with reasons for his behavior (in an effort to make it seem more acceptable), and thus reduce his overall anxiety level.

**118. A:** When working with a client with conduct disorder who has exhibited sociopathic behavior, the comments by the client of the most cause for concern is "That pretty little daughter of yours goes to Farmin School, doesn't she?" because this could be construed as an implied threat. The client should have no personal information about the counselor, especially about the counselor's children. This suggests that the client may be stalking the counselor.

**119. B:** If the counselor is seeing a client with a history of trichotillomania and plans to begin habit reversal training, the first step is awareness training during which the client pays close attention to hair pulling, describing in detail how and when it happens and the sensations the client feels. The next step is to develop a competing response, followed by contingency management, relaxation training to reduce stress, and generalization training. HRT may also be utilized with other disorders associated with repetitive behaviors.

**120. D:** A need to show a particular counselor's effectiveness is NOT generally cited as a reason for counseling program evaluation. Evaluation goals are to demonstrate how well a technique, process, or program of treatment works rather than how well an individual therapist works. Program evaluation has been stimulated by the increasing emphasis on accountability in the field of human services, which arose in the 1970s and currently continues. Evaluation speaks to a crucial need to demonstrate the effectiveness of counseling in general and the effectiveness of specific theories, approaches, and therapeutic techniques as well.

**121. B:** Individuals who go right into the workforce after high school graduation routinely earn substantially less than those individuals who go to college. Individuals who go to college would not be hired for unskilled positions, as they are overqualified. It would be hard to say whether or not the college-educated individuals would work longer hours than the non-college-educated individuals.

**122. B:** The severity of anorexia in adults is based on the client's BMI. If a female client has a BMI of 16 kg/m², the severity would be classified as moderate. Severity classifications:

- Mild: >17 kg/m².
- Moderate: 16-17 kg/m².
- Severe: 15-16 kg/m².
- Extreme: <15 kg/m².

**123. D:** Considering the 5-phase aggression cycle, the client is most likely in the phase of escalation. The 5-phase aggression cycle includes:

- **Triggering**: Client appears restless, irritable, pacing, tense, and exhibits increased perspiration, loud voice, and angry demeanor.
- **Escalation**: Client may begin yelling and swearing and making threatening gestures, exhibiting hostility and loss of self-control.
- **Crisis**: Client loses complete control and may begin hitting, spitting, throwing items, kicking, and screaming.
- **Recovery**: Client begins to relax physically and emotionally, lowering voice and acting more rationally.
- **Post-crisis:** Client experiences remorse and may cry or become withdrawn.

**124. B:** Verbal expressions are NOT included. Kinesics refers to nonlinguistic or nonverbal communication such as facial expressions, physical gestures and body movements. Proxemics refers to spatial features of the environment such as seating arrangements, furniture placement, and how our personal space is affected by such arrangements.

**125. B:** If a client who has been hospitalized for treatment is resistant to discharge because of fear that she will be unable to function independently, the most appropriate response is to review the progress the client has made, pointing out positive changes. This can help the client gain confidence in her ability to function outside of the hospital. The counselor should also review plans the client has made for the transition to the home environment.

**126. C:** An "n-score" is NOT a type of standardized score. Standard scores are obtained by converting raw score distributions into an accepted standardized format. The two most commonly used standardized scores are the z-score and the t-score.

**127. A:** A counselor who sees couples for sex therapy must first rule out any physical problems one or the other partner may or may not have. Therefore, one of the first courses of action is to have the couple see their physician to verify that there are no physiological reasons for the dysfunction.

**128. B:** Conducting a pilot study comes before developing a plan, operating the program, and evaluating the program. Critical steps identified in developing a counseling program are: 1) conceptualizing the system; 2) establishing a philosophy and assessing needs; 3) developing goals and objectives; 4) processing information; 5) conducting a pilot study; 6) developing a plan; 7) implementing the program, which includes hiring and training; operating the counseling program; 8) evaluating the program; and, 9) modifying the counseling program based on the evaluation.

**129. A:** It is the Rogerian therapist who is more likely to establish rapport the quickest with the client. The Rogerian therapist is warm and inviting, communicating to the client respect and the feeling of control. By contrast, the Freudian therapist is more likely to seem analytical and somewhat distant. Rational-emotive and Gestalt therapists are confrontational in their therapeutic approach, which may make the client feel less inclined toward a strong rapport at an earlier stage. Rogerian therapists don't force entry into the unconscious or confront or contradict the client. They simply mirror back what they see in the client, and guide them to an independent and self-directed state. This approach would certainly appeal to many clients, and would be more likely to encourage a swift and positive rapport between client and therapist.

**130. B:** If an adoptive parent complains to the counselor that the adoptive daughter never says, "Thank you," the situation in which the complaint suggests that the problem may lie with the parent rather than the child is if the child does not say "thank you" for room and board (bedroom and food). It is a parent's understood job to provide basic care for a child and not something that a child is ordinarily expected to explicitly thank the parent. On the other hand, special treats, lessons, and treating the child and her friends to a movie are situations in which the child should show gratitude.

**131. A:** A counselor needs to be able to understand the client's predicament, not feel sorry for the client. Understanding the client's predicament is called empathy. Feeling sorry for someone's predicament is sympathy and does nothing to empower the client. Although providing stability in the session is helpful, it is not what helps the client to work through the predicament. A counselor needs to keep his or her own emotions in check when working with a client. Emotionality on the part of the counselor usually serves to confuse the client or to add additional burden onto the client.

**132. C:** The role of the Gestalt therapist is to be authentically in the present while helping the client resolve unfinished business and to be congruent in verbal and nonverbal messages. In existential counseling, the role of the counselor is to be empathetic and understanding of the client while stressing the personal relationship and sharing experiences. The role of the behavioral counselor is to assist the client in clarifying goals and modifying behaviors while teaching, directing, and advising. The rational-emotive therapist teaches, confronts, and corrects the client's irrational beliefs and ineffective self-talk.

**133. A:** When a family enters into therapy, each family member must make adjustments, adjust to these changes, and maintain balance. The family wants to maintain homeostasis (balance), yet the family makes changes to which each family member must adjust and become stable again.

**134. D:** The counselor should be aware that digoxin (Lanoxin®) is a common drug that may be associated with depression, affecting about 5% of clients taking the drug. Depression may occur at therapeutic doses as well as toxic doses. Other drugs that may cause depression include carbonic anhydrase inhibitors, interferon-alpha, carmustine, busulfan, L-asparaginase, clonidine, and amiodarone, phenytoin, metronidazole, metoclopramide, H-2 blockers, steroids, and thiazide diuretics. Beta blockers, calcium channel blockers, and isotretinoin (Accutane®) are not associated with depression.

**135. D:** One method of assessing a client's ability to concentrate is to ask the client to count backward from 100 by serial 7s (100, 93, 86…). Other tests of concentration include asking the client to spell the word world backward, state the days of the week backward, or carry out a simple three-part task (pick up the card, fold it in half, and place it on the desk). Requests that require the production of facts, such as "give the name of the previous president," are used to assess memory rather than concentration.

**136. B:** The individual's relative competence is NOT one of the factors identified by career self-efficacy theory as likely to be affected by the individual's expectations. This theory states that the individual's expectations will influence: 1) choice or whether a behavior will be initiated; 2) performance, or how much effort will be expended; and, 3) persistence, or to what extent the individual will persevere when confronted by obstacles. Some theorists believe these explain gender differences in career choices. Higher self-efficacy seems related to choice and persistence in math and science careers.

**137. C:** Dual-career families generally are those in which both the man and the woman have some sort of professional career. Both members of the relationship usually are established in their careers before they start a family. Generally, these couples marry later than those who go directly into the workforce after high school. The key vocabulary to look at here is "career," rather than a "job," which often is part-time or flexible.

**138. C:** If a 30-year-old client with paranoia and schizophrenia states he does not want his parents (who are paying for his care) to visit because he believes they are "possessed by devils," the counselor should respect the client's request. Clients' rights are not determined by who is paying for care but remain with the person. Unless the client has been declared incompetent in a court proceeding and his parents granted conservatorship, the client can deny them visitation.

**139. B:** Evaluation is synonymous with appraisal. Both terms imply going beyond measurement to make inferences or judgments about human behavior and characteristics. Assessment refers to processes and/or procedures for gathering data or information on human behavior. Testing is a type of assessment.

**140. C:** Sexual misconduct yields the highest number of malpractice cases for all mental health professionals. The other malpractice cases usually focus on breaches of confidentiality.

**141. A:** The 18-year-old client away from home at a university is likely experiencing and maturational/developmental crisis. She has retained a dependent role with her mother and is finding it difficult to function independently and to make decisions as an adult, resulting in increasing anxiety and somatic complaints. In some cases, parents encourage this type of relationship because it makes them feel needed or because they want to exercise control over their child.

**142. B:** The SEM is NOT a measure of validity but of reliability. It is also known as confidence band or confidence limits.

**143. A:** A client on the autism spectrum who cannot pick up clues from another person's tone of voice or eye contact is an example of hypomentalism. Mentalism is the ability to comprehend others actions and the world about one in mental terms, such as the ability to understand intention, belief, and emotions. Those with autism spectrum disorder tend to be hypomental while those with psychotic spectrum disorders tend to be overly alert and constantly "on-guard" or hypermental.

**144. D:** This act does NOT give students' parents access to their counseling records. Rather, it gives them access to their educational records. It also gives the students themselves this access providing they are 18 years of age or older. Answers A, B, and C are all correct.

**145. C:** While all of these are important, clients who are homeless require further assistance with discharge, as compliance with treatment and follow-up appointments is poor in the homeless population. Interventions that are most important include:

- Lists of safe shelters and places they can go to bathe, eat, and get mail.
- Assistance in applying for welfare assistance or Social Security.

**146. A:** Gender bias goes both ways. Men in female-dominated careers (nursing and fashion for example) and women in male-dominated careers (truck driving) can experience discrimination. A woman who works in human resources, a career field in which women outnumber men by more than 2 to 1, would be least likely to experience gender bias.

**147. C:** The Yerkes-Dodson law says that people tend to perform best under moderate levels of arousal. If arousal is too high for an individual, it may be difficult to maintain focus on a particular duty or activity. Too low an arousal level, and the individual may not feel motivated enough to complete a job, or lack the necessary energy to perform a given task. Of course, the optimal level of arousal for maximum productivity differs from person-to-person. For example, one person's high arousal may seem like moderate arousal to another. However, overall, moderate levels of arousal tend to be best for optimal performance.

**148. A:** B.F. Skinner, as a behaviorist, attributed all behavior to external (rather than internal) causes. He would likely have viewed religious belief as a result of early parental conditioning. Skinner would have believed that religion gains control by attributing power to some supernatural force that punishes unacceptable behaviors (i.e., hell) and rewards desired behaviors (i.e., heaven). He did not believe that an individual had faith in a particular religion because of inner reasons, but rather simply because of the external reinforcements of the religion, such as parents and society.

**149. A:** The APA developed the cultural formulation interview as part of research and clinical evaluation to improve clinical understanding. The CFI includes a series of questions that are asked about four broad topics in the following order:

- Cultural definition of the problem.
- Cultural perceptions of cause, context, and support.
- Cultural factors affecting self-coping and past help seeking.
- Cultural factors affecting current help seeking.

**150. C:** Alfred Adler founded many child guidance clinics and thus is attributed with being one of the first family counselors. Ackerman and Satir would be considered psychoanalytic family therapists, and Rogers would be a family-centered therapist.

**151. D:** Closed-ended questions are those that can be answered with one- or two-word responses (e.g., yes or no). A client who is asked a closed-ended question generally does not add any other information other than answering the question asked directly, therefore personal information may not be disclosed, full answers to questions may not be communicated, and dialogue may not occur. While these are disadvantages of closed-ended questions, there is still purpose to closed-ended questions, including collecting important information in the client's history that can be successfully and efficiently communicated by clients answer direct closed-ended questions.

**152. C:** The DSM system is based on the medical model that looks at client's disease states or mental conditions. None of the other options are appropriate.

**153. B:** Maslow was a humanistic psychologist who developed a theory that included five basic, instinctual needs of all human beings. The strongest of the needs is "physiological," because the individual must have these met for basic survival. Once physiological needs are met, the individual can look to "safety" needs to ensure their well-being. Next on the list are needs for "love, affection, and belongingness." Once the most basic of needs are met, individuals can seek to end their loneliness by looking for love and a way to belong. The next need is "esteem" (from self and others), followed by "self-actualization" (to do what one was born to do in life).

**154. C:** The focus of psychodynamic therapy is bringing to the surface that which is unconscious. To achieve this goal, the therapist uses free association and transference. Psychodynamic therapy has roots in Freudian theory. Freud spent much of his time discussing early childhood experiences and defense mechanisms. Rational-emotive behavior therapy examines irrational thoughts and beliefs. Behavioral therapy examines observable behavior, and client-centered therapy focuses on making clients feel good about themselves.

**155. C:** The Rorschach test was introduced in 1921 by Herman Rorschach. It came to be known as the "inkblot test" because the test consists of ten cards, each with the picture of an inkblot on them. Most are shades of black and grey, but a few have some color on them. The client tells the clinician what he sees in each inkblot, and the test is used to determine information about the client's personality. It is a very popular test in psychology, but is considered by some to be unreliable. Other tests similar to it have also been developed in recent years.

**156. B:** HMOs (Health Maintenance Organizations) and PPOS (Preferred Provider Organizations) are managed care groups with strict policies regarding treatment including counseling. Professionals in private practice cannot receive referrals of clients whose health insurance is with one of these organizations unless the professionals have provider status with the organization. Counselors do not apply for provider status to enhance their reputations, but to increase the numbers of their potential clients. There are no national or state laws governing provider status in managed health care organizations. This is controlled by organizational policies. Counselors seeing clients insured through these organizations must obtain provider status (i.e., inclusion on the organization's list of allowed providers), not membership in the organization itself.

**157. D:** A "Blocker" is one of several "self-oriented roles" that involve the group member's concern about their own place in the group dynamics rather than the progress of the group as a whole. The Blocker tends to waste the group's time with old issues, and is almost always negative, as well as resistant to new ideas. Other self-oriented roles would be those who are aggressive or seek attention. Some members also avoid issues or remain passive in the group setting, and there are others who may tend to dominate the group discussion, turning discussions back toward themselves and their own issues.

**158. B:** According to Minuchin, the family is made up of subsystems that have boundaries between them. If the boundaries are too rigid, it leads to disengagement of the subsystems. If the boundaries are too diffuse (loose or undefined), it can result in enmeshment. Insufficient boundaries can lead to unhealthy attachments and interactions. Overly strict boundaries can minimize healthy interactions. Transactional patterns are the evolved rules of the family structure, which may be general or individual. Alignments are the way family members join with or oppose one another. Coalitions are alliances between specific family members. Conflicts are disagreements or problems occurring within families. A structural map is a diagram or drawing showing the boundaries, alignments, coalitions, conflicts and other features or interactions within the family structure. The other terms in the answer choices are not specifically identified as terms used in structural family therapy.

**159. C:** Response A describes the technique called tracking (keeping track of what is going on). Response B involves communication skill building techniques, as does response D. The best example of reframing is C as the therapist tries to present another perspective or reframes the situation to show a different interpretation than the one that is being held by one or another person.

**160. C:** Bergan's consultation model is behavioral, not process oriented. The process model was developed by Schein, who was also responsible for identifying the purchase model and the doctor-patient model. Caplan developed the mental health consultation model, and Bandura is known for the social learning model. Therefore, these other answers all correctly pair each consultation model with the person who developed it.

**161. C:** A standardized test must have standard procedures for administering, scoring, and interpreting the test. There must also be a set of norms to which a particular score is compared. Not all tests are standardized. For example, unless it is a test like the NCE or GRE, it is probably a test that was developed by a teacher or company. Tests may be administered the same way to everyone and scored the same, but if there are no norms to which to compare an examinee, it is not considered a standardized test. If a test has questions with multiple correct answers it cannot be standardized because there is no clear way to grade these questions in an objective manner.

**162. C:** Gould believed that what he called "protective devices" are false assumptions and are triggered at different ages. They may certainly be used as coping strategies or defense mechanisms by individuals, but these are not the most accurate definitions. The important point about these devices is that Gould thought they were false assumptions; therefore, misleading and not productive. Being false, they are in no way absolute truths.

**163. B:** Positive uncertainty is H.B. Gelatt's later model of career decision-making. According to Bandura, personal agency reflects an individual's ability to achieve objectives. Self-efficacy is Bandura's term for an individual's belief that one can succeed at something. Vicarious learning is one of several learning experiences that Bandura states can strengthen self-efficacy.

**164. B:** Professional liability insurance is required by law in some states, but not others. It is highly recommended for counselors even in those states where it is not required, and it is not generally considered an unnecessary expense. There are several providers of this insurance. For example, the American Counseling Association (ACA) sponsors a professional liability insurance program for its members.

**165. B: Displacement:** Expressing strong feelings generated by one person to another who is less threatening. In this case, yelling at the counselor instead of the boss who fired him. **Identification:** Modeling behavior or attitudes on those of another, such as entering the same profession as a mentor. **Sublimation:** Substituting behavior that is acceptable for one that is not, such as chewing gum instead of smoking. **Projection**: Unconsciously blaming unacceptable feelings/actions on someone else, such as by attacking gay people to deny homosexual attraction.

**166. B:** Free Association is a fundamental rule of psychoanalysis and is meant to bring unconscious material into conscious awareness. Free Association differs from usual conversation. In social conversation, an individual carefully chooses what he will say, selecting material that will fit the conversation, or that is appropriate to the circumstances. In Free Association, the client is encouraged to say whatever comes into his mind, no matter how silly or inappropriate it may be. The therapist carefully attends to what is being said, analyzing the content and bringing the unconscious forward.

**167. B:** There is no mixed randomized sampling technique. A cluster sampling technique involves taking a smaller sample from a larger sample. In cluster sampling, the groups are randomized, not the individuals in the groups. A random chance sampling technique involves the simple randomness involved in choosing people at random regardless of any characteristics or group identities. Each person has an equal chance of being chosen. In a stratified sampling technique, different subpopulations are included in the random sample based on percentages of the subpopulations in the larger population. For example, if a researcher wants a representative sample from the general population, she would want an equal representation of males and females. Therefore, she would randomly choose half of her sample from the male subpopulation and half from the female subpopulation.

**168. B:** Clients who undergo amputations often experience Kübler-Ross's five stages of grief associated with death and other losses as they try to cope with physical disability and changes in their body image. During the stage of denial, clients may believe unrealistically that they need no assistance and can return to their routine lives with no problem. Other stages include anger, bargaining, depression, and acceptance. Clients may not go through all stages or may go through the stages in no particular order.

**169. C:** Konrad Lorenz is one of Austria's most famous scientists, but he is known in the field of psychology for his work on imprinting. He observed that newly hatched goslings and ducklings would imprint upon whatever they first saw after hatching. The baby birds would later follow and even try to mate with whatever they had imprinted on. Lorenz even tried inanimate objects, which the babies also imprinted on. He felt therefore that the baby birds didn't recognize their species or require reinforcement, so he saw this as innate behavior.

**170. D:** A time-out is the removal of the child from the situation so that all attention is withdrawn from the child. Coercion, by definition, is forcible manipulation of a person to do what you want the person to do. The Premack principle states that more-probable behaviors will reinforce less-probable behaviors. Shaping is another behavioral technique that involves successive approximations of a desired behavior being reinforced as a means to teach a desired response.

**171. D:** Personality characteristics are typically tested using psychological instruments such as the Minnesota Multiphasic Personality Inventory (MMPI) or the California Psychological Inventory, which are personality tests. Brain dysfunctions are typically measured using neuropsychological assessments such as the Luria-Nebraska Neuropsychological Battery which measures organic damage and its location(s); the Bender® Visual-Motor Gestalt Test, which is often used with children to measure brain dysfunction. The five areas covered by a formal mental status examination are: appearance and behavior; thought processes; mood and affect; intellectual functioning; and, sensorium. Sensorium refers to orientation to self, place, time and environment.

**172. B:** In a heterogeneous group, if the members are too different from one another they may find it harder to relate. However, heterogeneous groups are more representative of the real world, so answer C is incorrect; heterogeneity is likely to stimulate interactions among members, so answer D is incorrect. Answer A is incorrect because homogeneity, or having similar members in a group, does not preclude having effective group dynamics – otherwise, homogeneous groups would never be indicated, but they are often successfully used.

**173. C:** "Group content" refers to the content being discussed among the group members in the group therapy session. This is different from "group process", which refers to how the material and interactions between members are progressing in terms of the group's goals. Put simply, "group content" is what is said, and "group process" is the analysis of the content.

**174. D:** Frederick and Laura Perls developed Gestalt therapy. Its focus is on challenging clients to become more self-aware and face their problems. Frederick Perls was a student of psychoanalysis and was trained as a Freudian psychoanalyst. As such, he believed that many problems resulted from early conflicts. However, he also believed that those conflicts should be forced into the here and now for clients to deal with. He believed that counselors should confront clients with questions that would lead them to face their thoughts and feelings, and force them to choose if they will allow the past to control the present.

**175. C:** Suffice to say, dual-career families tend to have less free time due to work and family responsibilities. They may or may not be involved in expensive leisure activities, which are similar to those of other families. Because no one is at home to take care of household duties during the day, these activities must be done after work, thus, dual-career families have less time to spend on leisure activities.

**176. B:** Most counselors would be considered eclectic because few choose only one theory or method through which they practice their profession. Most mental health professionals will agree that there is value and worth in all of the various theories and research that has taken place in the field of psychology, but also would concede that there are shortcomings to each as well. For that reason, most counselors will rely on several theories for their practice and will adjust their choices based upon their experience and the population they are serving. Some counselors will base their work with one population on a particular theory, and then use another theory as the base for their work with another.

**177. A:** The statement by a client that is most likely to indicate suicidal ideation and risk for suicide is "My children would be better off without me." When clients make statement indicating possible suicidal ideation, the counselor should address it immediately by asking if the client has thoughts about dying and if the client has a plan. Clients who have formulated a plan (such as taking an overdose of medications) are at higher risk than those who simply think about wanting to die.

**178. C:** There are five stages in the group process: forming, initial, transition, working, and closing. In the forming stage, the group leader recruits, screens, and orients potential group members. The initial stage involves tasks such as setting the ground rules, introducing members, and discussing confidentiality. The transition stage includes storming (a time of anxiety and conflict as the members test the leadership) and norming (when the group falls into a rhythm with expected routines and roles established). During the working stage, members work on specific issues while sharing personal information. At the closing stage, the leader begins the termination process.

**179. C:** It is projected that by 2050, all of the minority groups combined will total a larger number than all of the Non-Hispanic White people in the country. It is not projected that the Hispanic population alone will outnumber the White population. Since it is projected that all minority groups combined will outnumber Whites, it is incorrect that Whites will be the largest number in the population.

**180. A:** A t-score has a mean of 50 and a standard deviation of 10. In this situation, the test taker received a t-score of 40. That score is one standard deviation below the mean. It is neither a very high nor a very low score. T-scores of 70 and 30 may be considered to be high and low, respectively. A t-score of 70 is two standard deviations above the mean, while a t-score of 30 is two standard deviations below the mean.

**181. B:** When diagnosing schizophrenia, there are active and passive symptoms. Active symptoms are exaggerated and passive symptoms are absent. In the daily functioning of persons with schizophrenia, they experience many distortions in their thinking processes and are usually unable or minimally able to address activities of daily living (dressing, preparing meals, etc.).

**182. B:** The principal researcher is ultimately responsible for any and all ethical breaches in the research study. All others involved in the research study are individually responsible for their unethical behavior. It is important to note that, individually, everyone involved in a research study must admit personal responsibility, but overall, the principal researcher is responsible for the entirety of the study and anything connected to it.

**183. D:** The distinction between group content and group process hinges on behavior. Group content involves the topics of discussion or the skills to be addressed. Group process involves looking beyond someone's words and instead observing the person's behavior. It's not what is said; it's how it is said. In the examples, Joe brought up a topic to be discussed (content). Randy reacted not so much to what Karen said, but rather to Karen herself. The act of rolling his eyes is a process (behavior pattern that he perpetuates). Sarah's constant monopolizing is her pattern of responding. It wasn't that she spoke often, it was that she dominated the discussion and didn't allow others to join in.

**184. D:** Haley's strategic family therapy focuses on how families use or abuse power, how they fail to communicate effectively and clearly, and how a symptom serves as a protection against something that is painful.

**185. B:** A 98% chance of statistical significance equates to a p-value of <0.02. Of the choices listed, B and C are both less than 0.02, but the question asks for the loosest bound, so the correct answer is 0.01.

**186. C:** Existential therapy looks at the human condition in its totality from birth to death and everything in-between. "Social interest" is a term synonymous with Adlerian counseling, while self-actualization is a term used by Maslow when he talked about his hierarchy of needs. Psychoanalysis looks at bringing what is unconscious to the conscious level.

**187. D:** Regression toward the mean, or reversion to the mean, expresses the fact that if an individual scores very high (85% or higher) or very low (15% or lower) on a pretest, that individual is likely to earn a score closer to the mean (average) on the posttest. The unusual pretest score is usually an error due to chance, personal and environmental factors, which are reliably likely to be different on the posttest. This term does not express that most individuals will score near the mean on standardized tests. It does not mean that posttest scores will be lower than pretest scores, since they could also be higher depending on the pretest score. It does not mean that individuals scoring close to the average on a posttest will score lower on the pretest.

**188. A:** Alfred Adler is considered by many as one of the founding fathers of psychology. Both Sigmund Freud and Carl Jung (the other two founding fathers) talked about intrapsychic dynamics, focusing on the internal processes of the individual and using individual therapy as a treatment modality. However, Alfred Adler did not. Adler looked at the individual in relation to his or her environment, and so it was natural for him to embrace a less individualized approach to therapy. As early as the 1920s, he was already involved in use of group therapy.

**189. B:** A client who is in the midst of a personal crisis, or is otherwise fragile, is initially best treated with individual therapy. If the individual treatment is ineffective or if the situation significantly worsens, an inpatient referral may be considered. Clients who enter a group situation before they are ready run the risk of dropping out or experiencing an exacerbation of their symptoms. They may also impede the group process for the other members. Vocational counseling may be appropriate at a later date once the client has successfully worked through the more acute issues.

**190. B:** Generally, co-leaders use a team approach. Each leader observes and processes what goes on in the group and provides feedback to participants. One leader usually cannot catch everything that goes on in a group. Leaders have to be aware of content, process, flow, and progress toward goals. Co-led groups give participants opportunities to observe how conflicts are handled between or among the leaders. The participants see the effectiveness of cooperation and harmony. Oftentimes, co-leaders are viewed as parental figures, and thus participants can learn more adaptive behaviors from well-functioning "parents."

**191. A:** Two primary determinants of educational effectiveness include:

- **Behavior modification** involves thorough observation and measurement, identifying behavior that needs to be changed and then planning and instituting interventions to modify that behavior. Techniques include demonstrations of appropriate behavior, reinforcement, and monitoring until new behavior is consistent.
- **Compliance rates** are often determined by observation, which should be done at intervals and on multiple occasions, but in some cases, this may depend on self-reports or reports of others. If education is intended to improve individual health and reduce risk factors and that occurs, it is a good indication of compliance.

**192. A:** The Wechsler Intelligence Scales include the WPPSI-IV (Wechsler Preschool and Primary Scale of Intelligence), the WISC-IV (Wechsler Intelligence Scale for Children), and the WAIS-IV (Wechsler Adult Intelligence Scale)—the Roman numerals refer to edition numbers. The Stanford-Binet IQ test has a number of subtests to assess various abilities, but does not have different versions for different age groups as Wechsler does. The MAT is a test of analytical ability given to many college students as a standard for admission to graduate school. As such, it does not have versions for different ages. The SAT is a test commonly given to high school students to measure their verbal and quantitative abilities via subtests, and thus needs no age-accommodating versions. It is used to help determine their eligibility for admission to college.

**193. D:** Donald Super did NOT identify the church as one of the theaters in which we play out our roles. Home, community, school, and workplace are the four theaters he identified.

**194. B:** Bipolar disorder most often manifests itself with alternating periods of depressed and elevated mood. While both need not be present for a diagnosis of bipolar disorder, depression and mania are common to many cases. The cycles in bipolar can be of varying lengths, with differing levels of severity. The client will have symptom-free periods where daily function is at an expected level. The cause of the symptoms must not be medication-related for the diagnosis to be bipolar disorder, and it is often treated with a combination of medication and therapy.

**195. B:** Albert Ellis' rational emotive behavior therapy (REBT) has all of the characteristics summarized prior to the question. Existential therapy (Rollo May, Victor Frankl, Irvin Yalom) is based on phenomenology, or the study of our direct experiences taken at face value rather than of our interpretations of them. William Glasser's reality therapy is based on choice theory and posits that we determine our own fates. Glasser states that we all have genetically based needs of survival, love and belonging, power or achievement, freedom or independence, and fun. Taking responsibility is a key concept of reality therapy. Arnold Lazarus' multimodal therapy is a holistic and eclectic approach with considerable behavioral influences. Lazarus identified seven interactive but discrete modalities for which he used the acronym BASIC ID: behaviors, affective responses, sensations, images, cognitions, interpersonal relationships, and drugs (i.e., biology, including nutrition).

**196. A:** Although resistance to change is a common human reaction and many adults in career transition may experience it, this is not identified as an issue in counseling adults in career transition. Thus, although it may certainly be an issue for counseling, it falls into the area of "identifying issues" as opposed to being a distinct issue of its own. Some people fear or resent change simply because it is a change. Others may resist change for more pragmatic reasons such as having outdated job skills. This can be remedied by counselors who can facilitate retraining. Still other individuals need to resolve issues around the changes in their physical capacities as they age learning to accept the reality that they may need a different kind of work or a different form of work in the same or a related field. Others will find that as they have grown older and times have changed, their values have changed as well. Finally, some may fear a transition because they lack the resources to obtain needed information and the skills to look for a new job. Career counseling can help people adjust to changes in themselves and their environment, as well as providing clients with the resources they need to make a successful transition.

**197. D:** The client most likely at risk is the man who shot himself in the chest while alone. A suicide risk assessment should evaluate some of the following criteria: Would the individual sign a contract for safety? Is there a suicide plan? How lethal is the plan? What is the elopement risk? How often are the suicidal thoughts, and has the person attempted suicide before? High-risk findings include:

**198. C:** Incorporating additional objects or events into the infant's existing schema or structure such as sucking on things other than a nipple is assimilation. When the infant later modifies its organization by forming new schemas in response to the environment this is accommodation. Adaptation is Piaget's term for adjustment to the environment. Assimilation and accommodation are two processes that are parts of adaptation. Organization is how we organize our knowledge and mental processes. Piaget said that we inherit two tendencies, which are organization and adaptation.

**199. C:** Neutrality was NOT a factor identified by Ponzo or by Yalom as being present in leaders of successful groups. Ponzo identified caring support, and Yalom identified caring as characterized by warmth and concern. Yalom identified executive leadership, which includes giving direction, and Ponzo identified participation. All of these would tend to contradict neutrality in a group leader. The additional factors Ponzo cited were: openness, participation, risk-taking, conflict-confrontation, and caring support.

**200. D:** Analysis of covariance (ANCOVA) is used when the influence of an independent variable or variables upon a dependent variable is statistically controlled. Since the seniors initially scored

higher in self-efficacy than the juniors before the counseling, the researcher evens out the differences in their scores to control the effect of grade level on the dependent variable of self-efficacy. An ANOVA does not control the influence of an independent variable or variables on a dependent variable. It also cannot be used when there is more than one dependent variable, as is the case here. A MANOVA would work for this researcher's analysis of two dependent variables (self-efficacy and optimism), but would not control for the effect of grade level on self-efficacy the way the ANCOVA does.

# NCE Practice Test #3

To take this additional NCE practice test, visit our bonus page:
**mometrix.com/bonus948/nce**

# How to Overcome Test Anxiety

Just the thought of taking a test is enough to make most people a little nervous. A test is an important event that can have a long-term impact on your future, so it's important to take it seriously and it's natural to feel anxious about performing well. But just because anxiety is normal, that doesn't mean that it's helpful in test taking, or that you should simply accept it as part of your life. Anxiety can have a variety of effects. These effects can be mild, like making you feel slightly nervous, or severe, like blocking your ability to focus or remember even a simple detail.

If you experience test anxiety—whether severe or mild—it's important to know how to beat it. To discover this, first you need to understand what causes test anxiety.

## Causes of Test Anxiety

While we often think of anxiety as an uncontrollable emotional state, it can actually be caused by simple, practical things. One of the most common causes of test anxiety is that a person does not feel adequately prepared for their test. This feeling can be the result of many different issues such as poor study habits or lack of organization, but the most common culprit is time management. Starting to study too late, failing to organize your study time to cover all of the material, or being distracted while you study will mean that you're not well prepared for the test. This may lead to cramming the night before, which will cause you to be physically and mentally exhausted for the test. Poor time management also contributes to feelings of stress, fear, and hopelessness as you realize you are not well prepared but don't know what to do about it.

Other times, test anxiety is not related to your preparation for the test but comes from unresolved fear. This may be a past failure on a test, or poor performance on tests in general. It may come from comparing yourself to others who seem to be performing better or from the stress of living up to expectations. Anxiety may be driven by fears of the future—how failure on this test would affect your educational and career goals. These fears are often completely irrational, but they can still negatively impact your test performance.

> **Review Video: 3 Reasons You Have Test Anxiety**
> Visit mometrix.com/academy and enter code: 428468

# Elements of Test Anxiety

As mentioned earlier, test anxiety is considered to be an emotional state, but it has physical and mental components as well. Sometimes you may not even realize that you are suffering from test anxiety until you notice the physical symptoms. These can include trembling hands, rapid heartbeat, sweating, nausea, and tense muscles. Extreme anxiety may lead to fainting or vomiting. Obviously, any of these symptoms can have a negative impact on testing. It is important to recognize them as soon as they begin to occur so that you can address the problem before it damages your performance.

> **Review Video: 3 Ways to Tell You Have Test Anxiety**
> Visit mometrix.com/academy and enter code: 927847

The mental components of test anxiety include trouble focusing and inability to remember learned information. During a test, your mind is on high alert, which can help you recall information and stay focused for an extended period of time. However, anxiety interferes with your mind's natural processes, causing you to blank out, even on the questions you know well. The strain of testing during anxiety makes it difficult to stay focused, especially on a test that may take several hours. Extreme anxiety can take a huge mental toll, making it difficult not only to recall test information but even to understand the test questions or pull your thoughts together.

> **Review Video: How Test Anxiety Affects Memory**
> Visit mometrix.com/academy and enter code: 609003

# Effects of Test Anxiety

Test anxiety is like a disease—if left untreated, it will get progressively worse. Anxiety leads to poor performance, and this reinforces the feelings of fear and failure, which in turn lead to poor performances on subsequent tests. It can grow from a mild nervousness to a crippling condition. If allowed to progress, test anxiety can have a big impact on your schooling, and consequently on your future.

Test anxiety can spread to other parts of your life. Anxiety on tests can become anxiety in any stressful situation, and blanking on a test can turn into panicking in a job situation. But fortunately, you don't have to let anxiety rule your testing and determine your grades. There are a number of relatively simple steps you can take to move past anxiety and function normally on a test and in the rest of life.

> **Review Video: How Test Anxiety Impacts Your Grades**
> Visit mometrix.com/academy and enter code: 939819

# Physical Steps for Beating Test Anxiety

While test anxiety is a serious problem, the good news is that it can be overcome. It doesn't have to control your ability to think and remember information. While it may take time, you can begin taking steps today to beat anxiety.

Just as your first hint that you may be struggling with anxiety comes from the physical symptoms, the first step to treating it is also physical. Rest is crucial for having a clear, strong mind. If you are tired, it is much easier to give in to anxiety. But if you establish good sleep habits, your body and mind will be ready to perform optimally, without the strain of exhaustion. Additionally, sleeping well helps you to retain information better, so you're more likely to recall the answers when you see the test questions.

Getting good sleep means more than going to bed on time. It's important to allow your brain time to relax. Take study breaks from time to time so it doesn't get overworked, and don't study right before bed. Take time to rest your mind before trying to rest your body, or you may find it difficult to fall asleep.

> **Review Video: <u>The Importance of Sleep for Your Brain</u>**
> Visit mometrix.com/academy and enter code: 319338

Along with sleep, other aspects of physical health are important in preparing for a test. Good nutrition is vital for good brain function. Sugary foods and drinks may give a burst of energy but this burst is followed by a crash, both physically and emotionally. Instead, fuel your body with protein and vitamin-rich foods.

Also, drink plenty of water. Dehydration can lead to headaches and exhaustion, especially if your brain is already under stress from the rigors of the test. Particularly if your test is a long one, drink water during the breaks. And if possible, take an energy-boosting snack to eat between sections.

> **Review Video: <u>How Diet Can Affect your Mood</u>**
> Visit mometrix.com/academy and enter code: 624317

Along with sleep and diet, a third important part of physical health is exercise. Maintaining a steady workout schedule is helpful, but even taking 5-minute study breaks to walk can help get your blood pumping faster and clear your head. Exercise also releases endorphins, which contribute to a positive feeling and can help combat test anxiety.

When you nurture your physical health, you are also contributing to your mental health. If your body is healthy, your mind is much more likely to be healthy as well. So take time to rest, nourish your body with healthy food and water, and get moving as much as possible. Taking these physical steps will make you stronger and more able to take the mental steps necessary to overcome test anxiety.

# Mental Steps for Beating Test Anxiety

Working on the mental side of test anxiety can be more challenging, but as with the physical side, there are clear steps you can take to overcome it. As mentioned earlier, test anxiety often stems from lack of preparation, so the obvious solution is to prepare for the test. Effective studying may be the most important weapon you have for beating test anxiety, but you can and should employ several other mental tools to combat fear.

First, boost your confidence by reminding yourself of past success—tests or projects that you aced. If you're putting as much effort into preparing for this test as you did for those, there's no reason you should expect to fail here. Work hard to prepare; then trust your preparation.

Second, surround yourself with encouraging people. It can be helpful to find a study group, but be sure that the people you're around will encourage a positive attitude. If you spend time with others who are anxious or cynical, this will only contribute to your own anxiety. Look for others who are motivated to study hard from a desire to succeed, not from a fear of failure.

Third, reward yourself. A test is physically and mentally tiring, even without anxiety, and it can be helpful to have something to look forward to. Plan an activity following the test, regardless of the outcome, such as going to a movie or getting ice cream.

When you are taking the test, if you find yourself beginning to feel anxious, remind yourself that you know the material. Visualize successfully completing the test. Then take a few deep, relaxing breaths and return to it. Work through the questions carefully but with confidence, knowing that you are capable of succeeding.

Developing a healthy mental approach to test taking will also aid in other areas of life. Test anxiety affects more than just the actual test—it can be damaging to your mental health and even contribute to depression. It's important to beat test anxiety before it becomes a problem for more than testing.

> **Review Video: Test Anxiety and Depression**
> Visit mometrix.com/academy and enter code: 904704

# Study Strategy

Being prepared for the test is necessary to combat anxiety, but what does being prepared look like? You may study for hours on end and still not feel prepared. What you need is a strategy for test prep. The next few pages outline our recommended steps to help you plan out and conquer the challenge of preparation.

## STEP 1: SCOPE OUT THE TEST

Learn everything you can about the format (multiple choice, essay, etc.) and what will be on the test. Gather any study materials, course outlines, or sample exams that may be available. Not only will this help you to prepare, but knowing what to expect can help to alleviate test anxiety.

## STEP 2: MAP OUT THE MATERIAL

Look through the textbook or study guide and make note of how many chapters or sections it has. Then divide these over the time you have. For example, if a book has 15 chapters and you have five days to study, you need to cover three chapters each day. Even better, if you have the time, leave an extra day at the end for overall review after you have gone through the material in depth.

If time is limited, you may need to prioritize the material. Look through it and make note of which sections you think you already have a good grasp on, and which need review. While you are studying, skim quickly through the familiar sections and take more time on the challenging parts. Write out your plan so you don't get lost as you go. Having a written plan also helps you feel more in control of the study, so anxiety is less likely to arise from feeling overwhelmed at the amount to cover. A sample plan may look like this:

- Day 1: Skim chapters 1–4, study chapter 5 (especially pages 31–33)
- Day 2: Study chapters 6–7, skim chapters 8–9
- Day 3: Skim chapter 10, study chapters 11–12 (especially pages 87–90)
- Day 4: Study chapters 13–15
- Day 5: Overall review (focus most on chapters 5, 6, and 12), take practice test

## STEP 3: GATHER YOUR TOOLS

Decide what study method works best for you. Do you prefer to highlight in the book as you study and then go back over the highlighted portions? Or do you type out notes of the important information? Or is it helpful to make flashcards that you can carry with you? Assemble the pens, index cards, highlighters, post-it notes, and any other materials you may need so you won't be distracted by getting up to find things while you study.

If you're having a hard time retaining the information or organizing your notes, experiment with different methods. For example, try color-coding by subject with colored pens, highlighters, or post-it notes. If you learn better by hearing, try recording yourself reading your notes so you can listen while in the car, working out, or simply sitting at your desk. Ask a friend to quiz you from your flashcards, or try teaching someone the material to solidify it in your mind.

## STEP 4: CREATE YOUR ENVIRONMENT

It's important to avoid distractions while you study. This includes both the obvious distractions like visitors and the subtle distractions like an uncomfortable chair (or a too-comfortable couch that makes you want to fall asleep). Set up the best study environment possible: good lighting and a comfortable work area. If background music helps you focus, you may want to turn it on, but otherwise keep the room quiet. If you are using a computer to take notes, be sure you don't have any other windows open, especially applications like social media, games, or anything else that could distract you. Silence your phone and turn off notifications. Be sure to keep water close by so you stay hydrated while you study (but avoid unhealthy drinks and snacks).

Also, take into account the best time of day to study. Are you freshest first thing in the morning? Try to set aside some time then to work through the material. Is your mind clearer in the afternoon or evening? Schedule your study session then. Another method is to study at the same time of day that you will take the test, so that your brain gets used to working on the material at that time and will be ready to focus at test time.

## STEP 5: STUDY!

Once you have done all the study preparation, it's time to settle into the actual studying. Sit down, take a few moments to settle your mind so you can focus, and begin to follow your study plan. Don't give in to distractions or let yourself procrastinate. This is your time to prepare so you'll be ready to fearlessly approach the test. Make the most of the time and stay focused.

Of course, you don't want to burn out. If you study too long you may find that you're not retaining the information very well. Take regular study breaks. For example, taking five minutes out of every hour to walk briskly, breathing deeply and swinging your arms, can help your mind stay fresh.

As you get to the end of each chapter or section, it's a good idea to do a quick review. Remind yourself of what you learned and work on any difficult parts. When you feel that you've mastered the material, move on to the next part. At the end of your study session, briefly skim through your notes again.

But while review is helpful, cramming last minute is NOT. If at all possible, work ahead so that you won't need to fit all your study into the last day. Cramming overloads your brain with more information than it can process and retain, and your tired mind may struggle to recall even previously learned information when it is overwhelmed with last-minute study. Also, the urgent nature of cramming and the stress placed on your brain contribute to anxiety. You'll be more likely to go to the test feeling unprepared and having trouble thinking clearly.

So don't cram, and don't stay up late before the test, even just to review your notes at a leisurely pace. Your brain needs rest more than it needs to go over the information again. In fact, plan to finish your studies by noon or early afternoon the day before the test. Give your brain the rest of the day to relax or focus on other things, and get a good night's sleep. Then you will be fresh for the test and better able to recall what you've studied.

## STEP 6: TAKE A PRACTICE TEST

Many courses offer sample tests, either online or in the study materials. This is an excellent resource to check whether you have mastered the material, as well as to prepare for the test format and environment.

Check the test format ahead of time: the number of questions, the type (multiple choice, free response, etc.), and the time limit. Then create a plan for working through them. For example, if you have 30 minutes to take a 60-question test, your limit is 30 seconds per question. Spend less time on the questions you know well so that you can take more time on the difficult ones.

If you have time to take several practice tests, take the first one open book, with no time limit. Work through the questions at your own pace and make sure you fully understand them. Gradually work up to taking a test under test conditions: sit at a desk with all study materials put away and set a timer. Pace yourself to make sure you finish the test with time to spare and go back to check your answers if you have time.

After each test, check your answers. On the questions you missed, be sure you understand why you missed them. Did you misread the question (tests can use tricky wording)? Did you forget the information? Or was it something you hadn't learned? Go back and study any shaky areas that the practice tests reveal.

Taking these tests not only helps with your grade, but also aids in combating test anxiety. If you're already used to the test conditions, you're less likely to worry about it, and working through tests until you're scoring well gives you a confidence boost. Go through the practice tests until you feel comfortable, and then you can go into the test knowing that you're ready for it.

## Test Tips

On test day, you should be confident, knowing that you've prepared well and are ready to answer the questions. But aside from preparation, there are several test day strategies you can employ to maximize your performance.

First, as stated before, get a good night's sleep the night before the test (and for several nights before that, if possible). Go into the test with a fresh, alert mind rather than staying up late to study.

Try not to change too much about your normal routine on the day of the test. It's important to eat a nutritious breakfast, but if you normally don't eat breakfast at all, consider eating just a protein bar. If you're a coffee drinker, go ahead and have your normal coffee. Just make sure you time it so that the caffeine doesn't wear off right in the middle of your test. Avoid sugary beverages, and drink enough water to stay hydrated but not so much that you need a restroom break 10 minutes into the test. If your test isn't first thing in the morning, consider going for a walk or doing a light workout before the test to get your blood flowing.

Allow yourself enough time to get ready, and leave for the test with plenty of time to spare so you won't have the anxiety of scrambling to arrive in time. Another reason to be early is to select a good seat. It's helpful to sit away from doors and windows, which can be distracting. Find a good seat, get out your supplies, and settle your mind before the test begins.

When the test begins, start by going over the instructions carefully, even if you already know what to expect. Make sure you avoid any careless mistakes by following the directions.

Then begin working through the questions, pacing yourself as you've practiced. If you're not sure on an answer, don't spend too much time on it, and don't let it shake your confidence. Either skip it and come back later, or eliminate as many wrong answers as possible and guess among the remaining ones. Don't dwell on these questions as you continue—put them out of your mind and focus on what lies ahead.

Be sure to read all of the answer choices, even if you're sure the first one is the right answer. Sometimes you'll find a better one if you keep reading. But don't second-guess yourself if you do immediately know the answer. Your gut instinct is usually right. Don't let test anxiety rob you of the information you know.

If you have time at the end of the test (and if the test format allows), go back and review your answers. Be cautious about changing any, since your first instinct tends to be correct, but make sure

you didn't misread any of the questions or accidentally mark the wrong answer choice. Look over any you skipped and make an educated guess.

At the end, leave the test feeling confident. You've done your best, so don't waste time worrying about your performance or wishing you could change anything. Instead, celebrate the successful completion of this test. And finally, use this test to learn how to deal with anxiety even better next time.

---

**Review Video: 5 Tips to Beat Test Anxiety**
Visit mometrix.com/academy and enter code: 570656

---

## Important Qualification

Not all anxiety is created equal. If your test anxiety is causing major issues in your life beyond the classroom or testing center, or if you are experiencing troubling physical symptoms related to your anxiety, it may be a sign of a serious physiological or psychological condition. If this sounds like your situation, we strongly encourage you to seek professional help.

# Tell Us Your Story

We at Mometrix would like to extend our heartfelt thanks to you for letting us be a part of your journey. It is an honor to serve people from all walks of life, people like you, who are committed to building the best future they can for themselves.

We know that each person's situation is unique. But we also know that, whether you are a young student or a mother of four, you care about working to make your own life and the lives of those around you better.

**That's why we want to hear your story.**

We want to know why you're taking this test. We want to know about the trials you've gone through to get here. And we want to know about the successes you've experienced after taking and passing your test.

In addition to your story, which can be an inspiration both to us and to others, we value your feedback. We want to know both what you loved about our book and what you think we can improve on.

**The team at Mometrix would be absolutely thrilled to hear from you!** So please, send us an email at tellusyourstory@mometrix.com or visit us at mometrix.com/tellusyourstory.php and let's stay in touch.

# Additional Bonus Material

Due to our efforts to try to keep this book to a manageable length, we've created a link that will give you access to all of your additional bonus material:

**mometrix.com/bonus948/nce**

Made in the USA
Monee, IL
06 February 2023

27247822R00234